Whaт oтheяs aяe sɑ
A Famıly Guıde тo тhe

In 34 years of publishing Messianic Catalogs we have never seen such a creative contribution to the body of Messiah ...!" —Manny and Sandra Brotman (founder of The Messianic Jewish Movement International.)

I enthusiastically endorse this exceedingly creative project. This family guide is a Christian exploration of Biblical Holidays adaptable for all ages. This impressive work is visually attractive and scripturally anchored. Here is a delightful educational tool serious students will appreciate, for it will provide them with a detailed understanding of one of the foundational instructional pillars of the earliest Jewish church. Explore wonderful basic foundational truths that are found in the only Bible the earliest church knew. The glossary is a real asset.

> –Dr. Marvin Wilson, Professor at Gordon College, Wenham, MA and author of _Our Father Abraham: Jewish Roots of the Christian Faith_.

Many books about the Holy Days have crossed my desk, most with only an explanation of the New Testament view. I was delighted to see that _A Family Guide to The Biblical Holidays_ includes the historical purpose and meaning of each holiday as well as the foreshadows of Christ. The authors have done an excellent job explaining each holiday to the fullest in an easy-to-understand text. These often overlooked teachings reveal significant insights to the predominantly Jewish early church.

> –Ron Mosley, Founder of the Arkansas Institute of Holy Land Studies, author of _The Spirit of the Law_ and _Yeshua: A Guide to the Real Jesus and the Original Church_.

The feasts of the Lord have been the "curriculum of faith" over 3,000 years. This comprehensive volume will enable you to effectively add this curriculum to your family's education.

> –Neil Lash, Director of Education, Sar Shalom Hebrew Academy, Host of "Jewish Jewels," nationally syndicated television program.

I like how you have handled the tough issues of "do we have to celebrate the holidays?" along with the issue of grace and law. I also like your format and the simplicity with which it reads. The content is easy to follow and to comprehend... I recommend this material for your audience.

> –Pastor Peter A. Michas, author of _God's Master Plan_.

I so appreciate the work you are doing regarding the Biblical Jewish roots of Christianity. Believers will see the light of Messiah and their lives will be magnified and enriched. The work is excellent in appearance, well written and a blessing to behold.

> –Pastor Rick Drebenstedt, Menorah Ministries

Numerous Christian, Jewish, and historical resources written by many scholars with various doctrinal opinions, were examined during the research for this book. Quotations are used from scholars that are experts in research of Church history. However, this does not mean the authors agree doctrinally with any of the specific ministries or persons quoted.

A Family Guide to the

Biblical Holidays

With Activities for All Ages

Robin Sampson & Linda Pierce

About the Authors

Robin Sampson

Robin Sampson is a mother of eleven, grandmother of twelve, and author of several acclaimed books including Ancient History: Adam to Messiah, What Your Child Needs to Know When, Wisdom: An Internet-Linked Unit Study, and The Heart of Wisdom Teaching Approach. Robin's husband, Ronnie, is an assistant deputy director for Homeland Security in Washington, D.C. They reside in northern Virginia.

Linda Pierce

Originally a public school teacher of English and Science, she has worked as an art director and commercial artist for an advertising agency, and as editor of the Owen County News-Herald. Linda holds a B.S. degree in Home Economics and Biology from Georgetown College, KY. She now enjoys writing Christian-based curriculum for home educated children and creating freelance artwork. Linda began home schooling her two youngest children in 1989. Linda is a proud grandmother of three.

A Family Guide to the Biblical Holidays with Activities for all Ages
By Robin Scarlata and Linda Pierce
Heart of Wisdom Publishing
Copyright © 1999 Reprint 2009

Published by:
Robin Scarlata Sampson
Heart of Wisdom Publishing
Shelbyville, TN

Printed in the U.S.A.
Unless otherwise stated, all Bible verses are from the KJV and are used by permission–Eph. 6:17.
First Edition Copyright © 1997

Dedication:

to the
Glory
of
God

Introduction

Section 1:
God's Holidays

Section 2:
Preliminary Activities & Crafts

Section 3:
The Spring Holidays

Table of Contents

A Family Guide to the Biblical Holidays©

Section 4:
The Fall Holidays

Feast of Trumpets (Rosh Hashanah)

Day of Atonement (Yom Kippur)

Section 5:
Post Mosaic Holidays

Purim

Section 6:
The Seventh Day Holiday

Sabbath

Section 7:
Holidays Across the Curriculum

Holidays Across the Curriculum - cont.

Appendixes

Back Matter

INTRODUCTION

- ◆ PREFACE
- ◆ WHAT THIS BOOK IS ABOUT
- ◆ HOW THIS BOOK IS ORGANIZED
- ◆ HOW TO USE THIS BOOK
- ◆ SPECIAL EXPLANATIONS

Heart of Wisdom Publishing

Preface

WE DECIDED TO CELEBRATE THE BIBLICAL HOLIDAYS

During Bible study, our family discovered something that we had heard very little about from church. We found out God had set apart special days to worship and honor Him. By learning about the practices of these special days, we could learn about and worship God. We spent some time studying the holidays from Scripture and decided it'd be fun to teach to our children. So our family started celebrating the Biblical Feast days. What a joy! These celebrations are wonderful! Not only was the celebration itself fun and informative, but even the preparation was full of lessons and prompted us into deeper Bible study. The children enjoyed these great "interactive" celebrations more than any man-made holidays (more than even gift-giving days). I was very excited about all we had learned and anxious to tell my Christian friends.

My enthusiasm was soon crushed. I was eagerly sharing with a friend how we celebrated a feast day and how much we had learned. I expected my friend to catch the enthusiasm. Instead I was met with a fierce frown and raised eyebrows. I was told the feast days have been done away with, are no longer necessary, and such nonsense was legalistic. "But, but, ...we didn't do anything wrong...it's just...it can't be wrong... we were just studying the Bible," I stammered. My friend explained, "You cannot keep the holidays. It is legalistic."

Celebrating the feasts was only a surface learning experience? Down deep, was I trying to earn my way to heaven? Whoa, I know salvation only comes through God's Son. This conversation led to many questions. What is legalism? Is the Old Testament relevant today? How can obeying Deuteronomy 6—teaching our children God's ways—be legalistic? How can righteousness be wrong? Time for another Bible study.

LEGALISM OR DESIRING TO PLEASE GOD?

Legalism is when a person does works stemming from prideful self-sufficiency that ignores trust and regards performing good deeds as doing God a favor. It is when one gets so involved in seeking to fulfill every minor detail of God's law or man-made laws that the heart of God is missed. If someone is under a yoke of legalism he is probably trying to meet some fence laws-- extra rules tacked on to God's ways-- prescribed by men (see Fence Laws page 38). The yoke of legalism is unbearable. This "earned righteousness mentality" is a nasty pride. The end result of legalism is a proud confidence in one's own righteousness and missing God's will.

A sample of legalism is in Acts 15:5. The Pharisees laid down the position that unless the Gentiles who turned Christians were circumcised after the manner of Moses, and thereby bound themselves to all the observances of the ceremonial law, they could not be saved. This is foolish, as if being circumcised could earn salvation. Jesus spoke firmly against legalism (see Matthew 23:2–4, Mark 7:5–13).

So what is the difference between trying to please God and legalism? A measuring stick that only measures the end result will identify anything pleasing to God as *legalism*. As with most things Jesus taught about, the difference between doing something to please God, and legalism, is found in the heart.

To have faith in Christ's saving grace one must have the knowledge that we are completely unrighteous without the atonement of Jesus, unworthy of receiving the gift of life Christ laid down for us. Responding to God in worship and obedience to His Word is evidence of our gratefulness for His gift to us.

- Legalism is focused on a system.
- Desiring to please God is focused on a relationship.
- Legalism is focused on what is required.
- Desiring to please God is focused on love from within.
- Legalism asks "How can I meet the requirements?"
- Desiring to please God asks, "What is the Lord telling me about His desires through His instruction?"
- Legalism is horrid, for if it were possible to earn a relationship with God, in and of ourselves, Christ's death was pointless.
- Desiring to please God is obeying His command—to love Him with all out hearts, minds, and souls. Loving God can *never* be legalistic!

A FRUIT TEST

Celebrating the holidays can become legalistic. So can going to church, wearing certain clothing, helping the poor, etc. Anything to earn righteousness or done for the outward appearances is legalism. Celebrating the feast days can become legalistic if your heart is not right. If you feel you *have to* do the holidays and you're in a frenzy trying to make everything just perfect, your house is a shambles, children crying, and everyone in a foul mood, you are defeating the point. Time to check your motives. The woman who decided to wear a head covering to show she was submissive—who wore it against her husband's wishes—was not right in her heart. Are you are being controlled by legalism—or a desire to please God? It is easy to find out if something is legalistic—examine the fruit produced. If it is from God the fruit will be patience, joy, peace, love, kindness, gentleness and self-control. The fruit of legalism is easily recognized—arguments, selfish ambition, unreasonable behavior, deceitfulness, and envy.

UNDER LAW OF GRACE?

The Jewish New Testament Commentary explains, the word *under*, in Greek *upo,* means "controlled by" or "in subjection to." If one is under legalism he is controlled by legalism. Being "under grace" is a subjection which, because of the nature of grace itself, does not have the usual oppressive characteristics of subjection. God's people, the people who are in a trust relationship with him, are and always have been under grace and under *Torah* (a gracious subjection) but never under legalism (a harsh subjection).

We are not in bondage, we are free, free in Christ—free enough to enjoy a cycle of annual celebrations that reminds us that God has done a wonderful work of redemption for us through Christ. Celebrating the biblical holidays is a privileged set apart time of Bible study or family devotions. Do you *have* to have Bible study or family devotions? No, but will you learn more about God, His ways and His paths if you do?

We can celebrate the Biblical holidays if we do it to learn about God or to worship God. If we celebrate the holidays to earn righteousness there is no reason to observe them. By celebrating the biblical holidays I am no better than my friend who chooses not to observe these days. Both of our righteousness is as filthy rags. We are only saved by Christ.

The purpose of this book is not to tell you whether or not you should celebrate the biblical holidays. The purpose of this book is help you make a special memory with your children, to give you options of different ways to have a fun celebration while teaching you God's Word.

What this Book is About

This Book is devoted to helping you teach your family (or Bible study class) how the Lord's festival celebrations were a beautiful foreshadow of Jesus the Messiah! What a wonderful way to learn the Bible–by means of these powerful teachings using visual aids! We can celebrate the fulfillment of these holidays in Christ, pay tribute to what God felt was so important to remember, make long-lasting, warmhearted memories for our families, as well as learn glorious secrets hidden in God's word!

God's people are realizing how important it is to understand our Hebraic roots–our spiritual heritage. There is a revival in the land! Believers all over the world are returning to worshipping God in the same manner as in times of the original church of believers. We are seeing new praises by singing the Psalms, displaying banners, Hebrew dances, family-centered worship in homes, and worship by means of the Biblical holidays.

These holidays are a picture–more than any other subject in the Bible–to teach us historical, spiritual, and prophetic lessons! It is amazing that most Christians do not know about the "Holy Days" of the Bible, in spite of the fact that these days were celebrated by Jesus, by the apostles (long after His death and resurrection), and by the early New Testament Church–including the Gentile congregations.

There is so much about God we need to teach our children. Studying these holidays is such a special way to learn. It is the way God taught His people to remember His concern, love, mercy, and protective care for us. Studying these holidays will teach our children about:

1. historical events of the Bible.

2. prophetic events yet to come.

3. our Christian walk.

4. God's plan of salvation.

5. the life and ministry of Jesus Christ, our Lord and Savior.

How This Book is Organized

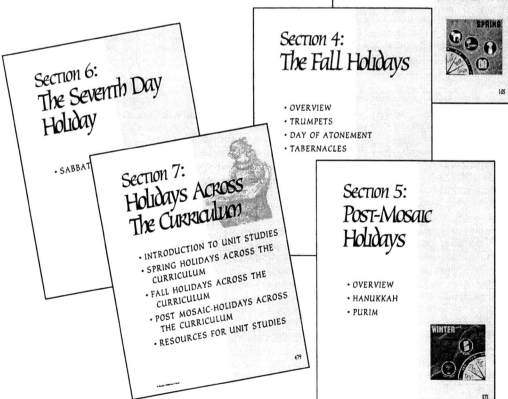

Section 1:
God's Holidays

...LIDAYS?
... THE HOLIDAYS?
... OLIDAYS
... IMES
... IE HEBREW

31

Section 2:
Preliminary
Activities & Crafts

• DISCUSSION ACTIVITY
• MULTI-HOLIDAY CENTERPIECE
• WALL HANGING
• FLAG DIRECTIONS & ILLUSTRATIONS
• HEBREW WORD
• RECIPE ROUND
• FOUR SEASONS
• FESTIVE FAMIL

Section 3:
The Spring Holidays

• OVERVIEW
• PASSOVER
• UNLEAVENED BREAD
• EARLY FIRSTFRUITS AND OMER

SPRING

105

Section 4:
The Fall Holidays

• OVERVIEW
• TRUMPETS
• DAY OF ATONEMENT
• TABERNACLES

Section 6:
The Seventh Day
Holiday

• SABBAT

Section 7:
Holidays Across
The Curriculum

• INTRODUCTION TO UNIT STUDIES
• SPRING HOLIDAYS ACROSS THE CURRICULUM
• FALL HOLIDAYS ACROSS THE CURRICULUM
• POST MOSAIC-HOLIDAYS ACROSS THE CURRICULUM
• RESOURCES FOR UNIT STUDIES

479

Section 5:
Post-Mosaic
Holidays

• OVERVIEW
• HANUKKAH
• PURIM

WINTER

375

21

How This Book is Organized-cont.

Each Chapter is divided as follows:

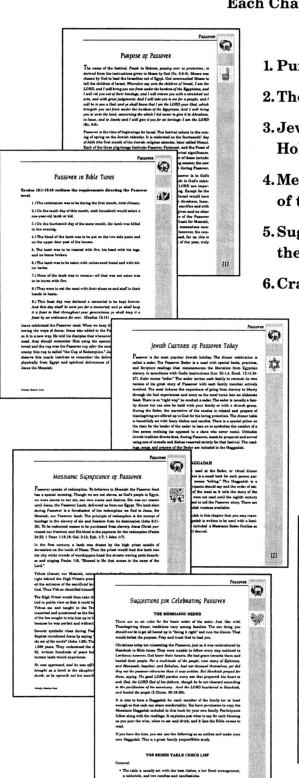

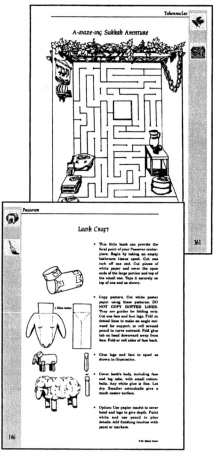

1. Purpose of the Holiday

2. The Holiday in Bible Times

3. Jewish Customs of the Holiday

4. Messianic Significance of the Holiday

5. Suggestions for Celebrating the Holiday

6. Crafts and Activities

How to Use this Book

This book is set up for parents and/or teachers to use as a study guide a few weeks before each holiday or as a thematic unit study for an entire year. Each section includes activities, crafts, recipes, and puzzles for you to choose from. You can use this book in several ways.

CELEBRATE THE HOLIDAYS

Make the holidays part of your family's tradition! Read through the Introduction section and Section One of this book first. The Preliminary Activities and Crafts section contain items including instructions for making a centerpiece, a recipe folder, a wall hanging, and other activities which can be used for each of the holidays. The holiday chapters start with the annual spring, fall, then post-mosaic holidays (winter) and finally, the weekly Sabbath holiday.

You need not wait for spring to start the holidays. You can start at any festival, but it would be helpful to read through the previous chapters, as the holidays do tell chronological events about Christ. The spring holidays tell of His first coming and the fall holidays describe His second coming.

This book includes a variety of suggestions, activities, and crafts for you to enjoy each holiday. Decide which activities will work well for your family and age group.

SMALL GROUP BIBLE STUDY

The renewed interest in the Hebraic roots of Christianity has caused an eager desire among churches as groups to study the holidays. This book can also be used to study fascinating topic at times other than the festival dates, as a small group Bible study.

Sample Eighteen Week Study

One example of a group study to get a quick overview of all the holidays would be to study one holiday for the duration of two two-hour classes (eighteen week study).

Week 1   Overview
Week 2   Purpose of Passover/Passover in Bible Times.
Week 3   Jewish Customs of Passover Today/Messianic Significance of Passover.
Week 4   Purpose of Unleavened Bread/Unleavened Bread in Bible Times.

Week 5   Jewish Customs of Unleavened Bread Today/ Messianic Significance of Unleavened Bread.

Decide on the format for your study. For example, a two-hour format may include: ten minutes prayer and overview, forty-five minutes leader guidance through Bible verses and information in this book, twenty minutes break, thirty minutes discussion, ten minute wrap-up and a closing prayer.

CHILDREN'S CHURCH SCHOOL

Plan on celebrating the holiday with a children's one-hour class by choosing very simple activities. The teacher should read through the Introduction and Section One. Start planning at least two to three weeks before the time of the holiday. Lesson Plan pages are included in the Preliminary Activities and Crafts section (page 68) for your convenience. The following is an example of a one-hour Bible or co-op class held each week for three weeks some time before Passover (or a class held each day for three days before Passover):

First Lesson: Read what the Bible says about Passover and the purpose of Passover. Make the Lamb craft or Lamb Centerpiece.

Second Lesson: Read the sections "Passover in Bible Times" and "Messianic Significance of Passover." Explain a seder. Play one of the suggested games, puzzles, or worksheets. Decorate the classroom for next week's seder.

Third Lesson: Have a mini seder. You won't have time for a full meal; however, you can have: matzo, bitter herbs, green vegetables, and cups of grape juice and go through most of the Haggadah.

HOME SCHOOLERS

There are also several ways to use this book while home schooling. You can incorporate the holidays into your regular studies or even make the holidays the central focus of study for an entire year. See the instructions and Lesson Plan sheets in the "Holidays Across the Curriculum" on page 481.

Special Explanations

Special explanations and details have been included in the back of this book for your convenience.

Appendix A: Controversies or Why All The Fuss?   Page 529

The mention of the biblical holidays can be a controversial subject among some Christians, as noted in the preface and first chapter. This appendix lists a few notes explaining why, and how to handle differences in a Christian manner.

Appendix B: The Festival Dates   Page 533

The festival dates from 2004 to 2011 according to the Jewish calendar are listed in this section. Once you have read the chapter "Understanding the Hebrew Calendar," and have studied God's word, you can decide if these may be the dates on which you would like your family to celebrate or study the holidays.

Appendix C: The New Moon   Page 536

The Biblical months begin on the sighting of the new moon. The new moon is a fairly detailed and somewhat debated subject. It is briefly discussed in the chapter "Understanding the Hebrew Calendar." To keep the "Calendar" section easy to understand, the "New Moon" details are listed in this appendix.

Appendix D: God's and Jesus' Names   Page 537

Throughout this book, several authors are quoted. Occasionally you will see God's and Jesus' Hebrew names, YHWH and Y'shua (Yehowshuwa, Yah Shua, or other spellings). Since this subject has come up often in relationship to returning to Hebraic roots, we have addressed this subject in detail in the Appendix.

Appendix E: Symbolism in Numbers   Page 545

The dates, number of sacrifices, number of times certain actions are performed, etc., are significant. This appendix includes a brief list of symbolic meanings of some of the numbers in Scripture.

Appendix F: Law   Page 547

The celebration of the biblical holidays tend to lead people into a study of God's law. Appendix F explains that spirit of the law is good, just, holy and natural and usually misunderstood. This section includes where to get further details of where and how so many misunderstandings about God's law. The Home School Section includes a thematic study on law (see page 499).

Appendix F: Law   **Page 547**

The celebration of the biblical holidays tend to lead people into a study of God's law. Appendix F explains that spirit of the law is good, just, holy and natural and usually misunderstood. This section includes where to get further details of where and how so many misunderstandings about God's law. The Home School Section includes a thematic study on law (see page 499).

Appendix G: Resources to Study Hebrew Roots   **Page 549**

There is a brief section about our fascinating Hebrew roots in the first chapter (page 47). If you feel the excitement of this subject and would like to learn more about our Hebrew roots or the church's history, we have an extensive list of illuminating materials in this appendix as well as a list of magazines and organizations dedicated to the study of Christian Judaic studies.

Appendix H: Home School Resources   **Page 557**

The authors, editors, publisher, and design artists involved in this book are teaching their children at home, and are very active in the home schooling community. Education in the public system is headed in a direction deeply influenced by Greek, Roman, Freudian, or New Age philosophies. If you are considering protecting your children from these influences (and much peer pressure, violence, or other problems your community school may face), see this appendix for more information about home schooling.

Glossary   **Page 567**

To make this book as simple as possible, we usually use the English translations of the Hebrew names of each holiday (Passover instead of Pesach, etc.). Occasionally, the Hebrew name will occur in parentheses after the English name. There are many variations of spellings of the holiday names because they are transliterations of the Hebrew word. We have chosen what we felt were the easiest. If you run into any words unfamiliar to you, see the Glossary. If you cannot find Hebrew words that sound as if they start with an *h* try looking under *ch*.

Chapter Symbols

Purpose of the Holiday

Agricultural and historical significance of each holiday.

The Holiday in Bible Times

How each feast was celebrated before the destruction of the temple (Old and New Testaments). This section usually includes sacrificial rituals which the Jews no longer do because there is no Temple. Believers in Jesus no longer need sacrifices because Jesus was the ultimate sacrifice.

Jewish Customs of the Holiday Today

Each chapter of this book includes a section describing the *Jewish Customs of the Holiday Today*. The Rabbis added some traditions to keep the holidays. Some of them are good and help explain the tradition, some are "fence rules" (see page 38), and some are borrowed from pagan rituals. We included this section so you can learn how the holidays are observed and decide for yourself whether or not you want to include parts of their ceremonies in your family traditions. The general guideline for observing any traditions that are not commanded in God's Word is that we must look at each tradition on its own. We must weigh it against scripture, to determine if there is any conflict, and we must guard ourselves against bondage to that tradition.

Messianic Significance of the Holiday

How Jesus celebrated the holiday and how the holiday points to the first or second coming of Jesus, and other symbolic meanings.

Suggestions For Celebrating the Holiday

A few favorite ideas the authors have used in their homes to help spark your imagination so you can teach your children about the holidays in your home.

Subject Symbols

Puzzles, crafts and art projects are found in each chapter. Academic subjects are found in the special Home School section to help home schoolers incorporate the study of the holiday into their curriculum.

Bible Study

Recipe

Art / Craft

Puzzle

History

Geography

Language Arts

Music

Health

Science

Math

Game

Field Trips

Agriculture

Industry

Section 1:
God's Holidays

- A PARABLE

- WHY STUDY THE HOLIDAYS?

- WHAT HAPPENED TO THE HOLIDAYS?

- OUR HEBREW ROOTS

- OVERVIEW OF THE HOLIDAYS

- GOD'S APPOINTED TIMES

- UNDERSTANDING THE HEBREW
  CALENDAR

Holiday Parable

nce upon a time there was a wonderful King that ruled a Kingdom. The King was always doing fine and wonderful things for His people. The people desired in their hearts to worship and glorify the King and His wonderful deeds. So the King planned appointed times each year: special times for celebrations to tell the stories of His deeds to the people's children and to glorify the King. The King wrote the instructions of how to observe the celebrations in a book called the Book of Wisdom. For many years the people enjoyed these celebrations. Each year they would learn more about their King and feel closer to Him. They realized the King's celebrations were not only to tell stories of the things the King had done for His people in the past, but also foreshadows of more fine things the King was planning to do for them in the future.

There was another kingdom that did not worship the King. They worshiped objects such as statues, animals, trees, and the sun. In this other kingdom, the people practiced several different annual parties that glorified the people and the objects instead of the King. Each party had a different theme. In some they dressed up like animals and other beings. In some they decorated their homes and gave gifts to each other.

Then a man from this other kingdom visited the King's kingdom and told the people the annual parties were much more fun than the King's celebrations. Some of the people wanted to continue celebrating the ceremonies that worshiped the King. Other people wanted to replace the special celebrations with the new celebrations. Through the years people started to combine both sets of celebrations. They would practice the annual parties, meant to worship objects such as statues, animals, trees, and the sun, but they would say that they were worshipping the King, not the object, so everyone would be happy. They changed the appointed times of the King's celebrations to new times that coincided with the annual parties. The people of both kingdoms were combining so many traditions that no one could tell that there were two kingdoms. The kingdoms blended into each other. This continued for many years until the most recent generations forgot the celebrations that the King planned that glorified the King and His wonderful deeds for the people.

One day a man was reading the Book of Wisdom. He came across a little known chapter that told about the King's appointed times each year: special times for celebrations to tell the stories of His deeds to the people's children and to glorify the King. He was *so excited*! He went to tell the people about the wonderful celebrations. This made the people very angry. They felt that the man was condemning them for traditions that they had innocently done all their lives. They did not understand.

The man was sad, but he decided to keep the King's celebrations in his own family. The man's family learned much about the King. In fact, each year the man and his family grew closer and closer to the King because of the wonderful stories they learned about during the celebrations. The man and his family learned that the King had special secrets that revealed foreshadows of more fine things the King was planning to do for them. That man wanted so much to share these stories with others. Even though the man was continually rejected, he continued to tell about the King's celebrations. After a while, a few other families (who had always felt uncomfortable about the annual parties they kept) listened to the man. They read the chapter in the Book of Wisdom and also got excited. Soon many people returned to celebrating the King's appointed times, worshipping and telling stories about the King. This made the King very happy!

Why Study the Biblical Holidays

"*To* every thing there is a season, and a time to every purpose under the heaven." (Eccl. 3:1).

How much would you know about the Pilgrims without the celebration of Thanksgiving? Think about it. Would you remember Plymouth Rock, the Indians, the Mayflower? God gave us instructions to learn about His Story (History) through fun celebrations!

Paul wrote to the Gentile believers in Colossians 2:16-17 that the holidays *"are a shadow of things to come."* Each of the spring holidays is a picture of Christ's first coming. Jesus was sacrificed for our sins on Passover, buried on Unleavened Bread, and arose on Firstfruits. The fall holidays are a picture of His second coming and the beginning of the Messianic reign.

BLUEPRINTS

The Festivals of God are blueprints for the plan of God. When you look at a set of blueprints for a house that is to be built, it is difficult to visualize what the house will look like when it is finished. It is hard to imagine all the details as a whole. But if you look at the blueprints for a house you are familiar with, perhaps the house you live in, then you can relate those plans to your own experience. You can fully visualize the whole of its completion, and the blueprints will help you see where the foundation is laid, where the pipes and cables run, and how the structure supports itself. It is the same with the Holidays of God. When we look at the spring festivals, we can look back at the first century and see how the prophetic elements of those festivals were fulfilled. We can see how the plan of God was carried out in perfection (Lancaster 1995).

Each of the biblical Jewish holidays teaches us about our wonderful relationship with God. His whole redemption story is portrayed for us in these festivals. Passover pictures salvation or deliverance from Egypt (flesh or sin). Unleavened Bread shows us that God saved us in order that we may be holy and set apart for Him by putting off the "old sin nature." Firstfruits teaches us the purpose of salvation: fruitfulness in the Kingdom of God (John 15:1-5) and putting on the "new man," the nature of God (Eph. 4:24). The Feast of Weeks instructs us further concerning the kind of fruit we must bear–spiritual fruit (Gal. 5:22-23) through the power of the Holy Spirit.

Quick Overview of the Biblical Holidays

FESTIVAL	PURPOSE	MESSIANIC SIGNIFICANCE
Passover Pesach Nisan 14 ❖	Remembering the deliverance from Egyptian bondage. An unblemished firstborn male lamb was sacrificed and its blood poured on the altar. A lamb was selected for each family, and four days before the lamb was to be slain it was brought into the home for a four-day examination period.	Jesus is the sacrificial lamb who died for our sins. On Nisan 15 at the exact time the lamb was to be slain, Jesus was slain. Jesus also had a four-day examination period before the religious leaders—and was found without blemish.
Unleavened Bread Nisan 15	Leaven symbolizes sin. Unleavened Bread speaks of sanctification. God told the Jews to cleanse all leaven from their homes and eat only unleavened bread, matzah, for seven days, symbolizing a holy walk with Him.	Jesus is the "Bread of Life" without sin. Born in Bethlehem. In Hebrew, Bethlehem means "house of bread." Just as matzah is striped and pierced, so was the Messiah. This Feast falls on the day Jesus was buried.
Day of Firstfruits Nisan 17	The first of the barley harvest was brought as an offering to the priest in the Tabernacle/Temple. The priest would present the first of the harvest unto the Lord by waving them back and forth. This reminded the Hebrews that God gave them the land, and the harvest belonged to Him.	Jesus is the Firstfruits (1 Cor. 15:20-23). Jesus' resurrection marked the beginning of the harvest of souls. John 12:23-24,32 shows Jesus was likened to a grain of wheat falling to the ground and dying to produce a great harvest. Jesus arose on Firstfruits.
Feast of Weeks Shavuot/Pentecost 50 Days after Firstfruits ❖	Fifty days after the Feast of Firstfruits, a rememberence of the giving of the Torah (law) to Moses on Sinai took place this day. Two loaves of leavened bread are presented to God. Also a reminder that the Jews were slaves to Egypt (Deut. 16:9-17). Three thousand were killed that day.	Fifty days after Jesus arose, a group of Messianic Jews received the Holy Spirit. Jesus said "Unless I go, the Holy Spirit will not come. But when I go (Firstfruits-His resurrection) I will send the Holy Spirit unto you." God wrote the law (Torah) on the hearts of the believers. Three thousand souls were saved.
Feast of Trumpets Rosh Hashanah Tishri 1	The Jewish New Year begins the high Holy Days in the Jewish month of Tishri (corresponding to September or October.) A celebration of the spiritual birthday of the world or creation. Blowing of the trumpets and coronation of the King.	Possibly depicts the rapture of the church, a regathering of believers at the sound of the trumpet (1 Thess. 4:16-18; Rev. 19) and judgment of the wicked, or possibility is that this is the day of the second coming. Jesus will be King of earth.
Day of Atonement Yom Kippur Tishri 10	The holiest day in the Jewish year is spent in fasting, prayer, and confession. This was one gracious day a year given by God that each individual could receive forgiveness. The high priest entered the holy of holies to make atonement for the nation by sacrificing animals including two goats.	Christ our Messiah was displayed as our sacrifice. We can use this as a time of self-searching, repentance, and recommitment to God. The goats represent Jews and Gentiles. Possibly points to the day of the Messiah's physically returning to earth. Or it is possible this is the Judgment Day.
Feast of Tabernacles Sukkoth Tishri 15 ❖	God told the people they should live in booths for seven days so that the generations would know that His people lived in booths when He brought them out of Egypt. Each Sukkoth, the Jews build and dwell or eat in booths or temporary dwellings for seven days. A joyful celebration!	Christ is our tabernacle or dwelling place (John 14:14). May represent the 1000-year reign of Christ on earth. Many believe Jesus was born during this Feast because He was born in the late fall in a "booth." Or this is possibly when we tabernacle (dwell) with God in heaven.

A Family Guide to the Biblical Holidays©

The Biblical holidays were instituted by God (all but Hanukkah and Purim instituted by God's people) as an integral part of the divine worship system of the church (Old and New Testament). They are not a matter of salvation or approval before God. They are, as He intended, a remembrance and memorial in honor of what God has done for His people. The holidays presented in this book have a deep abiding meaning for the Christian since their completeness is found in Jesus.

The Hebrew term for *feast* or *festival* is *mo'ed*: it means set time or appointed time. Studying the holidays will help you:

- better understand the Bible.
- rediscover the Jewish roots of Christianity.
- more fully comprehend God's plan of redemption.
- more deeply understand the revelation of Jesus.
- get greater insights into God's prophetic seasons.
- get clearer and more powerful teachings through visual aids.
- discover the Biblical Church calendar.
- learn hand's-on object lessons to communicate God's love and care to your children.
- make wonderful memories that your children will cherish.

The Bible is full of symbols. A symbol is a picture of a more complex "idea" or reality. It is true that a picture is worth a thousand words. Those who take the time to study the Holy Days and the "pictures" therein can fully understand the significance of Christ and God's original system of worship.

The whole basis of our teaching in Christian academics should be based on a knowledge of not only Old Testament, but a greater understanding of culture (Bean 1995). This in no way takes away from our basic belief in Jesus. It gives us a much deeper perspective of Christianity and the words of Jesus.

THE APOSTLES KEPT THE BIBLICAL HOLIDAYS

The Apostle Paul directed the church in Corinth, which was predominately Gentile, to keep the Feast of Passover (1 Cor. 5:7,8). Roughly thirty years after the death of Jesus (when most Christians believe the celebrations had ended), the Apostle Paul was still highly motivated with Christian zeal to return to Jerusalem and to celebrate The Day of Feast of Weeks (Pentecost). Obviously, Paul valued celebrating the biblical holidays.

Paul encourages the church of Corinth to keep Passover with a right spirit–with a focus on the New Covenant.

Purge out therefore the old leaven, that ye may be a new lump, as ye are unleavened. For even Christ our Passover is sacrificed: Therefore let us keep the feasts, not with old leaven, neither with leaven of malice and wickedness; but with the unleavened bread of sincerity and truth (I Cor. 5:7-8).

FENCE RULES

The early New Testament church tried to de-Judaize the church because of a fear of legalism. The church was right to get rid of what Jesus condemned— the *"fence rules"* the rabbis added to God's word. Jewish religious leaders added greatly to the details of the holiday requirements and to other laws. They sought to insure proper and careful observance by making certain that people did not even come close to violating any requirement. This substitution of human law for divine law (Matt. 15:9), made God's instruction a burden rather than a rest and delight (Luke 11:46).

The Pharisees were very devoted to God's Torah and prided themselves in denying everything impure and ungodly. They lived in total physical separation from the rest of the world. Their whole lives were spent in protecting and propagating the laws of God. But they did not stop there. In their zeal for God's law, they started adding to it. For example, God says not to work on the Sabbath, the Rabbis added to the command forty types of labor that were to be forbidden, such as untying a knot, lighting a fire, sewing, etc. These extra laws were called *seyag* which literally means *fence*. They would build fence laws around the scriptures. This stemmed from insecurity and not having a relationship with the living God. After a time, these laws became confused with the Bible itself. They also contradicted themselves continuously (Leaver, 1996).

Matt. 15:7-9, *Ye hypocrites, well did Esaias prophesy of you, saying, This people draweth nigh unto me with their mouth, and honoureth me with their lips; but their heart is far from me. But in vain they do worship me, teaching for doctrines the commandments of men.*

Jesus had no problem with them obeying the scriptures. In fact, he encouraged people to do what the Pharisees said to do if it was scriptural, Matthew 5:20, *For I say unto you, That except your righteousness shall exceed the righteousness of the scribes and Pharisees, ye shall in no case enter into the kingdom of heaven.* What the Lord objected to was the *seyag*—the fence laws! The adding to the Word of God.

What Happened to the Biblical Holidays?

The holidays contain more divine information of spiritual and prophetic value than any subject of scripture. Why aren't we taught these marvelous lessons in church? The answer is found during the first through the fourth centuries.

FIRST CENTURY CHURCH

In the first century there were literally hundreds of thousands of believing Jews (Acts 2:41, 47, 4:4, 6:7, 9:31, 21:20). Scripture tells us the apostles and the early church continued to celebrate the holidays with the new realization of the symbolism of Christ. Very few Gentiles converted before Peter and Paul were sent out. When God miraculously showed the believing Jews that Jesus was the Messiah for both Jew and Gentile alike, then Gentiles from every nation began to pour into this Jewish faith. The followers of Christ, whether Jewish or Gentile, were seen as one family. Both considered themselves part of Israel. The Gentiles saw themselves as grafted *into* Israel (Romans 11), not replacing Israel. The word *Christian* was not used until A.D. 42 in Antioch (Acts 11:26). Later it was adopted to set apart Jews believing in Jesus and unbelieving Jews. Ultimately it became an identity for the entire Church.

Paul makes it clear that Gentiles who trust in Jesus become children of God, are equal partners with believing Jews in the Body of the Messiah, and are declared righteous by God without their having to adopt any further Jewish distinctives (Rom. 3:22–23, 29–30; 4:9–12; 10:12; 11:32; 1 Cor. 12:13; Eph. 2:11–22; 3:6; Col. 3:11) (Stern, 1992).

SECOND CENTURY CHURCH

By the second century the Gentiles had taken control of the church, and there started the process of removing Jewish influences referred to as de-Judaizing. There was a growing spirit of resentment of the non-believing Jews and all Jewish customs. The first seeds of anti-Semitism were sown. As the church grew, it became increasingly Hellenized (Greek) and Latinized (Roman). The Gentile-dominated Church celebrated the Lord's resurrection, but to distance Christianity from Judaism they changed the resurrection date from the Jewish calendar from the third day of *Passover*, to Sunday—this is how Easter became separated from Passover.

FOURTH CENTURY

By the time of the Council of Nicea (325 A.D.), Constantine, Emperor of Rome, claimed conversion to Christianity and considered himself the leader in the Christian church. Things changed drastically for the Gentile believers. Gentile believers were no longer persecuted. It became an economic advantage to be a Christian. Constantine also supported paganism with Christianity. In 314 he placed the symbol of the cross on his coins with the marks of Sol Invictus and Mars Conservator. Constantine retained the title of chief priest of the state cult until he died.

Under Constantine things got better for the believing gentiles; however, now the Christians persecuted the Jews. The Jews who accepted Jesus as the Messiah were forced to give up all ties with Judaism, Jewish practices, Jewish friends and anything Jewish. Constantine issued laws forbidding Jewish believers to keep Saturday as Sabbath, circumcise their children, celebrate Passover, etc. The punishments included imprisonment and even death. Constantine replaced the Biblical Holidays with alternative forms of celebrations adopted from other religions.

The Jewish New Testament Commentary reports that the Jewish believers were told to ignore the way commanded by Moses or they could not be saved! "You Messianic Jews should not separate yourselves from us Gentile Christians by having Messianic synagogues! Don't you know that 'in Christ there is neither Jew nor Greek?' So be like us, give up your Jewish distinctives, stop observing the *Torah* and the Jewish holidays, put all that behind you; and worship with us in our Gentile-oriented congregations, living our Gentile lifestyle." The misuse is in concluding that because there is no distinction in God's sight between the forensic righteousness of believing Gentiles and of believing Jews, therefore Jews are prohibited from observing God-given commandments. Such a conclusion defies both logic and the practice of the early believers.

The anti-semitic attitude toward the Jews flourished. During the Middle Ages, bands of Crusaders destroyed many Jewish communities. The raiders demanded the Jews convert but the majority preferred to die for their faith. In the late thirteenth century half of the world's Jewish population were living in Western Europe, over five hundred thousand. By 1500 there were no more than 150,000 Jews in this region due to riots, plagues and expulsions.

TWO PEOPLES, ONE CHURCH

Galatians 3:28 says, *There is neither Jew nor Greek, there is neither bond nor free, there is neither male nor female: for ye are all one in Christ Jesus.* This isolated verse has been misinterpreted to say a Jew must give up his heritage. It really explains that Jewish and Gentile believers must treat each other as equals before God, of equal worth as human beings. Notice how Paul ends the chapter. *And if ye be Christ's, then are ye Abraham's seed, and heirs according to the promise* (v. 29).

[The sentence in the verse above] contains three parallel pairs: Jew ... Gentile, slave ... freeman, male ... female. Obviously there are still observable physical, psychological and social distinctions between male and female and between slave and freeman (even today there remains in the world tens of millions of slaves), even though in union with the Messiah Yeshua they are all one, so far as their acceptability before God is concerned. The same is true of Jews and Gentiles: the distinction remains; the verse does not obliterate it (Stern 1992).

The Bible does teach differences between Jews and Gentiles and between other groups. There are different commands for men and women, husbands and wives, parents and children, slaves and masters, leaders and followers, widows and other women as well as special requirements for offices such as pastors, elders, deacons, and evangelists (1 Cor. 11:2–16, 14:34–36; Eph. 5:22–6:9; Col. 3:18–4:1; Titus 3:1–13, 5:3–16; 1 Peter 3:1–7).

Much of the Church continues to insist on this view that once a Jew is saved he is no longer a Jew. Christians can be a better witness to a Jew once they understand how a religious, non-believing Jew thinks. For example, an invitation to Sunday church or to a ham dinner for Christmas would not be the best way to win Jewish converts.

THROWING OUT THE BABY

Unfortunately, while trying to separate from the non-believing Jews the Church threw out the baby (Biblical holidays) with the bath water (un-Biblical customs)! There was no reason to stop the Holidays. These days did not bring bondage—they brought people closer to God. Jesus and Paul both celebrated the holidays. The holidays should be analyzed according to the Bible — not whether or not they are Jewish.

A non-Jew may choose voluntarily to conform to certain observances, celebrations, or customs which are both Jewish and rooted in Scripture. Such practice is not Judaizing. Following a Biblical custom is far different from being bound by a required practice (Wilson 1989, 26). Jesus' ministry, death, and resurrection, has made it possible for all believers, Gentiles and Jews, to maintain the righteous principles of the law without being encumbered with all the cultural baggage of Talmudic Judaism (Judaizing).

THE PURITANS

When the Puritans came to America they were deeply immersed in their Hebrew heritage. Marvin Wilson explains in his book, *Our Father Abraham* (pp. 127-128):

> The Reformers put great stress on *sola scriptura* (Scripture as the soul and final authority of the Christian). The consequent de-emphasis on tradition brought with it a return to the biblical roots. Accordingly, during the two centuries following the Reformation, several groups recognized the importance of once again emphasizing the Hebraic heritage of the Church. Among these people were the Puritans who founded Pilgrim America.

> The Puritans came to America deeply rooted in the Hebraic tradition. Most bore Hebrew names. The Pilgrim fathers considered themselves as the children of Israel fleeing "Egypt" (England), crossing the "Red Sea" (the Atlantic Ocean), and emerging from this "Exodus" to their own "promised land" (New England). The Pilgrims thought of themselves as "all the children of Abraham" and thus under the covenant of Abraham (Feingold n.d., 46).

> Thus, the seeds of religious liberty for the American Church did not come from New England leaders like Roger Williams and Anne Hutchinson—as noble as they and others were. Rather, it came from the Hebrews themselves, whose sacred Writings inspired the Puritans.

The Jewish New Testament Commentary says, "The Puritans, who took the Old Testament more seriously than most Christians, modeled the American holiday of Thanksgiving after *Sukkoth*" (Stern 1992).

The Puritans wanted to abolish pagan religious ceremonies that had crept into the Roman Catholic church from Babylonianism. To rid the church of all pagan superstitions, the Puritans did away with *all* the calendar days.

Christmas was outlawed in England in 1644 by an act of Parliament, for it was a lingering pagan element of the papal calendar, and they considered it disobedient to God's Word (Deut. 12:30, 31; 1 John 5:18-21; 2 Cor. 6-14-7:1). By 1659, Massachusetts had passed a law fining anybody who celebrated Christmas. Under the influence of puritanical thought, America suppressed the celebration of Christmas well into the nineteenth century.

By doing away with *all* the calendar days, the Puritans also threw out the baby (the Biblical holidays) with the bath water (pagan festivals such as Halloween, which is the ancient Samhain Festival of Death).

TODAY, GOD IS DOING A MARVELOUS THING

Richard Booker said it so well in *Celebrating the Lord's Holidays in the Church:*

> But in these last days, God is doing a marvelous thing. He is breaking down the walls of... misunderstanding that have divided the Jew and Gentile *believers*. [Just as He is tearing down the walls between black and white and other discriminations.] He is sovereignty pouring out His Spirit on thousands of Jews to prepare them for the coming of the Messiah. At the same time, God is stirring in the hearts of Christians a holy love for the Jewish people and awakening them to the Jewish roots of their Christian faith. Many Christians are realizing that the origin of our faith is Jerusalem, not Athens, Rome, Geneva, Wittenberg, Aldersgate, Azusa Street, Springfield, Nashville, Tulsa, etc. As a result, Christian Churches around the world are reaching out to the Jewish people in their communities, singing songs from the Old Testament, rediscovering their Jewish roots and celebrating the Jewish Holidays as fulfilled in Jesus. It is clearly God's appointed time to reconcile Jew and Gentile, binding us together by His Spirit in the Messiah (Booker 1987).

THE BIBLE IS ONE BOOK

The Bible is not a composite of two books nor sixty-six books with conflicting concepts and teaching. It is, rather, one book recording the acts of God under two primary covenants (Old and New Testaments). Doctrinally there is no conflict between the two. They are altogether compatible and in mutual agreement. We believe literally that "All Scripture is given by inspiration of God, and is profitable for doctrine, for reproof, for correction, for instruction in righteousness: that the man of God may be perfect, thoroughly furnished unto all good works" (2 Tim. 3:16-17) (Somerville).

The themes in the Old and New Testaments are the same: God's holiness, righteousness and mercy; and man's alienation and estrangement from God through disobedience. It might surprise you to know that the Jewish people do not rely on works for salvation—they know the only way to salvation is through the Messiah. The basic significance of the New Testament is uniquely a Jewish one: the fulfillment of the messianic hope. The New Testament writers, with perhaps the exception of Luke, are all Jews. The early Apostles and followers of Jesus are also Jewish. There is nothing in the New Testament that is non-Jewish or anti-Jewish. Quite the contrary, Jesus' entire message taught that:

> Only the merciful were to receive mercy, only the forgiving could expect forgiveness and that *love* would be the sign of His true disciples.

LET NO MAN JUDGE YOU

Let no man therefore judge you in meat, or in drink, or in respect of an holyday, or of the new moon, or of the sabbath days: Which are a shadow of things to come; but the body is of Christ
Col. 2:16-17.

This passage refers to God's Holy Days as "shadows." When Jesus came the first time He fulfilled the first three holidays. This does not mean the days are now irrelevant, unnecessary, and should not be kept. Wedding anniversaries are not irrelevant, unnecessary. They are set times to remember a special day. We don't mistake the anniversary as the reality of marriage. The anniversary is a symbol of the marriage. It can be a special time set aside to focus on the meaning of the marriage and maybe to speak of memories over the years. The anniversary is not a substitute for the marriage.

The Holidays days are set apart special times to remember, to look ahead, and to look at our spiritual walk. The Holy Days and their observance, incorporating all five of our senses, give us a better understanding of God. Just as

God asked His people to remember the Exodus by observing Passover. Jesus, on the night He was betrayed (during Passover), asked us to remember Passover. 1 Corinthains 11:23-26 *For I received from the Lord...that He took bread and blessed it and said 'take and eat, this is my body which is broken for you. Do this in remembrance of me.' Also the cup after supper saying 'this cup is the new covenant in My blood. This do, as often as you drink it, in remembrance of me. For as often as you eat this bread and drink this cup, you proclaim the Lord's death till He comes.'* The taking of the bread (His body) and drinking of the wine (His blood) is a special set apart time to remember just like an anniversary.

But what about this verse? *Ye observe days, and months, and times, and years. I am afraid of you, lest I have bestowed upon you labour in vain"* (Gal. 4:10-11).

Here is a classic example of faulty interpretation of scripture. This reference has nothing to do with Biblical memorial days. Paul's statement to the Galatians is concerning their returning to former pagan or heathen practices. Clearly he is not speaking of Biblical celebrations, which is borne out in the very structure of the letter itself. Notice that this was something they were reinstituting which they had been practicing when they worshiped false gods (see verse nine). The Galatians had never celebrated Biblical (Jewish) holy days, because they were Gentiles (Somerville 1995).

BIBLICAL WORSHIP

There is a revival in the land! Many are turning away from man-conceived concepts of worship to Biblical patterns. The motive for celebrating the holidays should be as God originally intended; a memorial, a remembrance and honor for what He has done. We don't need to be concerned with ancient ritualism customs, but we should focus on the basic principle of the holidays' prophetic and spiritual meanings as is revealed under the New Covenant (Rom. 7:6).

Anyone can celebrate the holidays if they do it for the right reasons. *But it is good to be zealously affected always in a good thing, and not only when I am present with you* (Gal. 4:18).

Web Sites to Learn More About Our Hebrew Roots

Arkansas Institute of Holy Land Studies
http://www.haydid.org/aihs1.htm

Awareness Ministries
http://www.awareness.org

Bridges for Peace
http://www.bridgesforpeace.com/

Chosen People Ministries
http://www.chosen-people.com

Christian Friends of Israel (CFI)
http://www.yashanet.com/CFI.htm

Christian Jew Foundation (CJF)
http://www.cjf.org http://www.cjf.org

Christnet Global Resources
http://www.christnet.org

Christian Renewal Ministries International
http://www.shalom-crmi.org/html/books.htm

Crosstalk
http://www.crosstalk.org/

Echad
http://www.echad.com

First Fruits of Zion
http://www.teshuvah.com/ffoz

Friends of Israel (FOI)
http://www.foigm.org

Gospel Research Foundation
http://www.gospelresearch.org/

Hakesher Inc (Messianic Resources)
http://www.hakesher.org/hakesher2/

HaY'Did Ministries, Inc.
http://www.haydid.org

Hear Oh Israel
http://www.hoim.com

Hebrew Roots Journal
http://www.geocities.com/~hebrew_roots/

Hebrew Calendar
http://messianic.com/heb-cal.htm

Heart of Wisdom (publisher of this book)
http://www.heartofwisdom.com

Integrity Music's Messianic Praise!
http://messianic.com/integrty

International Christian Embassy Jerusalem
http://www.intournet.co.il/icej

International Messianic Directory
http://www.messianic.com/pchome.htm

Institute Jerusalem Post
http://www.jpost.co.il

Jerusalem Perspective
http://www.jerusalemperspective.com

Jewish Jewels
http://www.jewishjewels.org/

Jews for Jesus
http://www.jewsforjesus.org/

Koinonia
http://www.khouse.org/index.html

Lion and Lamb Ministeries
http://www.telepath.com/rhadkins/yavoh/home.htm

Messianic Events Calendar
http://messianic.com/announce.htm

Messianic Jewish Alliance of America
http://www.mjaa.org/

Messianic Messages
http://www.messianicmessages.com/

Messianic Vision
http://www.sidroth.org/

Menorah Ministries
http://www.rmii.com/~menorah

Messianic Gathering Place
http://home.att.net/~tmgp/

Olive Tree (listing over 600 Messianic sites)
http://www.saltshakers.com/home.htm

Petah Tikvah
http://www.etz-chayim.org/petah1.htm

Restore Magazine
http://www.restorationfoundation.org.

Return to G_d
http://www.iclnet.org/pub/resources/text/rtg/rtg-home.html

Shofar International
http://www.shofar.org/index.htm

Sounds of the Trumpet
www.rbooker.com

Union of Messianic Jewish Congregations
http://www.umjc.org/

Virtual Jerusalem
http://www.virtual.co.il/vjindex.htm

Our Hebrew Roots

The Biblical holidays are part of our Hebrew heritage. To fully comprehend our Christian faith, we should know about this fascinating heritage. We study a Hebrew book–written by Hebrews; we serve a Hebrew Lord–who had Hebrew disciples; we desire to follow the first century church–which was first predominately Hebrew; and through Christ, we are grafted into a Hebrew family! It makes sense to study the Hebrew culture.

This is a refreshing, new, exciting way to view the Bible! Much of the Bible is mysterious to most Americans. The perplexing phrases, puzzling actions, the sometimes difficult-to-understand words of Jesus, unconventional holidays, and parables are only understood with an awareness of the Hebrew culture. A Christian's roots are deep in Judaism through Christ, all the way back to Abraham! *And if ye be Christ's, then are ye Abraham's seed, and heirs according to the promise* (Gal. 3:29).

Studying Scripture from our Western/American/Greek view is like looking for gold in a dark mine with a dim pen light--you can see enough to stumble around but you need more light to see clearly. A good grasp of the ancient Hebraic customs and terminology would allow you to reexamine Scripture in this powerful light, exposing intricate details and treasures. Take a look at the examples below. One is a familiar Bible story, the other a familiar Bible phrase. Examine each with a light shed from Hebraic understanding.

The Woman with the Issue of Blood

The woman described in Matthew 9:20 had faith. She believed she would be healed if she did but touch the very *hem of his garment.* If you understand Hebrew thought you'll understand the significance of the story. Why did the woman touch the hem?

The hem of a Hebrew's prayer shawl is very important. The prayer shawl worn by Hebrew men is called a *tallit.* The fringe on the corner of the tallit is called a *tzitzit.* In Numbers 15 God directs the Hebrews to make fringes on the borders (also called corners or wings) of their garments to remind them of God's law!

... Speak unto the children of Israel, and bid them that they make them fringes in the <u>borders of their garments</u> throughout their generations, and that they put upon the <u>fringe of the borders a ribband of blue</u>: And it shall be

unto you for a fringe, that ye may look upon it, and <u>remember all the com-mandments</u> of the LORD...(Numbers 15: 38-39).

There are 613 actual commandments in the Torah–248 positive and 365 negative. Each tzitzit consist of five double knots and eighteen threads for a total of 13 elements. The numerical value of the word tzitzit is 600. So the total is 613. During the first century, a tradition associated with the tallit is that the tzitzit of the Messiah had healing powers. *The Sun of righteousness arise with healing in his wings* (Mal 4:2). The woman must have known of this tradition and in faith touched the wings of His garment! (For more on this subject see *The Hem of His Garment* by John Garr on page 550.)

The Kingdom of Heaven of Kingdom of God

The Kingdom of Heaven or Kingdom of God is the central theme of Jesus' preaching. The Hebrews did not use the sacred name of God. Many times they used the expression Kingdom of Heaven or Kingdom of God—just as today we say, "Heaven help me." We are not asking for heaven's help. We are asking for God's help.

Look at the phrase "The Kingdom of God has come near you" (Luke 10:9-11). The Kingdom of Heaven or God is described by most commentaries as God's kingdom *to come* sometime in the future. Some teach it means the second coming of Christ (Jesus called the second coming "the coming of the Son of Man").

The Greek word *engiken* means "about to appear" or "is almost here". However, if it is translated back to Hebrew–the verb *karav* means "to come up to," "to be where something or someone is." In the Greek the Kingdom is at a distance. In the Hebrew–it is here! Jesus' Messiahship is present here and now.

The "Kingdom of Heaven" is not futuristic, but rather a present reality wherever God is ruling...when one is able to put [Greek] passages back into Hebrew, it is immediately obvious that the Kingdom has already arrived, is in fact already here–almost the exact opposite of the Greek meaning (Bivin, Blizzard 1995).

Jesus Himself proclaimed that the Kingdom was at hand. This proclamation involved an awakening cry of sensational and universal significance. He was referring to Himself as the King being at hand—being present. He was already present in his person, He is the King. For one to follow Him he had to make Him his King and follow His rules. *Not every one that saith unto me,*

Lord, Lord, shall enter into the kingdom of heaven; but he that doeth the will of my Father which is in heaven (Matt. 7:21) takes on a whole new meaning. It is not heaven that they won't be entering. It is His Kingdom now, of peace, following His ways (Wilson 1989). *Blessed are the poor in spirit: for theirs is the Kingdom of Heaven* also takes on a new meaning.

Reread the following verses with this new light. It may change your opinion of these teachings: Mark 4:30-32; Matt. 13:33; 18:3; Luke 13:20-21, Matt. 12:28; Luke 11:20; Luke 17:20-21.

Jesus did not come right out and say, "I am the Messiah," In Hebrew there are far more powerful ways of making that claim (Bivin, Blizzard 1995). Seeking first the Kingdom of God is making Jesus Lord of your life today!

STUDYING OUR HEBREW ROOTS

Several fascinating books are available explaining Hebrew thought (see Appendix G page 549). *Yeshua: A Guide to Jesus and the Original Church* by Ron Mosley explains misunderstood idioms in Jesus' teaching such as: binding and losing, the parable of the reed and oak, the golden vine, the good eye, and many more. *Understanding the Difficult Words of Jesus*, by David Bivin and Roy Blizzard, explains that a proper Hebraic understanding of the words of Jesus would stop most theological controversies!

Our Father Abraham: Jewish Roots of the Christian Faith by Dr. Marvin Wilson is a in depth, detailed look at the Hebraic thought patterns as well as a study of Hebrew culture, worship, law and every aspect of family life. Here Dr. Wilson explains the contour of Hebrew thought:

> Modern man in the Western world thinks he has an image to defend. He is supposed to be macho and keep his cool. He is expected to be made of steel, always in control. He does not allow himself to become vulnerable by revealing much of his emotions. It is usually considered unmanly for him to cry. Yet Jesus, the exemplary man, wept (Luke 19:41; John 11:35). This display of emotion was in sharp contrast to the Greco-Roman world of the Stoics, who sought to be indifferent to pleasure or pain; they were determined never to submit or to yield; they were resolved to overcome their emotions and desires. The Hebrews, however, were a very passionate people; they did not hide or suppress their emotions.

The Hebrews, both men and women, were able to affirm their full humanity. They gave vent to their feelings, for each emotion had "a time" appropriate for its expression: being angry, crying, laughing, singing, feasting, dancing, hand clapping, shouting, embracing, and loving (see Eccl. 3:1-8). A brief summary of the holidays described in the Bible reveals a decisive emphasis on the release of emotion, especially joy. The weekly Sabbath is a time of rejoicing as God is celebrated as Creator (Isaiah 58:13-14; cf. Exod. 20:8-11). The entire annual calendar of festivals shows that the Hebrews were not afraid to release their emotions, in collective historical memory, before God and one another. The Hebrews were hardly halfhearted or reserved in their approach to life.

DIGGING THROUGH THE LAYERS

What we now consider "The Church" is almost nothing like the Early New Testament Church. Author/speaker Richard Booker once explained this, by giving the example of an archeologist digging through layers to find out what life was like in ancient times. To understand the Early Church we must dig through layers of a mountain of man's influences shoveling off and discarding man's traditions, theories, interpretations, and philosophies from Greek and Roman civilizations, Constantine, Marcion (see Appendix F), Catholicism, etc., to be able to examine the Early Church. During the Reformation, men such as Wycliffe and Calvin were digging in the right spot. They dug up and discarded many theological errors and found a view of God's plan of salvation by grace, but anti-semitic layers remain and now there are new layers of tradition, interpretations, western thought (a return to the Greek and Roman thought) and conditioning that need removal. Only then can we have a clear view of the Early Church worship.

BIBLICAL WORSHIP IS FAMILY WORSHIP

God has specific ways that He wants us to serve and worship Him. Those ways are pointed out for us by Jesus and the first church. They are the old paths. *Thus saith the LORD, Stand ye in the ways, and see, and ask for the old paths, where is the good way, and walk therein, and ye shall find rest for your souls...* (Jer. 6:16). Unfortunately these "old paths" have been paved with man's influences, opinions, traditions and interpretations of interpretations of interpretations of interpretations... and sometimes, like the holidays, simply ignored.

Christians can learn much from the Biblical Hebrew's strong family/worship lifestyle[1]. Everything is centered around the home–family, education *and* worship. Every area of the Hebrew world view is entirely saturated and encompassed with God. The Hebrews make no distinction between their spiritual life and the physical areas of life. They see all of life as an entirety. It is all God's domain. Everything that happens is an opportunity to praise Him. He is in control of everything–pains and joys. God's Word explains this Hebrew reasoning: *I have set the Lord always before me* (Psalms 16:8), and in Proverbs 3:6, *In all thy ways acknowledge him and he shall direct thy paths.* There were times of Temple worship; however, most of the worship centered around the home.

If you were to visit a religious Jew's home on a typical Friday you would find everyone in the home in a hurried state preparing for the coming Sabbath. Setting a fine table and special meal. At sundown, all the hurrying stops. The Mother of the home prays and dedicates this special day unto God as she lights the Sabbath candles to begin the Sabbath. The Father leads the family in prayers, Torah readings, and singing praise and worship. He prays a special blessing over each child. The rest of the twenty-four hour period is spent resting, enjoying family, growing spiritually as individuals, and growing closer together as a family.

We should ask ourselves, "Is there a time, if someone entered our home, that they would see such devotion to God?" How ashamed we should be when those who don't even know Jesus as the Messiah, show such devotion.

Professing Christians in America, in general, tend to view "The Church" as a part of their life–only a small part. Life and relationships are divided into quarters, into four distinctly different locations: partly religious (a few hours a week at church), partly educational (school), partly professional (workplace), and partly leisure (home). Each person in the family is going in separate directions and rarely at home together. Even in the church, the only family time spent together is on the ride to and from church. Upon arrival the family divides into their proper classes. It is hard to find all the members of a family together in one area at the same time in church–much less worshiping and interacting together or praying together as a family.

By examining the holidays, we can get a taste of the almost forgotten family worship–worship lead by father, in our homes, teaching our children God's Word (Deut. 6), with our families, singing and praising God, learning of His ways–growing, in Him, together!

Three holidays are considered pilgrim feasts. There are three festivals which the Israelites were commanded to celebrate *"in the place the Lord you God will chose"* (Deut. 16:16). These are Passover, Shavuot, and Sukkot, all have agricultural and national significance.

Overview of the Holidays

There are three major festivals, Passover (Pesach), Feast Of Weeks (Shavuot or Pentecost), and Feast of Tabernacles (Sukkot). On Passover, Jesus sacrificed Himself for our sins. On the Feast Of Weeks, God sent the Ten Commandments and the Holy Spirit. The Feast of Tabernacles speaks of a future time when men will again tabernacle with God. The three major festivals are pilgrimage festivals. Every male Jew was commanded to go to the Temple to observe these holidays. The promise that God would protect their homes (Exod. 34:23,24) while all the males were absent in Jerusalem at these holidays was always fulfilled.

From the time of Moses to the time of Christ, there never was a recorded instance of enemies invading the Hebrew homes during the period the men went to Jerusalem for the pilgrimage feasts.

Each of the three pilgrimage feasts had a historical and agricultural aspect. God planned the times perfectly. The holidays never interfered with the people's industries. Passover was kept before the harvest, Weeks was at the the end of the corn harvest (before the vintage), and Tabernacles was after all the fruit had been gathered (Eastman's Bible Dictionary).

When you add the three major festivals to the minor festivals associated with them, it makes seven in all. Seven is the biblical number of perfection or completion.

The spring holidays are Passover, the Feast of Unleavened Bread, Firstfruits and (fifty days later) the Feast of Weeks or Pentecost (Shavuot). The fall holidays include the Feast of Trumpets (Rosh Hashanah), the Day of Atonement (Yom Kippur), and the Feast of Booths or Tabernacles (Sukkot). All of these feast days are laid out in Leviticus 23 and other places in the Bible.

Everything in the Torah (or the Pentateuch, the Five Books of Moses) has a prophetic as well as historical significance and merits our careful attention. Torah means instruction. Paul also emphasized this in Romans 15:4: *For whatsoever things were written aforetime were written for our learning. . .* Everything that came about in the relationship between God and the Israelites happened mainly as a foreshadowing and an example to future generations.

God's Appointed Times

And God said, Let there be lights in the firmament of the heaven to divide the day from the night; and let them be for signs, and for seasons, and for days, and years (Gen. 1:14).

The "seasons" in this verse are not the seasons we usually think of: summer, fall, winter, and spring. God created a plan for the division of time. Our generation is so accustomed to referring to the modern clocks and Gregorian calendars that we forget God's original plan. We need to reexamine the scriptures relating to time through the eyes of the ancient Hebrew to fully understand every aspect of how creation was formed to lead us to Christ.

APPOINTED TIME IS TRANSLATED FEAST

The Hebrew word for *feasts* is *mow`ed. Speak unto the children of Israel, and say unto them, Concerning the feasts of the LORD, which ye shall proclaim to be holy convocations, even these are my feasts* [mow`ed] (Lev. 23:2).

Strong's Number Hebrew 04150 mow`ed {mo-ade'} or mo`ed {mo-ade'} or (fem.) mow`adah (2 Chr. 8:13) {mo-aw-daw'}from 03259; Theological Wordbook of the Old Testament - 878b; noun

1a). appointed time
1a1). appointed time (general)
1a2). sacred season, set feast, appointed season
1b). appointed meeting
1c). appointed place
1d). appointed sign or signal
1e). tent of meeting

HERE ARE JUST A FEW OF THE VERSES DEMONSTRATING GOD'S DESIGNATED TIMES:

1. Gen. 1:14; 17: 21; 18:13-14; 21:1-3

2. Exo. 9:5; 23:15

3. Lev. 23:-7

4. Num. 9:1-3

5. Ps. 81:3

6. Ps. 104:19

7. Jer. 5:24; 8:7

8. Ezek. 4:6

9. Neh. 10:34

10. Dan. 8:19; 12:6-7

11. Est. 9:3

12. Matt. 8:28-32; 13:29-30

13. Luke 1:18-20

14. Acts 17:31

15. Rom. 9:9

16. 1 Tim. 2:5-6

17. Acts 17:24-26

18. Gal. 4:4

19. Eph. 1:10

20. 2 Peter 3:8

To every thing there is a season,and a time to every purpose under the heaven: A time to be born, and a time to die; a time to plant, and a time to pluck up that which is planted; A time to kill, and a time to heal; a time to break down, and a time to build up; A time to weep, and a time to laugh; a time to mourn, and a time to dance; A time to cast away stones, and a time to gather stones together; a time to embrace, and a time to refrain from embracing; A time to get, and a time to lose; a time to keep, and a time to cast away; A time to rend, and a time to sew; a time to keep silence, and a time to speak; A time to love, and a time to hate; a time of war, and a time of peace.

What profit hath he that worketh in that wherein he laboureth? I have seen the travail, which God hath given to the sons of men to be exercised in it. He hath made every thing beautiful in his time: also he hath set the world in their heart, so that no man can find out the work that God maketh from the beginning to the end. I know that there is no good in them, but for a man to rejoice, and to do good in his life. And also that every man should eat and drink, and enjoy the good of all his labour, it is the gift of God. I know that, whatsoever God doeth, it shall be for ever: nothing can be put to it, nor any thing taken from it: and God doeth it, that men should fear before him.

Eccl. 3:1-14

Hebrew Month	American Month	Season	Feast	Weather in the Holy Land	Agriculture in the Holy Land
Aviv or Nisan	March April	Harvest begins	PASSOVER UNLEAVENED BREAD FIRSTFRUITS	Fall of the latter or spring rains (Deut. 11:14). The melting snows and rains fill its channel, and Jordan overflows in places its "lower plain" (Zech.10:1)	Barley harvest begins in sub-tropical plain of Jericho and in the Jordan valley; wheat coming into ear. Uplands brilliant with short-lived verdure and flowers.
Zif or Iyar	April May	Summer		Showers and thunderstorms very rare (1 Sam.12:17,18). Almost uninterruptedly cloudless, till end of summer.	Principal harvest month in lower districts. "Barley harvest" general. Wheat and apricots ripen. In Jordan valley, hot winds burn up vegetation.
Sivan	May June		FEAST OF WEEKS or FIRST FRUITS N.T. PENTECOST	Air motionless and brilliantly clear.	Wheat harvest begins in upland districts. Almonds ripe. Grapes begin to ripen. Honey of the Jordan valley collected in May-July.
Tammuz	June July	Hot Season		A dry, hot, and depressing wind. Air motionless and brilliantly clear. Heat becomes intense. Heavy dew still falls.	Wheat harvest on highest districts. Various fruits ripe. Elsewhere the country is parched, dry and hard, with withered stalks and burnt-up grass.
Av	July August	Hot Season		Air motionless and clear. Heat becomes intense. Heavy dew falls.	Main fruit month. Grapes, figs,walnuts, and olives, etc. (Lev. 26:5).
Elul	August September	Hot Season		Heat intense (2 Kings 4:18-20), much lightning, rain rarely.	Harvest of doura and maize. Cotton and pomegranate ripen.
Ethanim or Tishri	September	Seed Time	TRUMPETS DAY OF ATONEMENT TABERNACLES	Heavy dew. Early autumn rains begin to soften the hard ground (Deut. 11:14). Nights wintry (Gen. 31:40).	Plowing and sowing begin (Prov. 20:4; Eccl. 11:4). Cotton harvest.
Bul or Heshvan	October November			Rainy month.	Wheat and barley planted. Rice harvest. Fig tree full with fruit. Orange and citron blossom. Almost all vegetation has gone.
Chisleu or Kislev	November December	Winter begins	CHANUKAH or HANUKKAH	December, January, and February have greatest amount of rain in the year.	The plains and deserts gradually become green pastures.
Tevet	December January	Winter		In the winter the temperatures can fall into the forties. Near the Dead Sea region, temperatures stay in the seventies and the water is warm and inviting.	Mild winters support the growth of such crops as dates, bananas, and citrus fruits.
Sebat or Shevat	January February	Winter		Weather becomes warmer. End of month is the pleasant cool season.	In warmer and sheltered localities almond and peach trees blossom. Oranges ripen.

UnðeRStanðing the HebRew CalenðaR

The western world uses the Gregorian calendar based on the sun. The Jewish calendar is split into twelve months based on the lunar cycle. To bring it in line with the seasons, however, a thirteenth month, Adar Sheni (Adar II) is regularly added. The dates of Jewish holidays do not change from year to year. It just seems that way to us because feast dates fall on different days on the Gregorian calendar.

The Jewish calendar is based on a lunar year of twelve months, each month of twenty-nine or thirty days. The year lasts approximately 354 days. Since the biblical festivals relate to the agricultural seasons of the 365-day solar year, the shortage of eleven days between the lunar and solar years has to be made up. To overcome this problem, a thirteenth month is added in certain years. In Temple times this was done periodically, twelfth month. In a later period the additional month was introduced automatically seven times in a lunar cycle of nineteen years; in the years 3, 6, 8, 11, 14, 17, and 19 of the cycle (Encyclopedia of Judaism 1989).

God called the months by the ordinal/numerical names: first, second, and so on. The names of the twelve months are of Babylonian origin. Israel adopted all twelve months of the Babylonian calendar as their civil calendar, but not all of the twelve months are listed in the Bible. The seven that occur are: Nisan, the first month; Sivan, the third month; Elul, the sixth month; Kislev, the ninth month; Tevet, the tenth month; Shevat, the eleventh month; and Adar, the twelfth month.

Month	Length	Gregorian Equivalent
Nisan	30 days	March-April
Iyar	29 days	April-May
Sivan	30 days	May-June
Tammuz	29 days	June-July
Av	30 days	July-August
Elul	29 days	August-September
Tishri	30 days	September-October
Heshvan	29 or 30 days	October-November
Kislev	30 or 29 days	November-December
Tevet	29 days	December-January
Shevat	30 days	January-February
Adar	29 or 30 days	February-March
Adar II	29 days	March-April

(In leap years, Adar has 30 days. In non-leap years, Adar has 29 days.)

THE CIVIL AND RELIGIOUS CALENDARS

There are two calendars in the Bible, the civil calendar (Genesis 1:1 to Exod. 12) and the religious calendar. The first month in the civil calendar is Tishri starting in the fall, about September. The seventh month is Nisan (Aviv) starting in the spring, about the time of our March and April.

God changed the civil calendar to the religious calendar in Exodus 12:1 *And the LORD spake unto Moses and Aaron in the land of Egypt, saying, This month shall be unto you the beginning of months: it shall be the first month of the year to you.* So, now Nisan is the first month of the religious calendar and Tishri is the seventh month (Exod. 13:4). This book starts with the first feast of the religious calendar, Passover.

Civil Calendar	Religious Calendar
1. Tishri	1. Nisan (Aviv)
2. Heshvan	2. Iyar
3. Kislev	3. Sivan
4. Tevet	4. Tammuz
5. Shevat	5. Av
6. Adar	6. Elul
7. Nisan	7. Tishri
8. Iyar	8. Heshvan
9. Sivan	9. Kislev
10. Tammuz	10. Tevet
11. Av	11. Shevat
12. Elul	12. Adar

It is very interesting that the number of days between Nisan and Tishri is always the same. Because of this, the time from the first major festival–Passover in Nisan–to the last major festival–Feast of Tabernacles in Tishri–is always the same.

A Hebrew Year, Season, Week, Day & Times

THE BIBLICAL YEAR

Creation is the starting point for the Jewish year. Based on the biblical genealogical tables, the length of lives as recorded in Scripture, and the creation of the world in six days, the Jews have calculated the exact year of the Creation was 3761 B.C.E. Thus the years 1997 to 1998 C.E. are equal to 5758 in the Jewish calendar.

When Jews refer to secular years, they do not use B.C.—"before Christ" or A.D.—Anno Domini, "in the year of Our Lord," for that implies accepting Jesus as Messiah. They call these times C.E., common era and B.C.E., before the common era.

The Hebrew word for *year* comes from the idea of change or repeated action. Thus the year expresses the concept of "a complete cycle of change." Due to the repeated seasons, man set up a calendar to account for yearly events and to alert him of the coming seasons. The calendar revolved around the agricultural cycles. Man observed the climactic changes and the length of days in his planting and harvesting. Religious festivals were also established to parallel the agricultural year. No major religious festival, for example, was celebrated during the busy harvest season. Man observed that there were four seasons and that the year was about 365 days long. Although the calendars were not always precise, adjustments were made periodically to account for the lack of precision (Nelson Illustrated Bible Dictionary 1986).

THE BIBLICAL SEASONS

The Bible refers to the four seasons we normally think of as spring, summer, autumn and winter. *While the earth remaineth, seedtime and harvest, and cold and heat, and summer and winter, and day and night shall not cease* (Gen. 8:22). The seasons are regulated by the position of the sun or the tilt of the earth in its orbit around the sun, but normally when the Bible refers to seasons, it is referring to the Biblical holidays.

The word in Hebrew that is translated *seasons* is *moedim*, and it more specifically means "appointed times" by God, specifically, a festival; conventionally a year; by implication, an assembly (as convened for a definite purpose). In the King James Version, seasons mean— appointed (sign, time), (place of, solemn) assembly, congregation, (set, solemn) feast, (appointed, due) season, solemn (-ity), synagogue, (set) time (appointed).

THE BIBLICAL MONTHS

The month was marked by the first sighting of the crescent of the new moon at sunset. The first day of each month was viewed as a holy day. The day was to be announced with the blowing of trumpets. Jews had special sacrifices (Num. 28:11-15) at each first new moon.

Jewish years have twelve lunar months of twenty-nine or thirty days. The lunar month is 29 $\frac{1}{4}$ days long, so sometimes the new moon is visible on the twenty-ninth day, and sometimes not until the thirtieth. The standard month is twenty-nine days long, and when there needs to be a thirtieth day, it is called "new moon," as well as the first day of the following month. In addition, since lunar years are eleven days shorter than solar years, they need adjustment to keep the seasons the same in both calendars. Months were "declared" after sighting the new moon (Hillel Foundation). For more information on the new moon see Appendix C.

THE BIBLICAL WEEK

A week is any seven consecutive days or the period between two Sabbaths (Lev. 12:5; Jer. 5:24; Luke 18:12). The Jews observed the seventh day of the week, from Friday evening (beginning at sunset) to Saturday evening, as their Sabbath, or day of rest and worship (Ex. 16:23-27).

THE BIBLICAL DAY

All Jewish holidays begin the evening before the date specified. This is because a Jewish "day" begins and ends at sunset, rather than at midnight. This is from the Bible records, *And the evening and the morning...* in that order (Gen. 1:5, 8, 13). For example, Monday actually begins on Sunday evening at sunset.

THE BIBLICAL TIMES OF THE DAY

Dawn was the twilight before sunrise (1 Sam. 30:17; Matt. 28:1). The evening was the late afternoon (Deut. 16:6) between the day and the night (Jer. 6:4; Prov. 7:9), or it could mean literally "late" in the day (Mark 11:19)

the stars came out (Neh. 4:21). Noon was the end of the morning (1 Kings 18:26) which marked mealtime (Gen. 43:16). Noon was also referred to as "midday" (Neh. 8:3), "broad daylight" (Amos 8:9), and "heat of the day" (2 Sam. 4:5). The day was divided into three parts: evening, morning, and noon (Ps. 55:17). Midnight was the midpoint of the night (Matt. 25:6; Acts 20:7). In the Old Testament the night was divided into three watches (Judg. 7:19; Ex. 14:24), while it was divided into four watches in the New Testament (Matt. 14:25; Mark 13:35). The term hour was used to mean "immediately" (Dan. 3:6,15), or it could express the idea of one-twelfth of daylight (John 11:9). (ibid)

WHICH DAYS TO CELEBRATE?

The Biblical months begin on the sighting of the new Moon. The new moon listed in the calendars are modern interpretations with astronomical equipment, not sightings. As stated above, the modern Jewish calendar, Ancient Hebrew calendar and our Gregorian calendar differ. A few groups of Christians and/or Messianic Jews celebrate the holidays according to their calculations of the new moon in Israel, which are the actual dates. Most Jews and Gentiles who celebrate the holidays use the Jewish calendar dates.

God knows our hearts and desire to learn about Him. Hezekiah kept the Feast of Passover at the wrong time. He even added a full week's celebration, making a second Passover week (2 Chronicles 30:3-27) ...*Hezekiah prayed for them, saying, The good LORD pardon every one that prepareth his heart to seek God, the LORD God of his fathers, though he be not cleansed according to the purification of the sanctuary. And the LORD hearkened to Hezekiah, and healed the people* (2 Chron. 30:18-20).

More information on the calendar, holiday dates, special notes, new moon (including resources to calculate the new moon), etc. can be found in Appendix B page 533.

Section 2:
Preliminary
Activities & Crafts

- ◆ DISCUSSION ACTIVITY

- ◆ MULTI-HOLIDAY CENTERPIECE

- ◆ WALL HANGING

- ◆ FLAG DIRECTIONS & ILLUSTRATIONS

- ◆ HEBREW WORDS

- ◆ RECIPE ROUND-UP

- ◆ FOUR SEASONS

- ◆ FESTIVE FAMILY GAME

Introducing the Holidays: Discussion Activity

Use this discussion activity with your family or class to understand why you will be studying these new holidays.

BRAINSTORM AND DISCUSS:

- What celebrations does your family celebrate every year?
- What is your favorite time of the year?
- How much do you know about the Pilgrims? How much has celebrating Thanksgiving affected your knowledge of the Pilgrims?
- What are you most thankful for in your life?
- Imagine coming from a foreign country and never seeing a Fourth of July picnic. How would you explain it to someone from another country who had never seen a Fourth of July picnic? If you had only been to one Fourth of July party, do you think that you could prepare your own party? Would it be easier to study the reason and purpose for the holiday first?
- What is it like to attempt to assemble something without an instruction manual?
- Why do airplanes have detailed emergency exit plans?
- What happens when people fail to follow instructions?

BRAINSTORM AND MAKE A LIST

Brainstorm and make a list of something special that has happened in your family's lives (include as many details as you can): the birth of a baby, moving, finding a home, a special relative's visit, etc. Ask the children to make another list of things that you could do to celebrate the occasion and to help you remember what happened, like a family day at a lake swimming and picnicking. What things could you do in your home during winter to remind you of that treasured day?

- Each member of the family could tell his or her version of the day, how it felt, what each remembers.

- Prepare and eat the same meal.

- Turn the heat up (or air conditioning off) to remind you of the warm day.

- Wear summer clothing.

- Play the same games, only indoors (if possible).

- Display a large bowl of water somewhere in the house to remind you of the lake water.

- Make summer decorations from construction paper and hang around the room.

- Look on a map and trace the route from your home to the lake.

DESIGNATE A HOLIDAY

Create your own holiday! Brainstorm and make another list. Make a list of rituals to use if you were to keep this ceremony each year.

Example:

- Decide on January 29th.

- Always start at 12:00 noon.

- Eat the meal on the floor using a red checked tablecloth.

- Have potato salad and baked beans for lunch.

- Mom must always wear her straw hat.

- Dad should always toss a nerf ball with the children.

Do you think that doing these special things will help you to remember the occasion?

Lesson Planer

Holiday:

Date of Celebration: Date to Start: No. of Weeks:

Material Needed List

Lesson #   **Date:**   **Lesson #**

Read Aloud Pages:

Activity Sheet Pages:

No. of Copies to Make:

Bible Verse to Memorize:

Lesson #   **Date:**   **Lesson #**

Read Aloud Pages:

Activity Sheet Pages:

No. of Copies to Make:

Bible Verse to Memorize:

Lesson #   **Date:**   **Lesson #**

Read Aloud Pages:

Activity Sheet Pages:

No. of Copies to Make:

Bible Verse to Memorize:

Lesson #   **Date:**   **Lesson #**

Read Aloud Pages:

Activity Sheet Pages:

No. of Copies to Make:

Bible Verse to Memorize:

Lesson #   **Date:**   **Lesson #**

Read Aloud Pages:

Activity Sheet Pages:

No. of Copies to Make:

Bible Verse to Memorize:

Lesson Planer

Holiday:

Date of Celebration: Date to Start: No. of Weeks:

Material Needed List

Lesson #   **Date:**   **Lesson #**

Read Aloud Pages:

Activity Sheet Pages:

No. of Copies to Make:

Bible Verse to Memorize:

Lesson #   **Date:**   **Lesson #**

Read Aloud Pages:

Activity Sheet Pages:

No. of Copies to Make:

Bible Verse to Memorize:

Lesson #   **Date:**   **Lesson #**

Read Aloud Pages:

Activity Sheet Pages:

No. of Copies to Make:

Bible Verse to Memorize:

Lesson #   **Date:**   **Lesson #**

Read Aloud Pages:

Activity Sheet Pages:

No. of Copies to Make:

Bible Verse to Memorize:

Lesson #   **Date:**   **Lesson #**

Read Aloud Pages:

Activity Sheet Pages:

No. of Copies to Make:

Bible Verse to Memorize:

MULTI-HOLIDAY CENTERPIECE

Centerpieces provide a visual focus at the dinner table throughout each holiday. You can make one base and ten flags. Simply change the base cover, add a central craft and select two or four flags. Flag-making instructions follow in this section. Craft instructions, which flags to use, and symbols appear in each holiday chapter.

Materials suggested are listed below. Please *read through all three methods* of construction to determine which choices you will make for the flags:

1. 10" *styrofoam base*, may be circle, oval, square, or 8" x 10" rectangle.

2. *Fabric* approximately 15" square (or 13" x 15" if you use rectangle base) to cover base, drape down and allow 1/2" hem. Suggested color choices are **dark red** for Passover Week, **blue** for Pentecost, **purple** for Feast of Trumpets and Atonement, floral **calico** for Feast of Tabernacles, **white** for Hanukkah, and **colorful print** for Purim.

3. Any *fringe* (optional) for edge of dark red, blue or purple pieces.

4. *Spanish moss* or paper grass (optional) for area under lamb at Passover, trumpet at Rosh Hashanah.

5. One-quarter inch wood dowel sticks to cut into ten 9" flag supports. Four pieces will cut out of a 36" dowel.

CHOICES:

White fabric (smooth weave that can be ironed or painted easily) for ten flags. Each flag is 6-1/2" x 9" including hem allowances, so a total of 2/3 yd. is needed.

If you use the iron-on, machine or hand appliqué approaches: Assorted 4 inch scraps of green, tan, gray, blue, black, purple and red for flag designs in this section (prints that are predominately these colors are satisfactory), PLUS two-sided iron-on *bonding material*, 1/4 yd. (ask the clerk for choices, such as *Wonder Under*® used in decorating sweatshirts). Optional: gold, silver, or pearl *fabric paint* to seal edges and decorate designs.

If your artistic youth choose to paint the flags, you could use *acrylics*. An artistic youth or older child may also use *fine tip markers* to add details or color the entire design. Markers are generally not satisfactory for younger children because they require a quick stroke or will bleed on the fabric.

A *fine-tip black marking pen* is recommended, however, to highlight shadows, small details, or Hebrew words.

If you are in a hurry or have very young children, use this simple paper method. Use five sheets of white typing or similar *paper*. (Or purchase a disposable *white vinyl* tablecloth.) You will need *rubber cement* to secure paper parts to paper or *glue* for securing vinyl to itself and the flag dowel.

CENTERPIECE DIRECTIONS

- Mark the center of your base. Mark, then make four holes equally distant from the center. Slant your tool at the same angle away from the center as shown. This will allow the flags to hang slightly away from the craft which will sit in the center. You can use a dull pencil that is the same diameter or smaller than the flag dowel to get started, or have an adult taper the end of one of the dowels to use as your piercing tool. Try to make all your holes the *same depth*. They do not have to go to the bottom, but should be deep enough that the flag is secure. Remove flag dowels.

- Turn under ½" and machine stitch or use iron-on hem tape to finish the edge of draping cloth. Add fringe if desired. If using knit fabric, you may not need a hem. Center cloth over base and mark hole locations with chalk. Have parent cut a *very small* ¼" slit with x-acto knife, or snip with sharp scissors, or use an awl to make four holes in the red, blue, purple or calico cloths.

  The white and colorful print draping cloths for Hanukkah and Purim should have only two holes at diagonal corners.

- At each holiday, insert flags (instructions follow) and place craft in the center. Craft instructions appear with each holiday.

Flag Directions and Illustrations

For *all* flags, use flag designs in this section to create patterns on both sides of each flag. Use the mirror image for the back of the flag, so that the centerpiece will be fun to look at from every angle regardless of where the flags are placed.

For Fabric Flags

1. Cut ten pieces 6-1/2" x 9" from your white fabric. Parent may need to assist with, or do the next steps.

2. On both long sides and one short side, turn under 1/4" and press with iron to hold. Turn additional 1/4" and stitch to hold hem.

3. Turn remaining short side under 1/4" and press, then fold additional 5/8" and press. Stitch 1/2" from outside edge to form casing for dowel.

CHOOSE ONE OF THE FOLLOWING METHODS:

I. Iron-on Appliquéd Flags

1. To use iron-on procedure, copy or remove design and mirror image from book and trace onto paper face of *Wonder Under*® bonding material. Cut and iron onto reverse side of fabric scrap. Cut out.

2. Peel paper face off bonding material. Center design on flag and press ten seconds with damp press cloth, or according to bonding instructions included with material. When flag cools, turn and repeat for mirror image on other side of flag.

3. Add details with pen or fabric paint and seal edges with *FrayCheck* or fabric paint to prevent fraying and give festive touch.

4. Stain bottom half of dowel with brown marker, or paint. Let dry, then slide unpainted end through the flag casing.

II. Machine Appliquéd Flags

Machine appliqué may be done with a zig zag satin stitch to overcast cut edges. A piece of paper placed behind the quilt fabric will stabilize the satin stitch and should be carefully removed after stitching. Otherwise, cut your pieces allowing 1/4" seam allowances (as far as hand appliqué). The turned under edges may then be straight stitched close to the edge. A tiny machine zig zag or blind stitch may be used with invisible thread along the edge to resemble hand appliqué.

III. Hand Appliquéd Flags

Use a whipping stitch or embroidery stitches and/or intricate design of quilting stitches. Turn under edges along traced line and blind stitch.

IV. Fabric Painted Flags

To paint designs, trace image onto flag fabric, turn flag and trace matching mirror image on back. To make any words appear readable on back side, make on separate piece of fabric, then glue on last.

1. Use paint carefully.

2. When dry, turn and finish opposite side. Some color may bleed through to the back.

3. Finish dowel as above. Let dry, then slide unpainted end through flag casing.

V. Easy No-Sew Flags

For a money-saving approach, or for construction by very young children, you can make "quick" flags using paper, felt, or vinyl:

1 . Copy the flag illustrations in the pages that follow (two of each). Color with crayons or markers.

2. Cut 5-1/2" x 8-1/2" rectangles of white paper (two from 8-1/2" x 11" sheet), or white felt, or white vinyl (fabric from a disposable tablecloth) The felt or vinal would hang more naturally.

3. Finish dowel as above. Glue flag onto it, rolling paper or fabric entirely around dowel. Use rubber cement to secure designs on each side.

"HISTORY REPEATS ITSELF"

A tradition among many Jews is to save some element of a holiday's celebration to carry over to the next. Example: the leaves from a palm branch may be saved from Tabernacles and used to brush the crumbs from the Passover table. In this "carryover" theme, we will be repeating one or two of the flags in each following holiday. When the year is ended with Tabernacles, the **Palm Branches** and **Lamb** flags will come forward to the Passover. **Cup & Bread** and **Branches** carry into Firstfruits. The **Grain Sheaf** added at Firstfruits will carry over to Pentecost. **Ten Commandments** carries over from Pentecost to Trumpets. **Bible** and **Crown** flags continue into Atonement. From this observance, the **Bible** flag will go forward to Tabernacles. Since Hanukkah and Purim were added by the Jews themselves at a later time, we do not include them in this pattern. In a way to make them appear unique unto themselves, we have chosen to use only two flags at each of the added festivals.

Store items carefully for years of continued enjoyment. Lay flags flat if possible. As children mature, replace flags or crafts by using different techniques or by repeating, as children may wish to display maturing skills. Our motto is: *"make a memory."* As the Israelites did on repeated special occasions, your family is making a "monument of stones" to say "Remember this. God was here...and still is!"

TEN COMMANDMENTS
Make gray with black pen details; silver outline, if available.

CROSS
Make brown with black details or tan with brown details. Have red heart; suggest gold outline on cross, *FrayCheck©* on heart.

PALM BRANCHES
Make green with contrasting light details if your green is dark. Use black or dark green details if your green is grass-colored or lighter; FrayCheck©, pearl or gold outline.

CUP & BREAD
Make cup yellow or tan to simulate gold with fabric paint touches and outline and brown and/or black details; make juice purple, cloth blue, plate gray, and bread brown with black details and silver outline on plate, FrayCheck© on bread and cloth elements.

BIBLE
Make black binding and words, red or contrasting ribbon marker; pearl or silver outline.

LAMB
Make black details on white piece; purple oval. Use silver or pearl fabric paint outline.

DOVE
Make black details on piece of white cloth; blue box. Use silver or pearl fabric paint outline.

GRAIN SHEAF
Make tan or yellow with brown and/or black details. Red ribbon binding; gold outline.

STAR OF DAVID
Make blue or two shades of blue. Use silver fabric paint outline or gold, OR one triangle of each if fabric paint is available. You could also have solid gold and silver triangles. Be careful at intertwined, overlapping areas.

CROWN
Make yellow or tan with brown or black details and gold fabric paint touches. Gems may be of assorted colors such as red, green, blue and purple. Make delicate black details; gold outline. Option: purchase craft "gems."

TEN COMMANDMENTS

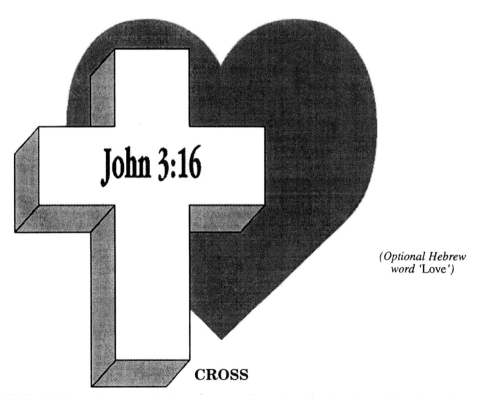

John 3:16

(Optional Hebrew word 'Love')

CROSS

NOTE: *For fabric version, cut* *entire* *heart, box or oval out of a color. Iron that on first, then add top design with same iron-on technique. For painted or paper versions, trace as shown.*

This page left blank for tracing

PALM BRANCHES

CUP & BREAD

*NOTE: For fabric version, it may be easier to cut <u>entire</u> plate and cloth out of a color. Iron plate on
first, then add cloth, then bread on top with same iron-on technique.
For painted or paper versions, trace as shown.*

This page left blank for tracing

BIBLE

LAMB

<u>NOTE</u>: *For fabric version, cut <u>entire</u> heart, box or oval out of a color. Iron that on first, then add top design with same iron-on technique. For painted or paper versions, trace as shown.*

This page left blank for tracing

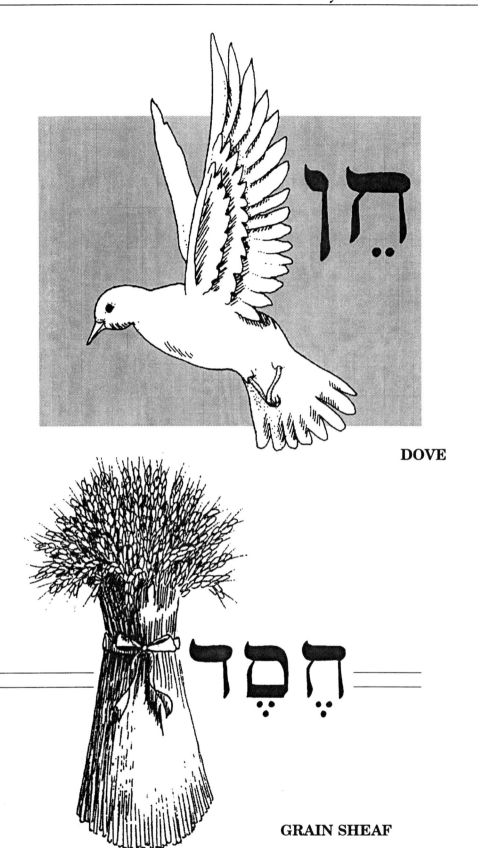

DOVE

GRAIN SHEAF

NOTE: For fabric version, cut entire heart, box, or oval out of a color. Iron that on first, then add top design with same iron-on technique. For painted or paper versions, trace as shown. Suggestions are given for colors of fabric paint outlines.

This page left blank for tracing

STAR OF DAVID

CROWN

NOTE: For the Star of David: Cut out as separate triangles, and iron onto fabric. Cut each apart close to a corner, and interlock them before pressing them onto flag.

Hebrew Words

You may wish to use some of these Hebrew words on various crafts or painting activities in this book. To associate with alphabet studies, remember the letters appear backward to English users (right to left).

A. To use on Watercolor Banner:

　1. Enlarge on copy machine as desired, and trace or copy by hand.

　2. Use felt-tip marker or paint brush to fill in, or use iron–on approach and cut from contrasting fabric. See activity instructions.

B. To use on Centerpiece Flags:

　1. Trace from this page onto <u>separate</u> white cloth or <u>separate</u> piece of paper with black felt-tip pen, fine point, and draw box around as shown.

　2. Cut out fabric and secure in place with ironing technique described in this section.

　3. If paper, secure with rubber cement described in flag construction, this section.

BRIT (Covenant)

Hokmah (Wisdom)

Shalom (Peace)

Mashiach (Messiah)

Chesed (Mercy)

Ahavah (Love)

Chen (Grace)

Simcha (Joy)

Kavod (Glory)

Wall Hanging

This beautiful quilted wall hanging makes a great conversation starter and witnessing tool for home or church. If you're an experienced quilter, you can easily make this using your own methods and the appliqué patterns in this book. Lamb, Cup and Bread, Sheaf of Grain, Law Tablets, and Tree Branches appear in the Flag Patterns section. Ram Horn, Balance Scales, Menorah, and Scepter With Scroll appear on the following pages. Use their original size or take them to a copy shop to have them enlarged.

OTHER PROJECTS

The patterns in this book are wonderful to use for any project. You're only limited by your creativity. Use fabric, markers, construction paper, glitter, and/or puff paint to make or decorate:

- napkins
- paper plates
- place mats*
- T-shirts
- sweatshirts
- walls
- windows
- bulletin boards
- gift wrap

*For durable placemats: decorate cardstock and laminate (available at most copy centers).

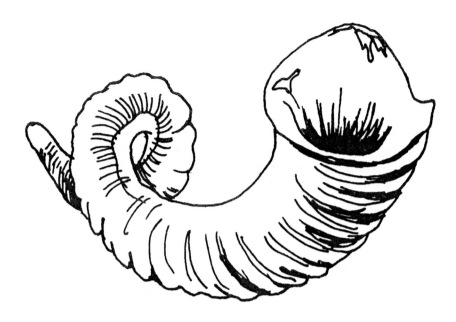

RAM'S HORN

GAVEL

NOTE: For fabric version, cut __entire__ heart, box or oval out of a color. Iron that on first, then add top design with same iron-on technique. For painted or paper versions, trace as shown.

This page left blank for tracing

MENORAH

SCEPTER

NOTE: For fabric version, cut <u>entire</u> heart, box or oval out of a color. Iron that on first, then add top design with same iron-on technique. For painted or paper versions, trace as shown.

This page left blank for tracing

Celebrate the Holidays

Remembering all the holidays names and order may be difficult at first. This little song to help you remember. Sing to the tune of Deck the Halls. Use the illustration on the back cover of this book to make a poster showing the seasons the holidays occur. Hang it in a prominent place until the children learn the song.

♪   ♪   ♪   ♪   ♪

Passover, Unleavened Bread,

Celebrate the holidays and learn of Christ

♪   ♪   ♪   ♪   ♪

Day of Firstfruits, Feast of Weeks,

Celebrate the holidays and learn of Christ

♪   ♪   ♪   ♪   ♪

Feast of Trumpets then Yom Kippur,

Celebrate Christ is King, Lord of all!

♪   ♪   ♪   ♪   ♪

Tabernacles, then for more light,

Hannukah and Purim's festive times.

♪   ♪   ♪   ♪   ♪

Recipe Round-Up

You can make a handy recipe keeper with a page of discontinued wallpaper (or use some excess off a roll you may have). You will also need ten or eleven large index cards (5x7).

Use the remaining cards as dividers at the beginning of each holiday's group of recipes. You can color the dividers with the holiday's name and add illustrations or other designs as you like. Younger children can help with this, too. You may want to include a divider for Yom Kippur, which is a fast. Younger children may have special menus this day, and your family may want to have a special supper to break the fast. You may or may not want to include the Sabbath. Your hallah recipe could be inserted, plus recipes or a list of any foods that your family may want to reserve for this weekly special occasion.

Students can use their best handwriting to copy recipes from cookbooks or mom's personal file. (You could even have a dictation lesson.) Use a copier if you prefer. Recipes, in a magazine that youngsters clip, need to be checked by mom to make sure you have all the instructions.

1.-2.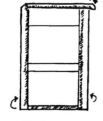

1. Cut the wallpaper to 9" x 16". If the piece you have is slightly smaller, like 8" x 14", you can make it work. Begin at the bottom and place the first index card 1/2" up from the bottom and centered between the two sides. Fold the half-inch edge and glue to the card. If your card has lines, turn it over so the white shows.

3.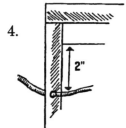

2. Skip 1/2" to 1", depending on how many recipes you plan to include. Center the next card. Use clear tape to secure the top of the first card and top and bottom of the second card.

4.

3. Fold the right and left sides over and glue full length. Fold a 1" edge at the top and glue.

4. Punch a hole on each side, in at least 1/4", about 2" down from the top of the top card.

5. Thread a 50" ribbon through to the inside and back out.

6. Insert recipes, fold flap over and tie like a package.

5.-6.

Four Seasons

On the following pages are illustrations to copy for coloring. Use sharp colored pencils. Cut and frame in standard 4" by 5" photo frame(s). If you wish to use 5" by 7" frames, cut a construction paper mat from the <u>dimensions</u> below. Center behind the mat and tape in position. You may display the current season alone, or make a grouping.

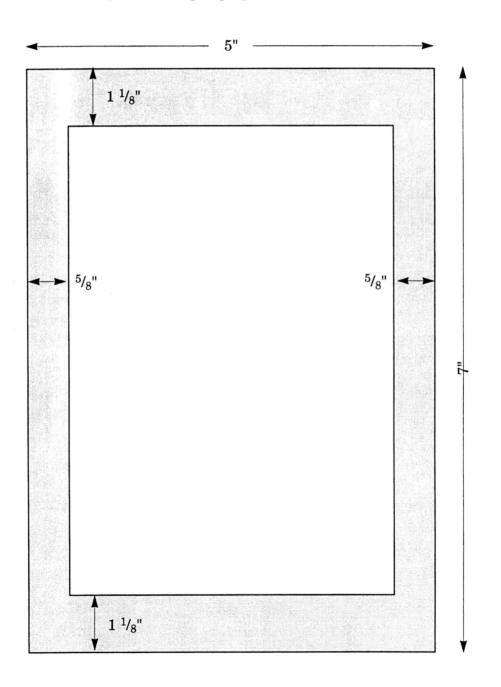

Directions:

Use sharp color pencils to change the seasons for your Jewish picture calendar.

Options:

Make different birds for seasons when they are active or most colorful. Example: red cardinals in winter, robins in spring, gold finches in summer, blue jays in autumn.

Four Seasons - Continued

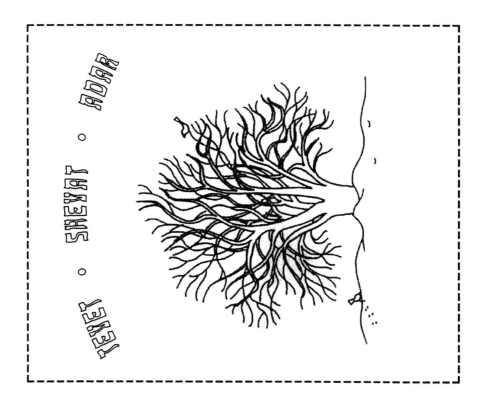

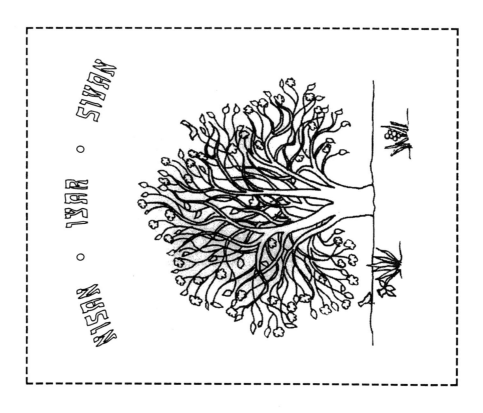

This page left blank for tracing

Four Seasons - Continued

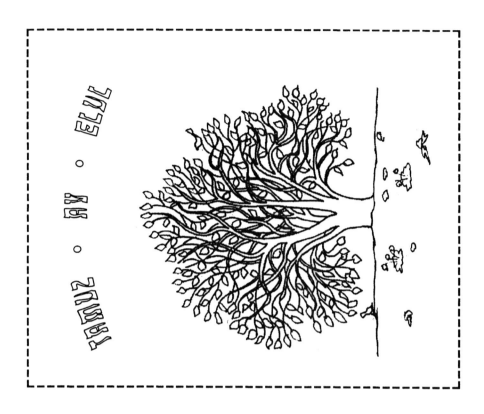

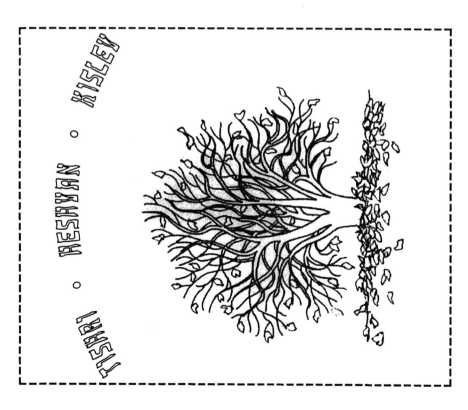

This page left blank for tracing

Festive Family Game

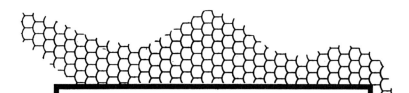

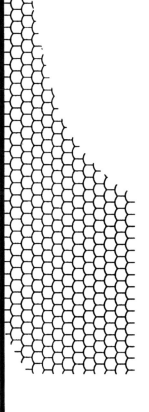

Rules for Play

Begin at the top of the board at Sabbath. Use dried beans, buttons, or color paper markers.

•For each turn, the player tosses one coin, die, or dice and draws a card from the face down pile.

•Heads up and even numbers move to the NEAREST letter marked by ○.

•Tails up and odd numbers move to the NEAREST letter marked by □.

•You may have to move backwards sometimes.

•You must land on the S at the end of Tabernacles to finish.

•The lines move from left to right, just as if you were reading. That means that when you are at the right end of a row, the next nearest letters begin the left of the next row.

Play until one or more have finished. When you have ample time, read the scriptures as you go, and Revelation 19:9 when you finish for a peek at the biggest holiday of all.

NOTE:
Cards on next page, board at end of book.

CARDS FOR FESTIVE FAMILY GAME

Cut out or copy these cards. Color and cover with clear contact-type paper. You may want to glue an envelope or closeable sandwich bag at end of book to hold your coin, cards and markers for playing.

DEUTERONOMY 16:10-15	NUMBERS 9:9-14	NUMBERS 9:1-2	EXODUS 34:22-24
EZRA 3:3-5	EZEKIEL 36:37-38	1 SAMUEL 1:19-22	2 CHRONICLES 30:21-23,26
JOHN 4:23	LUKE 2:41-42	ZECHARIAH 8:19	NEHEMIAH 8:15-18
ACTS 20:16	ACTS 20:6	JOHN 10:22	JOHN 4:45

You will find the game board at the back of the book for ease of copying. Laminate game and cards if desired, or cover with clear contact-type paper, *after* you have colored the illustrations.

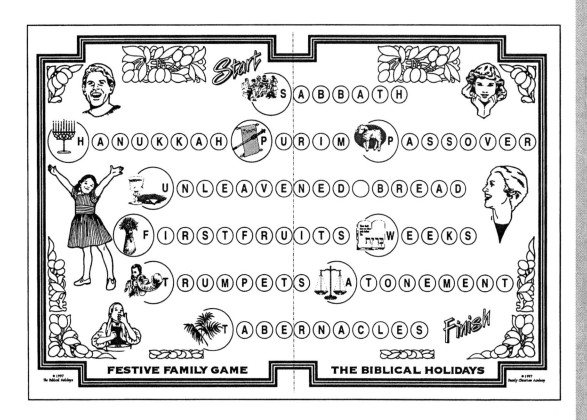

104

Section 3:
The Spring Holidays

- ◆ OVERVIEW
- ◆ PASSOVER
- ◆ UNLEAVENED BREAD
- ◆ EARLY FIRSTFRUITS AND OMER
- ◆ FEAST OF WEEKS

	DAY	6:00 P.M. - 6:00 P.M.	Events of Jesus	Matthew	Mark	Luke	John
Sixth Day Before Passover	Nisan 9	Thursday/ Friday	Approaches Jerusalem from Jericho. Spends Thursday night at Zacchaeus's home. Sends two disciples ahead for animals. Entry to Bethpage. Cleanses the Temple.	21:1-17	---	19:1-28	12:1
Weekly Sabbath before Passover	Nisan 10	Friday/ Saturday	Sabbath at Bethany. First of three suppers, two anointings.	---	---	---	12:2-11
Fourth Day Before Passover	Nisan 11	Saturday/ Sunday	Triumphal entrance into Jerusalem. Weeps over city. Enters Temple. Returns to Bethany.	---	1:8-10 11:1-7, 11	9:29-35 19:36-40 41 44	12:12-19
Third Day Before Passover	Nisan 12	Sunday/ Monday	Returns to Jerusalem. Curses the fig tree. At Temple for further cleansing and teaching.	21:18-22	11:12-19	19:45-48	12:20-50
Second Day Before Passover	Nisan 13	Monday/ Tuesday	Returns to Jerusalem. Parables and questions. First great prophecy in the Temple. Second great prophecy on Mt. of Olives. Returns to Bethany. Second supper with Simon. Second Anointing.	21:23-28 23:39 24:1-51 25:1-46	11:20-33 12:1-44 13:1-37 14:1-9	20:1-9 21:38	---
Passover Day of Crucifixion	Nisan 14	Tuesday/ Wednesday	Preparation of last supper. Passover supper. Gethsemane, led away to be crucified. Crucified at 9:00 A.M., died at 3:00 P.M., buried at 6:00 P.M.	26 27	14 15	22 23	13 19
Sabbath of Unleavened Bread	Nisan 15	Wednesday/ Thursday	First night, first day in the tomb.	---	---	---	---
Second Day of Unleavened Bread	Nisan 16	Thursday/ Friday	Second night, second day in the tomb.	---	---	---	---
Weekly Sabbath Firstfruits	Nisan 17	Friday/ Saturday	Third night, third day in the tomb. Arose at the end of the Sabbath at sunset.	28:1-10	16:1-18	24:1-49	20:1-23

A Family Guide to the Biblical Holidays©

Overview of the Spring Holidays

Three of the four spring holidays are celebrated within an eight-day period (Abib 14-21). The spring holidays of Passover, Unleavened Bread, and Firstfruits are a portrait of the death and resurrection of Y'shua (Jesus). He sacrificed Himself on Passover, was buried on the Feast of Unleavened Bread, and was resurrected on Firstfruits. The fourth and final spring feast is the Feast of Weeks (Shavuot or Pentecost). The Feast of Weeks is held seven weeks or fifty days following the morrow after the Sabbath of Passover.

Passover and the Feast of Unleavened Bread are held in immediate sequence. The lamb was slain on the fourteenth and the Feast of Unleavened bread began on the fifteenth day of the first month. *And in the fourteenth day of the first month is the Passover of the LORD. And in the fifteenth day of this month is the feast: seven days shall unleavened bread be eaten* (Num. 28:16-17). This passage might account for why Jesus began His Passover seder on the fourteenth. These are distinctly different holidays falling on different days; however, due to their closeness they are usually treated as one festival. (The scriptures seem to teach that these are two names for the same festival. See Exodus 13:3-8.)

These three spring festivals overlap or run into each other:

1. Passover (Pesach)

2. Unleavened Bread (Hag HaMatzah)

3. Day of First Fruits and Omer

   ... And fifty days later ...

4. Feast of Weeks

As you study the Spring Festivals, you will see the plan of God fulfilled in such dramatic detail that you cannot help but be stricken by the awesomeness of our Eternal King. The spring festivals clearly prophesy the first coming of Messiah and the fall festivals are prophetic of His second coming.

Our feet shall stand within thy gates, O Jerusalem.

Feast of Passover

Pesach

Passover Observance	Messianic Significance
The lamb was without blemish.	Jesus was examined and found without blemish (Mat 21:23; 27:1-2; 11-14; 17-26; Luke 3:2; John 11:49-53).
The lamb was a male of the first year.	Jesus was the firstborn Son of God.
The lamb was set aside for four days on the tenth of Nisan.	Jesus entered Jerusalem and the temple on public display for four days on the tenth of Nisan.
The penalty was imposed the moment the lamb was chosen.	Christ received the death penalty for our sin before He was born.
The lamb was killed between the evenings at 3:00 P.M.	Jesus died in the seventh hour, 3:00 P.M. (Mark 15:33-37).
The lamb's bones were not broken (Ex. 12:46, Num. 9:12).	Jesus' bones were not broken. (Ps. 34:20; John 19:31)
The blood of the lamb applied to the door saved the Israelites' firstborn.	The blood of Christ saves us.
The body of the lamb must be eaten the same night (Ex. 12:8).	Jesus was crucified, suffered, and died in the same night.
No work was to be done on the Passover. The Israelites could not save themselves. Even if they should have spent all the night in prayer, the destroying angel would have broken in upon them, and slain their first-born if the blood was not on the door.	The blood of Jesus saves us, not our works. (1 Peter 1:18-21).

Purpose of Passover

The name of the festival, *Pesach* in Hebrew, *passing over* or *protection*, is derived from the instructions given to Moses by God (Ex. 6:6-8). Moses was chosen by God to lead the Israelites out of Egypt. God commanded Moses to tell the children of Israel, *Wherefore say unto the children of Israel, I am the LORD, and I will bring you out from under the burdens of the Egyptians, and I will rid you out of their bondage, and I will redeem you with a stretched out arm, and with great judgments: And I will take you to me for a people, and I will be to you a God: and ye shall know that I am the LORD your God, which bringeth you out from under the burdens of the Egyptians. And I will bring you in unto the land, concerning the which I did swear to give it to Abraham, to Isaac, and to Jacob; and I will give it you for an heritage: I am the LORD* (Ex. 6:6-8).

Passover is the time of beginnings for Israel. This festival ushers in the coming of spring on the Jewish calendar. It is celebrated on the fourteenth[1] day of Abib (the first month of the Jewish religious calendar, later called Nisan). Each of the three pilgrimage festivals–Passover, Pentecost, and the Feast of Tabernacles—has an agricultural basis as well as an historical significance. Many different things are celebrated during Passover. A few of these include: the end of the rainy season and the beginning of the growing season; the new lambing time, and the Exodus of the Israelites from Egypt during Passover.

It cannot be overemphasized as to how foundational Passover is in God's eternal redemption plan. Only Nisan can be the first month in God's calendar. Though other cycles and other aspects of life in the LORD are important, it is the sacrifice of the Lamb that gives it all meaning. Except for the sacrifice of the Passover and the blood on the doorposts, Israel would have suffered the same fate as the Egyptians. The promises to Abraham, Isaac, and Jacob would have then become void. With no Passover sacrifice and with no blood on the doorposts, then no Torah could have been given and no other celebrations could have followed. Apart from the sacrifice of the Passover and the blood on the door posts, there would have been no basis for Messiah, our Passover, to be sacrificed on the anniversary of that momentous occasion. We would have no hope and remain dead in our sins; however, the command was obeyed and deliverance was accomplished. Indeed, for us, this is most certainly the first of all the months, the first month of the year, truly the real beginning of all spiritual life (Michael 1996).

God directs parents, this special night of the year, to take on the role of teacher, and pass down His story of the exodus from Egypt to future generations. This ceremony not only looks back to the miraculous story of God delivering His people, but it also presents the promise of Messiah's death and resurrection. It is an exciting experience centering on a mixture of ritual foods. The matzah, bitter herbs, wine, and the rest, provide a lasting link through the march of history.

ISRAEL'S REDEMPTION FROM EGYPT (EXODUS 1:1-18:27)

The Old Testament story of Passover has more light, more splendor, more vividness, and a richer application to life than any other story in the book of Exodus. Moses and his brother Aaron went to Pharaoh and told him that the Lord said to let the Israelites go. Pharaoh refused to release the Israelites, even for a brief visit to the desert to worship their God. In fact, he made life for the Israelite slaves even worse. Moses had warned Pharaoh that God would send a series of plagues upon Egypt unless the people were freed.

God sent the plagues to show the people that He is the one true God. He confronted the things that the Egyptians called gods. The ten plagues were righteous plagues, and justly inflicted upon the Egyptians because each plague had something to do with the false gods that the Egyptians worshipped. God makes those false things that we worship a burden to us.

The word *plague* is from the Hebrew word *oth*, which means "sign." The Egyptians believed in magic. They were always trying to override the laws of nature to perform their "tricks." God used the laws of nature to bring about His signs and wonders.

The entire episode of the plagues is supposed to have happened within eight to ten months. Each of the plagues spoke as a sign to the Egyptians, showing them that He is greater than their so-called gods. The first three plagues affected all the people, even the Hebrews. The next three plagues were much more intense and only happened to the Egyptians (*I will put a division between my people and thy people* v. 23). Before each plague, God commanded Moses and Aaron to warn Pharaoh, *Let My people go or I* [God] *will bring a plague upon you.* Before each plague, for three weeks, Moses warned Pharaoh. The actual plague lasted one week.

FIRST PLAGUE: THE NILE WATERS TURN TO BLOOD

The Nile, the river of Egypt, was the Egyptians' idol. The Nile's waters nourished the land and determined the welfare of all the people. The Egyptians thirsted after blood when they slaughtered the Hebrews' children, and now God gave them blood to drink. Now the source that brought the Egyptians life brought death instead (Exod. 7:14-25).

SECOND PLAGUE: THE FROGS

The frogs represented the fertility goddess, Isis, that was supposed to help women in childbirth. Frogs were everywhere: in their houses, in their beds, and at their tables. They could not eat, drink, or sleep without their precious god. The frog that symbolized life was left to be raked in heaps of rotting piles of death (Exod. 8:1-15).

THIRD PLAGUE: THE LICE

The lice which came up to live out of the dust of the earth represented the Egyptians' god of the earth, Seth. Matthew Henry notes that lice were small despicable, inconsiderable animals, and yet, by their vast numbers, they rendered a sore plague to the Egyptians. God could have plagued them with lions, or bears, or wolves, or with vultures or other birds of prey; but He chose to do it by these contemptible instruments (Exod. 8:16-19).

FOURTH PLAGUE: THE FLIES

The stinging, disease-carrying flies ruined the land. Beelzebub, the prince of the power of the air, has been glorified as the god of flies, the god of Ekron. The fly was always present at idolatry sacrifices. It seems that the god partook of those in this manner. This fourth plague came upon the Egyptians only. It made Israel a separate and Holy People (Exod. 8:20-32).

FIFTH PLAGUE: THE DISEASE OF LIVESTOCK

A great number of cattle died by a sort of pestilence. The Egyptians made the Hebrews poor and so God caused great loss to the Egyptians. This disease afflicted only the Egyptian livestock. The Egyptians believed animals were possessed by the spirits of gods. The bull was sacred in Egypt, identified in it markings to their god Apis. This pestilence, God's Word tells us, did not affect the Hebrew livestock (Exod. 9:1-7).

SIXTH PLAGUE: THE BOILS

Again God demonstrated His ability to control nature. When the death of their cattle didn't convince the Egyptians, God sent a plague that seized their own bodies. *And they took ashes of the furnace, and stood before Pharaoh; and Moses sprinkled it up toward heaven; and it became a boil breaking forth with blains upon man, and upon beast* (Exod. 9:10). Sores in the body were looked upon as punishment for sin, a means by which to call one to repentance. None of the Hebrews had any boils. This plague was a direct attack on the shamanism of the medico-mystical processes in Egypt (Exod. 9:8-12).

SEVENTH PLAGUE: THE HAILSTORM

Moses gave the people a one-day warning before this plague. The notice was given because the sorcerers of Egypt were also agricultural shamans who supposedly controlled the weather. Those who feared the Lord went into shelter (showing us that God had mercy on some of the Egyptians). Those who did not believe God and took no shelter died in the fields (Ex. 9:21). There was ice and fire mingled with the hail, very grievous, such as there was none like it in all of the land of Egypt. The hail killed both men and cattle, and battered down the herbs, vegetable gardens, fruit trees, and other plants. God, in His judgment, caused it to rain or hail on the Egyptians and not on the Hebrews (Exod. 9:13-35).

EIGHTH PLAGUE: THE LOCUSTS

By this time, Pharaoh's people, his magicians, and advisors, began to rebel. Pharaoh stood alone against God. *Moses stretched forth his rod over the land of Egypt, and the LORD brought an east wind upon the land all that day, and all that night; and when it was morning, the east wind brought the locusts. And the locusts went up over all the land of Egypt, and rested in all the coasts of Egypt: very grievous were they; before them there were no such locusts as they, neither after them shall be such.* The plague was then sent which devastated the land and hence the power of the gods and shamans of agriculture. Pharaoh sent for Moses and pretended to repent. He asked Moses to pray to God to take the locusts away. *And the LORD turned a mighty strong west wind, which took away the locusts, and cast them into the Red Sea; there remained not one locust in all the coasts of Egypt* (Exod. 10:13-14, 19).

NINTH PLAGUE: THE DARKNESS

The Egyptians rebelled against the light of God's Word and they were justly punished with darkness. This thick darkness was over Egypt three days, but the people of Israel had light where they dwelt. What a picture of dark and light, of being lost and saved. The children of God walked in the light while Pharaoh and his people wandered in the darkness.

Matthew Henry's Commentary states,

> The cloud of locusts, which had darkened the land (v. 15), was nothing to this. It was a total darkness. We have reason to think, not only that the lights of heaven were clouded, but that all their fires and candles were put out by the damp or clammy vapors which were the cause of this darkness; for it is said (v. 23), *They saw not one another.* It is threatened to the wicked (Job 18:5-6) that the spark of his fire shall not shine, even the sparks of his own kindling, as they are called (Isa. 50:11), and that the light shall be dark in his tabernacle. Hell is utter darkness. The light of a candle shall shine no more at all in thee (Rev. 18:23).

This plague was an attack on the power of the supreme deity of Egypt, the sun god Re or Amun-Re. The Egyptians could do nothing but stay in their homes and consider what they had experienced up to now, regarding the power of the God of the Israelites. Even then, Pharaoh refused to yield (Exod. 10:21-29).

TENTH PLAGUE: THE DEATH OF THE FIRSTBORN

God said in Exodus 13:2, *Sanctify unto me all the firstborn, whatsoever openeth the womb among the children of Israel, both of man and of beast: it is mine.*

Purpose of Passover - Continued

Nelson's *Illustrated Bible Dictionary* explains the importance of the first-born: God placed a special claim on the firstborn of man and beast (Ex. 13:11-13). This meant that the nation of Israel attached unusual value to the eldest son and assigned special privileges and responsibilities to him. Because of God's claim on the first offspring, the firstborn sons of the Hebrews were presented to the Lord when they were a month old. Since the firstborn was regarded as God's property, it was necessary for the father to redeem, or buy back, the child from the priest. Early Hebrew laws also provided that the firstlings of beasts belonged to the Lord and were turned over to the sanctuary (Ex. 13:2; 34:19; Lev. 27:26). The firstborn's birthright was a double portion of the estate and leadership of the family. As head of the home after his father's death, the eldest son customarily cared for his mother until her death, and provided for his unmarried sisters until their marriages. He was the family's spiritual head and served as its priest. In figurative language, the term *firstborn* stands for "that which is most excellent."

The significance of the death of every firstborn in Egypt, from the house of Pharaoh to the slaves and the livestock, was great. But Israel would be spared so that there would be an obvious distinction between those who belong to the YAWH and those who do not (Exod. 11:1-10).

And it came to pass, that at midnight the Lord smote all the firstborn in the land of Egypt, from the firstborn of Pharaoh that sat on his throne unto the firstborn of the captive that was in the dungeon; and all the firstborn of cattle. And Pharaoh rose up in the night, he, and all his servants, and all the Egyptians; and there was a great cry in Egypt; for there was not a house where there was not one dead. And he called for Moses and Aaron by night, and said, Rise up, and get you forth from among my people, both ye and the children of Israel; and go, serve the Lord, as ye have said. Also take your flocks and your herds, as ye have said, and be gone; and bless me also. And the Egyptians were urgent upon the people, that they might send them out of the land in haste; for they said, We be all dead men. And the people took their dough before it was leavened, their kneading troughs being bound up in their clothes upon their shoulders. And the children of Israel did according to the word of Moses; and they borrowed of the Egyptians jewels of silver, and jewels of gold, and raiment: And the Lord gave the people favour in the sight of the Egyptians, so that they lent unto them such things as they required. And they spoiled the Egyptians (Exodus 12:29-36).

SEDER

During the Passover celebration, Jews and Christians remember this great event by eating special foods associated with the bitterness of slavery and the sweetness of freedom. The entire meal, called the *seder*, is eaten as the story of Israel's freedom is told. Everything in the Seder is directed toward the prime command from the Bible: *And thou shall shew thy son in that day saying, This is done because of that which the LORD did unto me when I came forth out of Egypt* (Exod. 13:8). See a *Messianic Seder Process* in the next chapter.

REDEMPTION

The great miracle of the splitting of the Red Sea is the climax of the departure from Egypt and the inspiring wonder that forged a group of slaves into a nation. The redemption from Egypt is not only that of Israel but also a salvation by faith in general. The celebration of redemption from Egypt will be a pattern for salvation from all other evil.

During this God-ordained night we celebrate the doctrines of our salvation. Thus, like ancient Israel, we are sovereignty brought to the edge of the "sea" with no hope except to trust His deliverance and to follow Him. We marvel at His overwhelming sufficiency. Like ancient Israel, when we trust Him for deliverance and walk through the "sea" with Him, we end up singing and dancing on the other side. That's Pesach! (Berkowitz 1996)

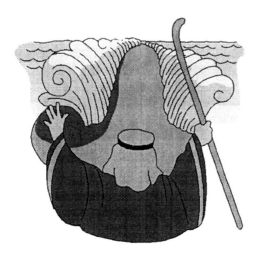

PASSOVER REMEMBRANCE THROUGH THE BIBLE

Numbers 9 is the first anniversary of the Passover. God made special alternative rules for persons unclean, or on a journey, for service to be held on the 14 of the second month. This made it possible for all to keep the feast. This chapter also outlines the penalty for disregarding the Passover observance.

Deuteronomy 16 restates the command to keep Passover, adding the appointed location where the Temple was to be established.

In Joshua 5:10-11 Passover is renewed by the Israelites upon their entering Canaan.

Ezra 6:19 and 20 tells of Passover after return from captivity.

For the first time in decades Hezekiah restores Passover. The people were so moved that the festival was extended an extra seven days (2 Chronicles 30-32).

2 Kings 23 and 2 Chronicles 35 describe a restoration of the Passover by Josiah after four hundred years of interruption.

Ezekiel reinstituted Passover (Ezekiel 45:21-24).

Luke 2:41-52 tells of Mary, Joseph, and twelve-year-old Jesus going to Jerusalem for Passover.

Matthew 21-28 focuses on Passover week, replacing ceremony with reality.

1 Corinthians 5:7 calls Christ our Passover.

Acts 12:3 tells us that Peter was imprisoned at the time of Passover.

Passover in Bible Times

OLD TESTAMENT

Many years before Israel's redemption from Egypt, God revealed the importance of the shedding of blood of a lamb. Consider the story of how Abraham obediently offered his beloved son, Isaac, to God (Gen. 22:1-19).

> "Father, where is the lamb?" These timorous words were first uttered by Isaac. Abraham, his father, in obedience to God, was taking him to the land of Moriah to be sacrificed (Genesis 22:1-7). Abraham's answer to Isaac's question was a prophetic promise as well as an illustration of faith, "God will provide himself a lamb for a burnt offering" (Genesis 22:8). Passover was God's provision of salvation for the nation of Israel to leave Egypt. That freedom was purchased at a great price—the death of the firstborn of Egypt. Passover demanded faith; it demanded obedience. Failure to provide the lamb, failure to put the blood of the lamb upon the doorposts and lintel in the prescribed manner meant death for the firstborn of that house (Exodus 12:1-13). The emphasis of God's Word has always been that, without the shedding of blood, there can be no remission of sin (Leviticus 17:11; Hebrews 9:22). Thousands of years later, God would provide Himself a Lamb (Sevener 1995).

The Bible records Passover kept the second year after the Exodus, then again when the Jews reached the promised land (Joshua 5:10). The requirements directing the Passover meal in the Exodus 12:1-13:16 outline were followed:

1.) The celebration was to be during "the first month," Abib (Nisan).

2.) On the tenth day of this month, each household would select a one-year-old lamb or kid.

3.) On the fourteenth day of the same month, the lamb was killed in the evening.

4.) The blood of the lamb was to be put on the two side posts and on the upper door post of the houses.

5.) The lamb was to be roasted with fire, his head with his legs, and no bones broken.

6.) The lamb was to be eaten with unleavened bread and with bitter herbs.

7.) None of the lamb was to remain—all that was not eaten was to be burnt with fire.

8.) They were to eat the meal with their shoes on and staff in their hands, in haste.

9.) This feast day was declared a memorial to be kept forever.

During the Temple times, the pilgrims came joyously in bands, singing psalms and bringing offerings. What a sight! Josephus records the number of lambs slain from 256,500 and later (a.d. 65) no fewer than three million. A sign hung on each lamb's neck bearing the name of the family. What an impression must have been made on the children. The glorious Temple, the robed priests, the smoke of the sacrifice, then a special supper with symbols and the re-telling of the story of the greatest night in all history. The special preparation for the Passover commenced on the evening of the thirteenth of Nisan, with which, according to Jewish reckoning, the fourteenth began, the day always being computed from evening to evening. The head of the house was to search with a lighted candle all the places leaven was usually kept. A reference to this search is seen in Zephaniah 1:12: *And it shall come to pass at that time I will bring Jerusalem with candles...*From early forenoon of the fourteenth of Nisan, the Feast of Passover may be said to have begun. In Galilee, no work would be done all that day. The next care was to select a proper Paschal lamb which, of course, was free from all blemishes (Edersheim 1994).

The crowd would lead their sacrificial lambs up to the Temple to be slain around 2:30 p.m. to 3:30 p.m. The priest blew the trumpet when the lambs were slain. The priests caught the blood of the lamb in a special bowl of silver or gold. While hymns were sung, the bowls were passed on to the priest at the altar. The Hallel was recited (Psalms113 to 119). The lambs were cleaned out and burnt on the altar. The service ended with burning of the incense. No work was allowed except the preparing of the Passover meal.

The lamb was roasted on a spit made of pomegranate wood. Special care was taken so the lamb did not touch the oven or any type of foreign matter. The bones were not broken. All that was not eaten was burnt with fire until none remained.

Passover is mentioned during the time of Solomon, Hezekiah, Josiah, and under Ezra. The earliest records (the Mishnah) explain the service of this supper was very simple including only the lamb, the unleavened bread, the bitter herbs, and red wine mixed with water.

PASSOVER OBSERVED BY JESUS

Unleavened Bread and Passover are used in the Gospels interchangeably. Strictly speaking, the Passover was Nisan 14 and the Unleavened Bread Nisan 15 through 21.

On the preparation day before the Passover (Mark 15:42), early in the day, Jesus sent Peter and John before Him to prepare for the Passover. Jesus ate His last Passover meal in the Upper Room in the evening in accordance with the original Passover observance in Leviticus 23:5, Numbers 9:1-5 and Exodus 12:6-13. Jesus washed the feet of His disciples. He broke the unleavened bread, symbolizing His offering of Himself as the bread of heaven. "In the evening He cometh with the twelve" (Mark 14:17) and ate the Passover lamb supper with them—all but Judas, who left before the meal (Matt. 26:26-29; Luke 22:14-23).

The Passover celebration took place yearly at the temple in Jerusalem. Every Jewish male was expected to make a pilgrimage to Jerusalem during this time (Deut. 16:16). This was a week-long festival.

And the Jews' Passover was at hand, and Jesus went up to Jerusalem, And found in the temple those that sold oxen and sheep and doves, and the changers of money sitting: And when he had made a scourge of small cords, he drove them all out of the temple, and the sheep, and the oxen; and poured out the changers' money, and overthrew the tables; And said unto them that sold doves, Take these things hence; make not my Father's house an house of merchandise. And his disciples remembered that it was written, The zeal of thine house hath eaten me up.

Then answered the Jews and said unto him, What sign shewest thou unto us, seeing that thou doest these things? Jesus answered and said unto them, Destroy this temple, and in three days I will raise it up. Then said the Jews, Forty and six years was this temple in building, and wilt thou rear it up in three days? But he spake of the temple of his body. When therefore he was risen from the dead, his disciples remembered that he had said this unto them; and they believed the scripture, and the word which Jesus had said.

Now when he was in Jerusalem at the Passover, in the feast day, many believed in his name, when they saw the miracles which he did. But Jesus did not commit himself unto them, because he knew all men, And needed not that any should testify of man: for he knew what was in man (John 2:13-25).

Now before the feast of the Passover, when Jesus knew that his hour was come that he should depart out of this world unto the Father, having loved his own which were in the world, he loved them unto the end (John 13:1).

(See also Matthew 26:17-28; Mark 14:12-25; and Luke 22:7-20.)

Jesus celebrated the Passover meal. When we keep the Passover we are following the ways of Jesus. Jesus also added to the Passover. He expounded on it in a new way. He told his disciples that whenever they ate the Passover meal, they should remember Him using the special unleavened Passover bread, and the cup was the Passover cup *after* the meal. In the Passover ceremony this cup is called "the Cup of Redemption." Jesus wants believers to observe this yearly institute to remember the deliverance of God's people physically from Egypt, *and* to recall the *spiritual* deliverance of God's people through Jesus the Messiah.

Jewish Customs of Passover Today

Passover is the most popular Jewish holiday. The dinner celebration is called a seder. The Passover Seder is a meal with special foods, practices, and Scripture readings that commemorate the liberation from Egyptian slavery, in accordance with God's instructions (Lev. 23:1,4, Exod. 12:14,24-27). *Seder* means "order." The seder invites each family to recount its own version of the great story of Passover with each family member actively involved. The meal induces the experience of going from slavery to liberty through the food experiences and story as the meal turns into an elaborate feast. There is no "right way" to conduct a seder. The seder is usually a family dinner but can also be held with your family or with a church group. During the Seder, the narrative of the exodus is related and prayers of thanksgiving are offered up to God for his loving protection. The dinner table is beautifully set with fancy dishes and candles. There is a special pillow on the chair for the leader of the seder to lean on to symbolize the comfort of a free person reclining (as opposed to a slave who never rests). Orthodox Jewish tradition directs that, during Passover, meals be prepared and served using sets of utensils and dishes reserved strictly for that festival. The readings, songs, and prayers of the Seder are included in the Haggadah.

THE HAGGADAH

The Haggadah is the prayer book used at the Seder, or ritual dinner observed at Passover. Sometimes there is a small book for each person participating in the seder. *Haggadah* means "telling." The Haggadah is a "script" of what the leader and participants should say and the order of eating and drinking during each part of the meal as it tells the story of the Exodus from Egypt. The haggadahs were not used until the eighth century A.D. before this oral tradition was used to tell the Passover story. There are over three thousand different Haggadah versions available.

We have included a Messianic Haggadah in this chapter that you may reproduce, for your family only. This Haggadah is written to be used with a family with small children. We have also included a Messianic Seder Outline so you can make your own Haggadah, if desired.

Jewish Customs of Passover Today - Continued

THE SEDER PLATE

There is a special plate in front of the leader called the seder plate. The Seder consists of three directive foods listed in Exodus 12 and customary foods later added by the Rabbis. Each of the foods symbolizes some aspect of the ordeal undergone by the Israelites during their enslavement in Egypt.

FOODS LISTED IN EXODUS 12

Bitter Herbs (usually horseradish) representing the bitterness of bondage

Shank Bone of a Lamb symbolizes the lamb eaten before they fled Egypt.

Matzah — must be made solely of special flour and water (no leaven).

CUSTOMARY FOODS LATER ADDED BY THE RABBIS

Haroset (it looks unappetizing but is delicious) is a mixture of apples, nuts, grape juice, and cinnamon. It represents the mortar the Israelites used to build the Egyptian cities and the sweetness of a better world.

Roasted Egg is said to be the symbol of life, but we believe it came in with the pagan fertility rituals (Boaz 1996). (Our family decided to leave off the egg.)

Karpas or fresh greens (usually parsley or celery) symbolizes the new life for the Jewish people and the hyssop used to sprinkle blood on the door post. The parsley is dipped into salt water representing the tears of slavery.

THE FOUR QUESTIONS

Jewish tradition requires the youngest child at the table to ask, usually in song, four questions about why this night is different from all other nights. The leader answers each question telling the Passover story.

> 1. Why do we eat unleavened bread on this night when all other nights we eat either leavened bread or matzah?

> 2. Why do we eat only bitter herbs on this night when all other nights we eat all kinds of vegetables?

3. Why do we dip our vegetables twice on this night when we do not dip our vegetables even once all other nights?

4. Why do we eat our meals reclining on this night when on all other nights we eat our meals sitting or reclining?

THE FOUR CUPS

The four cups of wine are customarily drunk at the Passover Seder. An innocent-looking choice between wine and grape juice for the Passover Seder can, under appropriate circumstances, become a focus for complex moral, political, and religious issues. This book will not attempt to go into this much-debated issue. We'll leave this debate up to you and your family.

During Passover, no food with leaven is permitted. Leavening is a fermenting process in which yeast turns the food sour. The rules of leavening apply to food prepared out of any of the five kinds of grain; barley, wheat, rye, oats, and spelt. Although wine is fermented, it doesn't enter into the category of leaven because it's not made from one of these five types. Some reports indicated that possibly unfermented "raisin-wine" was the only acceptable beverage for Passover. Today only kosher wine is used for Passover (Sarna 1988).

During the Seder, each participant drinks four cups of wine to recall the four expressions of redemption mentioned in the Bible (Ex. 6:6-7). God tells Moses to tell the people of Israel, *"I will **bring** you out from under the burdens of the Egyptians, and I will **rid** you from under their bondage and I will **redeem** you with a stretched out arm and with great judgments: and I will **take** you to Me for a people and I will be to you a God..."* The four cups at the Seder represent the four expressions of redemption—bring, deliver, redeem and take. The first cup is called the cup of sanctification; the second, the cup of judgment; the third, the cup of redemption; and the fourth, the cup of the kingdom.

A fifth cup was later added by rabbis, called the cup of Elijah. The custom of filling a fifth cup of wine for Elijah the Prophet at the seder table is relatively recent. Some families set a place at the table for Elijah and pour into a goblet called "Elijah's cup" to symbolize Elijah would be a welcome guest at the seder (Elijah never died. He ascended to heaven). Another custom is to open the door during the seder for Elijah, symbolizing bringing the

Messianic age into their lives. Elijah is expected to return at Passover time as we can deduce from Matthew 11:7.

THE MATZAH AND AFIKOMAN

Matzah is bread without leaven. The Jews have a ceremony they perform with the matzah bread. There are three pieces of matzah, two for the blessing and one to be broken. There is a special cloth holder with three sections called *matzah tash*. The three pieces of matzah are inside, one in each compartment. The leader takes the middle sheet of matzah and lifts it for everyone to see. He then breaks the bread in two. Next he takes one piece and places it back in the matzah tash. Then he takes the other piece and wraps it in a linen cloth. This linen-wrapped matzah is called the Afikoman. The leader "hides" the Afikoman.

The Jews teach that the matzah tash represents the three patriarchs of Israel: Abraham, Isaac, and Jacob *or* the High Priest, the Levites, and the Israelites *or* three tribes of Israel: Kohen, Levi and Yisrael. Yet we do not read in scripture that the Levites were broken, nor do we read that Isaac was broken. There is one explanation that does line up with scripture. We'll discuss this in the Unleavened Bread Chapter.

DAYENU

One of the traditional songs of the Seder is "Dayenu" [It would have been enough].

> If He had taken us out of Egypt but had not punished them, Dayenu. He killed their firstborn ... He split the Red Sea ... He allowed us to pass through it ... He buried our oppressors ... He supplied our needs ... He fed us the Manna ... He brought us to Mount Sinai ... He gave us the Torah .. He brought us to the promised land ... He built the Holy Temple for us .. [and all to the ever recurring refrain of "Dayenu, Dayenu, Dayenu—it would have been enough!"]

If you have access to the World Wide Web, you can download the music for Dayenu and other Passover music at: http://members.aol.com/melizo/ or http://www.holidays.net/Passover/.

Messianic Significance of Passover

Several symbolic clues during Passover are fulfilled in Christ. John the Baptist introduced Jesus by saying *"Behold the Lamb of God who takes away the sin of the world."* (John 1:29). The Jews had been celebrating Passover for 1,500 years. They understood the significance of John's statements.

Isaiah 53, written hundreds of years before Christ, records the suffering the human lamb would experience.

> *He was oppressed, and he was afflicted, yet he opened not his mouth: he is brought as a lamb to the slaughter, and as a sheep before her shearers is dumb, so he openeth not his mouth. He was taken from prison and from judgment: and who shall declare his generation? for he was cut off out of the land of the living: for the transgression of my people was he stricken. And he made his grave with the wicked, and with the rich in his death; because he had done no violence, neither was any deceit in his mouth. Yet it pleased the LORD to bruise him; he hath put him to grief: when thou shalt make his soul an offering for sin, he shall see his seed, he shall prolong his days, and the pleasure of the LORD shall prosper in his hand (Isa. 53:7-10).*

TRIUMPHAL ENTRY OF THE LAMBS

In the first century, a lamb was chosen by the high priest outside of Jerusalem on the tenth of Nisan. Then the priest would lead this lamb into the city while crowds of worshippers lined the streets waving palm branches and singing Psalm 118, "Blessed is He that comes in the name of the Lord."

Jesus our Messiah entered Jerusalem this same day, on a donkey (usually ridden by a king), probably right behind the High Priest's procession. The crowds that had just heralded the entrance of the sacrificial lamb heralded the entrance of the Lamb of God. Accordingly, Jesus identified himself with the Passover sacrifice (John 12:9-19). The next day, as Jesus entered Jerusalem, His entry fulfilled prophecy.

Enthusiasm filled the air. All Israel knew that it would be in Jerusalem where Messiah would be enthroned as their King. Edersheim writes,

> Everyone in Israel was thinking about the Feast, Everyone was going to Jerusalem, or had those near and dear to them there, or at least watched the festive processions to the Metropolis of

Judaism. It was a gathering of universal Israel, that of the memorial of the birth-night of the nation, and of its Exodus, when friends from afar would meet, and new friends be made; when offerings long due would be brought, and purification long needed be obtained—and all worship in that grand and glorious Temple, with its gorgeous ritual. National and religious feelings were alike stirred in what reached far back to the first, and pointed far forward to the final Deliverance.

The High Priest would then take the lamb to the Temple, where it would be tied in public view so that it could be inspected for blemish. In the same way, Y'shua sat and taught in the Temple courtyard for four days. He was inspected and questioned as the Sadducees, the Pharisees, and the teachers of the law sought to trip him up in His words and entrap Him. They could not, because He was perfect and without blemish (Lancaster 1996).

Passover pronounces redemption. To believers in Messiah, the Passover feast has a special meaning. Though we are not slaves, as God's people in Egypt, we were slaves to our sin, our own wants and desires. Sin was our master until Jesus, the Passover Lamb, delivered us from *our* Egypt. The lamb slain during Passover is a foreshadow of the redemption we find in Jesus, the Messiah, our Passover lamb. The principle of redemption is the concept of bondage to the slavery of sin and freedom from its domination (John 8:31-36). To be "redeemed" means to be "purchased from slavery." Jesus Christ purchased our freedom with His blood as the payment for the redemption (Ps. 34:22; 1 Peter 1:18,19; Gal. 3:13; Eph. 1:7; 1 John 1:7).

Jesus ate the Passover meal with eleven of His disciples (see Passover in Bible Times). Just as the priest was to teach, pray, and offer sacrifice, Christ, *the* High Priest, taught, prayed, and then offered Himself as our sacrifice.

AFTER THE MEAL

When Jesus had spoken these words, he went forth with his disciples over the brook Cedron, where was a garden, into the which he entered, and his disciples. (John 18:1).

Jesus went to the Garden of Gethsemane. The garden has many ancient olive trees today, some of which may have grown from the roots of the trees that were present in Jesus' time. (All trees in and around Jerusalem were cut down when the Romans conquered the city in 70 a.d. Olive trees can regenerate from their roots and live for thousands of years.) The name

Gethsemane comes from the Hebrew *Gat Shmanim*, meaning "oil press" (Kollek). Since *oil* is used in the Bible to symbolize the Holy Spirit, it may be said that the garden is where "the Spirit of God was crushed" (Missler 1995).

It was here that Jesus agonized in prayer over what was to occur. It is significant that this is the only place in the King James Version where the word *agony* is mentioned (Strong's concordance). The Greek word for *agony* means to be "engaged in combat" (Pink). Jesus agonized over what He was to go through, feeling that He was at the point of death (Mark 14:34). Yet He prayed, "Not my will, but thine be done" (Terasaka 1996).

Of medical significance is that Luke mentions Him as having sweat like blood. The medical term for this, *hemohidrosis,* or *hematidrosis,* has been seen in patients who have experienced extreme stress or shock to their systems (Edwards). The capillaries around the sweat pores become fragile, and leak blood into the sweat. A case history is recorded in which a young girl who had a fear of air raids in World War I developed the condition after a gas explosion occurred in the house next door (Scott). Another report mentions a nun who, as she was threatened with death by the swords of the enemy soldiers, "was so terrified that she bled from every part of her body and died of hemorrhage in the sight of her assailants." (Grafenberg) As a memorial to Jesus' ordeal, a church which now stands in Gethsemane is known as the Church of the Agony (ibid).

Immediately thereafter, He was betrayed by Judas (Mark 14:43), and captured by the high priest and taken for trial before Caiaphas (Luke 22:54). Consequently, Jesus was crucified between two thieves, fulfilling His own prediction that "as Moses lifted up the serpent in the wilderness, even so must the Son of man be lifted up" (John 3:14). Most of His disciples fled at His arrest; only a group of women and one disciple, called "the disciple whom He loved," were present at the cross when He died (John 19:25-27; compare Matthew 27:55-56; Mark 15:40; and Luke 23:49).

JESUS' TRIAL, DEATH, AND RESURRECTION

Many of us have a hard time grasping the pain and suffering Christ went through on the crucifixion day. Television today has de-sensitized our feelings pertaining to the horrifying violence of the torture and slow death of Jesus.

The following is just a portion of an article by Dr. C. Truman Davis, M.D., M.S., titled: **"The Crucifixion Of Jesus:** The Passion Of Christ From A

Medical Point Of View," which explains some of the agony of Christ:

> In the early morning, Jesus, battered and bruised, dehydrated, and exhausted from a sleepless night, is taken across Jerusalem to Pontius Pilate. The prisoner is stripped of His clothing and His hands tied to a post above His head. A short whip consisting of several heavy, leather thongs with two small balls of lead attached near the ends of each is brought down with full force again and again across Jesus' shoulders, back and legs.
>
> The condemned man was forced to carry the patibulum [cross bar], apparently weighing about 110 pounds, from the prison to the place of execution. Without any historical or Biblical proof, medieval and Renaissance painters have given us our picture of Christ carrying the entire cross. Many of these painters and most of the sculptors of crucifixes today show the nails through the palm. Roman historical accounts and experimental work have shown that the nails were driven between the small bones of the wrists and not through the palms. Nails driven through the palms will strip out between the fingers when they support the weight of the human body. The misconception may have come about through a misunderstanding of Jesus' words to Thomas, "Observe my hands." Anatomists, both modern and ancient, have always considered the wrists as a part of the hand. A titilus, or small sign, stating the victim's crime was usually carried at the front of the procession and later nailed to the cross above the head. A small bundle of flexible branches covered with long thorns (commonly used for firewood) are plaited into the shape of a crown and this is pressed into His scalp. The heavy patibulum [crossbar] of the cross is tied across His shoulders, and the procession headed by a centurion, begins its slow journey along the Via Dolorosa. In spite of His efforts to walk erect, the weight of the heavy wooden beam, together with the shock produced by copious blood loss, is too much. He stumbles and falls. The centurion, anxious to get on with the crucifixion, selects a stalwart North African onlooker, Simon of Cyrene, to carry the cross.
>
> The crucifixion begins. The legionnaire drives a heavy, square, wrought-iron nail through the wrist and deep into the wood.

The patibulum is then lifted in place at the top of the stipes and the titulus reading, "Jesus of Nazareth, King of the Jews" is nailed in place.

Hours of this limitless pain, cycles of twisting, joint-rending cramps, intermittent partial asphyxiation, searing pain as tissue is torn from His lacerated back as He moves up and down against the rough timber; then another agony begins. A deep crushing pain deep in the chest as the pericardium slowly fills with serum and begins to compress the heart.

The body of Jesus is now in extremis, and He can feel the chill of death creeping through His tissues. This realization brings out possibly little more than a tortured whisper, "It is finished."

His mission of atonement has been completed. Finally He can allow His body to die.

With one last surge of strength, He once again presses His torn feet against the nail, straightens His legs, takes a deeper breath, and utters His seventh and last cry, "Father, into thy hands I commit my spirit" (Truman 1965).

Jesus died as the lambs for the Passover meal were being slain. Not a bone was to be broken in these sacrificial lambs (Ex. 12:46; Num. 9:12). Jesus, the Lamb of God, was the perfect sacrifice for the sins of the world (1 Cor. 5:7).

During the Passover time, a sign hung on each lamb's neck, bearing the name of the owner of the lamb. Jesus was crucified with a sign hung over His head with the name of His Father. Studies have shown the Tetragrammaton probably appeared over Jesus when He hung on the cross. During Bible times, messages were commonly written with the first letter of each word. An example in English: UPS, stands for United Parcel Service. The phrase "Jesus of Nazareth and King of the Jews" was written in three languages on a sign above Jesus as He hung on the cross (John 19:19). The Hebrew initials for "Jesus of Nazareth and King of the Jews" was YHWH. That is why the priest asked Pilate to change the writing. *Then said the chief priests of the Jews to Pilate, Write not, The King of the Jews; but that he said, I am King of the Jews. Pilate answered, What I have written I have written* (John 19: 21-22).

The story does not end with the death of Jesus. His body was placed in a new tomb that belonged to a man named Joseph of Arimathea (Luke 23:50-56; John 19:38-42). The greatest event that separates Jesus from all others is the fact that He overcame death. In three days He rose again and lives today. He arose from the grave on the Feasts of Firstfruits!

On Nisan 17, when Israel emerged from the Red Sea, this emergence was a shadow of the fulfillment of the day of Firstfruits (Lev. 23:9-14). This was the first of God's people to emerge from sin (Egypt). It was fulfilled 1,478 years later on Nisan 17, 30 a.d. when Jesus was resurrected and ascended to heaven as our high priest, the Firstfruit of the resurrected (John 20:17).

TWO PASSOVERS

The gospels appear to say that the Messiah ate a Passover meal with the twelve on the evening beginning Nisan 14, and John appears to say Jews were having their Passover meal one day later. There are different theories to explain this.

1. The Sadducees and Pharisees disagreed on the day of Passover. The Sadducees (more conservative group) believed the Feasts of Passover and Unleavened Bread were separate feast days. They held Passover on the fourteenth as God decreed in Exodus, Leviticus, and Numbers. Those of the majority opinion, including the Pharisees, held Passover on the fifteenth. Jesus may have been following both dates by having Passover with the disciples on the fourteenth and becoming the Passover lamb on the fifteenth.

2. Thousands of people would come to Jerusalem to have their lambs ritually slain in the Temple. If they only had one day in which to prepare for the Passover, it would have been extremely difficult to have slaughtered all the lambs brought in to be sacrificed. Therefore, they worked on two different time scales. The northern part of the country went with the old way of dating (starting from morning and going to the following morning). The southern part of the country followed the official dating method (from evening to evening). Thus, there were two times when lambs were being killed in the Temple for sacrifice.

This controversy as to what day Passover should be is not the purpose of this. You must study to decide for yourself which day is correct. Some families celebrate both days, one with their church and one at home.

Suggestions for Celebrating Passover

THE MESSIANIC SEDER

There are no set rules for the basic order of the seder. Just like with Thanksgiving dinner, traditions vary among families. In this chapter is an example of:

1.) a very simple seder with no specific readings.

2.) a traditional seder outline. This outline consists of eighteen traditional steps you can adapt for your family.

3.) an easy-to-use twenty-four page step-by-step Haggadah (you may reproduce for your family's use) that explains just what to say for each blessing as you pour the wine, when to eat and drink, and a list of the Bible verses to read. The leader simply reads aloud the text from the grey box on each page as the rest of the group follows the directions.

4.) a basic checklist of what you need to have at (or close by) the dinner table.

The one thing you should *not* do is get all bound up in "doing it right" and ruin the dinner. That would defeat the purpose. Pray and trust God to lead you. Passover was reintroduced by Hezekiah in Bible times (Numbers 9). They were unable to follow every step outlined in Leviticus; however, God knew their hearts. He had grace towards them and healed their people.

A SIMPLE SEDER

Don't be reluctant to observe Passover because it seems like a fancy elaborate meal. Families with many small children may enjoy a simple seder that doesn't last quite as long as the traditional seder. The main focus is to teach the children about both Passovers–the Exodus and Christ.

A seder can be this simple: Let the children decorate by coloring and hanging pictures from this book. Dinner can include the three elements from scripture such as broiled lamb chops, bitter herbs (horseradish or raw turnip greens), and bread. Make a regular bread recipe without the yeast (roll flat and pierced with a fork before baking). You really don't even need to have lamb. You may want to just place a shank bone from your butcher on a seder plate, or put a small stuffed lamb as a centerpiece, add some candles and festive dishes for this special meal. During dinner, read the Passover story from the Bible or a storybook and asked the children to retell their favorite parts. Explain how Christ is our Passover Lamb. Play the Afikoman game explaining how it relates to Christ's burial and resurrection.

TRADITIONAL SEDER OUTLINE

1. This begins with a sanctification blessing over grape juice in honor of the holiday. The grape juice is drunk, and a second cup is poured, which is symbolic of the blood of Jesus (Matt. 26:28; Mark 14:23,24; Luke 22:20; John 6:53-56).

2. The father or leader pours water into a basin and washes his hands. This symbolizes the foot washing Jesus did before He ate the Passover meal. *After that he poureth water into a bason, and began to wash the disciples' feet, and to wipe them with the towel wherewith he was girded* (John 13:5).

3. The Karpas (a vegetable—usually parsley) is dipped in salt water and eaten. The vegetable is said to symbolize the lowly origins of the Jewish people; the salt water symbolizes the tears shed as a result of our slavery.

4. There are three pieces of matzah, two for the blessing and one to be broken. There is a special cloth holder with three sections called *matzah tash*. The three pieces of matzah are inside, one in each compartment. The leader takes the middle sheet of matzah and lifts it for everyone to see. He then breaks the bread in two. This symbolizes Christ. Next he takes one piece and places it back in the matzah tash. Then he takes the other piece and wraps it in a linen cloth. This linen-wrapped matzah is called the Afikoman. The matzah tash forms a unity of one which speaks of the unity of God: God the Father, God the Son, and God the Holy Spirit.

5. The leader hides the Afikoman. This is a picture of Y'shua (Jesus), the middle part of the tri-unity, which was broken, wrapped up in cloth, buried and brought forth again (as bread brought forth from the earth.) Y'shua (Jesus), the bread of life, was without sin (leaven), pierced, and striped just as the unleavened matzah. *And when Joseph had taken the body, he wrapped it in a clean linen cloth, and laid it in his own new tomb...*(Matt. 27:59-60).

6. There should be a retelling of the story of the Exodus from Egypt and

the first Passover. This may begin with the youngest person asking The Four Questions. Then the leader reads the Passover story in Exodus 12. We should try to motivate our children to ask their own chain of questions, by pointing out small items that will lead them along a path of discovery to ever bigger and more important items.

7. A blessing is recited over the second cup of wine and it is drunk.

8. A second washing of the hands, this time with a blessing, in preparation for eating the matzah.

9. A blessing specific to matzah is recited, thanking God for bread that symbolizes the body of Christ (Matt. 26:26). Then a piece of matzah is eaten.

10. A blessing is recited over a bitter herb (usually raw horseradish), and it is eaten. This symbolizes the bitterness of slavery and the bitterness of our sin. The bitter vegetable should be eaten together with matzah.

11. The bitter vegetable is eaten again, but with a mixture of apples, nuts, cinnamon and wine, which symbolizes the mortar used by the Jews in building during their slavery. This mixture symbolizes how the sweetness of Y'shua can overcome bitter sin.

12. A festive meal is eaten. There is no particular requirement regarding what to eat at this meal except that leaven cannot be eaten. Traditionally, some Jews eat gefilte fish and matzah ball soup at the beginning of the meal.

13. The piece of matzah set aside earlier is eaten as dessert, the last food of the meal. The children look for the Afikoman. Once it is found it is ransomed to the leader for a price as the Messiah was our ransom.

14. The third cup of wine, called the redemption, cup is poured. Grace is recited afterward. Then a blessing is said over the third cup and it is drunk.

15. The fourth cup is poured.

16. Some items are set aside for the prophet Elijah (see previous section "Jewish Customs of Passover Today.") The door is opened for awhile at this point for Elijah.

17. Several psalms of praise are recited. A blessing is recited over the last cup of wine and it is drunk.

18. The Passover is completed with the phrase: Lashanan Haba'ah Bi Yerushalayim! (Next Year in Jerusalem!) This is sometimes followed by various hymns and stories.

SEDER CHECK LIST

General

❑ The table is usually set with the best dishes, a low floral arrangement, a tablecloth, and two candles and candlesticks.

❑ Place a haggadah at each setting (or every other setting.)

On the table near the leader

❑ Seder Plate. You can purchase a seder plate or use a fancy dish, or even let the children color a paper plate. On the seder plate are usually: A shankbone of a lamb (some leave off the shank bone and serve a different main dish because Jesus was the ultimate sacrifice. Others like the symbolism—you choose): bitter herbs (usually horseradish); charoset (a green vegetable, usually parsley or celery.)

❑ Three pieces of matzah, in the specially designed matzah cover or within three cloth napkins.

❑ A small basin of water for the handwashing (or the leader can bring it to the table when it is time) and a towel to dry the hands.

❑ On the chair should be a pillow or cushion for leaning.

On the table within everyone's reach

❑ Small bowls of salty water.

❑ Wine goblet or glass.

❑ Extra bitter herbs and Charoset for a large family or gathering.

❑ A plate of matzah.

❑ A bottle of wine or grape juice (one bottle per every six to eight people).

FOLD

Jesus gasped a dying cry, "I thirst." The second drink, which He accepted moments before His death, is not a cup of wine. They filled a sponge, put it upon a hyssop-stalk and with this put it to His mouth, the same type stalk used to apply the blood to the wooden doorpost (Ex. 12:22JJ). This hyssop stalk was raised toward the Perfect Lamb who was hung on a wooden cross for the salvation of all mankind.

They wouldn't even give the Son of God one drop of water, yet He gave Himself for us. With one last bit of strength, in pain and agony, Jesus took a breath and uttered His last cry, "Father, into thy hands I commit my spirit."

On the third day, Nisan 17, the Day of Firstfruits, the greatest miracle occurred! Jesus Christ, Y'shua HaMashchiach, was raised from the dead, never to die again! Jesus became the Firstfruit of the dead that will rise (1Cor. 15:20–23). We rejoice in His victory over death and His gift of eternal life to those who believe and follow Him.

Blessed are YOU, Lord, our God, King of the universe, who has shown us a glimpse of your infinite grace and mercy. Thanks be to You for Your Son, our eternal Redeemer and Savior, the True and Perfect Lamb.

The Seder is Concluded.

Leh-shah-na Hah-bah-ah Be-ru-sha-law-yim
Next Year in Jerusalem!

24

Sanctify the Holiday

Leader's Action: Pray over this Festival of Freedom.

Leader Says: Tonight is a very special night; we are going to have a dinner celebration called a Passover Seder. This is a meal with special foods, practices, and Scripture readings that remind us of two very special true stories. The first story I will tell you, in a few moments, happened many years before Jesus. God instructed us to meet, as we are now, and have the older people tell the younger people how God delivered Moses and the Hebrew people from Egyptian slavery.

We will also be referring to another story, a special story about Jesus. The story of how God delivered the Hebrew people was a picture of how Jesus died for our sins. If you listen carefully you will see how the two stories are so much alike. Now we will start the Passover Seder as Mother lights the candles.

The Lighting of the Candles

Woman says: Blessed are you, O Lord our God, King of the universe, who sanctifies us by your commandments and has ordained that we kindle the Passover lights. Bring light into our hearts and minds as we honor and remember your son, the Light of the world, Y'shua Jesus.

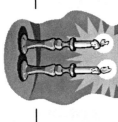

The woman lights the candles.

2

The Fourth Cup

Leader Says: After the disciples drank the third cup, "And when they had sung an hymn, they went out into the mount of Olives." (Matt. 26:30) The fourth cup was never drunk, not by Jesus, and perhaps not by the disciples. From the upper room, Jesus went outside of the city where He spent time in prayer at the Garden of Gethsemane. The name "Gethsemane," means "oil press" in Hebrew. Since "oil" is used in the Bible to symbolize the Holy Spirit, it may be said that the garden is where "the Spirit of God was crushed." Here Jesus was betrayed and arrested.

The next morning, Jesus, battered and bruised, dehydrated and exhausted, is taken in front of Pontius Pilate. Jesus was tried and condemned to scourging and crucifixion. The soldiers mocked Him, spit on Him, and beat Him. They struck Him with a heavy leather whip again and again across His shoulders, back, legs, and head. They braided flexible branches with long thorns and thrust them in His scalp.

"And they crucified him, and parted his garments, casting lots: that it might be fulfilled which was spoken by the prophet, They parted my garments among them, and upon my vesture did they cast lots. And sitting down they watched him there; And set up over his head his accusation written, THIS IS JESUS THE KING OF THE JEWS." (Matt. 27:27–35)

The fourth cup, the Cup of the Kingdom, reminds us that Jesus did not drink the wine offered to Him as He was dying. Let us not drink of the fourth cup. Let us wait to have this special cup with our Savior. After Christ's return we shall partake with Him—in His physical presence—in the kingdom (Matt. 26:29).

23

Display Seder Plate

Leader says: This special plate is called the Seder plate. Each of the foods symbolize some part of the Passover story. This story is not only a story of physical deliverance from bondage; it also is a story of our spiritual deliverance. Every part of Passover paints the portrait of that redemption. There are three foods God tells us to eat on this night and other foods later added by men to help us remember Passover.

The shank bone of a Lamb symbolizes the lamb eaten before they fled Egypt.

The Matzah is made with no leaven to remind us the Hebrews left Egypt in a hurry.

The bitter herbs represent the bitterness of bondage.

The Haroset is a mixture of apples, nuts, grape juice, and cinnamon. It represents the mortar the Israelites used to build the Egyptian cities and the sweetness of a better world.

The Karpas symbolizes the new life for God's people. The non-bitter vegetable is dipped into salt water representing the tears of slavery.

3

3

Dayenu
It Would Have Been Enough

If He had brought us out from Egypt, and had not carried out judgments against them
Dayenu, it would have sufficed us!

If He had carried out judgments against them, and not against their idols
Dayenu, it would have sufficed us!

If He had destroyed their idols, and had not smitten their firstborn
Dayenu, it would have sufficed us!

If He had smitten their firstborn, and had not given us their wealth
Dayenu, it would have sufficed us!

If He had given us their wealth, and had not split the sea for us
Dayenu, it would have sufficed us!

If He had split the sea for us, and had not taken us through it on dry land
Dayenu, it would have sufficed us!

If He had taken us through the sea on dry land, and had not drowned our oppressors in it
Dayenu, it would have sufficed us!

If He had drowned our oppressors in it, and had not supplied our needs in the desert for forty years
Dayenu, it would have sufficed us!

If He had supplied our needs in the desert for forty years, and had not fed us the manna
Dayenu, it would have sufficed us!

If He had fed us the manna, and had not given us the Shabbat
Dayenu, it would have sufficed us!

If He had given us the Shabbat, and had not brought us before Mount Sinai
Dayenu, it would have sufficed us!

If He had brought us before Mount Sinai, and had not given us the Torah
Dayenu, it would have sufficed us!

If He had given us the Torah, and had not brought us into the land of Israel
Dayenu, it would have sufficed us!

22

22

The Four Cups

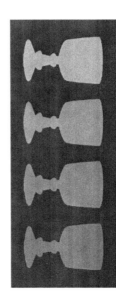

Leader says: There are four times we will drink from wine during this service, two times before dinner and twice after dinner. One of these cups is used to conclude the first half of the Seder (mark the end of the telling of the story part). The final cup is used to conclude the second half of the Seder.

These four cups represent four expressions of redemption mentioned in the Bible (Ex. 6:6-7). God tells Moses to tell the people of Israel, "*I will bring you out from under the burdens of the Egyptians, and I will deliver you from their bondage and I will redeem you with an outstretched arm and with great judgments; and I will take you to Me for a nation and I will be to you a God...*" The four cups at the Seder represent the four expressions of redemption - bring, deliver, redeem, and take.

* The first cup is the Cup of Sanctification
* The second, the Cup of Judgment
* The third, the Cup of Redemption
* The fourth, the Cup of the Kingdom

4

Children Hunt for the Afikoman

Leader Says: Dinner is finished but our seder is not over. The children can now look for the Afikoman. Whoever finds it can bring it to me to be ransomed. After the ransom, we will speak of the next two cups.

Grace After Meal and the Third Cup

Pour the third cup of wine called The Redemption Cup.

Leader Says: When Jesus ate the Passover meal as an obedient Jew, he drank from the first and second cups, however. He did not drink from the third cup. While drinking the second cup, Jesus said, "*Drink ye all of it: For this is my blood of the new testament, which is shed for many for the remission of sins. But I say unto you, I will not drink henceforth of this fruit of the vine, until that day when I drink it new with you in my Father's kingdom.*" The disciples drank the third cup, but Jesus could not because it represented redemption. Jesus was willing to drink the second cup, the cup of wrath, but He excluded himself of the redemption by not drinking the third cup. The next day, Jesus, who knew no sin, became sin for us and died in that sin to redeem us.

Blessed are you, O Lord, our God, King of the universe, who has given us the Cup of Redemption.

Everyone drinks from the third cup. (Pour the fourth cup, but do not drink from it.) The Passover meal concludes with singing. One of the traditional songs is Psalms 118:21-24 and Dayenu (It Would Have Been Enough). Sing your family's favorite praises.

21

  A Family Guide To The Biblical Holidays©

The First Cup

The Cup of Sanctification

Everyone stand to partake of the Kiddush (first blessing). The leader pours the first cup of wine. He lifts his cup and says a sanctification blessing over sweet wine (grape juice) in honor of the holiday.

Leader says: Please stand.

Leader prays: Blessed are You, O Lord, our God, King of the universe, who creates the fruit of the vine.

Leader says: This first cup is the Cup of Sanctification. Sanctification means to be set apart. We are setting apart this time to bring honor to our Lord.

Remember how God set apart His people in Egypt. *"Wherefore say unto the children of Israel, I am the LORD, and I will bring you out (set you apart) from under the burdens of the Egyptians, and I will rid you out of their bondage, and I will redeem you..."* Exodus 6:6

In the same way God has redeemed us from sin, set us apart, when we accept Jesus as our Lord. "God hath from the beginning chosen you to salvation through sanctification of the Spirit and belief of the truth" 2 Thessalonians 2:13.

We will drink the cup while leaning to symbolize freedom, as a slave cannot relax while eating or drinking. You may be seated.

Everyone drinks the cup of wine while seated, reclining on the left side as a sign of freedom. Pour the second cup of wine. (Do not drink the second cup at this time.)

5

Eating the Haroset

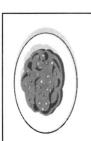

Leader says: Now we will eat the bitter herbs on the matzah again, this time with the Haroset. The Haroset symbolizes the mortar used by the Jews in building during their slavery. This mixture symbolizes how the sweetness of Jesus can overcome bitter sin.

Pass around the matzah, bitter herbs and haroset.

Leader Prays Over Meal: Blessed are you, O Lord, our God, King of the universe, who has ordained that we celebrate the Passover. Help us, God, to remember the two stories of how you give freedom to your people, first the freedom from Egypt, and now our freedom from sin through your precious son, Jesus.

Everyone enjoy the special Passover dinner.

20

20

Washing of the Hands

The leader washes his hands in a small basin.

Leader says: God commanded Aaron to wash his hands and feet before approaching the altar of the Lord. We wash our hands as a token of our desire to live a clean life of acceptable service to our Almighty God. This is also a reminder that Jesus humbled himself the night of Passover by washing the feet of the disciples. He said, *"If I then, your Lord and Master, have washed your feet; ye also ought to wash one another's feet. For I have given you an example, that ye should do as I have done to you. Verily, verily, I say unto you, the servant is not greater than his lord; neither he that is sent greater than he that sent him. If ye know these things, happy are ye if ye do them."*

Eating of the Karpas

Leader dips the vegetable (sprigs of parsley or celery) in salt water and distributes them to all present at the Seder table.

Blessed are you, O Lord our God, King of the universe, help us to remember to follow the example of your Holy Son, give us the love for others that He has shown us.

Leader says: The vegetable is said to symbolize the lowly origins of the people; the salt water symbolizes the tears shed as a result of slavery. May we also remember the tears Christ shed over His people?

Eating the Matzah

Leader Says: Now we will partake of the bread as Jesus did during Passover described in Luke 22:19 *"And he took bread, and gave thanks, and brake [broke] it, and gave unto them, saying, This is my body which is given for you: this do in remembrance of me."*

The Blessing: Blessed are you, O Lord, our God, King of the universe, who has sanctified us with His commandments and commanded us concerning the removal of leaven.

Eating the Bitter Herbs

Leader says: Blessed are you, O Lord, our God, King of the universe, who has commanded us to eat of the bitter herbs.

This symbolizes the bitterness of slavery and the bitterness of our sin. The bitter vegetable should be eaten together with matzah. Let us also remember the bitterness of the crucifixion Y'shua Jesus went through for our sins.

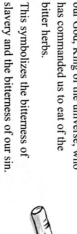

Everyone takes a small piece of matzah, dips it into the mixture of bitter herbs and eats it.

6

19

A color printable version of this Hagaddah is available from the Internet at http://BiblicalHolidays.com

A Family Guide to the Biblical Holidays©

Three Pieces of Matzah

Leader says: *(holding the Matzah)* This bread is called unleavened bread. See how flat it is; it has no leavening in it. The Hebrews had to leave very fast and they were unable to wait for their bread to rise. It is the bread of affliction that our fathers ate in the land of Egypt.

In the Bible leavening is a symbol of sin, so unleavened bread is a symbol of having no sin. This bread is also a portrait of Jesus, who had no sin. He is the bread of life. Jesus said, *"I am that bread of life. Your fathers did eat manna in the wilderness, and are dead. This is the bread which cometh down from heaven, that a man may eat thereof, and not die. I am the living bread which came down from heaven: if any man eat of this bread, he shall live for ever: and the bread that I will give is my flesh, which I will give for the life of the world."* John 6:48-51

The three pieces of Matzah represent the Father, Son, and Holy Spirit. Jesus, the middle part of the tri-unity was broken, wrapped up in cloth, buried and brought forth again as the bread brought forth from the earth.

I break the bread to represent that Christ was broken for us. I will wrap it in linen just as Jesus was wrapped in linen for his burial.

The leader takes the middle Matzah and breaks it into two, one piece larger than the other. The larger piece is wrapped in a linen napkin and set aside to serve as afikoman. The smaller piece is put back, between the two Matzah.

7

Drink from the Second Cup

The Leader lifts his cup and says a sanctification blessing over the grape juice in honor of the holiday.

Leader Says: Blessed are You, Lord, our God, King of the universe, who creates the fruit of the vine.

This second cup is the Cup of Judgment. When Jesus went to pray in the Garden of Gethsemane, He prayed, " *'Father, if thou be willing, remove this cup from me; nevertheless, not my will, but thine, be done.' And there appeared an angel unto him from heaven, strengthening him, And being in an agony he prayed more earnestly: and his sweat was as it were great drops of blood falling down to the ground."* (Luke 22:42-44). He did not want to drink of this Cup of Judgment, but did because He knew the will of His Father was best.

Jesus had a Passover Seder the night before He died for our sins. While drinking the second cup, Jesus said in Matthew 26:28 "For this is my blood of the new testament, which is shed for many for the remission of sins."

Jesus drank from the Cup of Judgment so we will not have to.

18

18

Hiding the Afikoman

Leader says: We call this bread wrapped in linen the afikoman. Afikoman is a Greek word meaning "that which comes after," such as the dessert of a meal.

Now, the children will close their eyes as I hide the afikoman, just as Jesus was hidden in the tomb for three days and three nights. After this special dinner you children may look for the Afikoman. Whoever finds it will receive a reward!

Children close their eyes as the leader hides the afikoman and returns to the table.

Leader says: God's word says that we should have this Passover meal, partly so that we can have a special time to tell you children about the things God has done for his people. *"And it shall come to pass, when ye be come to the land which the LORD will give you, according as he hath promised, that ye shall keep this service. And it shall come to pass, when your children shall say unto you, 'what mean ye by this service?' That ye shall say, It is the sacrifice of the LORD's Passover, who passed over the houses of the children of Israel in Egypt, when he smote the Egyptians, and delivered our houses."* Exodus 12:25-27

Leader says: Now it is time for the youngest child to ask the four questions.

8

Jesus, Our Passover Lamb

The lamb was a male of the first year.	Jesus is the firstborn of God.
The lamb was set aside for four days, on the tenth of Nisan.	Jesus was on public display for four days, on the tenth of Nisan.
The lamb had no blemish.	Jesus was without blemish.
The death penalty was imposed when the lamb was chosen.	Christ came to receive the death penalty to free us from the bondage of sin.
The lamb was killed at 3:00.	Jesus died at 3:00.
The lamb's bones were not broken.	Jesus' bones were not broken.
The lamb must be eaten the same night.	Jesus was crucified, suffered and died in the same night.
The blood of the lamb applied the door saved the Israelite's first born.	The blood of Christ shed on the cross saves all of us!
No work is done on Passover.	The blood of Jesus saves us— not our works.

17

 A Family Guide to the Biblical Holidays©

The Four Questions

Child asks:

1. Why do we eat only unleavened bread on this night when all other nights we eat either leavened bread or matzah?

2. Why do we eat only bitter herbs on this night when all other nights we eat all kinds of vegetables?

3. Why do we dip our vegetables twice on this night when we do not dip our vegetables even once all other nights?

4. Why do we eat our meals reclining or leaning on this night, when on all other nights we eat our meals sitting?

The leader answers the questions by reading the Passover story starting on the next page or from Exodus 12:3-49, or can tell the story in his own words, or (for small children) from an illustrated story book.

9

The Egyptians chased after them, and all Pharaoh's horses and horsemen followed them into the sea. God looked down from the pillar of fire and cloud at the Egyptian army and threw it into confusion. He made the wheels of their chariots come off so that they had difficulty driving. And the Egyptians said, "Let's get away from the Israelites! God is fighting for them against Egypt!"

Then God said to Moses, "Stretch out your hand over the sea so that the waters may flow back over the Egyptians and their chariots and horsemen." Moses stretched out his hand over the sea, and at daybreak the sea went back to its place. The Egyptians were fleeing toward it, and God swept them into the sea. The water flowed back and covered the chariots and horsemen-the entire army of Pharaoh that had followed the Israelites into the sea. Not one of them survived.

That day God saved Israel from the hands of the Egyptians. And when the Israelites saw the great power the LORD displayed against the Egyptians, the people feared the LORD and put their trust in him and in Moses his servant.

God said that Passover was a day to be celebrated for the generations to come. He said it was to be a festival to God every year, to remember that our fathers were once slaves in Egypt, but now we are free.

Can you see the symbolism of the first Passover and Jesus? When John the Baptist was baptizing people and He saw Jesus coming, he said, "Behold! The Lamb of God." That was a very special thing to say.

Jesus had the Passover Seder with His disciples on the eve of His death. The next day Jesus was beaten with a whip and at 3:00 Jesus was crucified on the cross for our sins. The blood shed on the cross was similar to the blood on the doorpost of the homes in Egypt. Because Jesus' blood was shed for us, we can be saved.

Look at the Matzah. Can you see how it reminds us of Jesus? The Matzah is striped and pierced just as Jesus was striped and pierced for us. The entire Passover story was a foreshadow, a picture of the coming of Christ!

16

The Passover Story

Leader says: This is the story of Passover. Listen carefully and you will hear where the name Passover came from.

Once upon a time, a long time before Jesus lived, the Hebrew people, who believed in the one true God, lived in Egypt. During that time there was a wicked king (or Pharaoh) ruling over Egypt. Pharaoh was very cruel to Hebrews. He made them into slaves and made them work

very, very hard.

Pharaoh was very jealous and worried that one of the Hebrew boys may grow up and try to take over. So he ordered the soldiers to kill all the Hebrew baby boys.

One Hebrew mother decided to hide her very special small baby. She put the baby in a basket on the riverbank so the mean sol-

diers

wouldn't find him. The pharaoh's daughter went to the river and found the baby. She adopted him as her own baby and named him Moses, which means, "brought from the water," in Hebrew.

10

10

When Pharaoh let the people go, God led the people around by the desert road toward the Red Sea. The Israelites left Egypt.

By day the LORD went ahead of them in a pillar of cloud to guide them on their way and by night in a pillar of fire to give them light, so that they could travel by day or night.

When the king of Egypt was told that the people had fled, Pharaoh and his officials changed their minds about them and said, "What have we done? We have let the Israelites go and have lost all our slaves!"

Pharaoh took six hundred of the best chariots, along with all the other chariots of Egypt, with officers to go after the Israelites. The Egyptians—all Pharaoh's horses and chariots, horsemen and troops—chased the Israelites and caught up with them as they camped by the Red Sea.

As Pharaoh got closer, the Israelites looked up, and there were the Egyptians, marching after them. They were terrified and cried out to God. Moses told the people, "Do not be afraid. Stand firm and you will see the deliverance God will bring you today. The Egyptians you see today, you will never see again. The LORD will fight for you; you need only to be still."

Then God said to Moses, "Why are you crying out to me? Tell the Israelites to move on. Raise you staff and stretch out your hand over the sea to divide the water so that the Israelites can go through the sea on dry ground."

The angel of God, who had been traveling in front of Israel's army, withdrew and went behind them. The pillar of cloud also moved from in front and stood behind them, coming between the armies of Egypt and Israel. Throughout the night the cloud brought darkness to the one side and light to the other side; so neither went near the other all night long.

Then Moses stretched out his hand over the sea and all that night God drove the sea back and turned it into dry land. The Israelites went through the sea on dry ground, with a wall of water on their right and on their left.

15

15

    A Family Guide to the Biblical Holidays©

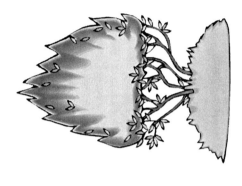

11

Moses grew to be a man. He wanted to help the Hebrew people, but he couldn't. He left Egypt and became a shepherd in a faraway land.

Now Moses kept the flock of Jethro, his father-in-law, the priest of Midian. While Moses was taking care of his sheep, he came to the mountain of God. There the angel of God appeared to him in flames of fire from with in a bush. Moses saw that though the bush was on fire, it did not burn up. So Moses thought, "I will go over and see this strange sight—why the bush does not burn up." God called to Moses from within the bush, "Moses! Moses!" And Moses said, "Here I am."

God said, "Do not come any closer, take off your sandals, for the place where you are standing is holy ground."

11

After nine of the ten plagues, God told Moses to tell all the Hebrew people that each man was to take a lamb for his family, one for each household. These were very special lambs. They had to be one year-old males without any sickness, disabilities, or blemishes.

They were to kill the lambs and take some of the blood and put it on the sides and tops of the door frames of the houses where they eat the lambs. That same night they were to eat the meat roasted over the fire, along with bitter herbs, and bread made without yeast. They were to eat the lamb with their cloaks tucked into their belts, their sandals on their feet and a staff in their hand. They were to eat in a hurry.

God said that on that night He would pass through Egypt and strike down every firstborn-both men and animals. When He saw the blood on the houses where His people were He would pass over them. He promised He would not harm anyone who had the blood on the door-post thatnight while He struck Egypt.

That night, death came to all of Egypt's firstborn.

Pharaoh and all his officials and all the Egyptians got up during the night, and there was loud wailing in Egypt, for there was not a house without someone dead. During the night Pharaoh summoned Moses and Aaron and said, "Up! Leave my people, you and the Israelites! Go, worship God as you have requested. Take your flocks and herds, as you have said, and go."

The sad and frightened Egyptians insisted the Hebrew people hurry and leave the country. "For otherwise," they said, "we will all die!" So the people took their dough before the yeast was added, and carried it on their shoulders wrapped in clothing. The sun baked it into hard bread called Matzah.

14

14

Then he said, "I am the God of your father, the God of Abraham, the God of Isaac, and the God of Jacob." Moses hid his face, because he was afraid to look at God. God said, "I have indeed seen the misery of my people in Egypt. I have heard them crying out because of their slave drivers, and I am concerned about their suffering. So I have come down to rescue them from the heard of the Egyptians and to bring them up out of that land into a good and spacious land, a land flowing with milk and honey. So now, go. I am sending you to Pharaoh to bring my people the Israelites out of Egypt."

Moses did not feel worthy but God told him, "I will be with you. And this will be the sign to you that it is I who have sent you. When you have brought the people out of Egypt, you will worship God on this mountain."

God told Moses to return to Egypt and free the Jewish slaves, and lead them away from Pharaoh. Moses did return to Egypt, went to Pharaoh and told him: "This is what the LORD, the God of Israel, says: 'Let my people go, so that they may hold a festival to me in the desert.'" But Pharaoh would not listen to him.

Pharaoh said, "Who is this God, that I should obey him and let Israel go? I do not know the LORD and I will not let Israel go." Moses told the Pharaoh if he didn't let the people go, great plagues would come upon Egypt. Pharaoh did not listen and God did send ten horrible plagues.

12

Leader says: Let us dip our fingers in the wine, putting a drop of wine on a plate for each plague as it is recited.

Everyone recites the names of the plagues together, while dipping a finger into the second cup of wine and placing one drop of wine on the plate (ten drops).

Blood	Lice	
Flies	Boils	
Hail	Blight	
	Locusts	Darkness
		Death of First Born

13

A Family Guide to the Biblical Holidays©

Centerpiece

To assemble your centerpiece for Passover Week, cover the base with crimson (dark red) cloth (see instructions for "Multi-Holiday Centerpiece" in *Preliminary Activities & Crafts* section). Set **Lamb** craft (instructions follow) in center atop a bed of Spanish moss, or paper grass. Position **Lamb**, **Cross**, **Palm Branches**, and **Cup & Bread** flags.

SYMBOLISM IN THE CENTERPIECE

Crimson—represents the blood atonement or sacrifice (Isa. 1:18)

Lamb—Jesus, who became our perfect sacrifice for sin (John 1:29b, Ex. 12, Rev. 5:6-13); Christ the submissive One (Isa. 53:7-8, Acts 8:32-33)

Cup & Bread—wine is symbolic of the Holy Spirit or fullness of joy (Isa. 65:8, Jer. 31:12, Hos. 2:22, Judges 9:13, Ps. 104:15, Eph. 5:18). Bread represents Christ as our food (John 6, 1 Cor. 11:24).

Cross—place of extreme agony and death, where Jesus died for our sins (1 Cor. 1:17-18, 28, Heb. 12:2, John 12:32-33).

Palm Branches—the upright and faithful tree (Jer. 10:5), used in honor or praise (John 12:13, Rev. 7:9, Lev. 23:40)

Lamb Craft

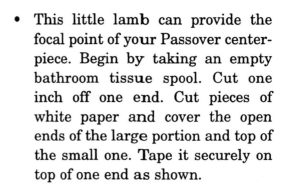

- This little lamb can provide the focal point of your Passover centerpiece. Begin by taking an empty bathroom tissue spool. Cut one inch off one end. Cut pieces of white paper and cover the open ends of the large portion and top of the small one. Tape it securely on top of one end as shown.

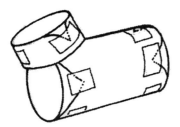

< Glue tabs>

- Copy pattern. Cut white poster paper using these patterns. DO NOT COPY DOTTED LINES. They are guides for folding only. Cut one face and four legs. Fold on dotted lines to make an angle outward for support, or roll around pencil to curve outward. Fold glue tab on head downward away from face. Fold or roll sides of face back.

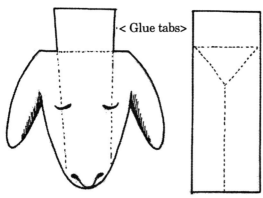

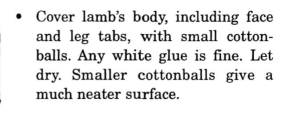

- Glue legs and face to spool as shown in illustration.

or

- Cover lamb's body, including face and leg tabs, with small cottonballs. Any white glue is fine. Let dry. Smaller cottonballs give a much neater surface.

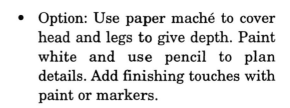

- Option: Use paper maché to cover head and legs to give depth. Paint white and use pencil to plan details. Add finishing touches with paint or markers.

The Ten Plagues Adventure

A fun activity to represent the ten plagues can be reenacted. Ten days before Passover begins, do something in your home to represent each one of the ten plagues. Here are a few examples. Be creative and make up your own symbols.

1. Nile waters turning to blood—put red food coloring in the water glasses at the dinner table, in the bathroom sinks, in the dog's water bowl, and anywhere else you can think of.

2. The frogs—Use green construction paper to cut out roundish frogs with thin green legs. Bend the legs to make the frogs look as if they are jumping. Put them everywhere, in cereal boxes, in the shower, refrigerator, drawers, etc.

3. The lice—Use a hole punch to make many small white "dots" out of plain white paper. Scotch tape them on your body and leave them on for a few hours. The appearance and irritation will make you think of itching lice.

4. The flies — Use clear scotch tape to tape pepper or small "dots" of black construction paper in different areas of the house, the windows, the bathroom mirrors, etc.

5. Disease afflicting the Egyptian livestock—put stuffed animals in different areas of the house, upside down.

6. Boils—Use a hole punch to make many small red "dots" out of red construction paper (or cut out circles). Cover each other with boils by scotch taping them on your body and leave them on for a few hours. The appearance and irritation will make you think of the boils.

7. Hailstorm —Put ice cubes around the outside of your house, the porch areas and on the outside window sills.

8. Locusts — Use brown construction paper to cut out oval-looking locusts. Put them everywhere as you did the frogs (you'll even think of some new places to surprise your family).

9. Darkness—Tape brown paper bags over all the windows, draw all draperies to keep it dark in the daytime, or don't turn on any lights in the evening.

10. Death—Put red ribbon on the sides and top of door post of your house to avoid the death plague. When the neighbors ask what the ribbon is for you can witness to them!

Family Drama: Moses and the Big Picture

Many families have a real flair for acting. Others haven't discovered it, but it is there waiting to be revealed. If any members of your family have good oral reading skills, or a knack for public speaking, inventing costumes, rigging props, or devising parts in a script, here's your chance! Encourage that brother or sister by staging a re-enactment of the Exodus.

You can start with Moses and the plagues and stage as much as your family size allows (multiple roles are O.K.). Invite extended family, church friends or home schoolers to join you or be an audience. All the plagues can be done with or without props, using complaints and gestures that convey the idea.

If you will perform this on an evening prior to your seder meal, it will enrich the "big picture" that surrounds this special observance.

*For a scaled-down version, Dad or Mom can condense the scripture account (or use a good Bible storybook) and read as a narrator while various children enter in costume, making gestures and those all-important facial expressions.

NOTE: When you discover which costumes (towels, bathrobes, fabric, etc.) and props work well—and those that don't—make a list and keep it in a file. You may want to refer to it if you decide to perform the Esther story at Purim, or something similar at Pentecost.

152

Don't "Passover" This Challenge

How many words can you make from the letters in Passover? There are at least enough to fill the lines below. Plurals and verb forms with **"s"** on the end **do not count** as separate words. You may show them as (S) at the end of the word. Example: PEAR(S). Other endings such as -er on some root words are acceptable, if found in the dictionary.

_____   _____   _____

_____   _____   _____

_____   _____   _____

_____   _____   _____

_____   _____   _____

_____   _____   _____

_____   _____   _____

_____   _____   _____

_____   _____   _____

                       _____

Bonus Words

_____   _____

_____   _____

Passover Questions to Discuss

1. What did God tell Moses and Aaron about a new Jewish calendar? (Exodus 12:1-2)

2. What specific command did God give Moses to tell all of Israel? (Exodus 12:3)

3. What was a family to do if their lamb was too big for them to eat? (Exodus 12:4)

4. How did God describe what the condition of the lambs must be? (Exodus 12:5)

5. What were the Israelites supposed to do with the lambs they got? (Exodus 12:6-7)

6. What were God's instructions about how the Passover meal was to be eaten? (Exodus 12:8-11)

7. What did God say He was going to do on the Passover night? (Exodus 12:12)

8. What would happen if the Israelites had blood on their door posts? (Exodus 12:13)

9. Why did God want bread prepared in a certain way? (Exodus 12:15)

10. How were God's instructions significant for Israel's future? (Exodus 12:24-27)

11. How did the Israelites respond to Moses and Aaron? (Exodus 12:28)

12. What happened at midnight in Egypt? (Exodus 12:29)

13. What was the final result of Pharaoh's hard heart against God? (Exodus 12:30)

14. Why did God give the Israelites detailed instructions about celebrating Passover?

15. How important was it for the Israelites to obey every detail of God's instructions?

16. What could have happened if the Israelites had disobeyed God?

17. What was the first feast the Lord told Moses about? (Lev. 23:1-3)

18. When were the Israelites to celebrate the Passover feast? (Lev. 23:4-8)

19. How many times a year were the Israelite men required to stand before the Lord? (Deut. 16:16)

20. What was the response of the disciples to Jesus' instructions? (Matt. 26:19)

21. What did Jesus and His disciples do that evening? (Matt. 26:20)

22. What did Jesus say about the bread on the table? (Matt. 26:26)

23. How did God respond to the problem of unclean people celebrating Passover? (Num. 9:9-14)

REINSTITUTION OF PASSOVER

24. What special celebration did Hezekiah reinstitute? (2 Chronicles 30:1-3)

25. Why hadn't the Passover been celebrated at the traditional time of year? (2 Chronicles 30:3)

26. What did the priests and Levites do with the blood of the Passover lamb? (2 Chron. 30:15-17)

27. How did the Lord respond to Hezekiah's prayer? (2 Chronicles 30:20)

28. How did the Levites perform as they reinstituted the Passover celebration? (2 Chron. 30:22)

29. What was the attitude of the people as the Passover celebration ended? (2 Chronicles 30:25-26)

30. In what ways did the celebration of the Passover in Hezekiah's day deviate from the instructions in the law, and how did God treat those deviations?

31. To whom did Josiah the king read the recently discovered book of God's law? (2 Kings 23:1-2)

A Family Guide to the Biblical Holidays ©

Recipe

PASSOVER PENNIES

1 cup	whole wheat flour
1 cup	shredded cheese
$1/3$ cup	butter, softened
$1/4$ tbs	salt
$1/2$ cup	sesame seeds toasted
$1/4$ tbs	garlic powder and/or celery seed or red pepper or onion powder
2 lbs	water or/as necessary

Combine all ingredients, except water with pastry blender or in mixer (or ambitious child may mix by hand). Add enough water to hold together but not feel sticky.

Form into roll about an inch in diameter. Roll in waxed paper: chill at least one hour. Slice into $1/4$ inch "pennies" (always pull knife in same direction to avoid breaking). Place on lightly greased sheet and bake for 10 minutes at 350° in preheated oven. Makes about sixty.

For mini-turnovers see *Hamantaschen* instructions in Purim recipe section. Use thickened fruit pie filling instead of jam, fold in half and bake a little longer.

Seder Supper Search

Find these hidden objects in the picture above.

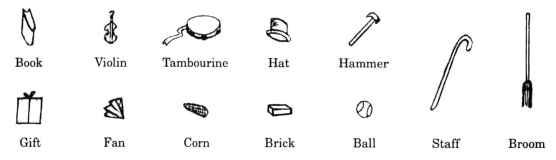

Book	Violin	Tambourine	Hat	Hammer		
Gift	Fan	Corn	Brick	Ball	Staff	Broom

A Family Guide to the Biblical Holidays©

Crossword Puzzle

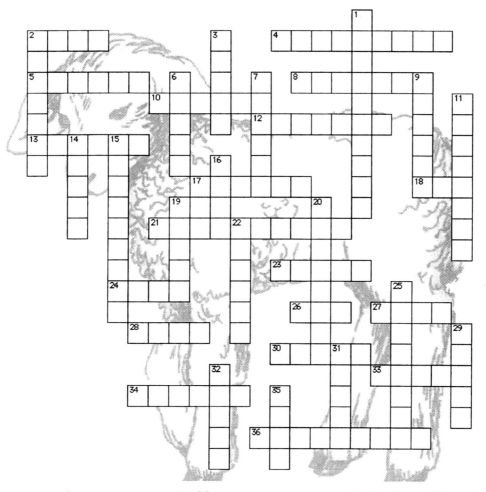

Across

2. Small, biting, body insects
4. Nailed to a cross
5. Cows, steers, bulls, and oxen
8. State of slavery
10. Widespread affliction
12. Servitude
13. Religious building
17. Sharply unpleasant taste
18. Disobedience
21. Payment of an obligation
23. Miriam's brother
24. Small drinking containers
26. Staff
27. Man
28. Food preservative
30. Clear liquid
33. Skin irritation
34. Fermentation agent
36. The oldest child

Down

1. Unsettled, uncultivated region
2. Migrating grasshoppers
3. Amphibians
6. Two-winged insects
7. Barren, desolate area
9. Departure of a large number of people
11. Having very little light
14. Confronted Pharaoh
15. Cattle
16. Egypt's principal tributary
19. Lord of Lords
20. Door frame
22. Unleavened bread
25. When Pharaoh's people lost their first born, and Moses' people did not
29. The seventh month
31. Pharaoh's kingdom
32. Family celebration during Passover
35. Frozen rain

Word Search

U	B	A	S	S	E	N	K	R	A	D	S	E	S	M
D	R	I	A	W	A	T	E	R	W	L	L	S	O	M
T	E	E	T	R	M	A	L	E	I	T	E	D	A	J
S	P	S	D	T	O	K	G	O	T	N	E	T	E	N
L	Y	Y	E	E	N	B	A	R	E	Z	S	L	I
A	X	T	G	R	M	R	C	E	R	A	U	R	I	S
V	L	L	Y	E	T	P	D	F	H	S	K	O	C	R
E	I	A	R	S	S	L	T	B	N	S	R	D	E	E
R	A	S	E	U	I	P	L	I	O	E	G	B	B	D
Y	H	I	D	W	L	E	S	O	O	N	V	O	Z	E
Z	L	O	J	A	L	N	M	I	C	N	D	A	R	S
F	X	H	G	P	I	U	R	O	B	U	C	A	E	F
E	R	U	M	S	E	L	I	N	S	B	S	A	G	L
T	E	E	A	G	I	S	P	U	C	E	A	T	H	E
S	T	N	D	O	O	R	P	O	S	T	S	R	S	U

AARON	FREEDOM	PLAGUES
BITTER	FROGS	RABBIS
BOILS	HAIL	REDEMPTION
BONDAGE	JESUS	ROD
CATTLE	LEAVEN	SALT
CUPS	LICE	SEDER
DARKNESS	LOCUSTS	SIN
DESERT	MALE	SLAVERY
DOORPOST	MATZAH	TEMPLE
EGYPT	MOSES	WATER
EXODUS	NILE	WILDERNESS
FLIES	NISAN	

Coloring Page

Jerusalem is builded as a city
that is compact together:
Psalm 122:3

Feast of Unleavened Bread

Hag HaMatzah

The Purpose of Unleavened Bread

Feast of Unleavened Bread (Hag HaMatzah) is the second spring festival beginning on the fifteenth of Nisan. When the Israelites fled from Egypt they took the dough before it had time to leaven. When they baked it, the next day, it was unleavened bread.

And Pharaoh rose up in the night, he and all his servants and all the Egyptians and there was a great cry in Egypt: And he called for Moses and Aaron at night and said: Rise up and get you forth from among my people, both ye and the children of Israel; and go serve the LORD as you have said...And the people took their dough before it was leavened, their kneading troughs being bound up in their clothes upon their shoulders (Exod. 12:30-31, 34).

Matthew Henry's explains,

> Of the provision made for the camp, which was very poor and slender. They brought some dough with them out of Egypt in their knapsacks, v. 34. They had prepared to bake, the next day, however, they were hastened away sooner than they thought of, by some hours, they took the dough as it was, unleavened; when they came to Succoth, their first stage, they baked unleavened cakes, and, though these were of course insipid, yet the liberty they were brought into made this the most joyful meal they had ever eaten in their lives.

The Egyptians urged the people to leave as fast as possible. As a result, their dough didn't have time to rise. So they carried it on their shoulders and made matzah. Every year, we commemorate this event during the Passover Seder, which is celebrated on the fifteenth of Nisan, the day that the Jewish people left Egypt.

The fermenting and permeating nature of leaven is commonly used as a metaphor for sin. As remembrance, God commanded His people to eat only pure, unleavened bread for seven days every year that they remember the "bread of affliction."

SYMBOLISM OF UNLEAVENED BREAD

The symbolic connection of matzah is twofold. On the one hand, unleavened bread is a symbol of freedom based upon Exodus 12:39; "*...They baked unleavened cakes of the dough which they brought forth out of Egypt, for it was not leavened; because they were thrust out of Egypt, and could not* *tarry..."* One Passover Haggadah explains, "It is because there was not time for the dough of our ancestors to rise, before the Ruler of All revealed Himself and redeemed them." Unleavened bread is also a symbol of the Egyptian slavery. *Thou shalt eat no leavened bread with it; seven days shalt thou eat unleavened bread therewith, even the bread of affliction: for thou camest forth out of the land of Egypt in haste: that thou mayest remember the day when thou camest forth out of the land of Egypt all the days of thy life* (Deut. 16:3). So unleavened bread is a reminder of both slavery and redemption from it.

Did You Know?

Lot's family baked unleavened bread for the two angels that came to Sodom, and they did eat.
(Gen. 19:3).

164

Unleavened Bread in Bible Times

During this week-long feast, nothing with leaven (yeast) in it may be eaten. In the Jewish religion, leaven is the symbol of all that is unclean and evil and therefore must scrupulously be removed from all houses before the Passover feast. Abstaining from leavened bread for seven days was symbolic of God's people separating themselves from sin and becoming a holy people and experiencing a holy walk with the Lord.

THE REQUIREMENTS DIRECTING THE FEAST OF UNLEAVENED BREAD (LEV. 23:6 AND EX. 12:15-17):

1.) The first day, all leaven should be removed from the home (Ex. 12:15).

2.) For seven days they were to eat unleavened bread (Lev. 23:6, Ex. 12:15).

3.) This feast was a high Sabbath (an extra Sabbath besides the weekly Sabbath). No work should be done the first day and the seventh day (except preparing food) (Ex. 12:16).

4.) This feast was declared a memorial to be kept forever. *And ye shall observe the feast of unleavened bread... therefore shall ye observe this day in your generations by an ordinance for ever* (Ex. 12:17).

Jewish Customs of Unleavened Bread Today

Spring house cleaning has its roots in the Passover preparation where, thirty days before the Festival, the women of every household began removing all leaven (*chametz*) from their homes. According to Leviticus 13:7, as long as leaven remains in the house one cannot celebrate Passover. It is a spiritual as well as a physical cleansing (Thompson 1984).

The symbolic ritual of searching for chametz begins at nightfall on the fourteenth day of the Jewish month of Nisan, the evening before the Passover. The leavened bread is removed from the household with the exception of ten small pieces, which the woman of the house hides throughout the rooms of the house. The man of the house lights a candle, and takes a feather, a wooden spoon and a paper bag to search the house for chametz. When a piece is found, he uses the feather to sweep the chametz onto the wooden spoon and then places it into the paper bag. This is done until all ten pieces are found. The bread is then taken outside and burned. (See how this ceremony points to Jesus in the next section.)

Afterwards, the following prayer is said:

"Any chametz which is in my possession which I did not see, and remove, nor know about, shall be nullified and become ownerless, like the dust of the earth."

Leavening is a fermenting process in which yeast turns the food sour. The rules of leavening apply to food prepared out of any of the five kinds of grain; barley, wheat, rye, oats and spelt. Although wine is fermented, it doesn't come into the category of leaven because it's not made from one of these five types.

Orthodox Jews of Ashkenazic background also avoid rice, corn, peanuts, and legumes (beans) as if they were chametz. All of these items have been used to make bread, thus use of them was prohibited to avoid any confusion.

Passover matzah (different from regular matzah) is made from wheat, but extreme care is taken to ensure that it's cooked very soon after being mixed with water so the yeast in it has no opportunity to begin to ferment.

To be quite certain the food is completely free from leaven there are products that bear the label of a reputable rabbinical authority, stating that they are "kosher" for Passover. All fresh fruit and vegetables are kosher for Passover and don't require any certification.

WHEN DOES THE LEAVENING PROCESS BEGIN?

During the first Passover the dough was made while in Egypt and baked it the next day. The rules the rabbis added to the holiday of Unleavened Bread is a good example of a "fence rule" (see page 38). The rabbis added a rule that says products can only be eaten on Passover if they are cooked before the leavening process even begins. This is reckoned to be eighteen minutes from the time they are mixed with water. Matzah is made from wheat, but extreme care is taken to ensure that it's cooked very soon after being mixed with water so the yeast in it has no opportunity to begin to ferment. Since it's very difficult to be certain that fermentation doesn't start even before this time, the Jews usually don't even try to prepare food themselves from things that have the potential to become leavened, as with their regular cooking utensils. To be extra sure they don't eat any leaven during this period, they have completely separate sets of utensils for this period: pots, pans, cutlery, and crockery.

If the purpose is to remember the unleavened bread of the Exodus, it would appear we can bake the dough any time, even the next day as the Israelites did.

Jesus spoke out against those who sought justification by keeping legal requirements. The scribes and Pharisees were so scrupulous about keeping the law of the tithe that they would not overlook the sprigs of seasoning herbs in their gardens–mint, rue, and dill (Matt. 23:23; Lk. 11:42). God's directive concerning tithing was not given because He had need of food or money, nor because God wanted to lay a burden on man to test him. God wanted this to be given for the welfare of His people. The Pharisees were looking for specifics as to how to keep the technicality of the law when they should have been using what they had to promote love, mercy, justice, and faith which the tithe was meant to promote. They were seeking to be justified by keeping law when they should have been seeking to accomplish its purposes.

Messianic Significance of Unleavened Bread

The matzah is a wonderful reminder of the Messiah. The bread is without leaven (without sin), striped, pierced, and bruised. The Messiah was wounded and bruised, and He suffered painful blows so that you may be healed from all sickness and diseases: He was wounded and bruised for our sins. *But he was wounded for our transgressions, he was bruised for our iniquities: the chastisement of our peace was upon him; and with his stripes we are healed. (Isa. 53:5) Who his own self bare our sins in his own body on the tree, that we, being dead to sins, should live unto righteousness: by whose stripes ye were healed (1 Peter 2:24).*

The Feast of Unleavened bread speaks of sanctification. The Messiah was set apart. His body would not decay in the grave. Christ spoke of leaven (yeast) as a type of sin. *Then Jesus said unto them, Take heed and beware of the leaven of the Pharisees and of the Sadducees. How is it that ye do not understand that I spake it not to you concerning bread, that ye should beware of the leaven of the Pharisees and of the Sadducees? Then understood they how that he bade them not beware of the leaven of bread, but of the doctrine of the Pharisees and of the Sadducees (Matt. 16:6, 11-12).*

Yeast is used in this analogy because just a small amount can puff up a large amount of dough. *A little leaven leaveneth the whole lump (Gal. 5:9).* In the same way a small sin can spread and grow in our minds and attitudes causing us to "puff up" with pride and arrogance (1 Cor. 4:18-19; 5:2; Col. 2:18).

As the leaven represents sin, the unleavened bread is a symbol of the body of Christ, without sin. The matzah also reminds us of Messiah because it is striped and pierced. Our Lord referred to Himself as the bread of God and as the bread of life (John 6:33, 35), and he chose the bread of the Passover to be the symbolic memorial of His broken body (Luke 22:19). Just as God sustained the children of Israel in the wilderness, His Son now feeds the believer with the true bread of heaven, Himself. John 6:32 and 33 says *"Then Jesus said unto them, Verily, verily, I say unto you, Moses gave you not that bread from heaven; but my Father giveth you the true bread from heaven. For the bread of God is he which cometh down from heaven, and giveth life unto the world."* It is also significant that Christ was born in *Bethlehem* which means "house of bread."

Paul used illustrations of the Passover lamb and unleavened bread to characterize Christ's sacrifice and our salvation. *Purge out therefore the old leaven, that ye may be a new lump, as ye are unleavened. For even Christ our*

Passover is sacrificed for us: Therefore let us keep the feast, not with old leaven, neither with the leaven of malice and wickedness; but with the unleavened bread of sincerity and truth (1 Cor. 5:7-8).

PUTTING OFF THE SIN NATURE

The unleavened bread is also a visual lesson instructing us how God wants us to change through Christ. When one accepts Jesus as the Passover Lamb who dies for our sins, his position before God changes to sinless (without yeast) because Jesus took on our sins. We are righteous through Jesus.

As believers in Christ we are to put off the sin nature within us. *That ye put off concerning the former conversation the old man, which is corrupt according to the deceitful lusts; And be renewed in the spirit of your mind; And that ye put on the new man, which after God is created in righteousness and true holiness* (Eph. 4:22-24).

This I say then, Walk in the Spirit, and ye shall not fulfill the lust of the flesh. For the flesh lusteth against the Spirit, and the Spirit against the flesh: and these are contrary the one to the other: so that ye cannot do the things that ye would. But if ye be led of the Spirit, ye are not under the law. Now the works of the flesh are manifest, which are these; Adultery, fornication, uncleanness, lasciviousness, Idolatry, witchcraft, hatred, variance, emulations, wrath, strife, seditions, heresies, Envyings, murders, drunkenness, revellings, and such like: of the which I tell you before, as I have also told you in time past, that they which do such things shall not inherit the kingdom of God. But the fruit of the Spirit is love, joy, peace, longsuffering, gentleness, goodness, faith, Meekness, temperance: against such there is no law. And they that are Christ's have crucified the flesh with the affections and lusts (Gal. 5:16-24).

SYMBOLISM IN THE FEAST OF UNLEAVENED BREAD

1.) Seven days—the Hebrew word seven is *shevah* from the root word *savah*, to be full or satisfied, to have enough of.

2.) Israelites fed on bread without leaven (sin)—believers feed on Y'shua (Jesus), the Word, without sin.

3.) Unleavened bread is used for consecration and separation—believers in Christ are to be consecrated and separated to live a holy life.

Suggestions for Remembering the Holiday

During the day of Passover, search for leavened bread (described below) before your Passover meal. The Bible's banning of leavened bread during Passover festival declares: ...*even the first day ye shall put away leaven out of your houses* (Ex. 12:15). Expounding on this precept, the Mishnah opens with the directive, "At (twi)light of the fourteenth day (of Nisan) we search for leaven bread by the light of the lamp." The Talmud explains that this is the time when everyone is at home and the light of a lamp is "good" for searching in the dark. It also quotes a series of biblical texts which relate this external search to an inner search of man's soul (relieving it of pollution).

Explain to the family that, after partaking of the Passover, we should ask God for power to choose his will and strive to live a sin-free life of obedience as we observe the seven days of Unleavened Bread. This is a symbol of our step towards righteousness and turning away from sin. The purity of the Feast of Unleavened Bread follows the blood-deliverance of Passover; we can only walk in purity before the Lord after we have had the blood-deliverance at the cross. We gladly clear our houses of all leavened products for seven days to remind us Jesus cleanses us of sin. We eat matzah for these seven days, allowing us to symbolically take in the unleavened bread of sincerity and truth (1 Cor. 5:7-8).

THE SEARCH FOR LEAVEN IS SYMBOLIC FOR BELIEVERS IN MESSIAH

The search process is described in the *1997 Encyclopedia Judaica*:

1) After Evening Service on the night before Passover eve, no work should be done or food eaten until the search for leaven has been undertaken. The householder first recites the benediction, "Who has sanctified us with His commandments and commanded us to remove the leaven."

(2) He then conducts a thorough search of the house (or premises), checking every place especially until the search for leaven has been undertaken. The householder first recites the benediction, "Who has sanctified us with His commandments and commanded us to remove the leaven."

(3) The search is conducted in silence. As an aid to concentration, it is cus-

tomary to switch off electric lights and only use an oil lamp or candle.

(4) Since pre-Passover "spring-cleaning" will already have disposed of most leaven, small pieces of bread and crumbs are left around the house in advance (usually on paper) for the searcher to find, so that his benediction should not have been recited in vain.

(5) All leavened bread discovered is carefully placed in a bag or other combustible container with the aid of feathers (some also use a disposable wooden spoon), tied up with the candle and feathers, and put to one side for burning the next day.

(6) Once the search has been completed, a formula renouncing any leaven that remains is pronounced.

(7) Before 10 A.M. the next morning (or as specified by the local rabbinate), the parcel of leavened bread is burned outdoors and a modified version of the previous formula is then recited.

THE SEARCH REPRESENTS JESUS

This search for leavened bread also represents the Messiah! Even Jewish tradition (not listed in the Bible) points to Jesus as Messiah! One day our Jewish friends will see Jesus as Messiah through these symbolic ceremonies.

1. The candle represents the Word of God who is the Light of the World, whose written word reveals to us our sin.

2. The feather represents the Holy Spirit (Ruach Ha Kodesh) directing us to the cross of Jesus.

3. The wooden spoon represents the tree of crucifixion.

4. The paper bag represents the grave.

5. The fire represents how our sin has been dealt with, never again to be remembered.

OUR FAMILY'S SEARCH FOR LEAVEN

One year, as we searched for leaven, I [Robin speaking] felt sure I had all the leaven out of the house, including the toothpaste, which had baking soda in it. I even remembered I had several small packets of yeast in our freezer, so I took those out. On around the fourth day of Unleavened Bread, I opened the freezer to pull out broccoli, and behind the broccoli was a 5-lb. bag of yeast! I had forgotten about it—it fell to the floor with a thud.

What a picture! Here I had searched and gotten rid of all the "little sins" but I did not see the biggest one in the house that needed to go. I had been angry at my husband for something and realized I needed to apologize. He forgave me and I got rid of the yeast. Praise God for symbolism.

One family's description of the seven days of Unleavened Bread:

Day One: Matzah tastes great! Why don't we have this more often?

Day Two: Let's make matzah appetizers with cream cheese and pickles.

Day Three: I made desert with chocolate and ice cream in between two matzah!

Day Four: Mom, Jimmy said cake has yeast in it. It doesn't does it Mom?

Day Five: I found an old peanut butter sandwich behind the sofa!

Day Six: Oh, plllllllllllllllllllease can I have a McDonald's hamburger?

Day Seven: Let's go watch for the sun to go down. Tonight we can have BREAD!!! Yeah!

EAT NO LEAVEN FOR SEVEN DAYS

This is a time to be creative. You'll never imagine how many things you eat that include leaven. Substitute unleavened matzah crackers to make sandwiches. Homemade unleavened bread is delicious shaped into bread sticks. Eat soups instead of sandwiches.

Each time you or your family go to get your regular leavened bread during this week, it is an opportunity to explain we are not eating leavened bread this week to remind us that:

1. The unleavened bread is a symbol of the speed and haste in which the Israelites were redeemed from Egypt, not having the time to bake full loaves of bread.

2. Jesus is the bread of life (John 6:26-58).

3. The days of Unleavened Bread were not joyless; the time began and ended with a feast–a party. A walk of purity in the Lord is not a joyless life!

4. Man shall not live by bread alone, but by every word of God. *And Jesus being full of the Holy Ghost returned from Jordan, and was led by the Spirit into the wilderness, Being forty days tempted of the devil. And in those days he did eat nothing: and when they were ended, he afterward hungered. And the devil said unto him, If thou be the Son of God, com-*

mand this stone that it be made bread. And Jesus answered him, saying, It is written, That man shall not live by bread alone, but by every word of God. And the devil, taking him up into an high mountain, showed unto him all the kingdoms of the world in a moment of time. And the devil said unto him, All this power will I give thee, and the glory of them: for that is delivered unto me; and to whomsoever I will I give it. If thou therefore wilt worship me, all shall be thine. And Jesus answered and said unto him, Get thee behind me, Satan: for it is written, Thou shalt worship the Lord thy God, and him only shalt thou serve. And he brought him to Jerusalem, and set him on a pinnacle of the temple, and said unto him, If thou be the Son of God, cast thyself down from hence: For it is written, He shall give his angels charge over thee, to keep thee: And in their hands they shall bear thee up, lest at any time thou dash thy foot against a stone. And Jesus answering said unto him, It is said, Thou shalt not tempt the Lord thy God. And when the devil had ended all the temptation, he departed from him for a season (Luke 4:1-13).

YEAST

Read the Parable of the Yeast found in Matthew 13:33 or Luke 13:20-21. This short parable is sometimes called the Parable of the Leaven.

Bakers' yeast is a microscopic one-celled plant that is nearly colorless. It has no chlorophyll and it is classified as a fungus. It is dependent on green plant starch or a sugar for food. It reproduces by developing a bud, which separates and grows into another yeast cell. Yeast produces two enzymes, invertase and zymase, which help to convert starch to sugar, and sugar to alcohol, carbon dioxide, and energy. This process is called fermentation. Breadmakers add yeast (and sometimes a sweetener) to dough and place the dough in a warm place. The carbon dioxide that is produced forms bubbles in the dough and causes the dough to rise. Baking causes the gas to expand even more, and most of the alcohol is driven off.

The yeast at first represents the Word of God, which becomes believers (the Word incarnate). The woman represents Christ. The flour is the world population. As yeast spreads throughout dough, so the kingdom of God spreads throughout the world. By interpreting this parable in scriptural context, the whole world will not be saved, although society will be affected positively. This parable does not teach universal salvation even though the salvation of everyone is a noble thought. Central Truth: As the Holy Spirit anoints the gospel of Christ, many will be converted and their Christlike nature will influence the world. Conclusion: Let us constantly sow the Word of God, which will penetrate the hearts of people who receive the Truth. Their Christlike lives, in turn, will permeate and influence society (Duthie 1996).

SUGGESTED BIBLE READINGS FOR EACH NIGHT:

Day One:

The Feast of Unleavened Bread: *And this day shall be unto you for a memorial; and ye shall keep it a feast to the LORD throughout your generations; ye shall keep it a feast by an ordinance for ever. Seven days shall ye eat unleavened bread; even the first day ye shall put away leaven out of your houses: for whosoever eateth leavened bread from the first day until the seventh day, that soul shall be cut off from Israel.*

And in the first day there shall be an holy convocation, and in the seventh day there shall be an holy convocation to you; no manner of work shall be done in them, save that which every man must eat, that only may be done of you. And ye shall observe the feast of unleavened bread; for in this selfsame day have I brought your armies out of the land of Egypt: therefore shall ye observe this day in your generations by an ordinance for ever. In the first month, on the fourteenth day of the month at even, ye shall eat unleavened bread, until the one and twentieth day of the month at even. Seven days shall there be no leaven found in your houses: for whosoever eateth that which is leavened, even that soul shall be cut off from the congregation of Israel, whether he be a stranger, or born in the land. Ye shall eat nothing leavened; in all your habitations shall ye eat unleavened bread (Exod. 12:14-20).

Day Two:

Manna from Heaven. *I have heard the murmurings of the children of Israel: speak unto them, saying, At even ye shall eat flesh, and in the morning ye shall be filled with bread; and ye shall know that I am the LORD your God. And it came to pass, that at even the quails came up, and covered the camp: and in the morning the dew lay round about the host. And when the dew that lay was gone up, behold, upon the face of the wilderness there lay a small round thing, as small as the hoar frost on the ground. And when the children of Israel saw it, they said one to another, It is manna: for they wist* *not what it was. And Moses said unto them, This is the bread which the LORD hath given you to eat.*

This is the thing which the LORD hath commanded, Gather of it every man according to his eating, an omer for every man, according to the number of your persons; take ye every man for them which are in his tents. And the children of Israel did so, and gathered, some more, some less. And when they did mete it with an omer, he that gathered much had nothing over, and he that gathered little had no lack; they gathered every man according to his eating. And Moses said, Let no man leave of it till the morning.

Notwithstanding they hearkened not unto Moses; but some of them left of it until the morning, and it bred worms, and stank: and Moses was wroth with them.

And they gathered it every morning, every man according to his eating: and when the sun waxed hot, it melted. And it came to pass, that on the sixth day they gathered twice as much bread, two omers for one man: and all the rulers of the congregation came and told Moses. And he said unto them, This is that which the LORD hath said, To morrow is the rest of the holy sabbath unto the LORD: bake that which ye will bake to day, and seethe that ye will seethe; and that which remaineth over lay up for you to be kept until the morning.

And they laid it up till the morning, as Moses bade: and it did not stink, neither was there any worm therein. And Moses said, Eat that to day; for to day is a sabbath unto the LORD: to day ye shall not find it in the field. Six days ye shall gather it; but on the seventh day, which is the sabbath, in it there shall be none.

And it came to pass, that there went out some of the people on the seventh day for to gather, and they found none. And the LORD said unto Moses, How long refuse ye to keep my commandments and my laws? See, for that the LORD hath given you the sabbath, therefore he giveth you on the sixth day the bread of two days; abide ye every man in his place, let no man go out of his place on the seventh day. So the people rested on the seventh day.

And the house of Israel called the name thereof Manna: and it was like coriander seed, white; and the taste of it was like wafers made with honey. And Moses said, This is the thing which the LORD commandeth, Fill an omer of it to be kept for your generations; that they may see the bread wherewith I have fed you in the wilderness, when I brought you forth from the land of Egypt. And Moses said unto Aaron, Take a pot, and put an omer full of manna therein, and lay it up before the LORD, to be kept for your generations. As the LORD commanded Moses, so Aaron laid it up before the Testimony, to be kept. And the children of Israel did eat manna forty years, until they came to a land inhabited; they did eat manna, until they came unto the borders of the land of Canaan (Exod. 16:12-35).

Day Three:

Miracles of the Loaves and Fishes: *And the passover, a feast of the Jews, was nigh.*

When Jesus then lifted up his eyes, and saw a great company come unto him, he saith unto Philip, Whence shall we buy bread, that these may eat?

And this he said to prove him: for he himself knew what he would do.

Philip answered him, Two hundred pennyworth of bread is not sufficient for them, that every one of them may take a little.

One of his disciples, Andrew, Simon Peter's brother, saith unto him,

There is a lad here, which hath five barley loaves, and two small fishes: but what are they among so many?

And Jesus said, Make the men sit down. Now there was much grass in the place. So the men sat down, in number about five thousand.

And Jesus took the loaves; and when he had given thanks, he distributed to the disciples, and the disciples to them that were set down; and likewise of the fishes as much as they would.

When they were filled, he said unto his disciples, Gather up the fragments that remain, that nothing be lost.

Therefore they gathered them together, and filled twelve baskets with the fragments of the five barley loaves, which remained over and above unto them that had eaten.

Then those men, when they had seen the miracle that Jesus did, said, This is of a truth that prophet that should come into the world. (John 6:4-14)

Peter's Imprisonment: *When he saw that this pleased the Jews, he proceeded to seize Peter also. This happened during the Feast of Unleavened Bread.*

After arresting him, he put him in prison, handing him over to be guarded by four squads of four soldiers each. Herod intended to bring him out for public trial after the Passover.

So Peter was kept in prison, but the church was earnestly praying to God for him.

The night before Herod was to bring him to trial, Peter was sleeping between two soldiers, bound with two chains, and sentries stood guard at the entrance.

Suddenly an angel of the Lord appeared and a light shone in the cell. He struck Peter on the side and woke him up. "Quick, get up!" he said, and the chains fell off Peter's wrists.

Then the angel said to him, "Put on your clothes and sandals." And Peter did so. "Wrap your cloak around you and follow me," the angel told him.

Peter followed him out of the prison, but he had no idea that what the angel was doing was really happening; he thought he was seeing a vision.

They passed the first and second guards and came to the iron gate leading to the city. It opened for them by itself, and they went through it. When they had walked the length of one street, suddenly the angel left him.

Then Peter came to himself and said, "Now I know without a doubt that the Lord sent his angel and rescued me from Herod's clutches and from everything the Jewish people were anticipating."

When this had dawned on him, he went to the house of Mary the mother of John, also called Mark, where many people had gathered and were praying.

Peter knocked at the outer entrance, and a servant girl named Rhoda came to answer the door.

When she recognized Peter's voice, she was so overjoyed she ran back without opening it and exclaimed, "Peter is at the door!"

"You're out of your mind," they told her. When she kept insisting that it was so, they said, "It must be his angel."

But Peter kept on knocking, and when they opened the door and saw him, they were astonished.

Peter motioned with his hand for them to be quiet and described how the Lord had brought him out of prison. "Tell James and the brothers about this," he said, and then he left for another place.

In the morning, there was no small commotion among the soldiers as to what had become of Peter.

After Herod had a thorough search made for him and did not find him, he cross-examined the guards and ordered that they be executed. Then Herod went from Judea to Caesarea and stayed there a while (Acts 12:3-19). NIV[1]

Day Four:

Jesus Explains He is the Bread of Life: *Jesus answered them and said, Verily, verily, I say unto you, Ye seek me, not because ye saw the miracles, but because ye did eat of the loaves, and were filled.*

Labour not for the meat which perisheth, but for that meat which endureth unto everlasting life, which the Son of man shall give unto you: for him hath God the Father sealed.

Then said they unto him, What shall we do, that we might work the works of God?

Jesus answered and said unto them, This is the work of God, that ye believe on him whom he hath sent.

They said therefore unto him, What sign showest thou then, that we may see, and believe thee? what dost thou work?

Our fathers did eat manna in the desert; as it is written, He gave them bread from heaven to eat.

Then Jesus said unto them, Verily, verily, I say unto you, Moses gave you not that bread from heaven; but my Father giveth you the true bread from heaven. For the bread of God is he which cometh down from heaven, and giveth life unto the world.

Then said they unto him, Lord, evermore give us this bread.

And Jesus said unto them, I am the bread of life: he that cometh to me shall never hunger; and he that believeth on me shall never thirst.

But I said unto you, That ye also have seen me, and believe not.

All that the Father giveth me shall come to me; and him that cometh to me I will in no wise cast out.

For I came down from heaven, not to do mine own will, but the will of him that sent me.

And this is the Father's will which hath sent me, that of all which he hath given me I should lose nothing, but should raise it up again at the last day.

And this is the will of him that sent me, that every one which seeth the Son, and believeth on him, may have everlasting life: and I will raise him up at the last day.

The Jews then murmured at him, because he said, I am the bread which came down from heaven.

And they said, Is not this Jesus, the son of Joseph, whose father and mother we know? how is it then that he saith, I came down from heaven?

Jesus therefore answered and said unto them, Murmur not among yourselves.

No man can come to me, except the Father which hath sent me draw him: and I will raise him up at the last day.

It is written in the prophets, And they shall be all taught of God. Every man therefore that hath heard, and hath learned of the Father, cometh unto me.

Not that any man hath seen the Father, save he which is of God, he hath seen the Father.

Verily, verily, I say unto you, He that believeth on me hath everlasting life.

I am that bread of life.

Your fathers did eat manna in the wilderness, and are dead.

This is the bread which cometh down from heaven, that a man may eat thereof, and not die.

I am the living bread which came down from heaven: if any man eat of this bread, he shall live for ever: and the bread that I will give is my flesh, which I will give for the life of the world.

The Jews therefore strove among themselves, saying, How can this man give us his flesh to eat?

Then Jesus said unto them, Verily, verily, I say unto you, Except ye eat the flesh of the Son of man, and drink his blood, ye have no life in you.

Whoso eateth my flesh, and drinketh my blood, hath eternal life; and I will raise him up at the last day.

For my flesh is meat indeed, and my blood is drink indeed.

He that eateth my flesh, and drinketh my blood, dwelleth in me, and I in him.

As the living Father hath sent me, and I live by the Father: so he that eateth me, even he shall live by me.

This is that bread which came down from heaven: not as your fathers did eat manna, and are dead: he that eateth of this bread shall live for ever (John 6:26-58).

Day Five:

They Kept the Seven Days With Gladness: *And there assembled at Jerusalem much people to keep the feast of unleavened bread in the second month, a very great congregation. And they arose and took away the altars that were in Jerusalem, and all the altars for incense took they away, and cast them into the brook Kidron. Then they killed the passover on the fourteenth day of the second month: and the priests and the Levites were ashamed, and sanctified themselves, and brought in the burnt offerings into the house of the LORD. And they stood in their place after their manner, according to the law of Moses the man of God: the priests sprinkled the blood, which they received of the hand of the Levites. For there were many in the congregation that were not sanctified: therefore the Levites had the charge of the killing of the passovers for every one that was not clean, to sanctify them unto the LORD. For a multitude of the people, even many of Ephraim, and Manasseh, Issachar, and Zebulun, had not cleansed themselves, yet did they eat the passover otherwise than it was written. But Hezekiah prayed for them, saying, The good LORD pardon every one That prepareth his heart to seek God, the LORD God of his fathers, though he be not cleansed according to the purification of the sanctuary. And the LORD hearkened to Hezekiah, and healed the people. And the children of Israel that were present at Jerusalem kept the feast of unleavened bread seven days with great gladness: and the Levites and the priests praised the LORD day by day, singing with loud instruments unto the LORD. And Hezekiah spake comfortably unto all the Levites that taught the good knowledge of the LORD: and they did eat throughout the feast seven days, offering peace offerings, and making confession to the LORD God of their fathers. And the whole assembly took counsel to keep other seven days: and they kept other seven days with gladness* (2 Chr. 30:13-23).

Day Six:

Paul said, "A little Leaven Leaveneth the Whole Lump." (Stay away from wicked people.) *It is reported commonly that there is fornication among you, and such fornication as is not so much as named among the Gentiles, that one should have his father's wife.*

And ye are puffed up, and have not rather mourned, that he that hath done this deed might be taken away from among you.

For I verily, as absent in body, but present in spirit, have judged already, as though I were present, concerning him that hath so done this deed,

In the name of our Lord Jesus Christ, when ye are gathered together, and my spirit, with the power of our Lord Jesus Christ,

To deliver such an one unto Satan for the destruction of the flesh, that the spirit may be saved in the day of the Lord Jesus.

Your glorying is not good. Know ye not that a little leaven leaveneth the whole lump?

Purge out therefore the old leaven, that ye may be a new lump, as ye are unleavened. For even Christ our passover is sacrificed for us:

Therefore let us keep the feast, not with old leaven, neither with the leaven of malice and wickedness; but with the unleavened bread of sincerity and truth.

I wrote unto you in an epistle not to company with fornicators:

Yet not altogether with the fornicators of this world, or with the covetous, or extortioners, or with idolaters; for then must ye needs go out of the world.

But now I have written unto you not to keep company, if any man that is called a brother be a fornicator, or covetous, or an idolater, or a railer, or a drunkard, or an extortioner; with such an one no not to eat.

For what have I to do to judge them also that are without? do not ye judge them that are within?

But them that are without God judgeth. Therefore put away from among yourselves that wicked person (1 Cor. 5:1-13).

Day Seven:

Paul Explains Passover: *For I have received of the Lord that which also I delivered unto you, That the Lord Jesus the same night in which he was betrayed took bread: And when he had given thanks, he brake it, and said, Take, eat: this is my body, which is broken for you: this do in remembrance of me. After the same manner also he took the cup, when he had supped, saying, This cup is the new testament in my blood: this do ye, as oft as ye drink it, in remembrance of me. For as often as ye eat this bread, and drink this cup, ye do show the Lord's death till he come. Wherefore whosoever shall eat this bread, and drink this cup of the Lord, unworthily, shall be guilty of the body and blood of the Lord. But let a man examine himself, and so let him eat of that bread, and drink of that cup. For he that eateth and drinketh unworthily, eateth and drinketh damnation to himself, not discerning the Lord's body. For this cause many are weak and sickly among you, and many sleep. For if we would judge ourselves, we should not be judged. But when we are judged, we are chastened of the Lord, that we should not be condemned with the world. Wherefore, my brethren, when ye come together to eat, tarry one for another. And if any man hunger, let him eat at home; that ye come not together unto condemnation. And the rest will I set in order when I come* (1 Cor. 11:23-34).

Centerpiece

You will continue to use the centerpiece you assembled for Passover Week (refer to the "Centerpiece" section in the "Passover" chapter). The base is covered with a crimson (dark red) cloth. The **Lamb** craft stands in the center atop a bed of Spanish moss, or paper grass. Also included are the **Lamb**, **Cross**, **Palm Branches**, and **Cup & Bread** flags.

SYMBOLISM IN THE CENTERPIECE

Crimson—represents the blood atonement or sacrifice (Isa. 1:18)

Lamb—Jesus, who became our perfect sacrifice for sin (John 1:29b, Ex. 12, Rev. 5:6-13); Christ the submissive One (Isa. 53:7-8, Acts 8:32-33)

Cup & Bread—wine is symbolic of the Holy Spirit or fullness of joy (Isa. 65:8, Jer. 31:12, Hos. 2:22, Judg. 9:13, Ps. 104:15, Eph. 5:18). Bread represents Christ as our food (John 6, 1 Cor. 11:24).

Cross—place of extreme agony and death, where Jesus died for our sins (1 Cor. 1:17-18, 28, Heb. 12:2, John 12:32-33).

Palm Branches—the upright and faithful tree (Jer. 10:5), used in honor or praise (John 12:13, Rev. 7:9, Lev. 23:40).

A Family Guide to the Biblical Holidays©

Crossword Puzzle

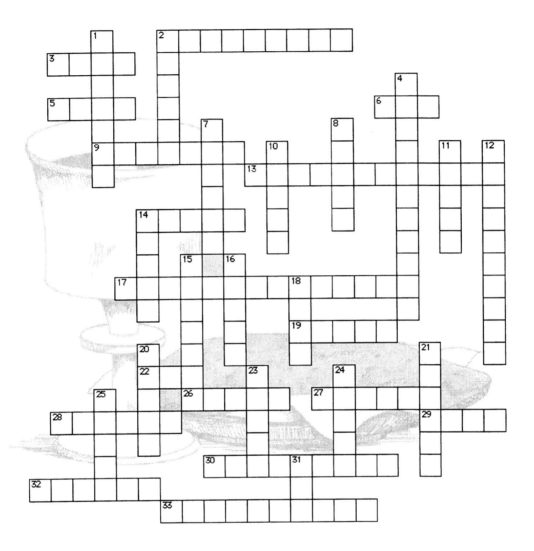

Across

2. Book in the Bible
3. Saul of Tarsus
5. Grain
6. Happiness
9. Liberator
13. Caused by agents such as yeast
14. Cooked in dry heat
17. A setting apart, separation
19. Miraculous food
22. Grain used to make flour
26. God's perfect integer
27. Baked bread
28. Innocence
29. Divine
30. Least among all of Judea
32. Aquatic vertebrates
33. Division

Down

1. Common traditions
2. Illuminations
4. A mandate from God
7. Grain, sometimes used for livestock
8. Edible grain, used to make certain breads
10. Leavening agent
11. Peter
12. Without yeast
14. Baked loaves
15. Wrote and copied manuscripts
16. Holy Book
18. Area with temporary shelters
20. Fact
21. Clean
23. Edible fungi
24. Kneaded, shaped, baked
25. Holy vengeance
31. One's fortune

Timbrel Time

After the Jews left Egypt and faced the miraculous parting of the Red Sea where they witnessed the drowning of their pursuing enemy, they paused for a celebration. See Exodus 15:1-19 for the song Moses and the people sang in praise. Miriam, Moses' sister, took up her timbrel (similar to a tambourine) and danced, with the other women joining her in verses 20-21. Pretend you are Miriam, or one of the other Israelites, and plan out a worship dance using a praise song you like.

Make the tambourine below and use it to make the music even more festive. Plan certain hand motions, body turns, graceful steps, shakes of the tambourine, or claps with it against your hand, etc., at certain parts of the song, so you can teach it to other members of your family. Read or sing Psalm 150. Search for other Psalms which speak of timbrels or tambourines and dancing.

Practice and use your song and dance again at each of the other holidays, if you remember, or make up new ones then.

TAMBOURINE DIRECTIONS

Materials needed: a 6-inch wooden embroidery hoop, 1 to 1-1/4 yds. each of two to four different colors of ribbon, 1/4" or less wide, one package of jingle bells (1/2" more or less), glue, markers or paint.

1.) Use markers or paint a trail of ivy or flowers around the outside of the largest ring and inside of the smallest ring (so both will show when you join the two parts).

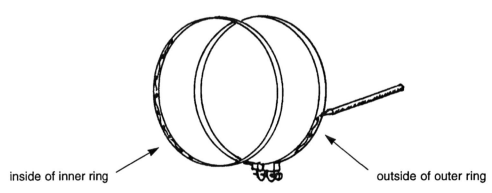

inside of inner ring   outside of outer ring

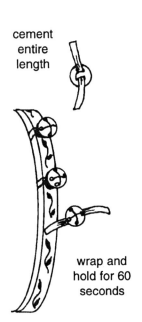

2.) Cut a 1 ½" piece of ribbon for each jingle bell you plan to use. Plan for six or more to go around the outside ring of your hoop. It really doesn't matter where you put them, except that you want to have room for your hand to hold the tambourine without going over the bells or bow. Hold the hoop and mark with a pencil where your hand comes, and arrange your bells and bow away from that area.

cement
entire
length

wrap and
hold for 60
seconds

3.) Thread ribbon through the clasp on the bell and apply glue to the clasp and backside of the ribbon. Wrap around the <u>outside</u> ring and hold in position a few minutes until secure. Repeat until all bells are attached.

4.) When glue is dry, join both rings and adjust the tension screw if necessary. Cut remaining ribbon in two parts, making one about 4" longer than the other. Wrap both around hoop or tension screw and tie tightly. Make bows with different size loops, or as desired, and put dots of glue between the bases of the loops, to prevent their coming untied. Let dry thoroughly before using. Trim ribbon ends with a slant to prevent fraying.

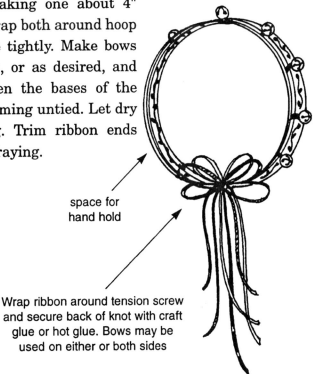

space for
hand hold

Wrap ribbon around tension screw
and secure back of knot with craft
glue or hot glue. Bows may be
used on either or both sides

Dancing the Horah

Here are the basic steps in the Horah, a popular Jewish dance, as performed by Christian friends of the author (Linda). Although the dance is commonly done holding hands and making a circle, it can also be done individually. If you are in a circle, you will be working clockwise.

This is a wonderful praise dance, done easily to such songs as "Jehovah Jireh" (translated: The Lord is Your Provider) and other peppy tunes.

Illustrations here are REAR VIEW to make it easier for the reader to do what is shown, i.e. LEFT on illustration is your LEFT also.

1. Balance weight on LEFT foot, making light hop as RIGHT foot is kicked forward.

2. Shift weight to RIGHT foot, making light hop as LEFT foot is kicked forward.

3. Put left foot down, balancing evenly, briefly.

4. RIGHT foot crosses behind LEFT.

5. Lift LEFT foot, stepping to the LEFT, moving balance off RIGHT to LEFT foot and repeat Step 1.

Do it in slow motion first, then maintain your sense of humor as you joyfully praise the LORD!

A Family Guide to the Biblical Holidays©

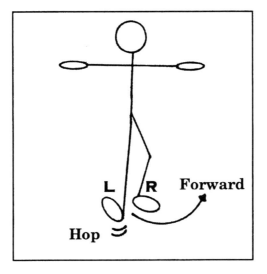

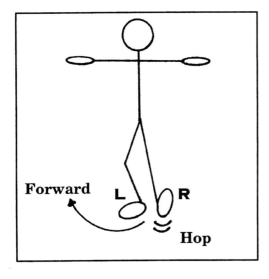

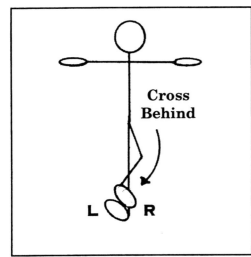

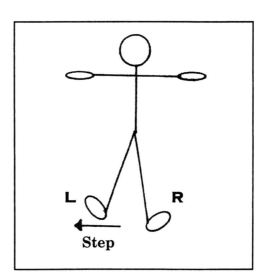

Unleavened Bread Recipes

Try having a special unleavened dessert or bread that you only serve during Unleavened Bread. This makes the family look forward to it.

SWEET CORN BREAD

1 cup whole wheat flour
1 cup corn meal
4 T honey
1/3 cup butter
1 egg
1 cup milk

Grease cookie sheet. Preheat oven to 400°. Mix flour and corn meal in plastic bowl. Add honey and butter, then microwave until melted. Mix, then add milk and egg mixture. Beat until smooth. Spread onto cookie sheet. Cook ten minutes. Cut while warm.

WHOLE WHEAT FLAT BREAD

4 cups finely ground whole wheat flour
1- 1/2 t salt
3 T butter
2 egg yolks
2 T olive oil
1 cup milk or water

Make the dough—sift flour, then add salt. Cut the butter into flour mixture. In another bowl, beat egg yolks, adding oil slowly. Pour this mixture into dough and stir with spoon or fork until it forms a ball of dough that comes away from the side of the bowl. Knead lightly on a floured board for about a minute to shape dough into soft ball.

Lightly flour the board again, pinch off about one-third cupful of dough and with the hands pat it as thin as can easily be done, then roll it thinner with rolling pin. Keep working the dough and rolling it until dough is so thin it just holds together without breaking when handled. Place rolled dough on ungreased baking sheet and mark into squares of any desired size with a knife or make bread sticks. Bake in preheated oven at 400° for 8-12 minutes until puffed, or very lightly browned.

APPLE BETTY CRISP

4 sliced apples

1/2 teaspoon cinnamon

1/4 teaspoon salt

1/4 cup water

1/3 cup butter

1 1/2 teaspoon lemon juice

1/2 cup whole wheat flour

1/2 cup rolled oats

1 cup brown sugar

Put apples in 9" pan, sprinkle with salt and cinnamon. Pour in water. Drizzle with lemon juice. In separate bowl, mix flour, sugar, and oatmeal. Sprinkle over apples, then drop butter over apples. Bake at 350° for one hour.

Word Search

A	S	B	B	D	S	I	B	B	A	R	P	I	B	S
E	P	A	A	S	O	S	A	U	L	M	L	R	T	G
L	G	P	N	K	U	O	V	T	U	K	E	S	R	R
A	T	Y	L	C	E	S	F	L	I	A	A	A	W	E
I	A	E	P	E	T	D	A	S	D	E	I	Y	H	V
R	R	A	D	T	S	I	R	B	F	N	J	Y	E	O
O	S	T	C	N	H	A	F	D	B	H	M	O	A	S
M	U	R	E	A	E	Z	P	I	E	A	A	J	T	S
E	S	V	Z	L	T	H	L	F	C	D	T	R	Z	A
M	E	T	I	E	A	E	H	R	I	A	A	H	O	P
S	A	T	M	R	R	E	A	N	E	S	T	E	Q	H
M	E	A	A	B	A	N	S	T	A	H	H	I	N	C
S	H	O	M	V	N	W	P	U	C	S	S	E	O	K
C	H	I	E	A	G	N	I	R	P	S	I	O	S	N
X	T	N	M	H	A	D	A	G	G	A	H	N	K	Y

APPLES	KOSHER
BAKED	LUMP
BREAD	MANNA
CHAMETZ	MATZAH
CUP	MEMORIAL
EAT	NISAN
EGYPT	PASSOVER
FEASTS	PHARAOH
FISHES	RABBIS
FOOD	SABBATH
GRAIN	SANCTIFICATION
HAGGADAH	SAUL
HEAVEN	SEVEN
HORAH	SPRING
ISRAELITES	TARSUS
JOY	TIMBREL
KNEADED	WHEAT

Coloring Page

Whither the tribes go up, the tribes of the LORD,
unto the testimony of Israel,
to give thanks unto the name of the LORD.

Psalm 122:4

Early FirstFruits & Omer

Yom Habikkurim

Purpose of Early First̄fruits & Omer

There are actually two Firstfruits. The Firstfruits celebration that occurs the day following the Sabbath after Passover is considered *Early Firstfruits*. Fifty days later the *Latter Firstfruits* occurs, called the *Feast of Weeks* (Pentecost). The fifty days in between are called *The Counting of the Omer*. Occasionally you'll see both the early and the latter firstfruits listed as one feast. This chapter is a combination of *Early Firstfruits* and *Counting the Omer*. *Latter Firstfruits* (Feast of Weeks) is addressed in the next chapter.

During Early Firstfruits, the firstfruits waved before the Lord were in the natural state—an omer of barley (and wheat, grapes, olives, etc.). During Latter Firstfruits (in the next chapter) the firstfruits waved before the Lord were in the prepared state—two loaves of bread (and wine, oil, etc.).

The day of Firstfruits is also called Yom HaBikkurim or Sfirat Haomer. The word *firstfruits* means "a promise to come." The very first of the harvest is waved before God to acknowledge the land He gave the Israelites. Early Firstfruits is celebrated on a very special day. On this day the Bible records miracles occurring over and over (the day that God seems to be drawing our attention to). No other day (except Passover) is mentioned as many times in the Bible.

The day of Firstfruits never received the status of high holy day just because the Priest had to offer the wave-sheaf. It remained an ordinary working day on which the high priest would wave the sheaf before the Lord. Therefore, some do not consider Early Firstfruits an actual feast day.

COUNTING THE OMER

God commanded His people to count from the day after the Sabbath until the day that the Torah was given. This counting demonstrated how great the desire is for the day that commemorates the most special occasion.

The offering of new barley was brought to the Temple on the second day of Passover. The omer measure is one tenth of an ephah (i.e., 2.2 liters), and therefore a relatively modest offering (see Lev. 23:9), but until the omer had been brought to the priest in the Temple, none of the new produce could be eaten.

TIMES GOD REQUIRED FIRSTFRUITS

Many times the firstfruits of the ground were offered unto God just as the firstborn of man and animals. The law required:

1.) **Early Firstfruits**— on the morrow after the Passover Sabbath, a sheaf of new corn should be waved by the priest before the altar (Lev. 23:5,6,10,12).

2.) **Feast of Weeks**—at the Feast of Pentecost two loaves of leavened bread, made from the new flour, were to be waved in like manner (Lev. 23:15,17; Num. 28:26).

3.) **The Feast of Tabernacles** — an acknowledgment that the fruits of the harvest were from the Lord (Ex. 23:16; 34:22).

4.) **Tithe**—Every individual was required to consecrate to God a portion of the firstfruits of the land (Ex. 22:29, 23:19, 34:26; Num. 15:20, 21).

Firstfruits & Omer in Bible Times

The Israelites were to bring a special thanks offering to the Temple. In Jewish literature the festival is frequently referred to as *Atseret,* translated as "a solemn assembly."

In Temple times, the order of Firstfruits and Counting the Omer was as follows:

1.) It was to be done the morrow after the Sabbath.

2.) They were to reap the harvest and "then ye shall bring a sheaf of the firstfruits of your harvest unto the priest."

3.) The priest would wave the sheaf before God.

4.) There followed the counting of seven weeks from the day it was brought.

5.) The law enjoined that no fruit was to be gathered from newly-planted fruit trees for the first three years, and that the firstfruits of the fourth year were to be consecrated to the Lord (Lev. 19:23-25).

Early Firstfruits was the first harvest of the spring, making it an excellent time to give the grain offering to the Lord. By this time of the year, in Israel, many fruits have ripened and are ready to eat. The owner of such fruit brought the first-picked fruit to the Temple as a special sacrifice. The sheaf (traditionally understood to be of barley, which is usually harvested by Passover) is to be "waved before the Lord," with accompanying sacrifices, and only after this ceremony may the grain of the new year be consumed.

The farmers in Israel were required to mark the fruits and grains designated that were most progressed in their growth. After marking them, sometimes with a red yarn, the farmer would declare them to be firstfruits. The marked samplings were taken to the Temple in Jerusalem as an offering to God. Rabbinic legislation set a minimum of one-sixtieth of the harvest of each species brought.

The Counting of the Omer was a time of great anticipation. This counting is comparable to that of a slave or prisoner, who counts the days to his freedom with great excitement. When one counts to a particular event or time, it demonstrates how deeply he wants to reach that point.

Jewish literature maintains that when the Israelites were told of their forthcoming liberation from Egypt, they were also informed that fifty days thereafter they would receive the Torah. The Israelites were so excited that they began counting the days till then.

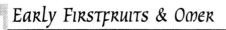

Jewish Customs of Firstfruits & Omer Today

Modern observance of Early Firstfruits excludes the elements of the ceremony which are dependent on the existence of the Jerusalem Temple.

The rabbis feel that the practice of counting seven weeks should still be performed even in generations which cannot wave the sheaf. Therefore, traditional Jews still continue to count the omer as their ancestors offered up the omer in the Temple area.

Today, most Jews start counting from the second day of Passover, the day after Unleavened Bread. (Jesus was slain on the fourteenth of Nisan and arose the seventeenth.) This would be the day after the weekly Sabbath during the week of Passover.

The procedure for counting is as follows:

While standing each evening, the following blessing is recited:

> "Blessed are You, Lord our God, Ruler of the universe who has sanctified us with His commandments, commanding us to count the omer."

This is followed by a count for the day. The counting was always started at day one and continued until day fifty as follows:

> Today is the first day of the Omer.
> Today is the second day of the Omer.
> Today is the third day of the Omer.
> Today is the fourth day of the Omer.
> Today is the fifth day of the Omer.
> Today is the sixth day of the Omer.
> Today is the seventh day. That is one week of the Omer.
>   etc.

Some recite Psalm 67 because it consists of seven verses and forty-nine words (in Hebrew).

This forty-nine-day period is considered semi-mourning because of several tragedies associated with this time of the year. Therefore, orthodox Jews do not shave, cut their hair, or perform weddings during this period.

Messianic Significance of Firstfruits & Omer

As strange as it may seem, the Israelites who performed this ritual year after year were never told what the wave sheaf symbolized. The wave sheaf is clearly symbolic of Christ, the Firstfruits. He is the Firstfruits of the harvest, the coming harvest of the souls of those who have fallen asleep in Christ on that wonderful resurrection day of the Lord.

Firstfruits speaks of resurrection. When the Pharisees asked Jesus for a sign (a miracle or wonder), Jesus rebuked them and then said the only sign would be three days and three nights in the center of the earth as Jonah was in the belly of the whale. Jesus died on Passover. Death could not hold our Messiah. On the third day He arose triumphantly from the grave!

Then certain of the scribes and of the Pharisees answered, saying, Master, we would see a sign from thee. But he answered and said unto them, An evil and adulterous generation seeketh after a sign; and there shall no sign be given to it, but the sign of the prophet Jonas: For as Jonas was three days and three nights in the whale's belly; so shall the Son of man be three days and three nights in the heart of the earth (Matthew 12: 38-41).

This sheaf of Firstfruits was typical of our Lord Jesus, who has risen from the dead as the *firstfruits of those that slept* (1 Cor. 15:20). That *branch of the Lord* (Isa. 4:2) was then presented to Him, in virtue of the sacrifice of Himself, the Lamb of God, and it was accepted for us. It is very observable that our Lord Jesus rose from the dead on the very day the Firstfruits were offered, to show that He was the substance of this shadow. We are taught by this law to *honour the Lord with our substance, and with the firstfruits of all our increase* (Prov. 3:9). They were not to eat of their new corn until God's part was offered to Him out of it (v. 14), for we must always begin with God, begin our lives with Him, begin every day with Him, begin every meal with Him, begin every affair and business with Him; *seek first the kingdom of God* (Henry 1991).

Paul wrote *"But now is Christ risen from the dead, and become the firstfruits of them that slept"* (1 Cor. 15:20). Our Messiah's resurrection is the firstfruits, or promise, of the believer's resurrection.

Verily, verily, I say unto you, Except a corn of wheat fall into the ground and die, it abideth alone: but if it die, it bringeth forth much fruit (John 12:24).

The Hebrew root of *bikkurim* (firstfruits) is the same as that of *bekhor* (firstborn). The firstfruits are dedicated to God because the first of everything, including the firstborn of man and beast, belong to God. Jesus was the firstborn. *And knew her not till she had brought forth her firstborn son: and he called his name JESUS* [Y'shua] (Matt. 1:25). *For whom he did foreknow, he also did predestinate to be conformed to the image of his Son, that he might be the firstborn among many brethren* (Romans 8:29).

The Bible tells us that God, the great husbandman, eagerly awaits the precious fruit of the earth and has long patience in waiting for it (James 5:7). Unfortunately, while God is focusing on fruit, we are often focusing on other things. Sometimes we even focus on gifts which God has given, instead of the fruit we are to produce as a result of God's gifts in our lives (Wagner 1995).

THE MORROW AFTER THE SABBATH

There are two different views about when Early Firstfruits occurs. This difference comes from different interpretations of Leviticus 23:11. *And he shall wave the sheaf before the LORD, to be accepted for you:* "on the morrow after the sabbath the priest shall wave it."

There are two kinds of sabbaths in the Bible. The seventh day of the week is the weekly Sabbath and the annual Holy Days are also considered Sabbaths. So the "morrow after the sabbath" would either mean 1.) the day after the weekly Sabbath after Passover or 2.) the day after the second day of Passover, which is a Holy Day. If you plan on celebrating the holidays you'll need to understand the two views, because which view you hold to will affect the date of Early Firstfruits, Counting the Omer and Latter Firstfruits (because it is fifty days from Early Firstfruits).

The Messianic and Sadducean method places the Early Firstfruits festival and the day of the start of the counting of the Omer as the day after the seventh-day (Saturday) Sabbath during Passover. The Rabbinic method places Firstfruits as the second day of Passover (i.e., the day after the sabbath *of* Passover instead of *during*).

Y'shua is the Firstfruits of those who rise from the dead. *But now is Christ risen from the dead, and become the firstfruits of them that slept. For since by man came death, by man came also the resurrection of the dead* (1 Cor. 15:20-21).

PUTTING ON THE NEW MAN

Firstfruits is also a visual lesson instructing us how God wants us to change through Christ (as Unleavened Bread). When one accepts Jesus as the Passover Lamb who died for our sins, our position before God changes to sinless (without yeast) because Jesus took on our sins. We are righteous through Jesus. Unleavened Bread teaches us to put off the old man and Firstfruits teaches us to put on the new man. *And that ye put on the new man, which after God is created in righteousness and true holiness* (Eph. 4:24). We put on the new man by allowing the Holy Spirit to live a life of Christ though us. As Paul said in Galatians 2:20, *"I am crucified with Christ: nevertheless I live; yet not I, but Christ liveth in me: and the life which I now live in the flesh I live by the faith of the Son of God, who loved me, and gave himself for me."*

Be ye therefore followers of God, as dear children; And walk in love, as Christ also hath loved us, and hath given himself for us an offering and a sacrifice to God for a sweetsmelling savour (Eph. 5:1-2).

AWAITING THE COMFORTER

Do you think the disciples were expecting the Holy Spirit fifty days after the resurrection—at Feast of Weeks (Pentecost)? Due to the significance of the Jewish holidays, I believe at least some of the disciples guessed the Holy Sprit would come at the end of the fifty days. Jesus had told them the Comforter was coming. *Nevertheless I tell you the truth; It is expedient for you that I go away: for if I go not away, the Comforter will not come unto you; but if I depart, I will send him unto you* (John 16:7). They knew the Holy Spirit was coming and they were in the process of counting the fifty days until the Feast of Weeks. Jesus told His disciples *"...ye shall be baptized with the Holy Ghost not many days hence."* (Acts 1:5) They must have at least wondered if maybe it was going to happen on the fiftieth day? On Pentecost they were gathered together: *And when the day of Pentecost was fully come, they were all with one accord in one place* (Acts 2:1).

We can only guess at the anticipation they had awaiting the promised comforter. Some Christians today have the same anticipation for Christ's second coming. Think about the anticipation. Do you know what is it like to wait for a guest who has not told you exactly when he or she will arrive? It is difficult to wait patiently for an exciting event. Jesus had to live by faith. We need to follow His example of living in complete faith and obedience to the Father. Can you imagine how they would have felt if Jesus told them He would not return for two thousand years? Sometimes a detailed outline of future events can be a hindrance instead of a help to our faith in God.

These things have I spoken unto you, being yet present with you. But the Comforter, which is the Holy Ghost, whom the Father will send in my name, he shall teach you all things, and bring all things to your remembrance, whatsoever I have said unto you. Peace I leave with you, my peace I give unto you: not as the world giveth, give I unto you. Let not your heart be troubled, neither let it be afraid (John 14:25-27).

For John truly baptized with water; but ye shall be baptized with the Holy Ghost not many days hence. When they therefore were come together, they asked of him, saying, Lord, wilt thou at this time restore again the kingdom to Israel? And he said unto them, It is not for you to know the times or the seasons, which the Father hath put in his own power. But ye shall receive power, after that the Holy Ghost is come upon you: and ye shall be witnesses unto me both in Jerusalem, and in all Judaea, and in Samaria, and unto the uttermost part of the earth (Acts 1:5-8).

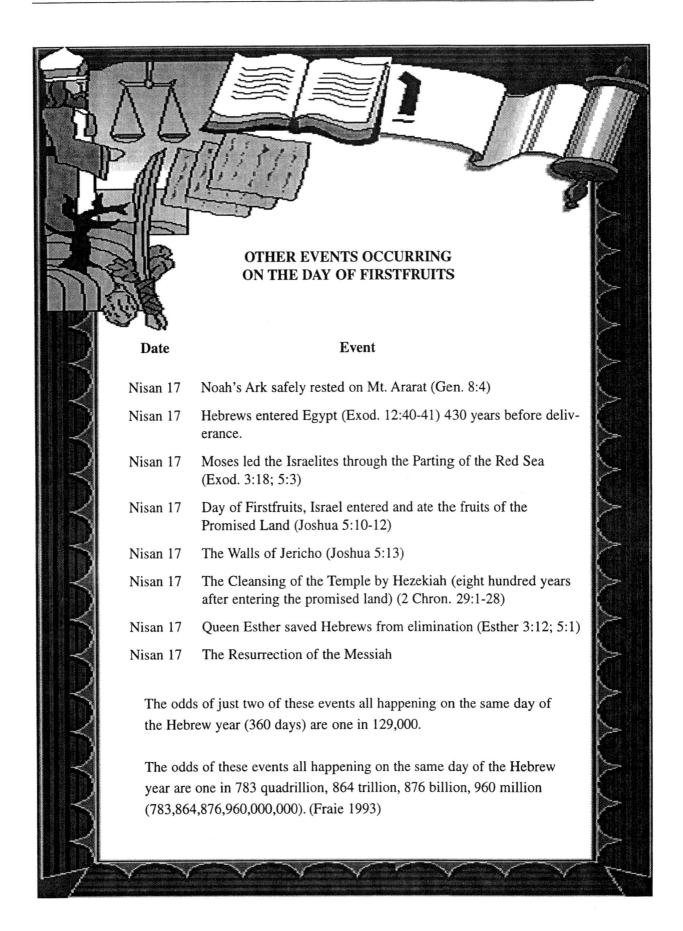

OTHER EVENTS OCCURRING
ON THE DAY OF FIRSTFRUITS

Date	Event
Nisan 17	Noah's Ark safely rested on Mt. Ararat (Gen. 8:4)
Nisan 17	Hebrews entered Egypt (Exod. 12:40-41) 430 years before deliverance.
Nisan 17	Moses led the Israelites through the Parting of the Red Sea (Exod. 3:18; 5:3)
Nisan 17	Day of Firstfruits, Israel entered and ate the fruits of the Promised Land (Joshua 5:10-12)
Nisan 17	The Walls of Jericho (Joshua 5:13)
Nisan 17	The Cleansing of the Temple by Hezekiah (eight hundred years after entering the promised land) (2 Chron. 29:1-28)
Nisan 17	Queen Esther saved Hebrews from elimination (Esther 3:12; 5:1)
Nisan 17	The Resurrection of the Messiah

The odds of just two of these events all happening on the same day of the Hebrew year (360 days) are one in 129,000.

The odds of these events all happening on the same day of the Hebrew year are one in 783 quadrillion, 864 trillion, 876 billion, 960 million (783,864,876,960,000,000). (Fraie 1993)

THE WEEK OF AND BEFORE THE CRUCIFIXION

	DAY	6:00 P.M. - 6:00 P.M.	Events of Jesus	Matthew	Mark	Luke	John
Sixth Day Before Passover	Nisan 9	Thursday/Friday	Approaches Jerusalem from Jericho. Spends Thursday night at Zacchaeus's home. Sends two disciples ahead for animals. Entry to Bethpage. Cleanses the Temple.	21:1-17	---	19:1-28	12:1
Weekly Sabbath before Passover	Nisan 10	Friday/Saturday	Sabbath at Bethany. First of three suppers, two anointings.	---	---	---	12:2-11
Fourth Day Before Passover	Nisan 11	Saturday/Sunday	Triumphal entrance into Jerusalem. Weeps over city. Enters Temple. Returns to Bethany.	---	1:8-10 11:1-7, 11	9:29-35 19:36-40 41 44	12:12-19
Third Day Before Passover	Nisan 12	Sunday/Monday	Returns to Jerusalem. Curses the fig tree. At Temple for further cleansing and teaching.	21:18-22	11:12-19	19:45-48	12:20-50
Second Day Before Passover	Nisan 13	Monday/Tuesday	Returns to Jerusalem. Parables and questions. First great prophecy in the Temple. Second great prophecy on Mt. of Olives. Returns to Bethany. Second supper with Simon. Second Anointing.	21:23-28 23:39 24:1-51 25:1-46	11:20-33 12:1-44 13:1-37 14:1-9	20:1-9 21:38	---
Passover Day of Crucifixion	Nisan 14	Tuesday/Wednesday	Preparation of last supper. Passover supper. Gethsemane, led away to be crucified. Crucified at 9:00 A.M., died at 3:00 P.M., buried at 6:00 P.M.	26 27	14 15	22 23	13 19
Sabbath of Unleavened Bread	Nisan 15	Wednesday/Thursday	First night, first day in the tomb.	---	---	---	---
Second Day of Unleavened Bread	Nisan 16	Thursday/Friday	Second night, second day in the tomb.	---	---	---	---
Weekly Sabbath Firstfruits	Nisan 17	Friday/Saturday	Third night, third day in the tomb. Arose at the end of the Sabbath at sunset.	28:1-10	16:1-18	24:1-49	20:1-23

From the Companion Bible, King James Version, 1990, Kregel Publications, ISBN 08254-2288-4. The Authorized Version of 1611 with structures and critical, explanatory and suggested notes with 198 appendixes.

Suggestions for Celebrating Firstfruits

Read the section titled "Messianic Significance of Firstfruits."

Read the resurrection story below or a storybook.

When the even was come, there came a rich man of Arimathaea, named Joseph, who also himself was Jesus' disciple: He went to Pilate, and begged the body of Jesus. Then Pilate commanded the body to be delivered. And when Joseph had taken the body, he wrapped it in a clean linen cloth, And laid it in his own new tomb, which he had hewn out in the rock: and he rolled a great stone to the door of the sepulchre, and departed. And there was Mary Magdalene, and the other Mary, sitting over against the sepulchre. Now the next day, that followed the day of the preparation, the chief priests and Pharisees came together unto Pilate, Saying, Sir, we remember that that deceiver said, while he was yet alive, After three days I will rise again. Command therefore that the sepulchre be made sure until the third day, lest his disciples come by night, and steal him away, and say unto the people, He is risen from the dead: so the last error shall be worse than the first. Pilate said unto them, Ye have a watch: go your way, make it as sure as ye can. So they went, and made the sepulchre sure, sealing the stone, and setting a watch. In the end of the sabbath, as it began to dawn toward the first day of the week, came Mary Magdalene and the other Mary to see the sepulchre. And, behold, there was a great earthquake: for the angel of the Lord descended from heaven, and came and rolled back the stone from the door, and sat upon it. His countenance was like lightning, and his raiment white as snow: And for fear of him the keepers did shake, and became as dead men. And the angel answered and said unto the women, Fear not ye: for I know that ye seek Jesus, which was crucified. He is not here: for he is risen, as he said. Come, see the place where the Lord lay. And go quickly, and tell his disciples that he is risen from the dead; and, behold, he goeth before you into Galilee; there shall ye see him: lo, I have told you. And they departed quickly from the sepulchre with fear and great joy; and did run to bring his disciples word. And as they went to tell his disciples, behold, Jesus met them, saying, All hail. And they came and held him by the feet, and worshiped him. Then said Jesus unto them, Be not afraid: go tell my brethren that they go into Galilee, and there shall they see me. Now when they were going, behold, some of the watch came into the city, and shewed unto the chief priests all the things that were done. And when they were assembled with the elders, and had taken counsel, they gave large money unto the soldiers, Saying, Say ye, His disciples came by night, and stole him away while we slept. And if this come to the governor's ears, we will persuade him, and secure you. So they took the money, and did as they were taught: and this saying is commonly reported among the Jews until this day. Then the eleven disciples went away into Galilee, into a mountain where Jesus had appointed them. And when they saw him, they worshiped him: but some doubted. And Jesus came and spake unto them, saying, All power is given unto me in heaven and in earth. Go ye therefore, and teach all nations, baptizing them in the name of the Father, and of the Son, and of the Holy Ghost: Teaching them to observe all things whatsoever I have commanded you: and, lo, I am with you alway, even unto the end of the world. Amen (Matt. 27:57-28:20).

Read Ephesians 4:24; 5:1-2 and Galatians 2:20. Explain how Unleavened Bread teaches us to put off the old man and Firstfruits teaches us to put on the new man.

DIRECTIONS FOR COUNTING THE OMER:

When we count the omer, we are looking forward to and anticipating joyfully our coming union with Christ the Messiah at His Coming! The daily "counting of the omer," then, beginning with the first Omer, representing Christ Himself, risen from the dead, continues for forty-nine days (until Pentecost) and spiritually symbolizes the firstfruits which have been "harvested" throughout the centuries and millennia leading up to the great day of Christ's coming, when Christ will complete the Harvest of Firstfruits and then marry His bride (the church)!

During the forty-nine days of the counting of the omer, we cleanse ourselves of our impurity by repenting. You will need a copy of the two Omer pages included and a glue stick or tape. Hang the page with fifty squares in a prominent area of your home. Each day, preferably during devotions, color and cut out the sheaf. One member of the family, or everyone at one time, can "count the days." You may decide to read Bible verses relating to agriculture, such as harvesting or planting. Custom has it to count by saying "Blessed are You, Lord our God, Ruler of the universe, who has sanctified us with His commandments, commanding us to count the omer. Today is the first day of the omer." Allow the youngest child to glue or tape a sheaf in the square. On day fifty, celebrate Pentecost! You could also make a counting of the Omer chart and cut sheaves from fabric as a sewing project you can use every year.

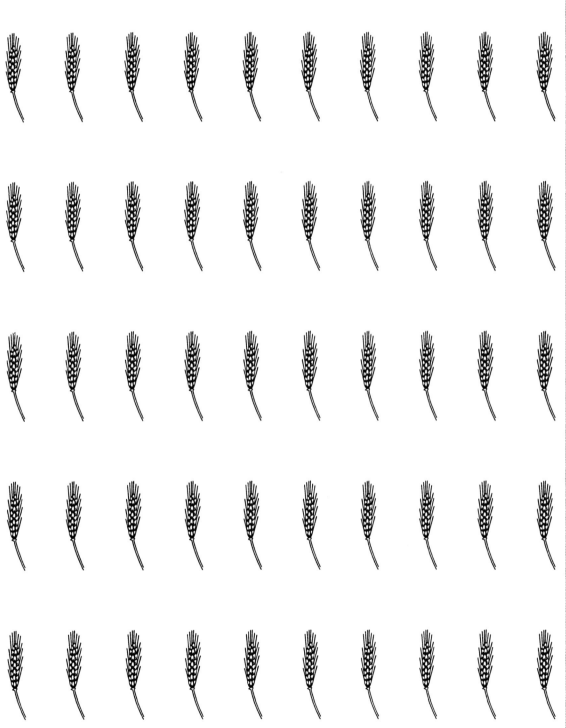

This page left blank for cut out

Counting the Omer Chart

1 First Fruits	2	3	4	5	6	7	8	9	10
11	12	13	14	15	16	17	18	19	20
21	22	23	24	25	26	27	28	29	30
31	32	33	34	35	36	37	38	39	40
41	42	43	44	45	46	47	48	49	50 Pentecost

Centerpiece

To change your centerpiece for Firstfruits, remove CROSS flag and replace it with the GRAIN SHEAF which represents Christ Who was the "firstfruit" from death to life eternal. Add the **Grain Sheaf** craft (instructions follow) to the center in place of the **Lamb**. Replace the LAMB flag with the CROWN. This represents Christ being lifted from a place of complete humility to a place of exaltation as King of Kings. You may wish to read Philippians 2:5-11. **Palm Branches** and **Cup and Bread** flags remain throughout Unleavened Bread week.

SYMBOLISM IN THE NEW FLAGS

Grain Sheaf flag—Firstfruits of barley were brought to the temple; harvest is a gift from the Lord (Hos. 2:22-23, Matt. 9:37-38).

Crown flag—royalty, throne, reigning (Ps. 21:3, Rev. 4:4, 9-11, Rev. 19:11-16).

Grain Sheaf Craft

If you live near a wheat, barley, or oat farmer this will be easy for you. Ask permission to gather alongside the road enough grain to make a large handful. The stem-to-head length should be at least 7 to 8 inches. It is best if the grain is full but a little green. Winter wheat or barley is ready in different parts of the world at different times, so you will want to ask and get it ahead of time. Sometimes you can still glean after harvest. It just isn't as pretty. Grain that is a little green should be stood loosely in a dry vase. As it matures, it will turn golden.

If you can't gather your own, craft stores often carry dried grain to use in dried flower arrangements.

Collect your bundle of stems so that the heads at the top of the center are straighter and higher than the sides. Tie securely with heavy thread, dental floss or thin string. Trim the bottom of the bundle evenly so that it will stand.

You can spray the entire bundle with a clear acrylic if you desire. Add a red ribbon to cover the string tie. If you have any trouble getting it to stand, insert a small ball of tissue or cloth into the center of the stems, making them spread to a large circle. Glue in place if necessary.

If you are unable to get a very large handful, tie together what you have with the red ribbon, and display laying on its side.

215

Memory Challenge

You may choose to learn a passage of scripture by building one word each of the fifty days. The Jews may use a Hebrew Psalm 67, but it has over twice as many English words. You will find that translations vary in exact number of words. Read through, divide, and collect extra words as needed if this is the passage you choose.

If you're brave, try for fifty *verses*. What an accomplishment to say them all on Pentecost! Remember, though, the point is to "hide them in your heart" and not just in your head. An interesting group would be Acts 1:7-9 and Acts 2. Another challenging group would be Isaiah 52:6-13, and the chapters 53, 54 and 55. The Sermon on the Mount has several possibilities for a fifty-word or fifty-verse selection.

Any number of the Psalms would also be excellent choices. Choose a combination that has fifty words, one hundred words (two per day), etc., or fifty verses. Some favorites for learning are Psalms 1, 8, 19, 23, 24, 27, 34, 67, 97, 100, 103, 107, 121, 126, 139, or parts of 119.

Joyful Junction

On the next page you will find a scrambled picture. Recreate the scene by drawing what you see in each numbered box, where it belongs (turn to the following pages). Number 16 is done for you. How many things come together at Joyful Junction?

Note: If your children are very young, you may allow them to cut the boxes and paste into position.

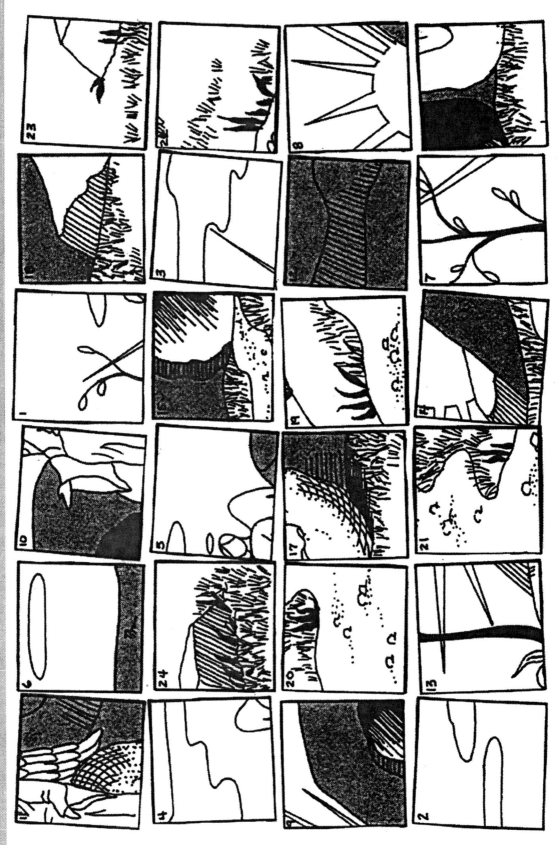

This page left blank for cut out

Early Firstfruits & Omer

Joyful Junction

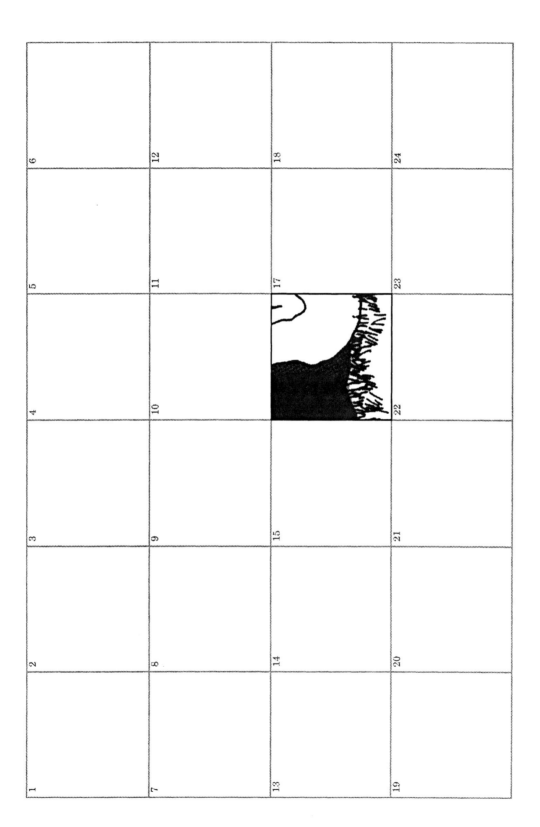

On the Six O'Clock News

To be ready for your production on Latter Firstfruits, you may need to begin this activity during Omer time. Using this idea from *Together at Home* by Dean and Grace Merrill, pretend you are the newscaster and write a script similar to a newspaper story. A hint for condensing your news story is to include only the most important and factual information you have. Set a sixty-second time limit and try to have the gifted talker in your family try to hit it.

If you want to have all the time you want, pretend you have a mini-documentary and talk slower. Be creative and add sound effects! (See "Family Drama" in Passover section.) Interview more disciples and visitors, maybe even a Gentile.

If you have or can borrow a video camera–use it! If not, use your regular camera and place the photos in a scrapbook you could make about the holidays.

TV CONSTRUCTION

Use a discarded window shade or a disposable white plastic tablecloth. Find a sturdy box and cut a hole for the picture tube area in front. The box should be a size where half of a broomstick handle will stick out some on each side. It could also be smaller, as a portable TV. You can buy a dowel stick if no broom or mop handle is available. Cut your shade or tablecloth to fit inside the box and fill your "viewing screen." Mark lines to show where picture "frames" end. Either a shade or a tablecloth would have to be cut apart and joined with tape to make a continuous long strip.

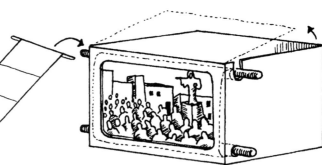

Create as many scenes as you want to go along with the newscast. Remember you will need more if you're making a documentary. As a suggestion, try to have one scene for every 5 to 10 seconds of news, or every 20 to 30 seconds of documentary.

Markers or acrylic paints work best. Use masking tape to anchor top end of your picture roll to a handle. Insert handle in bottom holes, then tape. You can remove tape from handle to change rolls.

NOTE

Some families may like these media ideas so well they could adapt them for other holidays. They would work well for Passover or Purim where the feast itself is based on a specific historic event. Home schoolers may want to use this idea to show a historical event.

A Family Guide to the Biblical Holidays©

Firstfruits Recipes

HONEY-BARLEY MUFFINS

1 cup barley flour

3/4 cup unbleached all-purpose flour

1/4 cup wheat germ or bran

1 T baking powder

1/2 tsp. salt

2 egg whites or 1 whole egg

1/4 cup oil

1/2 cup milk

1/2 cup honey

Mix all dry ingredients together and all wet ingredients together. Now put the two together and stir just until mixed. Pour into cupcake papers in muffin tin or grease the muffin tin. Bake in preheated 375° oven for 20 minutes. **NOTE**: For extra special touch, put a teaspoon of all-fruit jam or apple jelly in the center of each muffin before baking.

During Unleavened Bread:
Omit baking powder, increase to 3 egg whites, beat them until stiff and fold gently into batter last. Fill cups (11) nearly full. They won't rise much. Bake at 350° for about 25 minutes.

BARLEY VEGETABLE STEW

1/2 cup hulled barley (if you use pearled barley, see Note below)

4 cups water (or 2 to 2 1/2 cups if using prepared, pearled barley)

1/2 cup pizza/pasta sauce

1/4 cup onion, chopped, or 1 T dry flakes)

1/4 to 1/2 T garlic powder

2 T chicken-flavored powder or 2 bouillon cubes

1/2 T salt or to taste

2 carrots, diced

1 potato, diced

1 cup green beans or peas

1/2 cup to 1 cup bonded chicken pieces, optional

Soak hulled barley overnight in 2 cups of water. Add 2 more cups of water, pizza sauce, onion, garlic chicken powder or bouillon, and salt and bring to boil. Keeping covered, reduce heat and simmer for 1- 1/2 hours. Add chicken and diced carrots and return to boil for 15 minutes. Add potatoes and green beans, cooling an additional 15-20 minutes until potatoes are tender. Add water or remove lid to adjust liquid to desired consistency. Yields 6-7 cups.

Note: Pearled barley users prepare to yield 1-1/2 cups cooked. Add 2 cups water, pizza sauce and all seasonings and bring to boil. Simmer 5-10 minutes, then proceed to add vegetables and meat as above. Adjust liquid as above.

*To make wheat & barley biscuits, substitute 1/2 cup of barley flour for all purpose flour in a recipe using 2 cups of flour. In cornbread, use 2 tablespoons barley per cup of cornmeal mix.

Crossword Puzzle

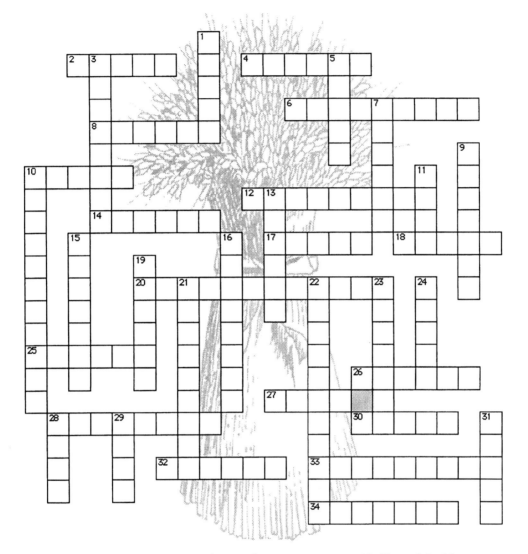

Across

2. First five
4. Grain used for cereals
6. Oldest heir
8. Large departure
10. Jonathan's best friend
12. The city
14. Clusters of edible berries
17. A tenth part
18. Edible plant product
20. Back to life
25. Important food, source of oil
26. An old language
27. Highness
28. To name or list one by one
30. A sacred song
32. Celebrations
33. Book of many edicts
34. Holy day

Down

1. More than one week
3. Contribution
5. Not late
7. Solomon built one
9. A declaration of commitment
10. Book in the Bible
11. You can count up to fifty of them
13. Queen
15. The origin
16. Unexplainable events
19. Responsible for Temple
21. Essence
22. Sanctuaries
23. Biblical book full of enumerations
24. A fine, powdery meal from a grain
28 Tall annual cereal grass bearing kernels
29 One of only eight survivors
31 Miriam's brother

223

Word Search

```
R  E  D  B  H  S  A  B  B  A  T  H  H  R  E
T  E  L  A  O  I  C  E  U  V  S  A  E  S  S
C  S  H  B  V  R  G  J  K  R  R  S  A  U  Y
O  H  R  T  I  I  N  H  E  V  U  E  D  L  N
M  E  C  I  S  B  D  B  E  R  R  O  R  R  G
F  B  P  O  F  E  M  S  R  C  X  A  O  O  S
O  R  Y  C  R  U  T  E  N  E  E  C  D  C  E
R  E  C  O  N  I  C  I  P  S  F  N  M  X  S
T  W  D  K  C  T  N  G  E  R  T  R  O  G  O
E  F  I  O  I  B  G  T  E  L  O  S  U  A  M
R  N  U  O  A  R  F  N  H  N  C  M  A  I  H
G  N  N  R  A  L  I  O  W  I  E  A  I  E  T
T  C  L  P  O  A  M  U  P  E  A  S  R  S  F
U  E  E  U  R  E  H  V  Q  I  E  N  I  I  E
Y  S  R  G  R  L  A  T  T  E  R  K  S  S  M
```

BARLEY	GENESIS	OLIVES
BIBLE	GOD	OMER
BORN	GRAIN	PRIEST
COMFORTER	GRAPES	PROMISE
CORINTHIANS	HARVEST	PSALM
CORN	HEBREW	RESURRECTION
COUNT	HIGH	SABBATH
DAVID	INCREASE	SHEAF
DEUTERONOMY	JERUSALEM	SPRING
EARLY	KING	SUBSTANCE
ESTHER	LATTER	TABERNACLES
EXODUS	LEVITICUS	TEMPLE
FEASTS	MIRACLE	TITHE
FIRST	MOSES	TORAH
FIRSTBORN	NOAH	WEEK
FLOUR	NUMBERS	WEEKS
FRUIT	OFFERING	

Coloring Page

FOR THERE ARE SET THRONES OF JUDGMENT,
THE THRONES OF THE HOUSE OF DAVID.
Psalm 122:5

Feast of Weeks

Thou shalt have no other gods before Me.

כְּרִית

Also called:

Shavuot
Pentecost
Latter Firstfruits
Feast of Harvest
Day of Congregation
Atserret

Purpose of the Feast of Weeks

There are many names for the Feast of Weeks. It is identified in the Old Testament as the Feast of Weeks (Ex. 34:22) and the Feast of Harvest (Ex. 23:16). As explained in the previous chapter, this feast is referred to as Latter Firstfruits. The Hebrew name is *Shavuot* (pronounced *sha-voo-ote*). The Greek name *Pentecost* is only found in the New Testament (Acts 2:1).

Pentecost is a major festival and has a dual significance: historical and agricultural, just as Passover and Tabernacles. Unlike Passover and Tabernacles, it is observed for only two days (only one in the Reform Movement). Pentecost marks the end of the barley harvest and beginning of the wheat harvest. Counting the days from the second day of Passover to Pentecost is called the "Counting of the Omer" (see previous chapter). The cutting of the omer of the new barley marked the beginning of the counting period; on the fiftieth day, Pentecost is observed. Pentecost is a Greek word meaning *fiftieth*.

Pentecost is considered the closing festival of the Passover season (Ex. 34:22; Lev. 23:15; Deut. 16:9-10). This day is further referred to as "latter firstfruits" of the spring harvest. The "early firstfruits" (barley) were waved before the Lord during the Feast of Firstfruits (see Passover chapter) and the "latter firstfruits" (wheat) were offered unto the Lord during the Feast of Weeks. It is also referred to as the Day of the Congregation (Deuteronomy 18:16). Another name is *Atserret*, meaning *stop* or *cease* or *conclusion* of seven weeks of counting.

Pentecost is the only festival for which no specific date is given in the Bible. Rather, the people were instructed to count seven weeks *"...from the morrow after the Sabbath, from the day that ye brought the sheaf [omer] of the wave offering* (Lev. 23:15). This holiday occurs in the months of May or June on the American calendar. It is the successful conclusion of the first wheat-growing season and the anniversary celebration of the giving of the Torah on Mount Sinai.

It is a celebration to reawaken and strengthen personal relationships with God by rededication to the observance and study of the Torah — the most precious heritage. When Yahweh revealed Himself on Mount Sinai, His people heard His voice proclaiming the Ten Commandments. Then the Israelites pledged their allegiance to Yahweh by saying, *"...All that the Lord has hath said will we do and be obedient"* (Exod. 24:7).

Passover freed God's people physically from bondage, but the giving of the Torah on Shavuot redeemed us spiritually from our bondage to idolatry and immorality. The Torah contains the Five Book of Moses, the Prophets, and the Writings.

Feast of Weeks in Bible Times

THE DAY MOSES RECEIVED THE TEN COMMANDMENTS

The Feast of Weeks not only marks the end of the grain harvest at Passover time, but also signifies the process of freedom started with the Exodus at Passover, and concluded with the proclamation of the Law at Sinai. The Feast Of Weeks is an observance of the giving of the Torah by Yahweh (God) to the Jewish people over three thousand years ago on Mount Sinai. Throughout the generations people have studied these works, commenting upon them, clarifying their meanings, deriving practical applications of these principles and codifying the laws derived from them. Thus, a continuous chain of tradition extends throughout the generations, connecting the scholars of the present day to the communication at Mount Sinai.

On that day (when Moses received the law) three thousand souls died due to disobedience. God has never taken His covenant with us casually. He is a jealous God. While on one hand, He desired and still desires intimacy with us, He also is a God committed in marriage to us by His rights as husband. When we violate Him, through types of spiritual adultery, we may indeed face His jealous wrath (Birnbaum 1996).

The Feast is one of the three times when all young men were required to appear before the Lord, a pilgrim festival (Exod. 23:17; 34:23, Deut. 16:16). Historically, the main activity on the Feast of Pentecost was the presentation of a wave offering to the Lord, two loaves of bread with leaven (Lev. 23:15-21). The bread was to be brought with seven male lambs, a young bull and two rams as a burnt offering (Lev. 23:18). The sin offering was a male goat (Lev. 23:19).

During the second Temple period, everyone gathered together in their home town and slept the night in the town streets (they didn't enter homes to prevent being exposed to impurities). In the morning the overseer would walk among the people saying, "Get up, let us go into the house of Zion, to the house of the Lord our God." Those in the Jerusalem area would join a procession carrying fresh dates, pomegranates, and grapes. Those at the back would carry dried fruit, figs, and raisins. The ox offering was led before them, whose horns were overlaid with gold, with an olive branch and a crown on his head. Each family brought two loaves of the finest bread.

Remember, only the best fruits were chosen. The men would go out before this festival to choose the best grapes and dates to give unto God. They tied a red thread to the fruit to mark them for the offering.

The wave offering expressed the Hebrews' dependence on God for the harvest and their daily bread. This was a thanksgiving offering. The link between Passover and Pentecost is the omer. The second night of Passover (Firstfruits) the barley is harvested and the first sheaf is waved before the altar in the Temple. On Pentecost two loaves are waved as an offering before the same altar.

This one day is to be kept with a holy convocation. It was one of the days on which all Israel was to meet God and one another, at the place which the Lord should choose. Some suggest that, whereas seven days were to make up the Feast of Unleavened Bread, there was only one day appointed for the Feast of Pentecost because this was a busy time of the year with them, and God allowed them speedily to return to their work in the country (Mays 1988).

Through the centuries the Jewish people have celebrated this important event. It was at Mount Sinai that this band of wearied travelers would become the nation known as Israel.

Jewish Customs of the Feast of Weeks Today

The Feast of Weeks has no colorful home ceremony that attracts attention. There is no sukkah or seder. Nevertheless, Shavuot is not without its own appeal. In many circles, it is celebrated by a lengthy study session from dusk to dawn.

Pentecost is usually celebrated on the sixth day of the Hebrew month of Sivan. Unlike the other festivals, Weeks is not necessarily celebrated on the sixth of Sivan, the anniversary of the giving of the Torah; it is celebrated on the fiftieth day after the beginning of the Counting of the Omer. In ancient times, there would never have arisen any doubts about the correct date of Shavuot before the institution of a fixed calendar, when the first day of each Jewish month was determined by the testimony of witnesses who had seen the new moon. Weeks could also be celebrated on the fifth of Sivan or on the seventh. The halakhic tradition decided to add a second day in order to maintain consistency among the various holidays.

The giving of the Torah was far more than an historical event. It was a far-reaching spiritual event—one that touched the essence of the Jewish soul then and for all time. The Jewish sages have compared it to a wedding between God and the Jewish people.

There are differing opinions about how Moses wrote the first Torah. Some sages say that Moses recorded the events at different times during forty years in the desert and at the end, combined them to give the Torah used today. Others say that Moses wrote the entire Torah at the end of the forty-year period. There are also different opinions as to who wrote the last eight verses of the Torah which record Moses' passing.

The Feast of Weeks is the special time of thanksgiving celebrated in homes and synagogues. One prevalent custom is that of staying up all night on the first night and learning Torah. It's customary to stay awake and recite a little of the beginning and end from each of the portions of the Torah, each book of the Prophets, Scriptures, and from the Mishnah (The first section of the Talmud—an oral tradition interpreting the Torah). They also touch on each of the 613 commandments (see Appendix F).

The Ten Commandments are read the first day of Shavuot. The night is spent studying, preparing, and praying in order to hear the Sinai Revelation at sunrise. There are two thoughts on the reason for this. It is either:

1.) to re-enact the great eagerness of the Jewish ancestors to receive the original Revelation, or

2.) it relates that the Jewish people did not rise early to be prepared for the account of the Torah given at daybreak, and that it was necessary for God Himself to awaken them. To compensate for their behavior, the Jews stay up all night learning the Torah which their forefathers had to be awakened to receive. *And it came to pass on the third day in the morning, that there were thunders and lightnings, and a thick cloud upon the mount, and the voice of the trumpet exceeding loud; so that all the people that was in the camp trembled...And when the voice of the trumpet sounded long, and waxed louder and louder, Moses spake, and God answered him by a voice* (Ex. 19:16, 19).

There is a custom to adorn the synagogue and home with flowers and greens. Jewish tradition says that although Mount Sinai was situated in a desert, in honor of the Torah the desert bloomed and sprouted flowers.

The Feast of Weeks is the day the fruit trees are judged as to how they will produce for the rest of the year. At one time Jews started a tradition to decorate with trees. It was thought if trees are there before them as they prayed, they would be reminded to pray for the fruit trees; however, most Jews have abandoned this custom because later pagan religions brought trees into their houses and decorated them on their holidays (Jer. 10:2-5).

During Pentecost two loaves of bread from wheat, known as the "Shtei HaLechem," are traditionally served. The custom commemorates the two loaves of bread which, in Temple times, were made from the new wheat and brought as an offering.

The prescribed readings for the festival include the Ten Commandments and the book of Ruth. Celebrations with colorful costumes, traditional readings (liturgical poems), folk dancing, and special foods are held on the festival of Pentecost. It is customary to invite guests and strangers in the community to celebrate with you, as the Torah says: "you shall rejoice before the Lord your God, you, your son, and your daughter...and the stranger, and the orphan, and the widow..." (Deut. 16:11). It is also customary during this time to help the widowed, the unmarried, and the orphan.

It is customary to eat dairy products (not hard cheese) before the main lunch meal to remember the situation of the Jewish ancestors at the time they received the Torah. This custom developed because, right after the nation of Israel received the Torah, they were faced with a quandary: What should they eat? They had just learned that there were food laws of "keeping kosher" which they had not followed before. As they did not know the laws well, dairy foods were the only option. Also, as all the food they had cooked previously was not kosher, the pots and other cooking utensils could not be used right away, as they had to be "koshered." Consequently, their meal was a dairy meal. Another reason is because sweet and nourishing milk and honey are symbolic of the Torah. Cheese blintzes are customarily served for this holiday, hot, with sour cream or applesauce.

Thou shalt have no other gods before Me.

בְּרִית

The Commandments Given	The Holy Spirit Given
Fifty days from the crossing of the Red Sea	Fifty days from the resurrection of Christ
Law of Yahweh written in Stone	Law of Yahweh written on our hearts
Three thousand slain	Three thousand receive salvation
The letter of the Law	The Spirit of the Law

Symbol	Represents
Grain of wheat	Messiah (John 12:23-24)
Two Loaves with leaven (Lev. 23:15-17)	Jewish and Gentile believers in Messiah
As the wheat is beaten and refined as fine flour (Lev. 23:17)	Messiah beaten, sifted, and crushed (Isa. 28:28, 52:14; 53:1-6)
Harvest	Salvation
Rain	Outpouring of the Holy Spirit

Messianic Significance of Feast of Weeks

Pentecost not only memorializes the first giving of the law written on tablets of stone, but it also memorializes, on the same day many years later, the giving of the Ruach HaKodesh (Holy Spirit), when the law of God is written in the heart of the believer. As it states in Jeremiah 31:33, *But this shall be the covenant that I will make with the house of Israel; After those days, saith the LORD, I will put my law in their inward parts, and write it in their hearts; and will be their God, and they shall be my people.*

Before His resurrection, Jesus told His disciples to wait for the Holy Spirit.

And, being assembled together with them, commanded them that they should not depart from Jerusalem, but wait for the promise of the Father, which, saith he, ye have heard of me. For John truly baptized with water; but ye shall be baptized with the Holy Ghost not many days hence (Acts 1:4).

THE DAY THE HOLY SPIRIT WAS GIVEN TO BELIEVERS

And when the day of Pentecost was fully come, they were all with one accord in one place. And suddenly there came a sound from heaven as of a rushing mighty wind, and it filled all the house where they were sitting. And there appeared unto them cloven tongues like as of fire, and it sat upon each of them. And they were all filled with the Holy Ghost, and began to speak with other tongues, as the Spirit gave them utterance (Acts 2:1-4).

The Feast of Weeks (Pentecost) commemorates this day on which the Holy Spirit was given to the believers (Acts 2). On that day three thousand souls were saved. It is the birthday of the church, when the Holy Spirit came to unite the believers in one body. All believers are baptized into the same body with Christ the head of the church.

From Luke's account in Acts 2 you see the marvelous timing of God. Thousands of Jews had journeyed to Jerusalem to celebrate the Feast of Weeks. It was then that the followers of Jesus waiting in the upper room were filled with the Holy Spirit. They then began to worship God in foreign languages that were spoken and understood by the Jewish pilgrims. There was such a loud noise accompanying this experience that it attracted the attention of the Jewish visitors who went to see what the commotion was all about. Peter then stood up and preached a bold sermon to this Jewish crowd. About three thousand responded to Peter's sermon by accepting Jesus as their Messiah and Lord (Somerville 1996).

THE TWO LOAVES OF BREAD

The outpouring of the Holy Spirit transpired on the very day that the Jews were offering the two wave loaves to God representing their reliance on Him. The two wave loaves with leaven offered to God may represent that Jews and Gentiles, both sinners (leaven in their lives), are able to receive the Baptism of the Holy Spirit through the Messiah. Promises made earlier by John the Baptist (Luke 3:16) and the risen Messiah (Luke 24:49; Acts 1:8) are now fulfilled on Shavuot (Pentecost): on that day, the Holy Spirit did indeed come upon the apostles and empowered them to witness of the Messiah. The first century church was mainly Jewish. The last century church will be mainly Gentile. This explains Paul's statement that the blessings of God were "to the Jew first and also the Gentile."

The two loaves may also represent two witnesses. *He that despised Moses' law died without mercy under two or three witnesses* (Heb. 10:28). The law of Moses is associated with two witnesses. Shavuot is associated with the law and the two loaves (witnesses).

Jesus said, *To whom also he shewed himself alive after his passion by many infallible proofs, being seen of them forty days, and speaking of the things pertaining to the kingdom of God: And, being assembled together with them, commanded them that they should not depart from Jerusalem, but wait for the promise of the Father, which, saith he, ye have heard of me. For John truly baptized with water; but ye shall be baptized with the Holy Ghost not many days hence. When they therefore were come together, they asked of him, saying, Lord, wilt thou at this time restore again the kingdom to Israel? And he said unto them, It is not for you to know the times or the seasons, which the Father hath put in his own power. But ye shall receive power, after that the Holy Ghost is come upon you: and ye shall be witnesses unto me both in Jerusalem, and in all Judaea, and in Samaria, and unto the uttermost part of the earth. And when he had spoken these things, while they beheld, he was taken up; and a cloud received him out of their sight.* Witnesses were always connected with the law, through the Bible; likewise the two loaves and the law are associated with Pentecost. Jesus said that they would become witnesses *after* they were baptized with the Spirit on Pentecost (Acts 1:3-9).

The two loaves were huge. *Ye shall bring out of your habitations two wave loaves of two tenth deals: they shall be of fine flour; they shall be baken with leaven; they are the firstfruits unto the LORD* (Lev. 23:17): An ephah is a measure of Egyptian origin and contained ten omers (an omer is about two quarts, so it would be approximately four quarts of flour). Four quarts of four cups each is about sixteen cups of fine flour. This would make the loaves approximately 12" x 21" x 3".

The followers of the Messiah obtained a mission through the dramatic descent of the Holy Spirit. From the moment of birth, this community—the early church—intended itself *not a new religion* but rather an awakening movement within Judaism. The church members continued to observe the Jewish laws and worshipped regularly in the Temple. What distinguished them from other Jews was their conviction that Jesus as the promised Messiah would reappear to restore the kingdom of Israel (Guinness 1988).

Suggestions for Celebrating Feast of Weeks

The fact that The Feast of Weeks is also identified as the Feast of Harvest gives us some spiritual insight concerning the harvest of souls that God desires to be reaped from the earth. The Bible teaches that Jesus was the Son of man who came to sow good seed—the Word of God (Luke 8:5-11). The church is the reaper sent forth for harvesting (John 4:38; Matt. 9:38). Through Spirit-filled witnessing, the harvest of earth will be reaped. It is for this reason that Jesus made the declaration "Ye shall receive power after that the Holy Ghost is come upon you and ye shall be witnesses unto me...unto the uttermost part of the earth" (Acts 1:9-8). The people of God can never be effective and productive in this harvest without an abundant anointing or baptism of the Holy Spirit. The Feast ofweeks symbolizes *anointing for the harvest.* A yearly observance of this biblical memorial day by the church serves to remind us of our total dependence upon the Holy Spirit to give us the guidance and anointing we must have for this spiritual harvest of earth. The apostle Peter referred to it as a "time of refreshing" (Somerville 1996).

Each year, Shavuot is the precious time for us to reawaken and strengthen our special relationship with God. We can do so by rededicating ourselves to the study of the Torah. We can declare our thanksgiving to God and belief on Him by celebrating the Feast of Weeks as fulfilled in Jesus.

DECORATE YOUR HOME

Decorate your home with flowers and greens. This is a great job for the children. This time of year there are beautiful wild flowers available. Send the children to gather them and put containers of wild flowers all over the house.

LIGHT THE CANDLES

Before sunset, the first day of Feast of Weeks, the woman of the home says a blessing and lights the two candles as for other Sabbaths.

BAKE TWO WAVE LOAVES

Ye shall bring out of your habitations two wave loaves of two tenth deals: they shall be of fine flour; they shall be baken with leaven; they are the firstfruits unto the LORD (Lev. 23:17).

241

DO NO WORK

The Feast of Weeks is a high Sabbath day; therefore, no work (business) is performed, although it is permissible for us to bake, to cook, to put away, to kindle a light, and to prepare and do on the Festival all that is necessary for the Sabbath.

EAT DAIRY

It is customary to eat a dairy meal at least once during Feast of Weeks. There are several different opinions as to how this custom started. Some say it is a reminder of the promise regarding the land of Israel, a land flowing with "milk and honey." We like to set out candy dishes full of Bit-O-Honey candy. This is a family tradition our children really look forward to. Cheese (not hard cheese) dishes are usually served such as cheese blintzes, hot, with sour cream or applesauce. Cheesecake with cherry or another fruit topping can be a special treat.

BLESS YOUR CHILDREN

Say a prayer over each of your children praying specifically for their needs, gifts, and talents.

PLANT A FRUIT TREE

Martha Zimmerman writes, in her book *Celebrate the Feasts,* about her family's special memory of planting a tree on the Feast ofweeks:

> Several years ago we all went to a nursery, chose a cherry tree ($5) and planted it on Shavuot. Richard dug the hole. After placing it and straightening it, we prayed and dedicated our little tree to the Lord. The next year on the afternoon of Shavuot we tied a red yarn around a branch that held our first green cherry. This year several branches had clusters of fruit and we chose the *best* one for the red ribbon. The children are expecting a *bushel* next year! They are also asking if we can plant an apple tree.

STAY UP ALL NIGHT

It is customary to stay up the entire first night of Shavuot and study the Bible, then pray as early as possible in the morning. If you choose to stay up all night you may want your children to just stay up very late—this will be a special memory for them. Let the children stay up until a late hour, 1:00 or 2:00 A.M., playing Bible games, working in this book, watching Bible videos, etc. The *Ten Commandments* would be a good choice. If you read the story before seeing the video you can point out the difference between God's Word and the Hollywood version.

Parents and older children may try staying up all night studying the Bible. Serve snacks and assign Bible portions from each book. Read aloud the Bible portions and discuss them. Take a few minutes each hour to walk around or do a few exercises to keep everyone awake.

STUDY THE BIBLE

You may not choose to stay up all night, but don't miss this excellent opportunity to go through a brief review of the books of the Bible and study short portions. You might try learning or finding at least one favorite verse or passage from each book, for example, Hebrews 3:17-19 or Zephaniah 3:17-20.

Include the story of the giving of the Commandments in the verses below, or from the Bible, or from a storybook.

And the LORD came down upon mount Sinai, on the top of the mount: and the LORD called Moses up to the top of the mount;

and Moses went up. And the LORD said unto Moses, Go down, charge the people, lest they break through unto the LORD to gaze, and many of them perish.

And let the priests also, which come near to the LORD, sanctify themselves, lest the LORD break forth upon them.

And Moses said unto the LORD, The people cannot come up to mount Sinai: for thou chargedst us, saying, Set bounds about the mount, and sanctify it. And the LORD said unto him, Away, get thee down, and thou shalt come up, thou, and Aaron with thee: but let not the priests and the people break through to come up unto the LORD, lest he break forth upon them.

So Moses went down unto the people, and spake unto them.

And God spake all these words, saying,

I am the LORD thy God, which have brought thee out of the land of Egypt, out of the house of bondage.

243

Thou shalt have no other gods before me.

Thou shalt not make unto thee any graven image, or any likeness of any thing that is in heaven above, or that is in the earth beneath, or that is in the water under the earth: Thou shalt not bow down thyself to them, nor serve them: for I the LORD thy God am a jealous God, visiting the iniquity of the fathers upon the children unto the third and fourth generation of them that hate me; And showing mercy unto thousands of them that love me, and keep my commandments.

Thou shalt not take the name of the LORD thy God in vain; for the LORD will not hold him guiltless that taketh his name in vain.

Remember the sabbath day, to keep it holy. Six days shalt thou labour, and do all thy work: But the seventh day is the sabbath of the LORD thy God: in it thou shalt not do any work, thou, nor thy son, nor thy daughter, thy manservant, nor thy maidservant, nor thy cattle, nor thy stranger that is within thy gates. For in six days the LORD made heaven and earth, the sea, and all that in them is, and rested the seventh day: wherefore the LORD blessed the sabbath day, and hallowed it.

Honour thy father and thy mother: that thy days may be long upon the land which the LORD thy God giveth thee.

Thou shalt not kill. Thou shalt not commit adultery.

Thou shalt not steal.

Thou shalt not bear false witness against thy neighbour.

Thou shalt not covet thy neighbour's house, thou shalt not covet thy neighbor's wife, nor his manservant, nor his maidservant, nor his ox, nor his ass, nor any thing that is thy neighbour's.

And all the people saw the thunderings, and the lightnings, and the noise of the trumpet, and the mountain smoking: and when the people saw it, they removed, and stood afar off (Exod. 19:20-20:18).

MEMORIZE THE TEN COMMANDMENTS

God's Word commands us to teach the commandments to our children.

Now these are the commandments, the statutes, and the judgments, which the LORD your God commanded to teach you, that ye might do them in the land whither ye go to possess it: That thou mightest fear the LORD thy God, to keep all his statutes and his commandments, which I command thee, thou, and thy son, and thy son's son, all the days of thy life; and that thy days may be prolonged. And thou shalt love the LORD thy God with all thine heart, and with all thy soul, and with all thy might. And these words, which I command thee this day, shall be in thine heart: And thou shalt teach them diligently unto thy children, and shalt talk of them when thou sittest in thine house, and when thou walkest by the way, and when thou liest down, and when thou risest up (Deut. 6:1, 2, 5-7).

If you haven't done so, memorize the commandments. Discuss each one with your children and answer any questions they may have.

1.) You shall have no other gods before Me.

2.) Do not make graven images.

3.) Do not take the name of the Lord your God in vain.

4.) Remember the Sabbath to keep it holy.

5.) Honor your father and mother.

6.) Do not murder.

7.) Do not commit adultery.

8.) Do not steal.

9.) Do not bear false witness.

10.) Do not covet.

READ THE BOOK OF RUTH

Ruth is the classic model of one who converted to Judaism out of love and responsibility. The book of Ruth is also the story of the community's care for the poor and the deprived, such as the orphan and the widow. Ruth's commitment to the people and the faith of Naomi constitutes a timely lesson for Shavuot, which itself commemorates Israel's acceptance of the Torah. David, who was descended from Ruth, has traditional associations with the festival (Encyclopedia of Judaism).

Centerpiece

To assemble your centerpiece for the Feast of Weeks, cover base with blue cloth (see "Multi-Holiday Centerpiece" in *Preliminary Activities & Crafts* section). Place **Bread Offering** craft in center (instructions follow). If you wish to also display your **Grain Sheaf** craft from Firstfruits you could choose a place in your home such as a mantel, between candles on a bookcase, etc., where younger children can't touch. In centerpiece, insert **Grain Sheaf**, **Ten Commandments**, **Star of David**, and **Dove** flags.

SYMBOLISM IN THE CENTERPIECE

Blue—heavenly origin (Torah and Holy Spirit given)

Bread—temple offering at this holiday which represents giving of ourselves.

Grain Sheaf flag—early wheat harvest (winter wheat) (Hos. 2:22-23, Matt. 9:37).

Ten Commandments flag—Christ, our lawgiver and keeper (Ex. 34:28, Jer. 31:33-34, Heb. 8:8-12, Matt. 5:17). Jews celebrate giving of Ten commandments.

Star of David flag—the nation of Israel. Although this symbol can have a political application as Israel's flag, we will use it to represent something spiritual. The triangle representing the Trinity has a tip "reaching down". It interlocks with a triangle representing the three patriarchs, Abraham, Isaac, and Jacob, who were the beginnings of a chosen people "reaching up" (Isa. 49:6, 66:18, John 10:16, Acts 13:47-48, and Heb. 1 and 12 where we see the "big picture" of God's chosen people).

Dove flag—Holy Spirit Who came in power at this feast (Matt. 3:16, Acts 2:1-4, Ex. 3:2-5, 2 Thess. 1:7-10, Heb. 12:29)

Bread Offering Craft

Loaves of bread were brought as offerings, then "waved" before the Lord by the priest. To make an offering loaf, prepare <u>half</u> of the hallah recipe (see the Sabbath section).

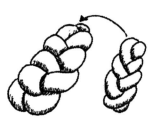

• Make two braids as directed. Do NOT brush with egg.

• You have a choice here. You can put the hallah on a cookie sheet OR...

...you can put it in a small loaf pan (approx. 4" x 7" or "one pound" size). **Remember, it will double in size**, some going up, some going out. Be sure you **bake the cookie sheet loaf before it gets too large** to fit on your centerpiece! (The loaf pan keeps the bottom dimensions safe.)

• Bake as directed in recipe. Remove from sheet or pan. Reduce heat to 200° or lower, leave door ajar a few seconds and place loaf in oven directly on rack. Continue to bake for another hour or more, then turn the oven off, but leave the bread in the oven to cool overnight. The hallah will be very hard, but should not be darker in color.

• Put loaf on old newspapers. You may want to go outside or open a nearby window. Use a clear acrylic spray or liquid and cover the top and sides of the challah. Let dry thoroughly. Read your can for drying time. **REPEAT TWO MORE TIMES.**

• Turn over and cover the bottom and any side portions you missed. Try to apply it evenly. If you notice any drips while doing the bottom, gently wipe them off. Dry thoroughly and **REPEAT TWO MORE TIMES**.

On The Six O'Clock News

If you did not begin this activity during Omer time (Firstfruits section), it may prove to be too time-consuming for this one-day holiday. If you have a week's notice and want to try, have fun with your production. Instructions are completed here for simplicity and continuity. Pretend you are the newscaster and write a script similar to a newspaper story. A hint for condensing your news story is to include only the most important and factual information you have. Set a sixty-second time limit and try to have the "gifted talker" in your family try to hit it.

If you want to have all the time you want, pretend you have a mini-documentary and talk slower. Be creative and add sound effects! (See *Family Drama* in Passover section.)

If you have or can borrow a video camera—use it! If not, use your regular camera and place the photos in a scrapbook or put them in the book you can make about the holidays.

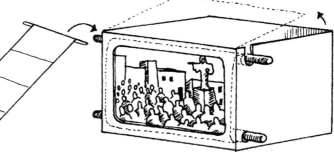

TV CONSTRUCTION

Use a discarded window shade or a disposable white plastic tablecloth. (The thin ones for picnics, etc.) Find a sturdy box and cut a hole for the picture tube area in front. The box could be a size where half of a broomstick handle will stick out some on each side. It could also be smaller, as a portable TV. You can buy a dowel stick if no broom or mop handle is available. Cut your shade or tablecloth to fit inside the box and fill your "viewing screen." Mark lines to show where picture "frames" end.

Create as many scenes as you want to go along with the newscast. Remember you will need more if you're making a documentary. As a suggestion, try to have one scene for every 5 to 10 seconds of news, or every 30 seconds of documentary.

Markers or acrylic paints work best. Use masking tape to anchor top end of your picture roll to a handle. Insert handle in bottom holes, then tape. You can remove tape from handle to change rolls.

NOTE

Some families may like these media ideas so well they could adapt them for other holidays. They would work well for Passover or Purim where the holiday itself is based on a specific historic event.

Headlines! Headlines!

The appearance of tongues of fire atop the disciples' heads at Pentecost (The Feast of Weeks) must have caused quite a stir! Foreigners from everywhere heard the gospel in their own language! The church grew by three thousand members in one day! Go to Acts 2 and read the account of the feast.

Invent your own headlines and write a main news story based on the events. Pretend you have interviewed some of the eyewitnesses present. Develop other related stories and use your imagination to go back in time. Artists in the family can develop "photos" for the front page. Don't forget large, bold (even interesting) headline lettering. Share with your family when the Feast of Weeks arrives.

JOURNALISM CLUE

Write the answers to Who, What, When, Where, and How in the beginning paragraph or two. Then add details starting with the most important, ending with least important. That way if something is too long it can be edited or omitted starting from the end and working backwards.

- Give your newspaper a clever title.

- Use 11" x 7" paper for a tabloid-size publication.

EXTRA! EXTRA! READ ALL ABOUT IT!

If you have access to a copy machine that will make 11" x 17" copies, you could make a few for fun and hand them out. Be prepared to tell folks that the same Holy Spirit is in the world today and was last seen in action at your church, your home, etc. ... doing...

Watercolor Banner

Create a lovely wall hanging with dramatic visual symbolism. For this craft you will need:

- One yard of 45" wide WHITE cotton fabric (or 1- 1/3 yards of 36" wide)
- 1/2 tablespoon blue watercolor paint (blue is suggested, other may be used).
- One 3/8" wooden dowel.
- 45" blue embroidery floss; additional floss for tassel, if desired .
- 1/4 yard contrasting fabric for Hebrew and other words.
- 1/2 yard iron-on bonding fabric (as used for centerpiece flags)
- Crystal sequins, Fray-Check® or optional fabric paint.
- Spray bottle with plain water
- Old newspapers

1. Hem the raw edges and create a 1" pocket at one 36-inch end. This will accommodate your 3/8" wooden dowel for hanging the banner vertically.

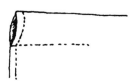

2. Dissolve the 1/2 tablespoon blue watercolor paint thoroughly in 2 cups water in a 5-6 qt. dutch oven or other pot (stainless steel recommended) approximately 10" wide.

3. Fold the fabric in half, half again, then in pie shapes from the center as shown.

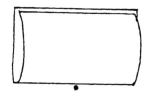

• Indicates center of fabric

4. Carefully set the folded fabric into the watercolor and watch it soak up the paint. When it is all blue, gently lift it over a clothes hanger, still folded, and hook it over a place where it can drip back into the pot for about 1 hour and 15-30 minutes, until it no longer drips but is not dry. Squeeze the center point with the folds gently to see if it is ready. NOTE: a good place to do the dyeing and hanging is on the floor in front of your kitchen stove where you can hook it onto the oven door handle to drip. Be sure to wash your hands and wipe up spills as soon as possible.

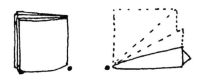

• Indicates center of fabric

251

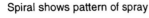

Spiral shows pattern of spray

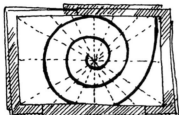

banner spread over newspapers

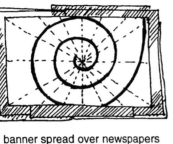

5. Spread a washable surface with 3 to 4 thicknesses of newspapers or put down a vinyl sheet under the papers. Spread the unfolded banner face down on them. With spray water bottle, spray a spiral design as shown and cover with more newspapers, pressing to blot design. The design will be a little more pronounced on the right side of the fabric (face down) than on the back which you see. Allow to dry. When completely dry, press with an iron on low setting.

6. Follow the manufacturer's instructions for bonding material. Patterns follow for using the Hebrew and English words for JOY (we suggest the English word JOY and the DOVE pattern be enlarged approximately two times the size shown, while the Hebrew pattern may be used as it appears—see illustrations). Other choices appear in the Preliminary Activities section of this book. Remember to reverse the letters for use on the bonding material. Trace off, iron onto back side of letter fabric about 6 seconds, cut out, then peel backing off. Position on banner, then use a damp pressing cloth to iron on, about 10 seconds in each area, overlapping strokes. (See bonding manufacturer's directions.)

7. Decorate with sequins. Fray-Check® or fabric paint letter edges as desired.

8. Stain or paint dowel ends which are visible (remove from banner for this). Have parent cut thin groove on each end with small saw or Exacto® knife. Make sure both grooves point the same way. Tie knot in each end of floss and slip into groove. Knot should be large enough to hold when banner is hung. Add tassels if desired.

TRACING PATTERNS

Below and on the next two printed pages are patterns for use on your watercolor banner. See photo or "SIMCHA" below to construct Hebrew word. Use as shown (right side up) if you wish to paint the words. If, however, you are using the iron-on procedure described in the craft, remember to trace pattern

"Simcha" (Joy)

upside down onto WonderUnder® bonding material. Press (dry iron) for 5 to 8 seconds onto the reverse side of the fabric you are using for the letters. Peel off paper backing and position onto banner. Tack lightly with iron, then cover with damp pressing cloth and press each area for ten seconds.

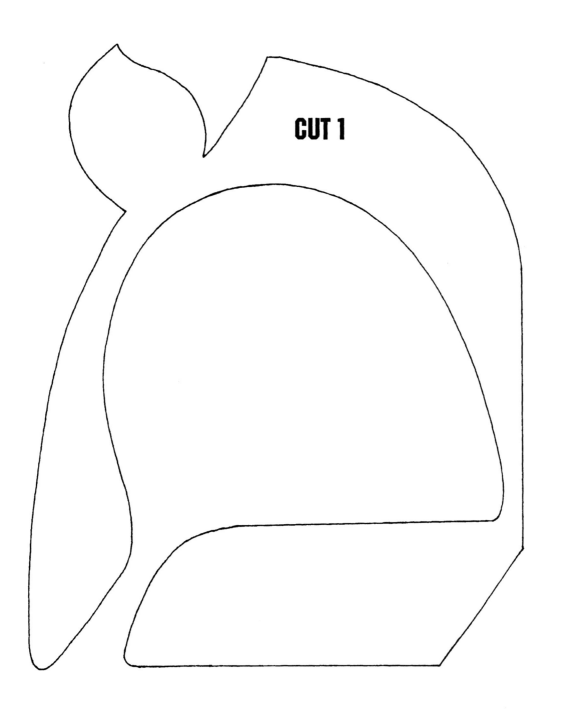

CUT 1

This page left blank for tracing

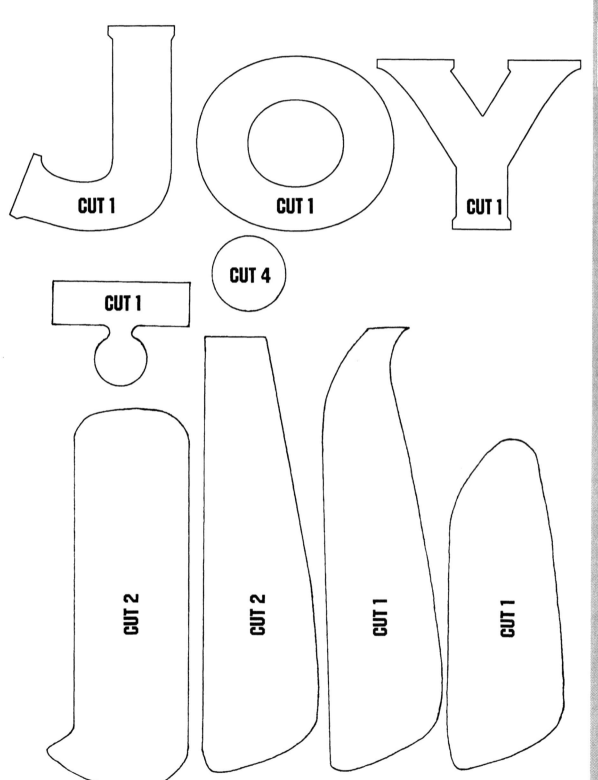

CUT 1

CUT 1

CUT 1

CUT 4

CUT 1

CUT 2

CUT 2

CUT 1

CUT 1

This page left blank for tracing

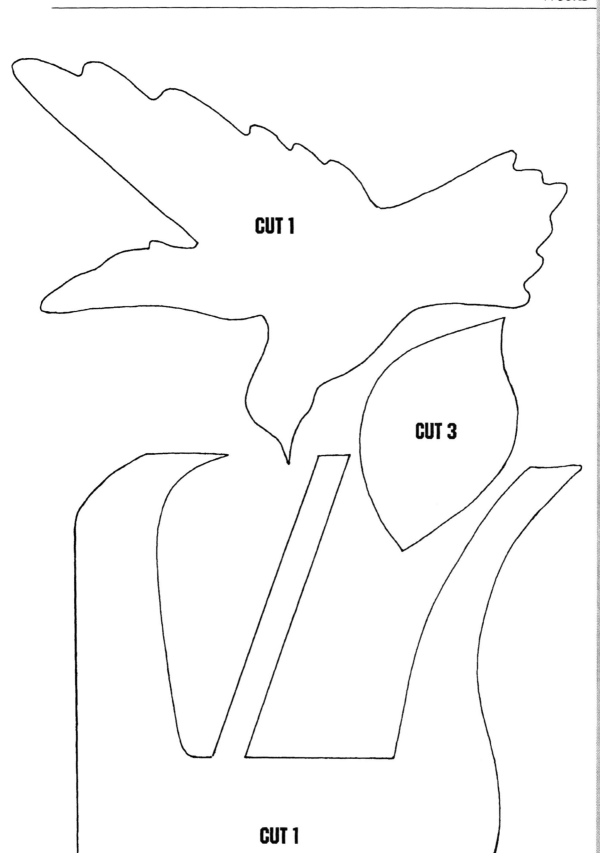

CUT 1

CUT 3

CUT 1

This page left blank for tracing

Recipes

Since 1 Peter 2:2 refers to our need of the "milk of the Word," Messianic Jews traditionally like to serve dishes with milk products such as blintzes and cheesecakes. Below is a recipe from American pioneer days which includes milk products and wheat harvested at this festival. All other ingredients were available in Bible times as well.

PATRIARCH PUDDING

We named this after the Patriarch Moses.

> 1 cup bulgar (cracked) wheat
> 1 quart water
> 1/8 tsp. salt
> 1/2 cup honey
> 3/4 cup milk
> 1/2 cup heavy cream
> 1/2 to 3/4 tsp. cinnamon
> 2 egg yolks

In 2-quart pot bring water to boil and add cracked wheat. Lower heat to above simmer, cover and cook for 30 minutes or until soft. Drain about 1/2 cup of water. Add all the rest EXCEPT yolks. Stir. Raise heat to bring back to near boil. Cover and reduce heat to near simmer again and cook for 30 more minutes. Beat yolks then add 1/2 cup of wheat mixture to them, stirring. Pour this mixture into the pot, stirring well. Cook another five minutes, stirring often. Serve drizzled with honey or maple syrup or top with whipped cream. Makes 5 cups.

During this festival you can heighten the awareness of wheat in your diet and boost your vitamin intake by using whole wheat in some of your favorite recipes. Below are some easy substitutions.

Pie Crust: 1 cup whole wheat, 1/2 cup white flour, 1/2 cup shortening, dash salt. Cut together with pastry blender until crumbs are pea size. Add enough cold water until crumbs begin to hold together. Roll out and use. Fills a nine inch deep pan, or makes great cinnamon/sugar-sprinkled "crust crackers."

Biscuits: 1 cup white flour, 1/2 cup whole wheat, 1/2 cup wheat bran in recipe that uses 2 cups of flour; or all whole wheat plus 1 tbsp. gluten.

Pancakes: Half the amount of flour in the recipe can be whole wheat without affecting the lightness. For even more nutrition, substitute wheat bran or wheat germ for 1/4 cup of white flour you plan to use. If you have barley flour on hand, you can use up to 1/4 cup of it, plus two tsp. gluten.

CHEESE BLINTZES

Batter:
    3 large eggs
    1 cup milk
    1 cup flour
    1 Tbsp. sour cream
    1/4 cup sugar
    1 package vanilla sugar
    pinch of salt

Filling:
    1 16-oz container cottage cheese
    2 egg yolks
    2 Tbsps. margarine or butter, melted
    2 Tbsps. sugar
    1 tsp. vanilla
    1/4 cup raisins (optional)

Mix eggs and milk, add sour cream and blend well. Add flour gradually. Mix until smooth. On a low flame, heat a small amount of oil in a small frying pan until hot. Scoop up a small amount of batter into pan, tipping pan in all directions until batter covers the entire surface of the pan. Fry on one side until golden, about 1 minute. Slip pancake out of pan and continue making very light, thin pancakes. Add oil to pan as required.

Filling: In another bowl mix ingredients below for filling. Fill each pancake on golden side with approximate 3 Tbsps. of filling. Fold in sides to center and roll blintz until completely closed. Replace rolled blintzes in pan and fry for 2 minutes, turning once.

Crossword Puzzle

Across
1. Rabbinic writings
4. A limb
5. Sixth month
7. One who furnishes evidence
9. Almighty
12. Rock
14. Start of a new day
15. The Feast of ___
19. A fruit with many seeds
24. Bestowed
26. Jubilee
27. Monetary standard
28. A bull
29. Days of the week
30. Principle
33. Peninsula in the Middle East
34. God is a ___
35. Gospel writer
36. Unit of weight

Down
2. Disciple
3. Thin slabs
6. Antlers
8. To sow
10. To propagate, strew, scatter
11. The physician
13. Scroll
16. A sovereign's realm
17. Fifth month
18. Those who have faith, confidence, trust
20. Raised by Pharaoh's daughter
21. Non-Jewish
22. Divinely inspired
23. The beloved
25. A commemoration
31. Four decades
32. At sunrise

Word Search

L	W	T	N	E	T	O	R	A	H	J	D	G	S	H
C	A	E	A	E	N	S	W	A	L	U	I	P	A	K
T	O	V	H	L	V	U	R	O	S	F	I	N	I	P
G	O	M	I	T	M	E	J	K	T	R	H	N	O	S
T	O	U	M	T	T	U	S	S	I	S	G	M	I	L
A	G	L	V	A	S	A	D	T	I	D	E	N	U	S
B	O	O	D	A	N	E	M	M	O	G	A	K	S	N
L	D	X	U	S	H	D	F	M	R	I	E	G	O	D
E	I	A	T	M	F	S	M	A	C	F	D	G	W	E
T	P	O	O	I	S	H	N	E	L	H	O	A	J	E
S	N	S	F	U	C	A	N	S	N	E	E	R	W	S
E	E	T	D	N	T	J	M	A	N	T	A	E	T	N
S	Y	O	A	E	O	W	T	A	V	R	Z	R	S	Y
K	X	R	S	H	O	Y	A	M	R	I	O	B	S	E
E	B	E	N	W	E	E	K	S	X	K	S	H	J	I

BELIEVERS	ISRAEL	PROPHETS
BRANCH	JOHN	SEED
CHEESE	JUNE	SEVEN
COMMANDMENT	KINGDOM	SHAVUOT
DAWN	LAW	SINAI
DUSK	LEVITICUS	SIVAN
EXODUS	LUKE	SOW
FESTIVAL	MARK	SPIRIT
FIFTY	MATTHEW	STONE
FORTY	MAY	TABLETS
GENTILES	MISHNAH	TALENTS
GIFTS	MOSES	TALMUD
GOD	OX	TORAH
GOLD	PASSOVER	WEEKS
HORNS	POMEGRANATES	WITNESS

Coloring Page

PASSOVER UNLEAVENED BREAD FIRSTFRUITS WEEKS
TRUMPETS ATONEMENT TABERNACLES PASSOVER
UNLEAVENED BREAD FIRSTFRUITS WEEKS TRUMPETS
ATONEMENT TABERNACLES PASSOVER UNLEAVENED
BREAD FIRSTFRUITS WEEKS TRUMPETS ATONEMENT
TABERNACLES PASSOVER UNLEAVENED BREAD FIRST-
FRUITS WEEKS TRUMPETS ATONEMENT TABERNACLES
PASSOVER UNLEAVENED BREAD FIRSTFRUITS WEEKS
TRUMPETS ATONEMENT PASSOVER UNLEAVENED
BREAD FIRSTFRUITS WEEKS TRUMPETS ATONEMENT
TABERNACLES PASSOVER PASSOVER UNLEAVENED
BREAD FIRSTFRUITS WEEKS TRUMPETS ATONEMENT
TABERNACLES PASSOVER UNLEAVENED BREAD FIRST-
TRUMPETS ATONEMENT TABERNACLES

Section 4: The Fall Holidays

- OVERVIEW
- TRUMPETS
- DAY OF ATONEMENT
- TABERNACLES

SPRING   FALL

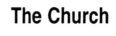

Christ's First Coming   **The Church**   **Christ's Second Coming**

Overheard:

"I know at one time I strongly believed in Pre-Trib, then I deeply believed in Mid-Trib, and finally I earnestly believed in Post-Trib. Today, all I know is that I was wrong twice."

Overview of the Fall Holidays

Most Christians don't know about the Fall Holidays of ancient Israel; Trumpets (Rosh Hashanah), Day of Atonement (Yom Kippur), and Tabernacles (Sukkoth). The Feast of Trumpets is the major fall holidays. If the spring festivals so clearly prophesied the first coming of Messiah, it stands to reason that the fall festivals are also prophetic of His second coming. The way these holidays are celebrated reveals specific information of the way they will be prophetically fulfilled.

Preparations for the Fall Holidays begin a full month in advance. On the Jewish calendar is a forty-day season called Teshuvah (return or repentance.) It begins on Elul 1 and ends on the Day of Atonement (Tishri 10). This forty-day season is a time for one to annually examine his life and restore relationships between God and man. The first thirty days of this season are the thirty days of the month of Elul. The last ten days of this forty-day season are the Feast of Trumpets and Day of Atonement, or the ten High Holy Days (Days of Awe).

The Jews start the celebration of the Fall Holidays thirty days prior to the Feast of Trumpets, which falls on the first day of the seventh month. For thirty days the shofar is blown every morning in the Synagogue to remind the people that the holy days are approaching, and that they should prepare themselves. Their preparation consists of confessing their sins and seeking forgiveness, and going back to fix mistakes made during the year. The ten days between the Feast of Trumpets and the Day of Atonement (Yom Kippur) are called the Days of Awe.

The long period between The Feast of Weeks and the Feast of Trumpets is symbolic of the long period between the formation of the church at the Feast of Weeks and the regathering of Israel to the trumpet blast calling all born again believers (see illustration).

FEAST OF TRUMPETS

The Feast of Trumpets (Rosh Hashanah) is the Jewish New Year, and begins the high Holy Days in the Jewish month of Tishri (corresponding to September or October). It is a celebration of the spiritual birthday of the world or creation, and is celebrated with blowing of the trumpets (Lev. 23:23-25). The Feast of Trumpets is a powerful prophetic look at the final days and

Messiah's return. Jewish eschatology teaches that on the Day of Atonement after six thousand years are complete, the Day of the Lord will come. On that day the shofar will sound and the righteous will be resurrected (Rev. 3:7-11).

THE DAY OF ATONEMENT

The holiest day in the Jewish year (a **fast** day not a feast day), the Day of Atonement (Yom Kippur), is spent in fasting, prayer, and confession. This was one gracious day a year given by God that each individual could receive forgiveness. The high priest enters the holy of holies to make atonement for the nation by sacrificing an animal (Lev. 23:26-32). Jesus has provided our atonement, *"for all have sinned and fall short of the glory of God..."* (Rom. 3:23) and are justified freely by his grace through the redemption that came by Him.

FEAST OF TABERNACLES

Feast of Tabernacles (Sukkoth or Booths) is celebrated Tishri 15 as outlined in Leviticus 23:33-43. This seven-day harvest festival, during which the Jewish people are told to live in "booths," or temporary shelters, is a reminder to future generations of how the Israelites had also lived in booths when God delivered them out of Egypt. A number of Christians believe this is the date of Christ's birth when He came to "tabernacle among us." We should look forward expectantly to the Feast of Tabernacles, just as we look forward to the coming of the Messiah to bring His government, His Kingdom, and His laws (Mic. 4:1).

Israel's Forty Years in the Desert	During the Fall Holidays	Jesus' Forty Days in the Wilderness
Israel wanted Bread	Bread is offered to God	Jesus was tempted with bread by Satan
Israel wanted to disregard God	Honors God	Satan tempted Jesus to disregard God
Israel doubted God's protection	Thankful for God's protection	Satan tempted Jesus to challenge God's protection
Deuteronomy tells story	Deuteronomy is read	Jesus quoted Deuteronomy three times
Israel led by pillar of fire.	Led by Torah	Jesus led by Holy Spirit

End Time Events

The Fall Holidays relate to end-time events. Different scholars have related the Fall holidays to major events to come such as the Rapture, the Judgment, the Tribulation, the Second Coming, and the Millennium; however, there is controversy about all of these events. This writer is not an expert in eschatology. Throughout the chapters, we will explain a few different theories about the fall holidays so that you can make your own decision about your personal belief. The purpose of this book is not to present any doctrine, but to motivate you to study God's Word to be able to recognize the signs of His coming. One thing we do know is that no one knows the exact time Christ will return (Matt. 24:27,36; Luke 12:40; 1 Thess. 5:2; and Rev. 3:3; 16:15.)

HOLIDAY	THEORY 1	THEORY 2	THEORY 3	THEORY 4
Trumpets	Rapture	Second Coming	Rapture	Second Coming
Atonement	Second Coming	Judgment	Judgment	Judgment
Tabernacles	Millennium	Millennium	Eternity in Heaven	Eternity in Heaven

Much of the symbolism described in the Bible was unclear until 1948 when Israel became a nation. The combined Arab forces should have annihilated the infant nation in 1948 but they were unable to. They were equally incapable in 1956, 1967, and 1973.

There are even some who believe that the Jews currently in Israel are not the real Jews, but that the "church" somehow replaced the Hebrews. That belief is not scriptural at all. The Bible is very clear that the Jews are the chosen people and they are the people who will usher in the Millennium.

The end-time events are briefly explained in the following pages, in no particular order:

RAPTURE

The Rapture refers to a coming of Christ, but not to the physical earth. It refers to the moment when Jesus comes in the clouds, the dead in Christ rise to meet the Lord in the air, and those who are alive are changed in an instant, in the blinking of an eye, to an eternal, immortal body. *For the Lord himself shall descend from heaven with a shout, with the voice of the archangel, and with the trump of God: and the dead in Christ shall rise first: Then we which are alive and remain shall be caught up together with them in the clouds, to meet the Lord in the air: and so shall we ever be with the Lord. Wherefore comfort one another with these words* (1 Thess. 4:16-18). Also see Matthew 24:30; Mark 8:38; Luke 21:26; 2 Thessalonians 1:7; 2 Thessalonians 1:8; and Revelation 1:7. Some believe there is no rapture and these verses are about the second coming.

THE LAST JUDGMENT

Matthew 25:31-32; 2 Corinthians 5:10; Hebrews 9:27; 2 Peter 2:9; 3:71; John 4:17; Jude 14-15; Revelation 20:12. Also see references to the Day of the Lord (Mal. 4:5; 1 Cor. 5:5; 2 Cor. 1:14; 1 Thess. 5:2; 2 Peter 3:10).

TRIBULATION

Jesus spoke of signs that would alert us to the nearness of the time to which He referred as the beginning of tribulation. *And Jesus answered and said unto them, Take heed that no man deceive you. For many shall come in my name, saying, I am Christ; and shall deceive many. And ye shall hear of wars and rumors of wars: see that ye be not troubled: for all these things must come to pass, but the end is not yet. For nation shall rise against nation, and kingdom against kingdom: and there shall be famines, and pestilences, and earthquakes, in divers places. All these are the beginning of sorrows* (Matt. 24:4-8).

A world leader shall rise to power with charisma unmatched in recent history. It is he and he alone who will persuade these bitter enemies to sign a seven-year peace treaty. As the world sinks into a deeper and deeper recession, he will have answers to virtually every economic, social, and political concern. He will become the next great leader of the world. He will be the leader of the united Europe. The Jews will embrace him and accept him as the Messiah. They will rebuild the Temple of God under his authority (Wiggins n.d.).

This man will be the antiChrist. The signing of this peace treaty will start the period known as the *Tribulation* (Dan. 9:27). For the first forty-two glorious months, Israel will experience peace and prosperity. Jews from all over the world will return to their homeland and rebuild Jerusalem. Midway through the tribulation, God's judgment will begin to rain on the nations of the world. The world has not seen, nor will ever see again, the devastation that the Tribulation will bring. Approximately 80 percent of the population that remains will be killed (Matt 24:21) (Hollaway 1995).

Also see Deuteronomy 4:30; Matthew 24:21; John 16:33; Acts 14:22; Romans 5:3; 1 Thessalonians 3:4; and Revelation 2:9; 7:14.

SECOND COMING

The Second Coming refers to Christ's future return to the earth at the end of the present age. Although the Bible explicitly speaks of Christ's appearance as a "second time," the phrase "second coming" occurs nowhere in the New Testament. Many passages, however, speak of His return. In fact, in the New Testament alone it is referred to over three hundred times. Careful examination of the New Testament makes it clear that the Second Coming will be a climactic historical event. The Lord will return in the same manner in which He left. His coming will be personal, bodily, and visible. The time of the Second Coming is unknown. In fact, Jesus stated that only the Father knew the time. Therefore, the return of the Lord should be a matter of constant expectancy. As He came the first time, in the "fullness of time" (Gal. 4:4), so will the Second Coming be. The believer's task is not to try to determine the time of the Second Coming. We should share the gospel message diligently until He returns (Acts 1:8-11) (Nelson Illustrated Bible Dictionary 1986). Also see Matthew 26:64; Mark 14:62; Luke 21:27; Acts 1:11; Hebrews 9:28; and 2 Peter 3:10.

MILLENNIUM

The millennium is viewed by interpreters in several different ways. One position holds that the millennium only refers to Christ's spiritual rule today from heaven. This symbolic view is known as the amillennial interpretation. Another position views Christ's spiritual rule as working through preaching and teaching to bring gradual world improvement leading up to Christ's return. This is the postmillennial view. The position that holds to an actual thousand year period in the future is known as the premillennial view. (Nelson's Illustrated Bible Dictionary)

THE POSTMILLENNIAL

The postmillennial view maintains that present gospel organizations will root out evils and the Gospel will spread until the entire earth is Christianized. Postmillennialist believe the righteous will be in charge of the church during the 1,000 year and Christ will return at the end. Then the second advent of Christ will initiate judgment and bring to an end the righteous order. This theory, largely disproved by the progress of history and no longer widely held, but is making a comeback in the recent years. Postmillennialism was declared by Daniel Whitby (1638-1726) in England.

AMILLENNIAL VIEW

The amillennial view advocates no Millennium is to be looked for except that which, it is claimed, is in progress now in this gospel age. This theological interpretation spiritualizes or, rather, gives a mystical meaning to the vast kingdom promises in the OT. Zion is construed not to mean Zion but to refer to the Christian church. It makes no trenchant differentiation between Israel and the church, a distinction that evidently underlies John the Baptist's prophecy of the baptism of the Spirit and Jesus' reference to this in (Acts 1:5). This spiritual ministry formed the church (Acts 2, 1 Cor. 12:13). The apostle Paul apparently makes a clear distinction between Israel and the church in (10:32), and he also outlines a future for Israel in (Rom. 11). Amillennialism does not seem to take full account of these facts. Moreover, the view contends that Satan is at present bound, a position that premillennialists maintain is hardly justified by conditions in the present age. (New Unger's Bible Dictionary).

PRE-MILLENNIAL VIEW

The position that holds to an actual thousand-year period in the future is known as the pre-millennial view. This interpretation does not diminish the power of Christ's present rule from heaven or limit that rule to the church only. That position sees the need for a thousand-year place in history for an earthly fulfillment of Israel's promises of land and blessing. It stresses that the one thousand years in Revelation 20 are actual years and are not symbolic (ibid).

PRE-MILLENNIALISM THEORIES

There are several theories that fall under the category of pre-millennialism. Pre-millennialism holds that Yeshua will set up a literal one thousand-year kingdom on earth after his return. At the end of the one thousand years, Satan will rebel and lead many astray with him (Rev. 20). Then Yeshua will bring in the eternal state and cast Satan into hell forever.

Pre-Tribulation Theory—This view is part and parcel of a theology called "dispensationalism." In that view, Messiah will come to take away the believers seven years before the final return. During that seven years, called the Great Tribulation, the Jewish people will receive Yeshua en masse and then He will return.

Mid-Tribulation Theory and pre-wrath rapture views hold that Yeshua raptures his people at some time in the middle of the process of the tribulation.

Post-Tribulation Theory or "Historic Pre-millennialism," holds that there are not two second comings, as in the pre-trib view, but that the rapture and the judgment occur all at the same time as one process.

WHAT WE SHOULD DO

No matter which theory you believe, the Bible tells us how to act while waiting Christ's return:

- Readiness (Matt. 24:44)
- Stewardship (Luke 19:13)
- Patient Waiting (1 Cor. 1:7)
- Charitableness (1 Cor. 4:5)

Pray for the peace of Jerusalem:
they shall prosper that love thee.

Psalm 122:6

Feast of Trumpets

Rosh Hashanah

Purpose of the Feast of Trumpets

The Feast of Trumpets (Rosh Hashanah) was celebrated at the beginning of the month Tishri, the first month of the civil year. It was one of the seven days of holy convocation. Tishri is the seventh month of the Biblical calendar, and as such parallels the Sabbath as a special and holy time to seek God. The previous month of Elul is the time of preparation just as Friday is the Day of Preparation for Shabbat. This season is a time of reflection, contemplation, and putting things in order and getting right our relationship with God.

God named the other holidays, Sabbath, Passover, Day of Atonement, etc.; however, this holiday has no name. It's simply referred to as Yom Teruah (the day of the sounding of the shofar), so it became known as the Feast of Trumpets, a special day calling attention to the coming holy day—the Day of Atonement (Yom Kippur). A shofar (ram's horn) is blown during the Feast of Trumpets service.

Leviticus 23 calls the blowing of trumpets a memorial but does not say what it is a memorial of. Many believe it is a memorial of God's grace to Abraham when He substituted a ram to be sacrificed instead of Isaac (Gen. 22). It is also regarded by both Jews and Christians as a memorial of the creation of the world, at which the sons of God shouted for joy (Job 38:7). This holiday was the new year's day, on which the people rejoiced in a grateful remembrance of God's benefits and implored His blessing for the future year.

The Feast of Trumpets and Day of Atonement (Yom Kippur) are the holiest days of the Jewish year. These ten days are called the Days of Awe or High Holy Days. Unlike other holy days, they do not celebrate a season or historical event. This season is a time for looking inward to spiritual growth. The themes surrounding this holiday include:

- Jewish New Year (Rosh Hashanah literally is "Head or beginning of the year.")
- God's Royalty (Coronation Day)
- Day of Judgment
- Remembrance (Yom Ha-Zikaron, the day of remembrance)
- Birthday of the world

NEW YEAR

The Feast of Trumpets is the Jewish New Year. There is little resemblance between the Feast of Trumpets, one of the holiest days of the year, and a typical New Year's Eve midnight drinking party. It is a celebration of the earth's physical birthday on Tishri 1, the seventh month of the religious calendar, the first month of the civil calendar. It is the first of the fall holidays and usually occurs in September.

Judaism has several different new years. This is similar to the calendar year starting in January, the new school year starting in September, and many businesses starting fiscal years in July and September. In Judaism, Nisan 1 is the new year for the purpose of counting the reign of kings and months on the calendar. Regardless when the king became ruler, the coronation was on Tishri 1. Elul 1 (in August) is the new year for the tithing of animals. Shevat 15 (in February) is the new year for trees (determining when first fruits can be eaten, etc.), and Tishri 1, the Feast of Trumpets (Rosh Hashanah) is the new year for years.

CORONATION DAY

Another theme of this holiday is God's royalty. The Jewish liturgical tradition has preserved tunes for many of the prayers that aptly accompany what the Chassidim called "Coronation Day." The shofar, in this light, announces God's Kingship: *With trumpets and sound of cornet* [shofar] *make a joyful noise before the LORD, the King* (Ps. 98:6). Through repentance we become God's subjects. It is said that the day that God manifests His Royalty, the day He created His world, is also naturally the day He sits in judgment. Coronation Day is a joyous day and world celebration.

JUDGMENT DAY

The history of the Feast of Trumpets as a "Day of Judgment" is from the legend that God sits in judgment between the New Year and the Day of Atonement over mankind to determine fates for the coming year. This symbolism is drawn upon to great effect by the authors of the liturgical poems written to heighten the prayers of the season. The sages say that destiny — whether financial, physical, or other– is pre-ordained on one day each year for the entire duration of that year (Talmud Rosh Hashanah).

It is said that on this day God has three books that are opened. Those who have returned to God are written in the Book of Righteousness. All other people are divided into two groups. The first is the wholly wicked whose names are written in the Book of the Wholly Wicked. The other group are considered intermediates. They are people who have not been judged and have ten more days to repent. If they repent by the Day of Atonement their names will be written in the Book of Righteousness. Hosea 14:1-9 expresses this theme.

> The sages of the Jerusalem Talmud (Rosh Hashanah 1:3) say, "Normally, someone standing in judgment would dress somberly, cloaking himself in black robes and not trim his beard. After all, he does not know how it will turn out. Israel is different, though. We dress in white and cloak ourselves in white and trim our beards and eat and drink and are joyous for we know that God will do miracles for us. Being judged by God is at once an awesome thing — He knows all — but He is a merciful God. Even judgment itself need not be devoid of joy (Talmud Rosh Hashanah 1:3).

REMEMBRANCE

The theme of "remembered" is thought to be from God remembering Sarah and Hannah. A Talmudic dictum (Rosh Hashanah 10b) says that on Yom Teruah, Sarah, Rachel, and Hannah were "remembered."

BIRTHDAY OF THE WORLD

Jewish tradition believes this day is the birthday of the world because the first part of Genesis, Bereishit, "in the beginning," when changed around, read *Aleph b' Tishri*, or "on the first of Tishri." Therefore the Feast Of Trumpets is known as the birthday of the world (Adapted Chumney 1994).

THE SHOFAR

The shofar has always had a special place for the Hebrew people. Trumpets were of a great variety of forms, and were made of diverse materials. Some were made of silver (Num. 10:2) and were used only by the priests in announcing the approach of festivals and in giving signals of war. Some were also made of rams' horns (Josh. 6:8). They were blown at special festivals, and to herald the arrival of special seasons (Lev. 23:24; 25:9, 1 Chron. 15:24, 2 Chron. 29:27, Ps. 81:3 98:6). *Trumpets* are among the symbols used in the Book of Revelation (Rev. 1:10 8:2) (Bushnell 1995).

Specific uses for the shofar:

- It was sounded to bring Moses to the top of the mountain to receive the Commandments. *And when the voice of the trumpet sounded long, and waxed louder and louder, Moses spake, and God answered him by a voice. And the LORD came down upon mount Sinai, on the top of the mount: and the LORD called Moses up to the top of the mount; and Moses went up* (Ex. 19:19-20).

- It was a signal during time of war. *And it came to pass, when he was come, that he blew a trumpet in the mountain of Ephraim, and the children of Israel went down with him from the mount, and he before them* (Judges 3:27).

- It was blown at the start of the Jubilee year. *Then shalt thou cause the trumpet of the jubilee to sound on the tenth day of the seventh month, in the day of atonement shall ye make the trumpet sound throughout all your land* (Lev. 25:9).

- It was blown during coronation services of a new King. *And let Zadok the priest and Nathan the prophet anoint him there king over Israel: and blow ye with the trumpet, and say, God save king Solomon* (1 Kings 1:34).

- It is a sign of the regathering of dispersed Israel. *And it shall come to pass in that day, that the great trumpet shall be blown, and they shall come which were ready to perish in the land of Assyria, and the outcasts in the land of Egypt, and shall worship the LORD in the holy mount at Jerusalem* (Isa. 27:13).

- It was sounded as a warning of danger. *Shall a trumpet be blown in the city, and the people not be afraid...* (Amos 3:6).

- And the greatest anticipation of all is the day of the arrival of the Messiah. *And the LORD shall be seen over them, and his arrow shall go forth as the lightning: and the Lord GOD shall blow the trumpet, and shall go with whirlwinds of the south* (Zech. 9:14).

The Feast of Trumpets in Bible Times

The Feast of Trumpets in biblical times was celebrated in a far more festive fashion than it is today (Amos 8:5). Although this is a two-day holiday, preparations for this feast begin a full month in advance. On the Jewish calendar is a forty-day season called *Teshuvah* (return or repentance). It begins on Elul 1 and ends on the Day of Atonement (Tishri 10). This forty-day season is a time for one to annually examine his life and restore relationships between God and man. The first thirty days of this season are the thirty days of the month of Elul. The last ten days of this forty-day season are the Feast of Trumpets and Day of Atonement or the ten High Holy Days (Days of Awe).

This holiday is one of mixed emotions. It is considered both a happy, joyous occasion and a somber occasion: joyous because it is celebration of the new year and somber because custom has it as a "Day of Judgment" in that it is a day of looking back and taking stock of one's life over the past year. No work is allowed on the Feast of Trumpets.

This festival has three expressions:

- A day of "solemn rest" to be observed on the first of the seventh month. (Cooking is permissible.)

- A memorial proclaimed with the blast of the horn (Zikhron Teru'ah).

- A day of blowing the horn (Yom Teru'ah) which indicates its chief observance, namely, the sounding of the shofar (ram's horn) (Num. 29:1).

ONE DAY OR TWO?

The Feast of Trumpets occurs at the time of the new moon. The entire Jewish calendar revolves around the moon, so it was very important to get the date of the new moon correct. In Bible times, as it is today, this feast is celebrated for two days instead of one. The Talmudic tradition maintains the second day was added during the time of the prophets (see Appendix C for more on the new moon).

A special blessing was said for the new moon: "Blessed are You, O Lord our God, King of the universe, whose word created the heavens, whose breath created all that they contain. Statutes and seasons He set for them, that they should not deviate from their assigned task. Happily, gladly they do the will of their Creator, whose work is dependable. To the moon He spoke: renew yourself, crown of glory for those who were borne in the womb, who also are destined to be renewed and to extol their Creator for His glorious sovereignty. Blessed are You, Lord who renews the months."

Notice that Ezra observed this feast for two days: *And Ezra the priest brought the law before the congregation both of men and women, and all that could hear with understanding, upon the first day of the seventh month. And he read therein before the street that was before the water gate from the morning until midday, before the men and the women, and those that could understand; and the ears of all the people were attentive unto the book of the law. 13And on the second day were gathered together the chief of the fathers of all the people, the priests, and the Levites, unto Ezra the scribe, even to understand the words of the law* (Neh. 8:2-3,13).

A PSALM IS DEVOTED TO THIS FEAST DAY

{To the chief Musician upon Gittith, A Psalm of Asaph.} *Sing aloud unto God our strength: make a joyful noise unto the God of Jacob. Take a psalm, and bring hither the timbrel, the pleasant harp with the psaltery. **Blow up the trumpet in the new moon**, in the time appointed, on our solemn feast day. For this was a statute for Israel, and a law of the God of Jacob. This he ordained in Joseph for a testimony, when he went out through the land of Egypt: where I heard a language that I understood not. I removed his shoulder from the burden: his hands were delivered from the pots. Thou calledst in trouble, and I delivered thee; I answered thee in the secret place of thunder: I proved thee at the waters of Meribah. Selah. Hear, O my people, and I will testify unto thee: O Israel, if thou wilt hearken unto me; There shall no strange god be in thee; neither shalt thou worship any strange god. I am the LORD thy God, which brought thee out of the land of Egypt: open thy mouth wide, and I will fill it. But my people would not hearken to my voice; and Israel would none of me. So I gave them up unto their own hearts' lust: and they walked in their own counsels. Oh that my people had hearkened unto me, and Israel had walked in my ways! I should soon have subdued their enemies, and turned my hand against their adversaries. The haters of the LORD should have submitted themselves unto him: but their time should have endured for ever. He should have fed them also with the finest of the wheat: and with honey out of the rock should I have satisfied thee* (Ps. 81).

The ceremony of the blowing of the shofar was a magnificent sight. The priest chosen to blow the shofar was trained from childhood. On the first day of this feast, the priest blowing the shofar stood outside the Temple with two trumpeters. The shofar represents, among other things, a call to awaken the conscience.

According to Jewish Tradition all the following happened on Tishri 1:

Adam and Eve were created

The Flood waters dried up

Enoch was taken by God (Gen. 5:24)

Sarah, Rachel, and Samuel (1 Sam. 1) conceived

Joseph freed from prison by Pharaoh

The forced labor of Hebrews in Egypt ended

Job contracted leprosy

Start of sacrifices on the altar built by Ezra (Ezra 3:1)

Jewish Customs of Trumpets Today

The Feast of Trumpets requires a preparing of the spirit. Each person is to take time to look back in self-examination over the events and emotions of the previous year. The shofar is blown each morning in the synagogue. Psalm 27 is recited twice a day. New Year's cards are sent, cantors and choirs practice, and a special collection is taken for the poor.

Most Jews celebrate this holiday for two days. As explained in the calendar chapter, the precise hour for the appearance of the new moon of Tishri could not always be ascertained, therefore, it was extended to two days. Reform Jews retained the practice of a one-day celebration.

This is a time of offering forgiveness and seeking reconciliation with others (family, friends, and business associates). Everyone is to seek out anyone who feels hurt or wronged and "clear the air" by asking for understanding for any harsh words said, or deeds done, during the past year. If anyone has treated someone unfairly, this is the time to correct it and make amends.

The night before Rosh Hashanah, a special midnight service is conducted called *Selichos* (Repentant Prayers), which helps to prepare the worshipper for the time of reverence and self-appraisal during the coming Days of Awe.

THE EVENING SERVICE

The holiday begins in the evening. Much of the ritual takes place in the synagogue, but most Jews celebrate a joyous feast in their homes with family. It begins as all Sabbaths, by the woman lighting the festival candles. The woman usually stays home to prepare the holiday as the men go to the synagogue.

The mood is mixed. It is a serious and somber yet festive occasion. Worshippers pull prayer shawls over their heads as they pray over God's judgment.

THE READINGS AND SONGS

The annual Torah cycle has the following readings for the first day of the Feast of Trumpets: Genesis 21:1-4, 5-12, 13-21, 22-27, 28-34; Numbers 29:1-

6; 1 Samuel 1:1 - 2:10. The theme of the readings is "remembered" because Sarah and Hannah were remembered by God.

The Jewish liturgical tradition has preserved songs for many of the prayers for "Coronation Day." The shofar, in this light, announces God's Kingship: *With trumpets and sound of cornet* [shofar] *make a joyful noise before the LORD, the King* (Ps. 98:6).

THE BLOWING OF THE SHOFAR

On both days of the Feast of Trumpets (except when the first coincides with a Sabbath) the blowing of the shofar is a high point of the services. Before the shofar is sounded, the Ba'al Tokea (the shofar blower) prepares himself for his task of blowing the shofar for the congregation and says: "I am prepared to fulfill God's commandment to blow the shofar, as it is prescribed in the Torah, a day of blowing unto you."

The sound from the shofar is broken, a series of staccato blasts. The broken sound is said to remind the people they need to break their evil inclinations. The shape of the shofar is not straight like a trumpet. The end is curved and bent as a reminder to bend in respect to God.

The sound is meant to be a rousing call to repentance on the part of each individual. It is meant to awaken everyone to make them remember the Creator and forsake evil ways and return to God. The sound is also meant to inspire. It is a reminder that man should strive to break the impulses of his heart which are evil with the sinful cravings of the world.

The sounds have been established in detail by centuries of tradition. There are four different sounds associated with the Feast of Trumpet's service. These sounds are explained as follows:

- Tekiah–A pure unbroken sound that calls man to search his heart, abandon his evil ways, and seek forgiveness through repentance.

- Shevarim–A broken, staccato, trembling sound. It typifies the sorrow that comes to man when he realizes his wrong and desires to change his ways.

- Teruah–A wave-like sound of alarm calling upon man to stand by the banner of God.

- Tekiah Gedolah–The prolonged, unbroken sound typifying a final invitation to sincere repentance and atonement.

A Family Guide to the Biblical Holidays©

A total of one hundred notes are sounded, beginning with thirty blasts immediately after the Reading of the Law. Sephardi, Eastern, and Hasidic Jews then blow thirty more during the silent Additional Service Amidah, another thirty during the reader's repetition of the Amidah, and the remaining notes at the end. In the Ashkenazi rite, however, there is no sounding of the shofar during the silent Amidah, only in the course of the reader's repetition (thirty), and at various points thereafter (thirty), usually concluding with a final sequence of ten blasts prior to Adon Olam (Avudraham, 71-72).

TEN REASONS FOR THE RAM'S HORN

Saadiah Gaon, a leading rabbi and scholar of the ninth century says there are ten reasons the Creator, be blessed, commanded us to blow the ram's horn on Rosh Hashanah.

1. The first is because Rosh Hashanah marks the beginning of Creation, on which the Holy One, be blessed, created the world and reigned over it. Kings do the same, who have trumpets and horns blown to let it be known and heard everywhere when the anniversary of the beginning of their reigns fall. So we, on Rosh Hashanah, accept the kingship of the Creator, be blessed. Thus said David: *"With trumpets and sound of cornet* [shofar] *make a joyful noise before the LORD, the King"* (Ps. 98:6)

2. The second reason is that, since Rosh Hashanah is the first of the ten days of Teshuvah, the ram's horn is blown to announce their beginning, as though to warn: Let all who desire to turn in Teshuvah, turn now; and if you do not, you will have no reason to cry injustice. Kings do the same: first they warn the populace in their decree, and whoever violates the decrees after the warning complains unheeded.

3. The third reason is to remind us of our stand at the foot of Mount Sinai, as it is said: *And when the voice of the trumpet sounded long, and waxed louder and louder...* (Exodus 19:19), in order that we may take upon ourselves that which our forefathers took upon themselves when they said *"will we do and be obedient"* (Exodus. 24:7).

4. The fourth reason is to remind us of the words of the prophets, which were compared to a ram's horn, as it is said: *"Then whosoever heareth the sound of the trumpet, and taketh not warning; if the sword come, and take him away, his blood shall be upon his own head...But he that taketh warning shall deliver his soul"* (Ezek. 33:4-5).

5. The fifth reason is to remind us of the destruction of the Temple and the battle alarms of the foe, as it is said: *"...because thou hast heard, O my soul, the sound of the trumpet, the alarm of war"* (Jer. 4:19). When we hear the sound of the ram's-horn, we beseech God to rebuild the Temple.

6. The sixth reason is to remind us of the binding of Isaac, who offered himself to heaven. So ought we to be ready at all times to offer our lives for the sanctification of His Name. And may our remembrance rise before Him for our benefit.

7. The seventh reason is that when we hear the blowing of the ram's horn, we fear and tremble and bend our wills to the will of the Creator for such is the effect of the ram's horn, which causes shaking and trembling, as it is written (Amos 3:6): *"Shall a trumpet be blown in the city, and the people not be afraid"*

8. The eighth reason is to remind us of the great Day of Judgment, that we may all fear it, as it is said (Zeph. 1:14-16): *"The great day of the Lord is near, it is near and hasteth greatly ... a day of the trumpet and alarm..."*

9. The ninth reason is to remind us of the gathering of the dispersed of Israel, that we may passionately long for it, as it is said (Isa. 27:13): *"And it shall come to pass in that day, that the great trumpet shall be blown; and they shall come which were ready to perish in the land of Assyria."*

10. The tenth reason is to remind us of the revival of the dead, that we may believe in it, as it is said (Isa. 18:3): *"All ye inhabitants of the world, and ye dwellers on the earth, see ye, when he lifteth up an ensign on the mountains; and when he bloweth a trumpet, hear ye."*

WISHING ONE ANOTHER A HAPPY NEW YEAR

Before leaving the House of Prayer on the night of Rosh Hashanah, it is customary to bless one another with the benediction, "May you be inscribed and sealed for a good year." Then it is customary to go home joyfully and to keep away from all grief and sighing, so as not to give the Accuser an opening, for the Accuser's only place is where there is grief and sighing. One ought to trust in God, as it is written: "For the joy of the Lord is your strength" (Neh. 8:10) (Seder haYom, 53-54).

THE DINNER

When the men return home for dinner, the table is beautifully set with a centerpiece of sweet fruits and cakes symbolic of the sweet year to come. The challah bread is baked for this holiday just as for the weekly Sabbath. However, the loaves are shaped symbolically. A round loaf signifies hopes for a good round year or a crown as a reminder of the kingship of this holiday. A ladder-shaped loaf symbolizes Jacob's ladder or man's effort to direct his life upward to God. A bird-shaped loaf symbolizes God's protection as in Isaiah 31:5. Sweet cakes are usually served, a custom traceable back to King David (2 Sam. 6:15,19). Sour and bitter foods are avoided, representing the avoidance of bitter times for the year ahead. Other traditional foods eaten during this holiday are gourds, fenugreek, leeks, beets, carrots, and dates.

APPLES AND HONEY

A popular observance during this holiday is eating apples dipped in honey, a symbol for a sweet new year. It is customary to dip an apple sweetened in honey during the evening meal, and to recite this blessing, "Be it thy will that a good and a sweet year be renewed for us." "Blessed are You, O Lord our God, King of the universe, creator of the fruit of the tree," is recited at the beginning, even though the apple may be eaten in the middle of the holiday.

THE NEXT MORNING SERVICE

The blowing of the shofar is incorporated into the service three times. Each one is followed by Biblical verses.

The annual Torah cycle has the following readings for the second day of the Feast of Trumpets: Genesis 22:1-3, 4-8, 9-14, 15-19, 20-24; and Jeremiah 31:1-19. These passages are to recall the faith of Abraham and Isaac. Because God used a ram as a substitute sacrifice for Isaac, the ram's horn is a reminder of how Isaac and Abraham were prepared to give up all their hopes and dreams for God's sake (Gen. 22:7). (This is traditionally read on the second day of Rosh Hashanah, but in most Reform synagogues it is read on the first day.)

CASTING THE STONES—TASHLIKH

A custom still widely observed is the ceremony of Tashlikh, consisting of the symbolic casting of one's sins into a river, lake, or other body of water on the afternoon of the first day of the Feast of Trumpets (or of the second day if the first coincides with a Sabbath). There is no record of this tradition until the sixteenth century in Germany, when the tradition became popular after the endorsement by Rabbi Isaac Luria. It is supposedly derived from Micah 7:19, *"He will turn again, he will have compassion upon us; he will subdue our iniquities; and thou wilt cast all their sins into the depths of the sea."*

Taking a brief break from the long hours in synagogue, the community gathers in the afternoon at a river to metaphorically divest their sins. The widespread practice in most Jewish communities today is to turn one's pockets inside-out, discarding crumbs that might be taken along for the occasion. The ceremony is symbolic of the determination to free oneself from sins and shortcomings during this special season. Some do this custom on the first day. Others wait until the second day to avoid working on the Sabbath.

Messianic Significance of Trumpets

The blowing of trumpets is a sign of the return of Christ and memorial of God's grace to Abraham when He substituted a ram to be sacrificed instead of Isaac (Gen. 22). Isaac is a type of foreshadowing of Christ. Just as Abraham offered his son on the altar, God offered His son on Calvary's altar. Hebrews 11:17-19 says *"By faith Abraham, when he was tried, offered up Isaac: and he that had received the promises offered up his only begotten son, Of whom it was said, That in Isaac shall thy seed be called: Accounting that God was able to raise him up, even from the dead; from whence also he received him in a figure."* Both Isaac's and Christ's births were miracles. Both were obedient to the point of sacrifice.

Trumpets were used in giving signals of war. Jesus is the commander of the army of God. The Jewish people were looking for a deliverer who would defeat the Roman army. Jesus came, the first time, to defeat the work of Satan and the sin in men's hearts. *And having spoiled principalities and powers, he made a shew of them openly, triumphing over them in it* (Col. 2:15).

In the same way this feast speaks to the Christian about spiritual warfare. *Put on the whole armour of God, that ye may be able to stand against the wiles of the devil. For we wrestle not against flesh and blood, but against principalities, against powers, against the rulers of the darkness of this world, against spiritual wickedness in high places. Wherefore take unto you the whole armour of God, that ye may be able to withstand in the evil day, and having done all, to stand.* Jesus is our armor because He defeated Satan. When we put on Christ we will triumph over evil forces (Eph. 6:11-13).

The Feast of Trumpets can be a very special time for believers in Christ. Our sins are not forgiven just when we "believe." James 2:19 says *"Thou believest that there is one God; thou doest well: the devils also believe, and tremble."* To be forgiven, we must have a repentant heart. We must come in submission to our Heavenly father, asking for forgiveness, knowing that He will forgive us, as a father forgives his child. That forgiveness which we seek has been guaranteed—bought and paid for by Jesus' atoning sacrifice on the tree.

BAPTISM?

Evidence shows that Jesus was born in the fall (see The Feast of Tabernacles chapter). It is believed that His baptism was also in the fall. After Jesus' baptism, He spent forty days in the wilderness. *Then was Jesus led up of the Spirit into the wilderness to be tempted of the devil. And when he had fasted forty days and forty nights, he was afterward an hungered* (Matt 4:1-2.) It is possible these forty days parallel the forty-day season called Teshuvah (return or repentance). Some believe that this is the time that Jesus began His ministry, at the end of the forty days when he began to declare His message. *From that time Jesus began to preach, and to say, Repent: for the kingdom of heaven is at hand* (Matt. 4:17).

PROPHETIC SIGNIFICANCE

The Feast of Trumpets is a major festival. The three major festivals are Passover, Pentecost and Feast of Trumpets. We know Passover represents the sacrifice of Christ, and Pentecost represents the coming of the Holy Spirit, so it stands to reason that the Feast of Trumpets represents a very special time.

The trumpet was the signal for the field workers to come into the Temple. The high priest actually stood on the southwestern parapet of the Temple and blew the trumpet so it could be heard in the surrounding fields. At that instant the faithful would stop harvesting, even if there were more crops to bring in, and leave immediately for worship service (Levitt 1979, 12). The Feast of Trumpets could be either the Rapture or the Second Coming of Christ. You'll have to study and decide for yourself.

On Rosh Hashanah, a series of one hundred trumpet blasts is sounded to announce the setting up of the eternal court, with the trumpets heralding God as the all-seeing, all-knowing Judge of the Universe. Jewish tradition says that this court date is to find out who are righteous and have their names in the Book of Life through the Messiah. All other people are a mixture of good and bad, and God in His mercy will delay their court date for a period of time to allow them to try and prepare a proper defense. The second court date is on Yom Kippur.

THE WEDDING

For the Lord himself shall descend from heaven with a shout, with the voice of the archangel, and with the trump of God: and the dead in Christ shall rise first: Then we which are alive and remain shall be caught up together with them in the clouds, to meet the Lord in the air: and so shall we ever be with the Lord (1 Thess. 4:16-17).

It is possible that Rosh Hashanah will be fulfilled when the Messiah comes on the clouds, the dead in Christ rise to meet the Lord in the air, and those who are alive are changed in an instant in the blinking of an eye to an eternal, immortal body. All of those whose names are in the Lamb's Book of Life have open and shut cases and are righteous, not by their own deeds, but by the blood of the Lamb (Wagner 1995).

An inexpensive booklet with illustrations titled *Unlocking Prophecy: Jesus Fulfills the Seven Feasts of Israel is* available (see Appendix G). This popular theory purports that Jesus will fulfill the fall holidays by coming on the Feast of Trumpets to catch away His Bride, the church to celebrate the Marriage Supper of the Lamb in Heaven, then return to earth seven years later on the Day of Atonement to establish His Kingdom beginning on the Feast of Tabernacles.

A portion from the booklet *Unlocking Prophecy: Jesus Fulfills the Seven Feasts of Israel*:

Rabbis have taught that after being resurrected on the Feast of Trumpets, the righteous would enter the chupah, or wedding canopy to spend seven years while the "day of trouble" [tribulation], the seven years of judgment occurs on earth. By examining an ancient Jewish wedding, we can more clearly see the picture of the union of the Church (the bride) with the Messiah.

When a man in ancient Israel married, he went to the bride's house with a "bride price" and made a contract (covenant) with the girl's father. If the father accepted the man and his bride price, the man would pour a glass of wine. If the girl drank it, it would indicate that she accepted the man's proposal and they were betrothed. The man would go away and prepare a wedding chamber for his bride. When the man's father deemed that the wedding chamber was ready, usually one to two years later, the man would return to the bride's house and "steal" her away "like a thief in the night" at an hour when no one would suspect. He would take her to the wedding chamber for seven days. During this time, the groom's father would hold a party to announce the marriage. At the end of the seventh day, the married couple would emerge from the chamber and partake of the marriage supper.

The ancient Jewish wedding is a picture of Jesus the Bridegroom and His bride, the church. The contract (covenant) was sealed at the Last Supper when Jesus shared the covenant cup with His disciples. *And he said unto them, This is my blood of the new testament, which is shed for many* (Mark 14:24). Jesus, in speaking to the Disciples after the last supper said the same words that any Jewish man would tell his betrothed. *In my father's house are many mansions; if it were not so, I would have told you. I go to prepare a place for you. And if I go to prepare a place for you, I will come again, and receive you unto myself; that where I am, there ye may be also* (John 14:2, 3). And, of course, Jesus paid the "bride price" with His life. *The marriage of the church to Jesus is described in several Bible texts. Let us be glad and rejoice, and give honour to him: for the marriage of the Lamb is come, and his wife hath made herself ready. And to her was granted that she should be arrayed in fine linen, clean and white: for the fine linen is the right-eousness of saints* (Rev. 19:7-8). The Jewish wedding ceremony is another beautiful shadow of Christ's return. For details see *Here Comes the Bride* by Richard Booker in the resources section of this book.

TESHUVAH AND DAYS OF AWE

The forty-day season called Teshuvah (return or repentance) starts thirty days before the Feast of Trumpets, and is a shadow of God's prophetic plan. The entire ten days from the first day of the Feast of Trumpets through the Day of Atonement are known as the Days of Repentance or Days of Awe. The days between may be a picture of the tribulation. The days between the Feast of the Trumpets and Day of Atonement reflect the seven-year period of Jacob's Trouble. *Alas! for that day is great, so that none is like it: it is even the time of Jacob's trouble; but he shall be saved out of it* (Jer. 30:7). One theory divides the days as follows:

- The thirty days of the month of Elul —the Church
- The Day of the Feast of Trumpets—the Rapture
- The days between the Feast of Trumpets and Day of Atonement—Tribulation
- The Day of Atonement—the Second Coming

For thirty days the shofar is blown every morning in the Synagogue to remind the people that the holy days are approaching, in order that they may prepare themselves. Their preparation consists of confessing their sins and seeking forgiveness along with a change in life, if needed. The Jews' earnest prayer is that their names may be written in the Book of Life (Wagner 1995). This might represent the period before the rapture—calling people to repentance. One's name is written in the Book of Life only when he or she has a repentant heart and comes in submission to our Heavenly Father, asking for forgiveness through Jesus' death and resurrection.

CORONATION OF Y'SHUA, OUR KING

Jewish eschatology teaches that on the Day of Atonement after six thousand years are complete, the Day of the Lord will come. On that day the shofar will sound, the righteous will be resurrected and will attend the coronation of the King. According to Jewish eschatology, the gates of heaven are opened on Rosh Hashanah and closed on Yom Kippur. This brings us to the book of Revelation, chapter 3:7-11. Note the two words here that relate to Rosh Hashanah: *open door* (as the gates of heaven are opened on Rosh Hashanah) and *crown* (as in a coronation). (Raisdanai 1945)

And to the angel of the church in Philadelphia write; These things saith he that is holy, he that is true, he that hath the key of David, he that openeth, and no man shutteth; and shutteth, and no man openeth; I know thy works: behold, I have set before thee an open door, and no man can shut it: for thou hast a little strength, and hast kept my word, and hast not denied my name. Behold, I will make them of the synagogue of Satan, which say they are Jews, and are not, but do lie; behold, I will make them to come and worship before thy feet, and to know that I have loved thee. Because thou hast kept the word of my patience, I also will keep thee from the hour of temptation, which shall come upon all the world, to try them that dwell upon the earth. Behold, I come quickly: hold that fast which thou hast, that no man take thy crown (Rev. 3:7-11).

Daniel 7:9-14 also speaks of the Messiah returning to reign as king: *I beheld till the thrones were cast down, and the Ancient of days did sit... thousand thousands ministered unto him, and ten thousand times ten thousand stood before him: the judgment was set, and the books were opened* [The Day of Judgment]. *I beheld then because of the voice of the great words which the horn spake: I beheld even till the beast was slain, and his body destroyed, and given to the burning flame. As concerning the rest of the beasts, they had their dominion taken away: yet their lives were prolonged for a season and time. I saw in the night visions, and, behold, one like the Son of man* [Jesus] *came with the clouds of heaven, and came to the Ancient of days, and they brought him near before him. And there was given him dominion, and glory, and a kingdom, that all people, nations, and languages, should serve him: his dominion is an everlasting dominion, which shall not pass away, and his kingdom that which shall not be destroyed.*

In Revelation, chapters 8 through 10, the seven trumpets and the "Mystery of God" are revealed at the final blast: *And the angel which I saw stand upon the sea and upon the earth lifted up his hand to heaven, And sware by him that liveth for ever and ever, who created heaven, and the things that therein are, and the earth, and the things that therein are, and the sea, and the things which are therein, that there should be time no longer: But in the days of the voice of the seventh angel, when he shall begin to sound, the mystery of God should be finished, as he hath declared to his servants the prophets* (Rev.10:5-7).

Remember, whatever theory you believe, you should have joyful expectations (Titus 2:13) and be patiently waiting in obedience (1 Cor. 1:7, 1 Tim. 6:14). Celebrate Rosh Hashanah by teaching your children about repentance, renewing your heart toward God, and looking forward to the Second Coming of our Lord!

Suggestions for Celebrating Trumpets

A FEAST

Have a joyous holiday in your home with family. Set a special table with your best tablecloth and dishes. Use the centerpiece explained in this chapter. The woman can light the festival candles. Include the traditional apples dipped in honey with your meal.

MAKE AMENDS

Seek out anyone who feels hurt or wronged and "clear the air" by asking for understanding for any harsh words said, or deeds done, during the past year. If anyone has treated someone unfairly, this is the time to correct it and make amends.

READ THE BIBLE

The annual Torah cycle has the following readings for the first day of the Feast of Trumpets: Genesis 21:1-4, 5-12, 13-21, 22-27, 28-34; Numbers 29:1-6; 1 Samuel 1:1 - 2:10. The theme of the readings is "remembered" because Sarah and Hannah were remembered by God.

BLOW THE TRUMPETS

Get a shofar or buy the children toy trumpets or make a paper maché shofar. The sound of the shofar is a call to alert and awaken us, but it is up to each and every one of us to repent and come closer to God.

MAKE AND SEND NEW YEAR'S CARDS

Use your imagination to make the cards. One version is provided for you in this chapter. Feel free to reproduce as many copies as you like. Be creative. Use puff paint, sparkles, jewels, and other decorations.

GAMES, MUSIC, DANCE

Play "pin the apple on the honey jar." Dance the Horah in a circle with family and friends (see Unleavened Bread activities). Play music tapes such as "Arise, O Lord" by Israel's Hope which also includes "Day of the Lord," and many others.

Centerpiece

To assemble your centerpiece for Feast of Trumpets (see instructions in "Multi-Holiday Centerpiece" in *Preliminary Activities & Crafts* section), cover the base with purple cloth. Place **Ram's Horn** craft or **World** craft in the center (instructions follow). You can nest your **Ram's Horn** in the Spanish moss, if available. Insert **Bible**, **Ten Commandments**, **Cup & Bread**, and **Crown** flags.

SYMBOLISM IN THE CENTERPIECE

Purple—royalty, kingship (Ps. 24).

Bible flag—God's word which contains the account of *creation* as well as glimpses into *future judgment and hope*, for which this feast is a preparation. From start to finish it is God's "love letter" offering us a new beginning and a wonderful "ending that never ends." This printed Word is also a reminder of the Living Word Who created the world (John 1).

Ten Commandments flag—Christ, our lawgiver and keeper (Ex. 34:28, Jer. 31:33-34, Heb. 8:8-12, Matt. 5:17). The original "law" flag is joined by the complete scriptures **Bible** flag to indicate the foreshadowing of fulfillment of God's covenant promises.

Cup & Bread flag—wine is symbolic of the Holy Spirit or fullness of joy (Isa. 65:8, Jer. 31:12, Hos.2:22). Grapes are harvested near the time of this holiday (John 15:1-11).

Crown flag—kingship over the earth (Psalms 47, 65, 97, 104, numerous others).

A Family Guide to the Biblical Holidays©

Ram's Horn Craft

To make a paper maché ram's horn, representative of a shofar, begin by cutting a piece of screen wire in a cone shape and taping the raw edges with masking tape to make it easier to handle. Use a needle and thread to sew the overlapped edges together to hold the horn shape. Twist and bend to make the cone form the curve of a ram's horn. Flatten a bit at the base.

Easy–and cheap–paper maché glue is made by putting 1 cup of flour in a quart jar with 2 cups of water. Put on a lid and shake. Tear thin strips of newspaper no more than 1 inch wide. Dip in the flour-glue, wipe <u>excess</u> glue off with fingers and apply to the wire horn. Be sure when you get to the end of the horn to fold the paper over the edge. Make a few layers inside the wide end so that the wire doesn't show.

You can use either of two methods. 1) Let each layer dry before applying the next layer, or 2) apply all three layers at once. A couple of days' air drying time will be needed. If you are in a hurry, however, you can set the oven on its lowest setting, put the horn on the middle rack and leave the oven door in its barely-open position 1 to 2 hours.

When it's dry, paint the horn with tempera or acrylics. Try to find a color photo to go by or make blended layers of light and dark gray, tan, or brown. Let dry. Seal with two coats of clear acrylic if you plan to pretend blowing it. Use your "shofar" for the ten days of Rosh Hashanah to Yom Kippur. It can rest among the centerpiece flags, or set beside it on the table if you decide to put a globe (see next craft) on the centerpiece.

1. Cone 12" high, 9" across, slightly rounded bottom. Cover edges with tape.

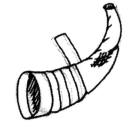

3. Wrap wet paper maché strips around, overlapping a bit as you go. Press layers together to conform to twisted shape and insure tight bond.

2. Stitch together, twist to resemble ram's horn (some have more curve than others).

4. Air or oven dry. Paint and dry.

5. Seal with 2 coats of clear acrylic spray. Let it dry out.

Create-a-World Craft

If you don't have a small globe, and want to use one on your centerpiece, you can make a simple facsimile yourself. It can be reused in connection with other school activities if you wish.

Purchase a <u>blue</u> 7" (approx.) foam rubber ball at a variety store (if blue is not available, mount ball on a tooth pick and insert it on a base heavier than the ball and spray paint). This size will fit comfortably between your flags. It can also be set on top of the Creation Ring (instructions follow).

Cut out simple continents from green or tan colored cloth. A teenager or older child may want to develop a relief map using green for the flat areas, and two or three shades such as light green, tan and brown for highlands and mountainous areas. Secure in position by wetting entire fabric map section in thinned craft glue. Suggested patterns are included in the following pages. Simplify further as needed for younger children. To make a relief map, see globe or encyclopedia for mountain and plateau areas.

Set the "South Pole" in the Spanish moss, on your centerpiece or atop the Creation Ring. You may also place it on a canning jar ring (underside up) to hold it in place.

When using your globe for the first time, an older child may want to give a dramatic reading of James Weldon Johnson's poem "Creation." This historical literature selection by an African American writer gives an intimate and interesting viewpoint to the account of creation.

1.) Pin through 5" square or larger cardboard. 2.) To make placement easier, wrap a thread in a straight line around the center of the ball and tie so it is snug but not pinching the foam ball. Use this "equator" as a guide for positioning continents. Glue the first continent over the knot. Place either South America or Africa first, then work around it (re-position ball on pin so that you are able to work on the top of the world each time you glue a continent). 3.) Leave in a safe place to dry (ball is not firm on this base, but will not roll).

Slits for overlapping to
accommodate for roundness
of foam rubber ball (globe).

This page left blank for tracing

Check Atlas for placement of
major islands. They are grouped
here for convenience.

This page left blank for tracing

Creation Ring

Use this ring to support your globe craft. If you choose not to make a globe, use it to close a vase of fall flowers, etc. A third option is to leave it in a long strip to display. To make the ring:

1. Use your color pencils to create excitement in the pictures below.

2. Cut out both strips and using rubber cement, secure them to a strip of poster board 16 inches long by 2¼ inches wide.

3. Overlap the extra inch on the poster board and staple or tape to secure.

4. Use this as a base for your creative world craft or for any other fun purposes you have in mind.

FLAP

THE SEVENTH DAY

THE THIRD DAY

THE SIXTH DAY

THE SECOND DAY

THE FIFTH DAY

THE FIRST DAY

THE FOURTH DAY

Heart of Wisdom Publishing
BiblicalHolidays.com

Each of the Biblical Jewish holidays teaches us about our wonderful relationship with God. His whole redemption story is portrayed for us in these festivals.

Paul wrote to the Gentiles believers in Col. 2:16-17 that the holidays, "are a shadow of the things to come."

Each of the springs holidays are a picture of Christ's first coming. Jesus was sacrificed for our sins on Passover, buried on unleavened bread and arose on Firstfruits.

The fall holidays are a picture of His second coming and the beginning of the Messianic reign.

The three fall holidays are: The Feast of Trumpets, Day of Atonement, and Feast of Tabernacles.

The Feast of Trumpets or Rosh Hashana is the seventh month of the religious calendar and the first month of the civil calendar.

The New Year is ushered in with the sound of a ram's horn.

It is traditional to eat apples dipped in honey on Rosh Hashana.

Wishing you a sweet New Year!

And the Lord spake unto Moses, saying,

Speak unto the children of Israel, saying,

In the seventh month, in the first day of the month,

shall ye have a sabbath,

a memorial of blowing of trumpets,

and holy convocation.

Ye shall do no servile work therein:

but ye shall offer an offering

made by fire unto the Lord

Leviticus 23:23-25

Happy New Year

A Sensible Story

Using all five senses, write a story to describe your favorite activities during this feast. This story can be written soon after the feast has happened. Remember to tell how things looked, sounded, smelled, tasted, and felt.

Shofar Number Network

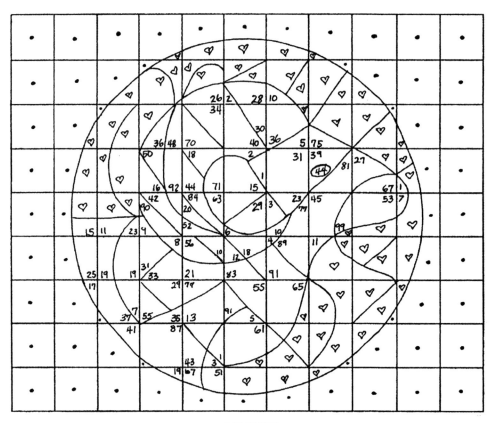

ABOVE

Color EVEN numbered areas gray. Leave ODD numbered areas white. make areas with ♥ blue. Color areas with • purple.

BELOW

Look at each number below. If it is EVEN, circle the letter in the even row. If it is ODD, circle the letter in the odd row. Put the letters in order on the lines at the bottom to discover who is being announced with a shofar. After working the puzzle, read Matthew 24:29-44 to see what is about to happen.

1	2	3	6	7	8	9	11	12	13	14	20	22	25	27	28	31	32	35	36	38
EVEN H	E	D	U	R	W	V	G	L	K	O	M	E	P	H	T	B	P	E	W	E
ODD J	O	S	K	S	Y	I	L	H	C	J	I	R	W	I	F	H	C	O	M	I

39	40	41	42	43	44	47	48	50
EVEN T	A	C	D	A	L	B	R	Y
ODD R	T	N	E	G	I	O	E	M

__ __ __ __ __ __ __ __ __ __ __ __ __ __,

__ __ __ __ __ __ __ __ __

__ __ __ __ __ __ __ __!

Painting The Universe

Make a recipe of this interesting, thick paint. Cover a large sheet of newsprint, shelf paper, or drawing paper well. A large 2" brush works best so you can cover the paper quickly. Use orange juice "sippers" (they have a zigzag piercing end that's great for twirling a pattern of several lines), pastry tools, fingernails and fingers to make swiggles, planets, moons, etc. Make a solar system replica or a galaxy. When you are finished, before it dries, scatter some silver glitter all around for background and stars. Wow!

DOODLE PAINT

½ cup all-purpose flour
½ cup liquid dish soap (not dishwasher)
¼ cup powdered tempera (or about 2 tbsps. liquid tempera)
½ cup water (or more)

Add sufficient water to make a thick gravy consistency.

This paint is similar to finger paint and can be used as such. Covering your page well allows for sharp designs in white to appear. Too thick of an application, however, may make the design hard to hold in white.

Note: You may use this procedure to make wrapping paper out of old desk calendar pages.

Crossword Puzzle

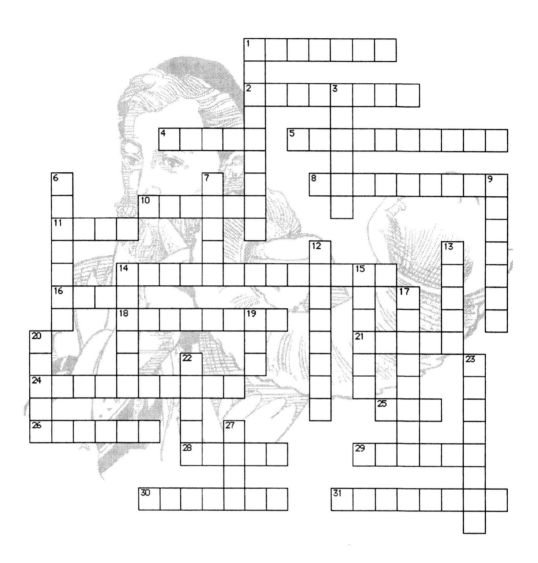

Across
1. First month
2. One of twelve
4. Serenity
5. Crowning ceremony
8. Covenant
10. Deeply sacred
11. Biblios
14. Morally upright
16. A prophet
18. An Act of God
21. Deluge
24. Dramatic disclosure
25. An upright man
26. Samuel's mother
28. His son was the oldest
29. First month
30. Sabbath
31. Remembrance

Down
1. Discernment
3. Jacob
6. Fiftieth year
7. A memorial
9. Musical wind instrument
12. God's created realm
13. The earth
14. The older was Leah, the younger was ___
15. Hebrew horn
17. Splendorous, magnificent
19. Antediluvian
20. She laughed at what Abraham said
22. Thirty-nine books, plus twenty-seven books
23. Based on God's Word
27. Crescent

Word Search

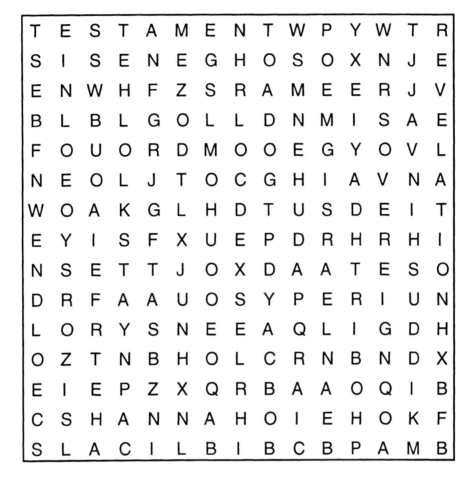

T	E	S	T	A	M	E	N	T	W	P	Y	W	T	R
S	I	S	E	N	E	G	H	O	S	O	X	N	J	E
E	N	W	H	F	Z	S	R	A	M	E	E	R	J	V
B	L	B	L	G	O	L	L	D	N	M	I	S	A	E
F	O	U	O	R	D	M	O	O	E	G	Y	O	V	L
N	E	O	L	J	T	O	C	G	H	I	A	V	N	A
W	O	A	K	G	L	H	D	T	U	S	D	E	I	T
E	Y	I	S	F	X	U	E	P	D	R	H	R	H	I
N	S	E	T	T	J	O	X	D	A	A	T	E	S	O
D	R	F	A	A	U	O	S	Y	P	E	R	I	U	N
L	O	R	Y	S	N	E	E	A	Q	L	I	G	D	H
O	Z	T	N	B	H	O	L	C	R	N	B	N	D	X
E	I	E	P	Z	X	Q	R	B	A	A	O	Q	I	B
C	S	H	A	N	N	A	H	O	I	E	H	O	K	F
S	L	A	C	I	L	B	I	B	C	B	P	A	M	B

BIBLE	JUDGMENT
BIBLICAL	KIDDUSHIN
BIRTHDAY	MOON
BOOK	OLD NEW
CITY	PEACE
CORONATION	PSALM
ELUL	REVELATION
ENOCH	RIGHTEOUSNESS
EZRA	ROSH
FEAST	SARAH
FLOOD	SOVEREIGN
GENESIS	TESTAMENT
HANNAH	WORLD
ISRAEL	YOM

Recipes

HONEY CAKE

Various versions of honey cake seem to be popular among Jews. Since apples dipped in honey are a customary treat at meal times, here is a recipe that uses both.

1 1/4 cup whole wheat flour	1 1/4 tsp. baking soda
1 tsp. cinnamon	1/4 cup barley flour
1/8 tsp. salt	1/2 tsp. nutmeg
1/4 cup oil	1 cup applesauce
1 egg white	1/2 to 2/3 cup honey

Mix all dry ingredients together and in a separate container mix all wet ingredients. Now combine the two, then pour into a greased 8" or 9" pan. Bake in preheated 325° oven for 30 to 35 minutes. Serve warm with an extra dollop of applesauce and sprinkle of cinnamon, or topped with whipped cream. It is also good as a snack plain, warmed with a little butter.

FESTIVE FEATURES

Foods that are customarily served at this feast are full of symbolism. A **round raisin challah** represents the desire of a sweet and full year of God's blessing. **Apples dipped in honey** repeat that theme and the incredible sweetness that comes from our Heavenly Father. The Hebrew word for **carrots** also means "increase," so carrots become a symbol for seeking God's abundant blessings in the new year. A **fish** cooked with the head on is symbolic of the time when Israel will become the "head and not the tail" (Deut. 28:13). Place it in front of father to represent his headship of your family, and his leadership under the Lord. Pray for him to have a year of "walking in Godly leadership." Fish in general biblical symbolism represent the souls of men. Christians can also think of a new year of people coming into the saving knowledge of Jesus Christ.

BIRTHDAY OF THE WORLD

For a special birthday party to honor God's creation, children can look through Mom's cookbooks and select something special, a multi-layered torte, specially filled or decorated cream puffs, or an exotic cheesecake... or a unique "creation" of your own. Remember the reason—you're making a memory!

A Family Guide to the Biblical Holidays ©

Coloring Page

Peace be within thy walls,
and prosperity within thy palaces.
Psalm 122:7

Day of Atonement

Yom Kippur

Purpose of the Day of Atonement

In the Bible, Yom Kippur bears three names: the Day of Atonement, the Day of Judgment, and the Sabbath of Sabbaths. Technically, Yom Kippur is not a feast in a traditional sense, but is so closley ted to Rosh HaShannah and the Biblical Hebrew calendar, we have decided to explain it. Yom Kippur occurs on the tenth day of Tishri. This is a holy day of the Lord that remains "a statute forever." Day of Atonement is the day in which the people of Israel are to be judged by God and the sins of the nation of Israel are atoned. The Day of Atonement is also referred to as "the Day of Redemption." This day pictures the transference of sin. It is a time of fasting, cleansing, and reflection which is to be observed once a year.

The Day of Atonement served as a reminder that the daily, weekly, and monthly sacrifices made at the altar of burnt offering were not sufficient to atone for sin. Even at the altar of burnt offering the worshipper stood "afar off," unable to approach the Holy Presence of God, who was manifest between the cherubim in the Holy of Holies. On this one day in the year, atoning blood was brought into the Holy of Holies, the divine throne room, by the high priest as the representative of the people (New Bible Dictionary).

It is customary to wear white on this holiday, which symbolizes purity and the promise that our sins shall be made as white as snow (Isa. 1:18). Some Jews wear a kitel, the white robe in which the dead are buried.

WEAKNESS OF THE LAW

The commandment itself explains the weakness of the law. *For the law having a shadow of good things to come, and not the very image of the things, can never with those sacrifices which they offered year by year continually make the comers thereunto perfect* (Heb. 10:1).

The Jew knew something was missing. There is a multitude of sacrifices. The sacrifices attempt to supplement one another but there is still something missing, because Hebrews 10:4 says: *For it is not possible that the blood of bulls and of goats should take away sins.* Obviously, this means of taking away sin was temporary. The sacrifices, are only a forerunner, like John the Baptist, or to prepare the way for the better hope (Edersheim 1994, 241) described in Hebrews 7:19: *For the law made nothing perfect, but the bringing in of a better hope did; by the which we draw nigh unto God.*

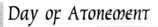

The Day of Atonement in Bible Times

The high priest is entirely responsible for the Day of Atonement. He began preparing for this day a week early. He stayed in the high priest chamber in the temple court and studied the laws of the Day of Atonement. It was very important the priest not make a mistake. An error could cost him his life and the nation of Israel's atonement. The high priest spoke a word this day that was unspeakable all other times. During the services he voiced the Holy name of God, YHWH or Yahweh ten times during the ceremony. When the people heard the Holy Name they fell on the ground in reverence.

The interior of Solomon's Temple was rectangular, about 35 feet wide and 140 feet long. It was divided into three parts. The priest would have entered the porch, which was about 17 feet deep. He would then pass through gilded Cyprus doors decorated with flowers, palm trees, and cherubim, and enter the main room of the Temple—often called the Holy Place. Beyond a set of olive wood doors lay the room no ordinary priest would ever see. This was the Holy of Holies. It was a perfect cube, with each side measuring nearly 35 feet. In it was the Ark, containing the two tablets of stone of the Ten Commandments (Guinness 1988).

The Holy of Holies was entered only once a year, on the Day of Atonement, when the high priest made atonement for the people.

This was the great solemn day that the high priest put aside his official robes and dressed in a simple white garment. To fulfill the law of the Bible, he wore eight garments on this day (Lev. 8:7; Ex. 28:33-35).

1. The golden crown on his forehead.
2. The breastplate on his heart.
3. The outer robe decorated with pomegranates and bells (the people listened for the bells while the priest was in the Holy of Holies to be sure the priest was still alive).
4. The apron or vest.
5. Four white garments made from white flax.
6. The belt.
7. The turban.
8. Pants.

He then offered a bullock as a sin-offering for himself and the priesthood. He would fill the censer with live coals from the altar, then enter into the Holy of Holies, where he placed incense on the coals. The incense sent forth a cloud of smoke over the mercy seat, which served as a covering for the ark of the covenant. The high priest took some of the blood of the bullock and sprinkled it on the mercy seat and on the ground in front of the ark cleansing them from defilement.

The burnt offerings were: seven male lambs, each a year old, one young bull, and one ram. The sin offering was one male goat. Every step the priest took was precisely scripted. According to the Talmud he made forty-three trips between the court and sanctuary on this respected day.

ORDER OF EVENTS

A Bible study by Greg Killian explains the high priest would:

1. Remove the ashes from the outer altar (1:8).
2. Immerse (baptize) himself for the first time. Put on the golden vestments (3:4).
3. Slaughter the daily morning elevation (burnt) offering (3:4).
4. Receive and throw the blood of the elevation (burnt) offering (3:4).
5. Prepare the five lamps of the menorah (3:4).
6. Offer the daily incense (3:5).
7. Prepare the remaining two lamps of the menorah.
8. Burn the limbs of the daily morning elevation (burnt) offering on the outer altar (3:4).
9. Offer the daily meal offering (3:4).
10. Offer the Chavitin offering (3:4).
11. Offer the wine libation (drink offering) (3:4).
12. Offer the Mussafim: The ox and the seven lambs - all elevation (burnt) offerings, along with their meal and drink offerings (7:3).
13. Immerse (baptize) himself for the second time and then don the linen vestments (3:6).
14. Do the first confession on the High Priest ox offering (3:8).
15. Draw the lots to select the he-goats for God and for Azazel (3:9, 4:1) [see the section titled "Two Goats" in the "Messianic Significance of the Day of Atonement" further in this chapter].

16. Do the second confession on the High Priest ox sin offering (4:2).

17. Slaughter his ox sin offering (4:3).

18. Perform the service of the special Yom HaKippurim incense: (a) scoop up some coal; (b) scoop up the incense into the ladle; (c) burn the incense in the Holy of Holies. This was his first entry into the Holy of Holies (4:3, 5:1-2).

19. Sprinkle the blood of his ox in the Holy of Holies. This was his second entry into the Holy of Holies (5:3).

20. Slaughter the he-goat for God (5:4).

21. Sprinkle the he-goat's blood in the Holy of Holies. This was his third entry into the Holy of Holies (5:4).

22. Sprinkle the blood of his ox on the curtain in the Holy place (5:4).

23. Sprinkle the he-goat's blood on the curtain in the Holy place (5:4).

24. Mix the blood of his ox and the he-goat (5:4).

25. Sprinkle the mixture on the inner altar (5:5-6).

26. Do the confession on the he-goat to Azazel and present the he-goat, to the designated person, for dispatch to azazel (6:2). This was not a sacrifice.

27. Remove the entrails of his ox and the he-goat and place them in a utensil (6:7).

28. Prepare the limbs of his ox and the he-goat for removal to the burning place (6:7).

29. Read from the Torah (7:1).

30. Immerse (baptize) himself for the third time, then don the golden vestments.

31. Perform the service of the he-goat sin offering of the Mussafim (7:3).

32. Offer his ram (7:3).

33. Offer the people's ram (7:3).

34. Burn the entrails of the ox and he-goat on the outer altar (6:7).

35. Immerse (baptize) himself for the fourth time, then don the linen vestments (7:5).

36. Remove the incense ladle and the shovel with burnt coals from the Holy of Holies. This was his fourth and final entry into the Holy of Holies (7:4).

37. Immerse (baptize) himself for the fifth time, then don the golden vestments (7:5).

38. Offer the daily afternoon elevation (burnt) offering (7:3).

39. Burn the daily afternoon incense (7:4).

40. Light the Menorah (7:5).

Ten times would the High Priest pronounce the Name of God on Yom Kippur: six times in connection with the bullock, three times in connection with the he-goat, and once in connection with the lots. Those who were near him would fall on their faces, and those who were far from him would say: "Blessed be His Name whose glorious kingdom is for ever and ever." Neither those who were near nor those who were far would move from their places until he had disappeared.

THE FAST

The fast, the penitential prayers, the Bible readings, the formulas of confession (viddu'i), and every part of the Atonement Day ritual emphasize this single theme—that would relieve one from the burden of sin—acknowledging the transgressions, declaring repentance through a process of confession, and then making atonement before God in order to obtain His forgiveness.

Yom Kippur is a time to atone for sin. While fasting is not explicitly mentioned, the Bible ordains for this day, "You shall afflict your souls" (Lev. 16:31; 23:27-32; Num. 29:7), and from early times the rabbis interpreted this to mean fasting. Part of the "affliction of the soul" included five statutory rules of mortification. These were abstention from: food and drink, marital relations, wearing leather shoes, using cosmetics and lotions, and washing any part of the body other than the fingers and eyes. The pleasure of such bodily comforts is seen as a prime source of opposing the "affliction of one's soul." In Biblical times, rending one's garments and putting on sackcloth and ashes were further signs of distress, accompanying abstention from food (Jonah 3:6; Ezek. 9:5). In other cases the fasting is clearly implied (Josh. 7:5-13; Jer. 6:26; Lam. 2:10).

Jewish Customs of the Day of Atonement Today

In modern Jewish usage the Day of Atonement, Yom Kippur, is the '10 Days of Awe' which began with The Feast of Trumpets (see previous chapter). This 10-day period is devoted to the spiritual exercises of penitence, prayer and fasting in preparation for the most solemn day of the year, the Day of Atonement.

The number ten (10) symbolizes perfect holiness as the aim on the most sacred day of the year. The Ten Days of Repentance are concluded on the tenth of Tishri. The Viddui (Confession of Sins) begins with an immersion (baptism) of repentance, and is recited ten times on the Day of the Atonement to coincide with the tradition that the High Priest pronounced the Name of God ten times when he invoked divine pardon on Yom HaKippurim. Yom HaKippurim also recalls the Ten Commandments, which serve as advocates before the Supreme Judge in behalf of the children of Israel, who accepted them with love after the nations of the world refused them (Killian n.d.).

Many Jews who do not observe any other Jewish custom will refrain from work, fast and attend synagogue services on The Day of Atonement. In modern Israel, this day is the one day in the year when restaurants, places of entertainment, stores, offices, factories, and even the radio and television close down for more than 24 hours.

The sacrificial aspects of the Day of Atonement have not been in effect since the destruction of the Temple; however, Jews still observe the day by fasting and refraining from all types of work. It is the only Jewish fast day that is never postponed if it coincides with a Sabbath. Everyone is permitted in the synagogue for the Day of Atonement, even those who have been previously barred. Just the presence of someone confirms their desire to make amends.

Fasting in Jewish tradition is a religious discipline involving the abstention from food, drink, and physical pleasures, for the purpose of enhancing spiritual experience in atonement for sin, in commemoration of national tragedies, or as part of a personal petition to God in seeking His help.

Various rabbinical laws are associated with fasting. The mandatory fasts have to be observed by all males over the age of 13 and females over the age of 12. In order to train the religious loyalty and self-discipline of younger people, the rabbis encouraged youngsters below those ages to observe partial fasts. Fasting is not done in order to rebuke oneself, but simply to focus the mind on the occasion. To the Jews, entertainment of any sort on a fast day is inappropriate. The denial of pleasurable acts during Yom Kippur was designed to focus on moral purification to cause total dedication to the pursuit of moral character rather than bodily comforts. Sick people may take medicine and small amounts of food and drink, on the advice of their doctors or rabbis. Those who are ill may even be forbidden to fast altogether.

THE EVE OF THE DAY OF ATONEMENT

A special meal is prepared to be eaten before sundown. The meal shows that enjoyment as well as deprivation can be the expression of holiness and that both have their place in the Jewish concept of holiness. Jews fast for twenty-five hours on Yom Kippur to help them to direct their thoughts to their spiritual rather than to their physical needs. Since one does not eat on Yom Kippur, the meal is eaten earlier than usual and then the candles are lit to begin the festival. Many families bless their children (parents, spouse) after the meal, prior to the departure for the synagogue.

The Day of Atonement starts, like Sabbath, at sundown, and there is a long evening service called *Kol Nidre*, as well as services throughout the day. The shofar, or ram's horn, is blown to assemble the people for worship in the synagogue. The impressive *Kol Nidre* (all vows) service is chanted (some synagogues hold the Kol Nidre the next day). This special prayer is sung to a sorrowful, traditional melody asking for forgiveness from God for breaking the vows which they were unable to fulfill. A rabbinical decree of reprieve is declared three times.

It is customary to wear white on the holiday, which symbolizes purity and calls to mind the promise that our sins shall be made as white as snow (Isa. 1:18). The furnishings in the synagogue are also draped in white (as on the Feast of Trumpets). The customary greeting for the day is: *"Gemar Hatimah Tovah"*–may you be finally sealed for good (in the Book of Life).

It is a custom (now only among the very Orthodox) to spend the night in synagogue reciting the entire Book of Psalms and other readings. Sephardi and Reform Jews recite memorial prayers on this night.

ON THE DAY OF ATONEMENT

Five services are held on the Day of Atonement, beginning with the initial evening service. Soon after, the fast commences, proceeding with festive morning, and afternoon prayers, and ending with the concluding service. Each service has its own special features and individual liturgy. Common to all of them, however, is the confession of sins. The confessions are written in the first person plural to emphasize shared responsibility for the individual, and the individual's responsibility for his community.

Services are held on the Day of Atonement from early morning until night. At sunset the day is ended by a single blast of the shofar, after which the worshippers return to their homes. In the thirteenth century a custom was established to open the Ark replica and remove two scrolls held by two individuals on either side of the reader. These three men compose a judicial court and proclaim the prayer the offenders are to recite. In most Jewish communities the doors of the Ark remain open and worshippers stand throughout the service.

IN THE HOME

A special memorial light is kindled to burn throughout the day and leather shoes are replaced by non-leather shoes or slippers before worshippers leave for the synagogue. The tallit prayer shawl is worn continuously at all services, including those held after dark. Since the color white is a traditional symbol of purity and forgiveness, a white curtain adorns the synagogue (Encyclopedia of Judaism).

A widespread custom is for construction of the sukkah (see Feast of Tabernacles in the next chapter) to begin at home, once people have broken their fast.

Messianic Significance of the Day of Atonement

Christians know that Jesus has provided our atonement: *"...for all have sinned and come short of the glory of God; being justified freely by his grace through the redemption that is in Christ Jesus"* (Rom. 2:23-24). God presented Him as a sacrifice of atonement, through faith in His blood. Jesus' death surpasses and replaces the atonement ritual of the Jewish Temple. The book of Hebrews explains the ceremonies of the Day of Atonement as a pattern of the atoning work of Christ. Jesus is our high priest, and His blood shed on Calvary is seen as symbolized in the blood of bulls and goats. As the high priest of the Old Testament entered the Holy of Holies with the blood of his sacrificial victim, so Jesus entered heaven itself to appear before the Father on behalf of His people (Heb. 9:11-12) (Killian n.d.).

The Old Testament tabernacle was designed, in part, to teach Israel that sin hindered access to the presence of God. Only the high priest, and he only once a year, could enter the Holy of Holies, and then not without taking blood offered to atone for sins (Heb. 9:7). Hebrews notes that the levitical offerings could effect only the purification of the flesh. They ceremonially cleansed the sinner, but they could not bring about inward cleansing, the prerequisite for fellowship with God. Just as the high priest had to be sinless to enter the Holy of Holies and live, so Yeshua had to be sinless to live after He entered the grave.

But Christ being come an high priest of good things to come, by a greater and more perfect tabernacle, not made with hands, that is to say, not of this building; Neither by the blood of goats and calves, but by his own blood he entered in once into the holy place, having obtained eternal redemption for us. For if the blood of bulls and of goats, and the ashes of an heifer sprinkling the unclean, sanctifieth to the purifying of the flesh: How much more shall the blood of Christ, who through the eternal Spirit offered himself without spot to God, purge your conscience from dead works to serve the living God (Heb. 9:11-14).

The high priest had to offer sin offerings each year for his own sins and the sins of the people. This annual repetition of the sacrifices served as a reminder that perfect atonement had not yet been provided. Jesus, however, through His own blood effected eternal redemption for His people (Heb. 9:12).

The Old Testament offerings served as a pattern and a prophecy of Jesus, who, through His better sacrifice, cleanses the conscience from dead works (Heb. 9:13-14). God always determined what was an acceptable offering and what was not. He finally provided His Son, the Lamb of God, as the sacrifice for the sins of the world (John 1:19; 3:16).

The moment Jesus died, the veil of the temple was torn in two, from top to bottom (Matt. 27:50-51). The earth quaked beneath men's feet. This event is important because it established Jesus as being the new High Priest and Lamb of God. No longer must there be an annual sacrifice for sin on our behalf; instead, He has made payment for us once and for all. Jesus, through a new and living way has entered heaven itself, the true Holy of Holies, where He ever lives to make intercession for His people. The believer need not stand afar off, as did the Israelite of old, but may now through Christ approach the very Throne of Grace! Yes, it is now possible for each of us to have direct access to God through the blood of Yeshua HaMashiah (Jesus Christ)!

THE TWO GOATS

After purifying the holy place and the altar of burnt offering with the mingled blood of the bullock, the High Priest went to the eastern side of the court in front of the Temple. Facing him were two identical goats. Nearby was a lottery box especially designed for this ceremony. In the box were two tablets (lots). One bore the name "For God," the other "For azazel" (the scapegoat). The high priest shook the box and withdrew the tablets, putting one tablet in front of each goat. The goat labeled "for God" was sacrificed. The priest laid his hands upon the goat's head labeled "for azazel" and confessed over it the sins of Israel. The scapegoat symbolically bore the sins of the nation of Israel away from the people. This goat, commonly called the scapegoat (*i.e.* escape goat), was then driven into the desert.

In the same way Jesus was brought before Pilate and stood before the people just as He was about to be led forth, bearing the iniquities of the people. These two goats were required for one sacrifice (Lev 16:17, 21-22). Both sacrifices were fulfilled in the death and resurrection of Messiah Yeshua. How can resurrection be portrayed in a sacrifice? By using two animals, one killed, the other set free, representing Jesus' death and resurrection.

And he shall take the two goats, and present them before the LORD at the door of the tabernacle of the congregation. And Aaron shall cast lots upon the two goats; one lot for the LORD, and the other lot for the scapegoat. And Aaron shall bring the goat upon which the LORD'S lot fell, and offer him for a sin offering. But the goat, on which the lot fell to be the scapegoat, shall be presented alive before the LORD, to make an atonement with him, and to let him go for a scapegoat into the wilderness (Lev. 16:7-10).

And he shall go out unto the altar that is before the LORD, and make an atonement for it; and shall take of the blood of the bullock, and of the blood of the goat, and put it upon the horns of the altar round about. And the goat shall bear upon him all their iniquities unto a land not inhabited: and he shall let go the goat in the wilderness (Lev. 16:18, 22).

Tradition states that a cord of red wool was tied on the horn of the scapegoat, before it was let go in the wilderness. When the red wool turned white, it was a sign that God forgave the people's sin. *Come now, and let us reason together, saith the LORD: though your sins be as scarlet, they shall be as white as snow; though they be red like crimson, they shall be as wool* (Isa. 1:18).

The Priests used to bind a shining crimson strip of cloth on the outside door of the Temple. If the strip of cloth turned into the white color, they would rejoice; if it did not turn white they were full of sorrow and shame (Tractate Yoma 67a).

Jewish literature explains the Shekhina glory of God left the Temple forty years prior to its destruction. Three signs occurred to show evidence of this: 1.) The western candle of the menorah refused to burn continually. 2.) The doors of the Temple would open of themselves. 3.) The red wool no longer turned white supernaturally. This is especially significant because it indicated that God was no longer forgiving the sins of His people. The people were sorrowful because they began to realize more and more that the sacrifice of Yom Kippur did not have the power to cleanse their sinful hearts. That very year Jesus was crucified, the very year that the blood of bulls and goats was no longer accepted as a sacrifice for the atonement of sin!

PROPHETIC SIGNIFICANCE

The Second Coming or Judgment?

The entire ten days from the first day of the Feast of Trumpets through the Day of Atonement are known as Days of Repentance or Days of Awe. These days are possibly a picture of the Rapture (Feast of Trumpets), the Tribulation (days in between), and the second coming (Day of Atonement). Another theory claims these are a picture of the Second Coming (Feast of Trumpets), the Judgment (Day of Atonement).

Second Coming?

Our Messiah made two promises before He returned to our Father. He would send the Comforter (Pentecost) and He would come again. *And if I go and prepare a place for you, I will come again, and receive you unto myself; that where I am, there ye may be also* (John 14:3). The Day of Atonement just may be the day of the Second Coming when Jesus will physically return to earth! The Bible clearly states Jesus will return immediately after the great tribulation. *But in those days, after that tribulation, the sun shall be darkened, and the moon shall not give its light, and the stars will be falling from heaven, and the powers that are in the heavens will be shaken. And then they will see the Son of Man coming in clouds with great power and glory* (Mark 13:24-26).

Day of Judgment?

The apostle Peter wrote about this awesome day of judgment. He declared, "But the day of the Lord will come like a thief. The heavens will disappear with a roar; the elements will be destroyed by fire, and the earth and everything in it will be laid bare. Since everything will be destroyed in this way, what kind of people ought you to be? You ought to live holy and godly lives as you look forward to the day of God and speed its coming."

But the day of the Lord will come as a thief in the night; in the which the heavens shall pass away with a great noise, and the elements shall melt with fervent heat, the earth also and the works that are therein shall be burned up. Seeing then that all these things shall be dissolved, what manner of persons ought ye to be in all holy conversation and godliness, Looking for and hasting unto the coming of the day of God, wherein the heavens being on fire shall be dissolved, and the elements shall melt with fervent heat? Nevertheless we, according to his promise, look for new heavens and a new earth, wherein dwelleth righteousness (2 Peter 3:10-13).

When the Son of man shall come in his glory, and all the holy angels with him, then shall he sit upon the throne of his glory: And before him shall be gathered all nations: and he shall separate them one from another, as a shepherd divideth his sheep from the goats: And he shall set the sheep on his right hand, but the goats on the left. Then shall the King say unto them on his right hand, Come, ye blessed of my Father, inherit the kingdom prepared for you from the foundation of the world (Matt. 25:31-34).

For we must all appear before the judgment seat of Christ; that every one may receive the things done in his body, according to that he hath done, whether it be good or bad (2 Cor. 5:10).

In the coming judgment, there is forgiveness and mercy and grace to those who have already received Jesus Christ our Lord and Savior, Who gave His life as a ransom for us! *Therefore being justified by faith, we have peace with God through our Lord Jesus Christ: By whom also we have access by faith into this grace wherein we stand, and rejoice in hope of the glory of God* (Rom. 5:1-2).

Suggestions for the Day of Atonement

EVENING MEAL

Before sundown, the day before the Day of Atonement, have a special light meal to prepare for the fast. After dinner, light the candles and say a blessing to begin the festival.

BLESS YOUR FAMILY

Many families bless their children (parents, spouse) after the meal. Say a prayer over each of your children praying specifically for their needs, gifts, and talents.

FAST

Traditionally the fast lasts for twenty-five hours. Children, pregnant women, and the elderly may want to try a "Daniel Fast" and only eat vegetables (Dan. 1:12-15) and water for the twenty-five hours. Spend time in prayer asking for forgiveness and praising God.

STUDY THE TABERNACLE AND TEMPLE

The Holy of Holies was so sacred that only the high priest could enter in, and only one day of the year, The Day of Atonement. To explain the dimensions and design of the temple would take another book. Sir Isaac Newton wrote volumes about Solomon's Temple. There are several good, illustrated books available from Christian bookstores about the symbolism of the Tabernacle and Temple and how each item relates to Christ.

WORSHIP

Find Psalms that you may have sung or sing other songs about forgiveness. Spend some time in personal prayer. A Bible concordance may be helpful in collecting verses related to forgiveness and atonement (a clue to the meaning is "at-one-ment").

PRAY FOR JERUSALEM

Another interesting idea to incorporate is a time of prayer for the nation of Israel (Rom. 10:1). This is once in the year when Jews the world over are packed into synagogues. Pray for light to come and the reality of Yeshua the Messiah to enter their hearts. The fasting and prayer are sure to make your gathering special.

BURN A CANDLE

Burn a large, white twenty-four-hour candle all day.

MUSIC

Play a music tape such as *Arise, O Lord* by Israel's Hope, which also contains other selections like "Shalom, Jerusalem," and "Holy, Holy, Holy." Or play a Scripture-based song collection by Marty Goetz or other similar artists.

OTHER READINGS

Reading *In His Steps* is an excellent choice to stimulate family discussions. It comes in original and abbreviated (pictorial) versions, and a children's adaptation. Richard Booker's *The Miracle of the Scarlet Thread* is an excellent choice for adult or older teen reading. You may need all the Days of Awe to complete the longer book choices. Begin now in anticipation of discussions on Day of Atonement.

Centerpiece

To change your centerpiece for Day of Atonement, replace **Ten Commandments** flag with **Cross** flag to remind that our Righteous Judge is also our Savior (Heb. 10). Use the **Dove flag** to replace **Cup & Bread** flag to remind of the fasting from food and inviting the presence of the Holy Spirit on this day of soul searching. Replace the **Shofar** with your large **white candle**. (If you can't keep an eye on it, get one made inside a glass container.) If your family is fasting, you may want to consider relocating the entire centerpiece away from the dining area to the room where you can see it.

SYMBOLISM IN THE CENTERPIECE

White candle—purity and light, the cleansing presence of the Holy Spirit within our hearts and minds on this day.

Cross and **Dove** flags—explained above. For further scriptures see Unleavened Bread and Pentecost centerpiece symbol sections.

The Secret Scroll Message

Use Morse Code to break the mystery on the scroll below.

MORSE CODE

A •-   B -•••   C -••   D -••   E •   F •••-   G ---   H ••••   I ••
J •---   K -•-   L •-••   M --   N -•   O ---   P •--•   Q ---•-   R •-•
S •••   T -   U ••-   V •••-   W •--   X -••-   Y -•--   Z --••

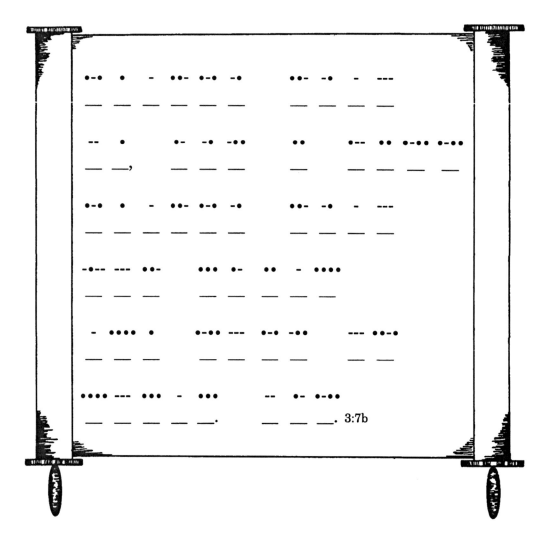

3:7b

Crossword Puzzle

Across

1. Of great elevation
3. Destroyed by fire
5. Male bovine mammals
7. Compassionate treatment
11. Head covering made of precious metals and jewels
13. Bovine mammal
14. Aromatic substance burned for its odor
15. Oil vessels that generate light
16. Young cow
17. Violation of a law
24. Only through the ___
25. Chest containing the Ten Commandments
27. A servant, administrator
28. The king's chair
29. A long, loose, flowing outer garment
30. Rule of conduct
31. Powdery residue left when something is burned
33. Perpetual, changeless, forever
34. A piece of armor that covers the chest

(Across 24 continues: "of the Temple")

Down

2. Worthy of worship
3. A flexible band worn around the waist
4. Members of the northern Semitic people
6. Surrendering something highly valued
7. A nine-branched candelabrum
8. Of lustrous, radiant, yellowish color
9. Yom ___
10. Color of purity
12. Precious gems
17. Moslem headdress
18. Integers
19. Domestic, bearded mammal
20. To scatter
21. A petroleum derivative
22. Holy of ___
23. To cleanse or purify
26. A primary color
32. A chair or bench

Word Search

```
N B T G T S E I R P H J L B F
L E L N O M L I O G I A R H J
N A D O R A Z L I N N E A E N
H O M L O U T H C R A R W W N
N O I P O D B E E S O E O L U
A C L S S G N T T N L R J A M
B N W Y S S E P E S C L I W B
R X Q R E E L M M S W T L O E
U O O B S A R B S O E H A G R
T B E L T H K G A W D I I E S
E L L E E A M I S P E G L T S
T U K I S E P O P N T R N O E
B R F H R E D E R P A I B I H
A E E C T H R O N E U R Z E K
R S Y C H E R U B I M R T E H
```

ARK	GOLDEN	MERCY
ASHES	HEBREWS	NUMBERS
BAPTIZE	HEIFER	OIL
BELT	HIGH	OX
BLOOD	HOLIES	PRIEST
BREASTPLATE	HOLY	RED
BULLS	INCENSE	ROBE
BURNT	JEWELS	SEAT
CHERUBIM	KINGDOM	THRONE
CROWN	KIPPUR	TRANSGRESSION
ETERNAL	LAMPS	TURBAN
GOAT	LAW	WHITE
	MENORAH	

Coloring Page

Add a red cord to one goat's neck.

For my brethren and companions' sakes,
I will now say, Peace be within thee.

Psalm 122:8

342

Feast of Tabernacles

Sukkoth

Purpose of the Feast of Tabernacles

The Feast of Tabernacles is a week-long autumn harvest festival. Tabernacles is also known as the Feast of the Ingathering, Sukkoth, Succoth, or Sukkot (variations in spellings occur because these words are transliterations of the Hebrew word pronounced "Sue-*coat*"). The two days following the festival are separate holidays, Shemini Atzeret and Simkhat Torah, but are commonly thought of as part of the Feast of Tabernacles.

The Feast of Tabernacles was the final and most important holiday of the year. The importance of this festival is indicated by the statement, *"This is to be a lasting ordinance."* The divine pronouncement, *"I am the Lord your God,"* concludes this section on the holidays of the seventh month. The Feast of Tabernacles begins five days after Yom Kippur on the fifteenth of Tishri (September or October). It is a drastic change from one of the most solemn holidays in our year to one of the most joyous. The word *sukkoth* means "booths," and refers to the temporary dwellings that Jews are commanded to live in during this holiday, just as the Jews did in the wilderness. The Feast of Tabernacles lasts for seven days and ends on the twenty-first day (3x7) of the Hebrew month of Tishri, which is Israel's seventh month.

This holiday has a dual significance: historical and agricultural (just as Passover and Pentecost). Historically, it was to be kept in remembrance of the dwelling in tents in the wilderness for the forty-year period during which the children of Israel were wandering in the desert.

It is expounded in Leviticus 23:43 *That your generations may know that I made the children of Israel to dwell in booths, when I brought them out of the land of Egypt: I am the LORD your God.*

What were they to remember? Matthew Henry's commentary explains,

> 1.) The meanness of their beginning, and the low and desolate state out of which God advanced that people. Note: Those that are comfortably fixed ought often to call to mind their former unsettled state, when they were but little in their own eyes. 2.) The mercy of God to them, that, when they dwelt in tabernacles, God not only set up a tabernacle for Himself among them, but, with the utmost care and tenderness imaginable, hung a canopy over them, even the cloud that sheltered them from the heat of the sun. God's former

mercies to us and our fathers ought to be kept in everlasting remembrance. The eighth day was the great day of this holiday, because then they returned to their own houses again, and remembered how, after they had long dwelt in tents in the wilderness, at length they came to a happy settlement in the land of promise, where they dwelt in goodly houses. And they would the more sensibly value and be thankful for the comforts and conveniences of their houses when they had been seven days dwelling in booths. It is good for those that have ease and plenty sometimes to learn what it is to endure hardness.

They were to keep this holiday in thankfulness to God for all the increase of the year; however, the emphasis is that Israel's life rested upon redemption which in its ultimate meaning is the forgiveness of sin. This fact separates this holiday from the harvest festivals of the neighboring nations whose roots lay in the mythological activity of the gods.

WAS THE FIRST THANKSGIVING A FEAST OF TABERNACLES CELEBRATION?

Many Americans, upon seeing a decorated sukkah for the first time, remark on how much the sukkah (and the holiday generally) reminds them of Thanksgiving. The American pilgrims, who originated the Thanksgiving holiday, were deeply religious people. As they were trying to find a way to express their thanks for their survival and for the harvest, it is quite possible that they looked to the Bible (Leviticus 23:39) for an appropriate way of celebrating and based their holiday in part on the Feast of Tabernacles.

Note: celebrating Thanksgiving on the third Thursday of November was established by the American government and may not necessarily coincide with the pilgrim's first observance.

The Feast of Tabernacles in Bible Times

As The Feast of Tabernacles approached, the entire Jewish nation started making preparations. Work crews were sent to repair roads and bridges for the thousands of pilgrims coming to Jerusalem. During the festival many Jews eat (and sleep, as well) in the booths or huts, which are built in the five days between Yom Kippur and this festival.

The Feast of Tabernacles is by far the most festive and joyous of occasions. History records that four huge candelabra were constructed, lighted, and attended by young men ascending ladders periodically with pitchers of oil to keep them burning. The light from these lamps illuminated the whole city, and around them danced distinguished men with torches in their hands, singing hymns and songs of praise. The dancing as well as the music continued until daybreak. It was an extravaganza (Somerville 1995).

The holiday was celebrated following the outline in Leviticus:

- They lived in booths made of boughs of trees and branches of palm trees for the seven days of the feast (Lev. 23:42).

- They rested from all regular work on the first and eighth days.

- The Priest offered sacrifices on the seven days, beginning with thirteen bullocks and other animals on the first day and diminishing by one bullock each day until, on the seventh, seven bullocks were offered.

- On the eighth day there was a solemn assembly when one bullock, one ram, and seven lambs were offered (Num. 29:36). The sacrifices offered during this time amounted to 189 animals.

- Men carried the cluster of branches to the synagogue to wave as they rejoiced before the Lord, as commanded by the Lord (Lev. 23:40).

Water was also an important part of the Feast of Tabernacles. Before the festival, the Rabbis taught on every passage in Scripture dealing with water. In Old Testament Biblical times, gold pitchers of water were brought from the pool of Siloam to the temple. The Priest would pour out the water over the altar to signify Israel's gratitude for the rain that had produced the harvest, and would pray for rain in the next year. The priest would recite Isaiah 12:1-3. *And in that day thou shalt say, O LORD, I will praise thee: though thou wast angry with me, thine anger is turned away, and thou comfortedst me. Behold, God is my salvation; I will trust, and not be afraid: for the LORD JEHOVAH is my strength and my song; he also is become my salvation. Therefore with joy shall ye draw water out of the wells of salvation.* This special libation was performed *only* during the seven days of the Feast of Tabernacles. This was done not only to remind God of the need for abundant rain during the winter season, but also to remind the people of the coming Messiah who had promised to pour out His Holy Spirit on the people.

This ceremony lasted seven days. The last day was called Hosha'na Rabba, meaning the Day of the Great Hosanna. As the celebration continued, the priests blew the trumpets and waved the branches and the people sang the Great Hallel (Psalms 113 through 118).

Jewish Customs of Tabernacles Today

The services in the synagogue today are modeled after the ancient services in the Temple (see Feast of Tabernacles in Bible Times). Sacrifices are no longer performed since the time of the destruction of the Temple.

It is usual practice to build and decorate the booth (sukkah). In the United States, Jews usually hang dried squash and corn in the sukkah to decorate it because these vegetables are readily available in the fall.

LULAV

Jewish tradition calls for a lulav (Four Species) made of a palm, myrtle, willow and fruit from the citron to be waved. The rabbis insist this is the only accepted lulav; however Scripture says, *"And ye shall take you on the first day the boughs of goodly trees, branches of palm trees, and the boughs of thick trees, and willows of the brook..." (Lev. 23:40).*

When Ezra reinstated the feasts, Nehemiah 8:15, he used olive branches. *And that they should publish and proclaim in all their cities, and in Jerusalem, saying, Go forth unto the mount, and fetch olive branches, and pine branches, and myrtle branches, and palm branches, and branches of thick trees, to make booths, as it is written.*

The Hebrew word for "goodly" in the verse in Leviticus above is *hadar* {haw-dawr'} [01926] meaning "ornament," "splendor," or "honor." The Hebrew word for "palm" in this verse is *tamar* {taw-mawr'} [8558] meaning "palm tree" or "date palm." The Hebrew word for "bough" in this verse is `anaph {aw-nawf'} [06057] meaning "bough" or "branch." The Hebrew word for "willows" in this verse is `arab {aw-rawb'} [06155] meaning "poplar, willow or a tree characterized by dark wood."

There is thought to be spiritual significance based on the characteristics of the lulav and citron:

> The palm bears fruit (deeds) but is not fragrant (spiritual blessing). This is like a person who lives by the letter of the law but does not have compassion or love for others.

> The myrtle only has fragrance, but can't bear fruit. This is like a person who is "so heavenly minded he is no earthly good." He (or she) may recite scripture, but he doesn't produce fruit.

The willow can neither produce fruit nor fragrance. This is like a person who is intrigued by different doctrines but never produces fruit.

The citron creates both fruit and fragrance. This is like a faithful believer who lives a balanced life in wisdom before God and man. Believers should strive to be like the citron.

THE TRADITION OF WAVING THE LULAV

1. While standing, the person picks up the lulav with its attached willows and myrtle in his right hand, holding the lulav so that its spine is toward them.

2. The etrog is picked up in the left hand, next to the lulav, with its tip (pitom) pointing down.

3. The blessings are said: "Blessed are You, O Lord our God, King of the universe, who has sanctified us by His commandments, and instructed us concerning the waving of the palm branch." Then the shehekeyanu is said: "Blessed are You, O Lord our God, King of the universe, for keeping us in life, for sustaining us, and for helping us reach this day."

4. The etrog is then turned right side up and shaken with the lulav.

Each day of the Feast of Tabernacles, the people in the Temple courtyard would hold their lulavs and make a circular procession around the altar. During the procession they would pray a prayer that came to be known as *Hoshanos.* It is a prayer for God's blessing, ending each phrase of the prayer with the word *hoshana* ("Please save" or "save now!"). On the first six days they would march around the altar one time. On the seventh day they marched around it seven times. Traditionally, Psalm 27 is recited at the service of the Feast of Tabernacles.

Bible prophecy tells us that people from the nations of the world will come up to celebrate the Feast of Tabernacles with the Jewish people in Jerusalem *And it shall be, that whoso will not come up of all the families of the earth unto Jerusalem to worship the King, the LORD of hosts... (Zech. 14:17).*

Messianic Significance of Tabernacles

JESUS CELEBRATED THE FEAST OF TABERNACLES

Jesus celebrated the Feast of Tabernacles. He taught in the Temple on the Feast of Tabernacles. Although His disciples had not expected Jesus to attend the feast, the vast majority of the pilgrims from afar who had heard of Him entertained the hope that they might see Him at Jerusalem. They were not disappointed, for on several occasions He taught in Solomon's Porch and elsewhere in the temple courts. These teachings were really the official or formal announcement of the divinity of Jesus to the Jewish people and to the whole world. Jesus risked His life to go to the Feast of Tabernacles, but the audacious boldness of Jesus in publicly appearing in Jerusalem over-awed his enemies; they were not prepared for such a daring challenge.

On the last day and greatest day of the Feast of Tabernacles (the day the Rabbis poured the water) Jesus stood (calling special attention to his message) and proclaimed Himself the very fountain of living water in John 7:37-38.

SPIRITUAL LESSONS FROM THE FEAST OF TABERNACLES
God is Our Shelter

This holiday reminds us not to hold too tightly to material things. We live in a very materialistic age. When the Israelites were wanderers in the desert, they all lived in tents—rich and poor alike. Material possessions can control and manipulate us; they become gods, or idols, over us. We must remember that this life is only temporary. We are also on a pilgrimage to a Promised Land in eternity. We need to seek God's kingdom, not earthly comfort. As we seek first the Kingdom of God (Luke 12:31), God is our shelter. *For thou hast been a strength to the poor, a strength to the needy in his distress, a refuge from the storm, a shadow from the heat, when the blast of the terrible ones is as a storm against the wall* (Isa. 25:4).

Jesus is the Living Water

Our spiritual thirst cannot be quenched with anything less than Christ. *But whosoever drinketh of the water that I shall give him shall never thirst; but the water that I shall give him shall be in him a well of water springing up into everlasting life* (John 4:14).

Jesus Washes Away Our Sins

Jesus is the true living water cleansing us from sin through His blood. *For if the blood of bulls and of goats, and the ashes of an heifer sprinkling the unclean, sanctifieth to the purifying of the flesh: How much more shall the blood of Christ, who through the eternal Spirit offered himself without spot to God, purge your conscience from dead works to serve the living God* (Heb. 9:13-14).

Jesus is the Light of the World

The light from the Feast of Tabernacles lamps illuminated the whole city. Scholars suggest that Jesus referred to this custom when he spoke those well-known words, *"I am the light of the world..."* (John 8:12) Also see John 1:1-9 and John 9:5.

Jesus is Preparing Our Permanent Home

These physical bodies we now occupy are only temporary dwelling places. Our bodies are frail, and will eventually begin to deteriorate. Life is short. Our hope is not in what the world has to offer, but in what God has already provided for us for eternity. Our permanent home is being prepared for us in eternity. Jesus said in John 14:2-3, *In my Father's house are many mansions: if it were not so, I would have told you. I go to prepare a place for you. And if I go and prepare a place for you, I will come again, and receive you unto myself; that where I am, there ye may be also.*

As the Israelites Left Bondage, We Leave the Bondage of Sin

God brought the Children of Israel out of the bondage of their Egyptian taskmasters into freedom. For Christians, we can celebrate that God redeemed us from a life of bondage to sin and brought us into His freedom in the Kingdom of God.

Was the Birth of Christ during the Feast of Tabernacles?

Many scholars believe Jesus was born during the Feast of Tabernacles. Matthew Henry states:

> It is supposed by many that our blessed Saviour was born much about the time of this holiday; then He left his mansions of light above to tabernacle among us (John 1:14), and he dwelt in booths. And the worship of God under the New Testament is prophesied of

under the notion of keeping the feast of tabernacles, Zec.14:16. For, [1.] The gospel of Christ teaches us to dwell in tabernacles, to sit loose to this world, as those that have here no continuing city, but by faith, and hope and holy contempt of present things, to go out to Christ without the camp, Heb. 13:13, 14. [2.] It teaches us to rejoice before the Lord our God. Those are the circumcision, Israelites indeed, that always rejoice in Christ Jesus, Phil. 3:3. And the more we are taken off from this world the less liable we are to the interruption of our joys.

The Bible does not specifically say the date of Jesus' birth. We know it was not during the winter months because the sheep were in the pasture (Luke 2:8). A study of the time of the conception of John the Baptist reveals he was conceived about Sivan 30, the eleventh week.

When Zechariah was ministering in the temple, he received an announcement from God of a coming son. The eighth course of Abia, when Zekharya was ministering, was the week of Sivan 12 to 18 (Killian n.d.). Adding forty weeks for a normal pregnancy reveals that John the Baptist was born on or about Passover (Nisan 14). We know six months after John's conception, Mary conceived Jesus (Luke 1:26-33). Therefore, Jesus would have been conceived six months later in the month of Kislev. Kislev 25 is Hanukkah. Was the "light of the world" conceived on the festival of lights?

Starting at Hanukkah, which begins on Kislev 25 and continues for eight days, and counting through the nine months of Mary's pregnancy, one arrives at the approximate time of the birth of Jesus at the Festival of Tabernacles (the early fall of the year).

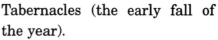

During the Feast of Tabernacles, God required all male Jews to come to Jerusalem. The many pilgrims coming to Jerusalem for the festivals would spill over to the surrounding towns (Bethlehem is about five miles from Jerusalem). Joseph and Mary were unable to find a room at the inn because of the influx of so many pilgrims. They may have been given shelter in a sukkah, which is built during a seven-day period each year accompanying the celebration of the Feast of Tabernacles. Due to the difficulties during travel, it was common for the officials to declare tax time during a temple Feast (Luke 2:1).

We know our Messiah was made manifest into a temporary body when He came to earth. Is it possible He also was put into a temporary dwelling? The fields would have been dotted with sukkoths during this harvest time to temporary shelter animals. The Hebrew word "stable" is called a *sukkoth* (Gen. 33:17).

And she brought forth her firstborn son, and wrapped him in swaddling clothes, and laid him in a manger; because there was no room for them in the inn (Luke 2:7).

Joseph and Mary took the child and flew to Egypt and remained there until they were told by God that Herod was dead. Joseph and Mary brought the baby Jesus into Jerusalem forty days from His birth for Mary's purification and the child's dedication (according to Torah this had to be done within forty days of the birth of a male child–not doing so is considered a sin). This indicates that Herod died within the same forty days, because as long as Herod was alive, they could not appear at the Temple. (According to Josephus' calculations, Herod's death occurred during the Autumn in the fourth year before the Common Era 4 B.C.E.).

Later in His life, Yeshua celebrated His birthday on a mountain with three of His disciples. In contrast to birthday parties, such as Herod's, where people were killed for entertainment, His was a celebration of life. On the Festival of Succoth, Moshe and EliYahu (Elijah), from centuries past, representatives of the Torah and the Prophets, appeared and talked with Yeshua. One disciple, Kepha (Peter), suggested building three succoth for Yeshua, Moshe, and EliYahu, because it was required for the festival, but he did not understand that these three were fulfilling that which the festival symbolized: they were dwelling in their succoth (temporary tabernacles) of flesh, awaiting their eternal resurrection temples (Killian n.d.)

A number of Christians are celebrating Christ's birth during the Feast of Tabernacles, complete with decorations and lights on the sukkah, a birthday cake, and music celebrating Jesus' birth.

Jesus preached three sermons in which he declared himself the "light of the world," and all three would be during the Festival of Lights (Hanukkah) in the winter of the year (December).

Prophetic Significance

These fall festivals speak of a future time when men will again tabernacle with God, when He will dwell with them and they with Him (Rev. 21:3). They speak of a day in which all nations will gather to Jerusalem (Zech. 8:22; 14:16). Curiously, even in the days to come, Bible prophecy tells us that people from the nations of the world will come up to celebrate the Feast of Tabernacles with the Jewish people in Jerusalem (Zech. 14). The stage is being set and prophecy is being fulfilled. The "coming-up" (*aliyah*, in Hebrew) is taking place now in Israel with the massive influx of Jews from over a hundred nations. Christians, also, are already visiting the land in record numbers—the majority of pilgrims coming to Israel are Christians! We believe this is all in preparation and building for future scriptural events. Jerusalem continues to be the focus of God's earthly pattern and plan, for ultimately it is to Jerusalem that Messiah is coming (Wagner 1996).

Jesus Christ is the tabernacle or dwelling place of God. In Him dwelled the fullness of God (John 1:14, Col. 2:9), and God dwells in our midst through Jesus Christ (Matt. 18:20). It may be that Jesus will ultimately fulfill the Feast of Tabernacles at His second coming. There will be a literal rest for planet earth and all its inhabitants. Until then we can find rest in our souls.

The Beginning of the Millennium

Most Bible scholars agree that Tabernacles represents the beginning of the Millennium. We should look forward expectantly to the Feast of Tabernacles, just as we look forward to the coming of the Messiah, to bring His government, His Kingdom, and His laws. *But in the last days it shall come to pass, that the mountain of the house of the LORD shall be established in the top of the mountains, and it shall be exalted above the hills; and people shall flow unto it. And many nations shall come, and say, Come, and let us go up to the mountain of the LORD, and to the house of the God of Jacob; and he will teach us of his ways, and we will walk in his paths: for the law shall go forth of Zion, and the word of the LORD from Jerusalem. And he shall judge among many people, and rebuke strong nations afar off; and they shall beat their swords into plowshares, and their spears into pruning hooks: nation shall not lift up a sword against nation, neither shall they learn war any more* (Micah 4:1).

Tabernacles and Passover are the only holidays mentioned in the millennial worship (Ezek. 45:21-25; Zech. 14:16). Note that the number of days between Nisan and Tishri is always the same. Because of this, the time from the first major festival (Passover in Nisan) to the last major festival (The Feast of Tabernacles in Tishri) is always the same. Could this have any connection to Christ's birth during Tabernacles and His death on Passover? Passover is in the first month in the religious calendar and Tabernacles is in the first month of the civil calendar. Hosea 6:3 explains Christ will come as the latter and former rain. *Then shall we know, if we follow on to know the LORD: his going forth is prepared as the morning; and he shall come unto us as the rain, as the latter and former rain unto the earth.* The spring holidays are during the former rain and the fall holidays are during the latter rain.

Zechariah chapter 14 introduces the millennial age. The chapter tells of the liberation of Jerusalem and how the Messiah will be king over the whole earth. It ends with all nations keeping the laws of the Most High. The Feast of Tabernacles–that great feast which symbolizes the very presence of Yeshua the Messiah (He is the very "Tabernacle of God"), will be kept by all the nations of the world. The prophet tells us that fearsome punishments and plagues will be meted out on nations that refuse to send delegates to Jerusalem for the Feast of Tabernacles.

And it shall be in that day, that living waters shall go out from Jerusalem; half of them toward the former sea, and half of them toward the hinder sea: ... And the Lord shall be king over all the earth; in that day shall there be one Lord and his name one ... And it shall come to pass, that every one that is left of all the nations which came up against Jerusalem shall even go up from year to year to worship the King, the Lord of Hosts, and to keep the feast of tabernacles. And it shall be that whoso will not come up of all the families of the earth unto Jerusalem to worship the King, the Lord of Hosts, even upon them shall be no rain. And if the family of Egypt go not up, and come not, that have no rain; there shall be the plague, wherewith the Lord will smite the heathen that come not up to keep the feast of tabernacles. This shall be the punishment of Egypt, and the punishment of all nations that come not up to keep the feast of tabernacles (Zech. 14:8-19).

Suggestions to Celebrate Tabernacles

BUILD A SUKKAH

Building and decorating a sukkah is a fun family project. Jim Gerrish, with *Bridges for Peace in Jerusalem*, describes one plan for building a sukkah:

> Actually it is not such a difficult job. You will need to start planning early though, in order to begin your construction as quickly as possible after Yom Kippur, the Day of Atonement. In Israel some devout Jews begin construction as soon as the sun is down on Yom Kippur, four days before the Feast of Tabernacles starts.
>
> Since the sukkah is not to be an elaborate or permanent structure, the most inexpensive materials may be used. You will need 4 sturdy posts (2 x 4s in the U.S.) for the corners, 4 smaller poles (2 x 2s) for the roof. All of these boards should be approximately 7 or 8 feet (2.5 meters) in length. To cover the roof you will need several slats or small boards capable of holding up light tree branches. For the sides, old bedsheets seem to work well. Other materials like canvas, cane matting or even light plywood are also fine. You will need enough to enclose three sides, with a drape for the entrance. For the top you simply need to trim a few trees in the back yard.
>
> Now for the actual construction. The tabernacle can be almost any size so long as it is large enough to sit in. A seven foot cube (2.5 meters) is recommened, since this will allow plenty of room for guests (make a larger Sukkah if you are blessed with a big family).
>
> First, you will need to sink four holes in the ground for the four upright corner poles. In lieu of this, you may anchor the uprights in the holes of stacked concrete blocks, or design other sturdy legs for them. If you want to do it the easy way, you may use an existing building for one side of your sukkah. Once the uprights are firmly in place, then attach the horizontal rods at the top along the outside. With this finished, you can now place the slats or other small support boards on the roof.
>
> The next step is to drape the bedsheets or other coverings around three sides. In the front, a bedsheet attached on a wire track works well for a door. Finally, place the tree branches on top, but if you like to see the stars, don't make the roof too thick. The sukkah can now be outfitted to your own taste. A table and chairs are a must. You may wish to decorate the walls with pictures or Bible verses. Fruit may be hung from the ceiling; paper chains and other decorations may be hung on the walls. Use your imagination, and by all means, let the children participate.

It is customary to decorate the inside of the sukkah with pictures, hangings, and the agricultural produce for which Israel is famous: wheat, barley, grapes, figs, olives, dates, and pomegranates.

All that is left now is the enjoyment. Invite your friends to see your masterpiece and rejoice with you. Try a meal out in the sukkah, or even spend the night there. It will be an unforgettable and blessed experience.

WHAT TO DO IN A SUKKAH

- Praise God through prayer.

- Praise God by singing praise songs.

- Invite relatives, friends, and neighbors to celebrate with you.

- Wave the Lulav (explained in the following pages).

- Eat, drink, relax, nap.

- Read the section titled "God is Our Shelter" and "Jesus is Preparing Our Permanent Home" from the "Messianic Significance of Tabernacles."

- Sing songs to celebrate the birth of Christ. Such as "Joy to the World," "Silent Night," "Away in a Manger," "The First Noel," "O Little Town of Bethlehem," etc.

- The light from the Feast of Tabernacle lamps illuminated the whole city. Decorate the sukkah with strings of light. Read Bible verses about Jesus being our light (John 1:1-9; 8:12; 9:5).

- Set up a nativity scene. Read the story of Christ's birth in Luke or one of the gospels.

- Pour water on the ground and read Jesus' proclamation (John 7:37).

- Read aloud the verses explaining this feast (Lev. 23:34-43 Deut. 16:13-15, and Num. 29:12-40).

- Read John 7:2-39 about Jesus celebrating the Feast of Tabernacles.

- Many Bible prophecies tell of the Messiah's reign over all nations. Read some of them aloud to your family (Psalms 2, 47, 93, 95, 96, 97, 98, 99, 110, and 126).

- Tell Bible stories.

A Lulav Theory for Today

Symbolism easily applied to the lulav is that of unity in diversity. The branches of four different types of trees are bound together as one to be held in the hand. Unity in diversity (different parts acting as a whole) is a picture of the body of Christ in the New Testament. Paul developed this in 1 Corinthians 12. Unity between all believers who proclaim Christ as Lord will only come as prejudices are laid aside. Prejudice simply reflects personal belief that others must be like us (an eye, a hand, etc.) to be accepted (verses 15-21). The reality is all must cooperate in honor and respect as Paul stated in verses 22-27.

A branch of a tree representing beauty (flowering or fruit) is bound with a branch noted for strength (hardwood such as oak or maple, etc.) and another representing endurance (palm or evergreen), and another noted for flexibility (willow).

Unity in diversity is also pictured in Revelation 7:9-10 when all nations, tribes, and tongues combine, and in 1 Peter 2:5 where believers are referred to as living stones. The same theme is found in Malachi 3:16-17, where they are described as jewels.

Jesus told his disciples that He was the "vine" or main trunk and they were the "branches" (John 15). The apostle Paul also discussed the olive branches of the Jews and Gentiles in Romans 11. The point of comparison which leads to prejudice is also addressed in verse 18. It would appear that God is more interested in cooperation than comparison with other persons, and focused on how we measure up to Christ Himself: "Fixing our eyes upon Jesus, the Author and Finisher of our faith..."

Symbolism in scripture reveals that willow as representative of sorrow or weeping (Ps. 137: 2), yet an unidentified tree "planted by the rivers of water" in Psalm 1:3 is portrayed as flourishing. It might represent people with a penitent heart (Isa. 66:2), or those who thirst after the Waters of Life (John 4:14).

The palm is representative of uprightness (Ps. 92:12), and is used in praise and worship in John 12:13 and Revelation 7:9. Carvings of it were made on the walls and doors in the temple (1 Kings 6:29, 32, 35) and seen in the temple vision of Ezekiel (Ezek. 40:16, 41:18). It might represent people with a heart of worship, or people of endurance, perseverance, or longevity.

Since Leviticus does not specifically name the other varieties, we suggest that the "pleasing" or fruiting tree may be any flowering or fruiting variety, and that it may represent people that show the gift of kindness or similar fruits of the spirit as in Galatians 5:22. The "goodly trees" also translated as thick or leafy trees may be any variety of hardwood. Oak, poplar, maple may represent people of strength or faith.

359

In this analogy, the grouping of four varieties in your lulav is simply stating that God likes diversity. There are 1,035 kinds of trees in the United States alone? This diversity can become a strength as we unite for a common purpose: serving in the Kingdom of God.

This may be a good teaching time to evaluate the strengths in each of your family members. You may want to use the list of suggestions below and initial those that seem to be apparent in each parent or child. Note how God has put variety in your own family and think of similar ways to recognize and appreciate differing character and personality traits (not just talents) in people within your church or neighborhood. Just like snowflakes, no two people are alike! Appreciating and building on each other's strengths can help us grow in cooperation while maintaining our uniqueness.

PERSONAL CHARACTER QUALITIES:

thoughtful	patient	thankful
generous	self-controlled	decisive
orderly	creative	plans ahead
helpful	careful	kind
loving	responsible	diligent
unselfish	good listener	friendly
prayerful	honest	wise
submissive	dependable	compassionate
good talker	encouraging	confident
well-mannered	content	humble
faithful	joyful	cooperative
gentle	resourceful	follows up

Waving the lulav in the four directions of the compass may symbolize a number of things. In general, including all directions at once, universality or the "four corners of the earth" is represented. Matthew 28:18-20, Acts 1:8, and Revelation 21:13 are examples.

Specifically, north is represented in scripture as a place of God's throne (Ps. 75:6-7, Isa. 14:13-14) or place of judgment (Jer. 1:13-14). South is seen as a place of refreshment (Ps. 126:4). East is a place of the glory of God in Ezekiel 43:1-2, and west is a place of sunset or setting down as in Isaiah 59:19, Psalm 103:12, and Matthew 8:11.

Even the motions of up and down have interpretation in scripture. Down represents spiritual decline as in Jonah 1:3 and 5 and Luke 10:15. On the other hand, up means spiritual ascension in Genesis 12:10-13:1. Wave your branches upward and bless the Body of Christ!

Centerpiece

To assemble your centerpiece for Feast of Tabernacles, cover base with floral calico cloth (see "Multi-Holiday Centerpiece" in *Preliminary Activities & Crafts* section). Place **Miniature Sukkah** craft (instructions follow) or a small collection of fruits and vegetables in the center. Position **Palm Branches**, **Grain Sheaf**, **Bible**, and **Lamb** flags around.

SYMBOLS IN THE CENTERPIECE

Floral calico print—enhances the "outdoorsiness" of your sukkah craft and adds a festive touch for this celebration time.

Palm Branches flag—God listed several trees, including the palm, to collect to make the roof of the sukkah. This may not be possible for you, so enjoy the representation on the flag. Palm also symbolizes rejoicing which is supposed to characterize this holiday (Rev. 7:9-10).

Grain Sheaf flag—final wheat harvest (spring wheat) is at this season and a reminder of the harvest of souls (Matt. 9:36-38 and 13:37-43).

Bible flag—Jews celebrate reading through the Torah annually. Christians can celebrate going through the scriptures as well. Three to four chapters a day will get you through the Bible in a year! Chronologically arranged Bibles are nice for seeing God's hand through history. See Simhat Torah party ideas later in this section. Celebrate the Word!

Lamb flag—living in tents was a humbling activity, and God showed us ultimate humility when He came as the humble Lamb of God and "tabernacled among us" (John 1:14).

LULAV

Building a Sukkah

The Bible only says "Build a sukkah (or booth)." Rabbis have added all details about size, materials, location, etc.

You might want to use any scrap lumber you have available, pitch your tent, or use old sheets to create an adventure for your children (attach tarps with bungee cords to your deck or swingset). One family had sick children and made a booth out of old sheets in their living room. Meals were eaten in it and they occasionally spent the night. The importance of this and each holiday is making a memory — not getting hung up on customs.

Get started, evaluate each year, and have fun.

Plan to eat at least one meal in your sukkah, and use it for your time alone with God, perhaps. Younger children will want to "play house" which is alright since the Israelites were "housed" in them for forty years.

TO MAKE A LULAV

Collect 1.) Hardwood deciduous, 2.) Flowering or fruiting, 3.) Evergreen or palm (depending on your geography as to what stays green all year, or is available from your florist), 4.) Leafy shrub or willow (as you have access). The point is to have a variety. If you want to see the trees as types of people, as some Jews think, remember God likes variety (hard, soft, high, low, pretty, and plain, etc.).

Miniature Sukkah Craft

This small version can become part of your centerpiece. Optional materials include:

- Half of a small shoebox or similar size (or)
  Small paper sack, shortened (or)
  Craft sticks.

- Use any of these to create your basic hut shape. Cut a doorway in the sack or leave a doorway if using sticks. The shoebox can be simply stood on the cut end. Use different shades of brown markers if you want a natural wood appearance.

- Use a collection of small twigs and leaves to make your roof. Glue on top, or leave loose if you want to store them separately later. Tiny metallic stars can be put on your top branches. If you want to hang "fruit" from the ceiling, use things like raisins, seeds, nuts, or beads on threads. Use your imagination for other small inside decorations. Stuff tiny cushions or use a wooden block for a table.

- If you like, thread spools or clothespins (half or whole) can become little people. Tiny manufactured people and furniture also work. A birthday candle on a button can set off your table.

- Many craft stores have doll house furniture available. We were able to find a tiny Bible, small fruit basket, and miniature fruit.

Note from Robin: This was our family's favorite craft! If you enjoy doll houses you'll love this one. (Thanks for the idea Linda.)

Orange Pomanders

A useful, good-smelling craft is a pomander made from an orange. It can be hung from the ceiling of your sukkah to remind you of the fruit harvest, then hung in your closet afterward to remind you of the holiday.

- Start on or before the first day of the holiday. Begin by taking a fruit and wrapping it around two times with masking tape. Have Mom secure at the bottom and top with long beaded pins (hat pins or corsage pins). You will remove it after the fruit shrinks in six to seven days.

- Pierce your design with a small nail first. Use whole cloves (purchase cheapest at a discount store or co-op that carries spices) to fill your design in the four sections of exposed fruit.

- Place in basket in your sukkah to enjoy the fragrance and ROTATE, daily rearranging each one to promote drying of the fruit. On the seventh day, remove tape and replace with ribbon. Knot at the top and glue where they overlap at bottom. Use a paper clip, straightened at one curve, if you wish to hang it from your ceiling.

- Make a bow with several loops and use a glue gun or sturdy craft glue to attach it to the top, securing it to <u>both</u> circles of trim.

- The fruit will continue to shrink some, but will smell good for several weeks or months. Hang in your clothes closet until thoroughly dry, or store in tissue paper in a drawer for a spicy scent after the holiday.

Scribes Do Not Scribble

Imagine you are the child of a scribe. You are learning your father's trade. Using your best penmanship, write your account of how your family plans to spend (or spent) this holiday.

A Simchat Torah Party

The eighth day of the Feast of Tabernacles is to be a Sabbath and holy assembly (Lev. 23:36). The Jewish community has added a ninth day called Simchat Torah or "rejoicing in the law." Kasdan in his book, *God's Appointed Times* says "this day celebrates the revelation of God as symbolized in the Torah scroll. It is a time of tremendous joy, with dancing and lively music... How much more so (to joyously celebrate) for believers of Yeshua Ha Mashiach, the Word who became flesh at this time of year!"

CELEBRATIONS

Invite other families to join you. As everyone gathers, the reason for the party is explained. Fathers and Mothers can carry **Bibles** and handmade **"scrolls."** The children get to carry banners and flags. Dowels supporting flags can be topped with apples with or without a small candle. Parents decide how far to carry this.

One Dad can read Revelation 22, another can read Genesis 1. Children may gather under a white "prayer shawl" (sheet or tablecloth) as parents surround them reading verses from Psalm 119 and praying blessings.

This is a last opportunity for a "sukkah open house." Serve fruit wedges, nuts, and/or small squares of honey cake (see *Trumpets* activities section).

BANNERS

The flags and banners suggested may be the ones you have made for your centerpieces.

Placemat-size flags can use a dowel on each end to create a banner for two children to carry. See flag instructions in "crafts" section.

Enlarge to 12x18" cloth and find a copy machine that enlarges or enlarge designs by hand to make banners if you wish. You may want to use designs that differ from your flag to add interest. Suggestions include:

- Grapes (fruit of the vine is harvested in the fall), etc.
- An oil lamp symbolic of the Word of God.
- A sun symbolic of the Glory of God the Father
  (Rev. 1:16, Matt. 13:43, Ps. 84:11).
- A rose for Rose of Sharon symbolizing the Church in Christ
  (Song of Solomon 2:1).

POLISH UP YOUR HORAH STEPS

See "Unleavened Bread" chapter to learn this dance. Or learn a new song. A suggestion for songs to use are those included on the tapes *Yeladim for Yeshua (Children for Jesus)*. Many Messianic Jewish groups' tapes (such as *Liberated Wailing Wall*) are available for a blend of joyful "parading" music and worshipful "blessing time" or dinner music. A "teens only" family may want to use Bible-oriented games instead of a parade. Remember the focus: making a meaningful memory.

READ TO HEAR

This is a good opportunity to *plan to read through the Bible* in the coming year. Three chapters a day is average. You may want to do more Psalms, or group them with some of the chapters in 1 and 2 Samuel as you read about David. Don't just read to be "doing it." <u>Read to hear from the Lord</u>. You won't be disappointed!

Recipe

HOMEMADE COCOA MIX

This is easy to make and can be taken out to your sukkah, stored in a jar or empty coffee can (decorate for another activity?). All you need is a tea kettle of hot water to warm the family up for your "look at the stars."

3 cups of powdered milk

1/4 cup of cocoa or carob powder

2/3 cup of sugar or 1/2 cup of fructose

Mix well. Use about 1/3 cup per mug. Add steaming water. Stir. Sometimes settles and needs re-stirring. Option: mix in quart jar with 1 to 1 1/2 cup boiling water. Shake vigorously. Use as syrup, measure quantity desired.

A simple meal consisting of one or two dishes is easiest to serve in a sukkah. Since weather may be nippy around the first of October, how about a big pot of HOMEMADE CHILI? Another possibility is a casserole - type dish featuring vegetables served with hot challah* and butter. For dessert try a warm fruit crisp.

CORN QUICHE

Corn, as Americans know it, was not a crop in Bible times, but it is a prominent grain that we eat as a vegetable and harvest during this festival. Here's an easily prepared, easy-to-eat idea.

1 1/2 cups corn (1 can or 3 medium ears, cooked & cut off cob)

1/4 cup chopped onion, sautéed (or 1 1/2 tsp. dry if you need to "hide" it)

1 tbsp. butter or margarine

1/2 cup shredded sharp cheddar cheese

5 eggs (or 3 whole eggs and 4 whites) beaten

1 cup + 2 tbsp. milk

1 tsp. seasoned salt or garlic salt

1/2 tsp. dry mustard

1 tsp. parsley flakes

Unbaked deep-dish pie shell (set on cookie sheet if aluminum pan)

Mix all ingredients: pour in pie shell. Bake at 350° for about 50 minutes. (Knife in center should cut clean.)

* Challah recipe appears in Sabbath section.

Crossword Puzzle

Across
1. ___ to the Highest
3. The art of arranging sounds with time
4. Living away from one's native country
5. Male sheep
7. Inner surface of the hand
10. Act of giving thanks
11. A body of principles and beliefs
13. Several young sheep
16. Son of David
20. Old Testament King

21. A season of the year
22. A sweet edible product of a producing plant
23. Gathered together for a common reason
24. A religious devotee who travels to a particular place
25. Portable sanctuaries

Down
2. Contributions or gifts
3. Complaining confidentially
6. A prophet

8. Waving the ___
9. The pool of ___
10. Perennial woody plants
12. A small body of still water
14. Small stalls used during a feast
15. Coming into public view
17. To mar or impair
18. A covering suspended over a throne
19. Moving to music
20. To gather a crop

371

Word Search

B	T	N	M	A	S	S	E	M	B	L	Y	E	B	C
A	L	G	M	U	R	A	M	S	X	L	X	O	A	F
P	S	E	N	U	S	B	D	F	C	I	O	B	R	S
P	D	B	M	I	T	I	Y	W	L	T	I	U	E	H
E	O	V	M	I	V	U	C	E	H	N	I	E	R	A
A	C	S	I	A	S	I	A	S	G	T	R	U	H	I
R	T	O	C	N	L	H	G	A	S	T	V	Q	G	K
A	R	O	X	Q	U	N	T	S	C	Y	P	A	H	E
N	I	Q	Y	V	O	H	D	H	K	A	M	R	X	Z
C	N	S	A	M	E	A	S	M	A	N	N	L	C	E
E	E	L	O	R	N	F	Z	H	A	R	A	O	A	H
L	U	L	I	C	F	K	A	Q	O	O	V	H	P	P
L	O	N	I	R	M	Q	L	O	O	P	L	E	T	Y
S	G	N	G	N	I	R	U	M	R	U	M	I	S	Q
C	G	T	A	B	E	R	N	A	C	L	E	S	S	T

APPEARANCE	LAMBS
ASSEMBLY	LULAV
AUTUMN	MURMURING
BLEMISH	MUSIC
BOOTHS	PALM
CANOPY	POOL
DANCING	RAMS
DOCTRINE	SILOAM
EXILE	SOLOMON
FRUITS	TABERNACLES
HARVEST	THANKSGIVING
HEZEKIAH	TREES
INGATHERING	

Coloring Page

PASSOVER UNLEAVENED BREAD FIRSTFRUITS WEEKS
TRUMPETS ATONEMENT TABERNACLES PASSOVER
UNLEAVENED BREAD FIRSTFRUITS WEEKS TRUMPETS
ATONEMENT TABERNACLES PASSOVER UNLEAVENED
BREAD FIRSTFRUITS WEEKS TRUMPETS ATONEMENT
TABERNACLES PASSOVER UNLEAVENED BREAD FIRST-
FRUITS WEEKS TRUMPETS ATONEMENT TABERNACLES
PASSOVER UNLEAVENED BREAD FIRSTFRUITS WEEKS
TRUMPETS ATONEMENT PASSOVER UNLEAVENED
BREAD FIRSTFRUITS WEEKS TRUMPETS ATONEMENT
TABERNACLES PASSOVER PASSOVER UNLEAVENED
BREAD FIRSTFRUITS WEEKS TRUMPETS ATONEMENT
TABERNACLES PASSOVER UNLEAVENED BREAD FIRST-
FRUITS WEEKS TRUMPETS ATONEMENT TABERNACLES

Section 5:
Post-Mosaic Holidays

- ◆ OVERVIEW
- ◆ HANUKKAH
- ◆ PURIM

Overview of Post-Mosaic Holidays

Post-Mosaic Holidays are those which were not instituted by God as given to Moses (the Leviticus 23 feasts).

HANUKKAH

The Festival of Lights is held on Kislev 25. This celebration observed the rededication of the Temple and the victory by a group of Jews led by Yehudah Maccabee against the Hellenizing rule and the defiling of the Holy Temple by the Greek ruler Antiochus IV. This occurred after the Old Testament and before the New (inter-testament period). The New Testament mentions that Jesus went to the Temple on that day (John 10:22-23).

PURIM

Feast of Lots is held on Adar 14 and celebrates the deliverance of the Jewish people from the evil plot of Haman to destroy them. The book of Esther (which tells the story) is read, and traditionally, Purim plays are put on which dramatize it.

Because of the house of the LORD our God
I will seek thy good.

Psalm 122:9

378

Hanukkah

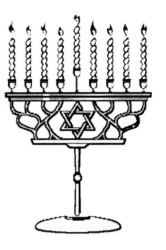

Purpose of Hanukkah

Hanukkah is an annual festival of the Jews celebrated on eight successive days to honor the restoration of divine worship in the Temple after it had been defiled by heathens. The return of their religious liberty was to them as life from the dead and, in remembrance of it, they kept an annual holiday on the twenty-fifth day of Kislev. Kislev is the third month of the Jewish calendar corresponding, approximately, to early December in the Gregorian calendar. Jesus kept this festival. The principal source for the story of Hanukkah is found in the Talmud. The biggest lesson of Hanukkah was the power of the spirit, the ability of God's people to live by God's commands. *...Not by might, nor by power, but by my spirit, saith the LORD of hosts* (Zech. 4:6).

In between the Testaments, around 164 B.C., the Maccabees (or Hasmoneans), led by Judah Maccabee, wrested Judea from the rule of the Seleucids–Syrian rulers who supported the spread of Greek religion and culture. Hanukkah commemorates the recapture of Jerusalem by the Maccabees and the establishment of the Temple. The Temple had been profaned by Antiochus IV Epiphanes, king of Syria and overlord of Palestine. The Maccabees ruled Judea until Herod took power in 37 B.C.E.

Hanukkah centers around a nine-branch menorah. The Temple menorah has seven branches. The Hanukkah menorah has nine branches, eight to remember the eight days of Hanukkah and one is the shamus, the candle used to light the other candles (this is usually either higher or separate from the other eight branches).

Hanukkah in Bible Times

Nearly twenty-two centuries ago, during the time of the Second Temple in Jerusalem, the events took place that the Jews memorialize each year at Hanukah time:

The Jewish people had returned to the Land of Israel from the Babylonian Exile, and had rebuilt the Holy Temple, but they remained subject to the reigning powers: first, the Persian Empire, then later, the conquering armies of Alexander the Great.

Alexander the Great was a kind and generous ruler to the Jews. He canceled the Jewish taxes during Sabbatical years, and even offered animals to be sacrificed on his behalf in the Temple. After the death of Alexander, his kingdom was divided among his generals. Judea was caught in the middle and ended up under the system of the Seleucid Dynasty, Greek kings who reigned from Syria.

THE JEWS UNDER SYRIAN RULE

A Syrian tyrant, Antiochus IV, was the new king who ruled Judea. He worshipped the Greek gods, but he did allow the Jews to worship YHWH.

During the years of Greek power, many Jews started to embrace the Greek culture and its Hellenistic, pagan way of life. These Jewish Hellenists helped Antiochus's goal to abolish every trace of the Jewish religion.

DESECRATED THE TEMPLE

Eventually, King Antiochus decided to go into Jerusalem and take the treasures in the temple and forbid the Jews from keeping their holy traditions, such as the Sabbath, kosher laws, studying their holy books, and the practice of circumcision. To prove his point he desecrated the Holy Altar by sacrificing a forbidden, unclean pig on it.

The Temple was dedicated to the worship of Zeus Olympus. An altar to Zeus was set up on the high altar. The Jews were forced to bow before it under penalty of death. The Holy Temple was invaded, desecrated, and pillaged of all its treasures. Many innocent people were massacred, and the survivors were heavily taxed. Antiochus went so far as to proclaim himself a god, taking the name Epiphanes—God manifest.

Flavius Josephus, a renowned historian who lived at the time of the Apostles recorded the horrifying event of that time in this way: (*Antiquities of the Jews* Book 12, Chapter 5)

> *And when the king had built an idol altar upon God's Altar, he slew swine upon it, and so offered a sacrifice neither according to the law, nor the Jewish religious worship in that country. He also compelled them to forsake the worship which they paid their own God, and to adore those whom he took to be gods; and made them build temples, and raise idol altars, in every city and village, and offer swine upon them every day (254). He also commanded them not to circumcise their sons, and threatened to punish any that should be found to have transgressed his injunction. He also appointed overseers, who should compel them to do what he commanded (255). And indeed many Jews there were who complied with the king's commands either voluntarily, or out of fear of the penalty that was denounced; but the best men, and those of the noblest souls, did not regard him, but did pay a greater respect to the customs of their country than concern as to the punishment which he threatened to the disobedient; on which account they every day underwent great miseries and bitter torments (256). For they were whipped with rods and their bodies were torn to pieces, and were crucified while they were still alive and breathed: they also strangled those women and their sons whom they had circumcised, as the king had appointed, hanging their sons about their necks as they were upon the crosses. And if there were any sacred book of the law found, it was destroyed; and those with whom they were found miserably perished also.*

A WICKED HIGH PRIEST

Some Jews drifted into the Greek Ways, changed their names from their Hebrew names, and followed the Greek "modern" practices, giving up the "old" ways of their ancestors. One hellenized Jew's Hebrew name was Joshua, but he changed it to the Greek name Jason. He offered King Antiochus a bribe so he could take over the position of the High Priest.

The "High Priest" Jason constructed a gymnasium near the Temple, and demoralized his fellow Jews with pagan customs and licentious behavior.

Another Hellinized Jew came along and offered a bigger bribe and Jason was replaced. Jason then gathered an army and attacked Menelaus in the Holy City, slaughtering many of the Jews. Antiochus interpreted this civil squabble as a revolt against his throne, and sent his armies into Jerusalem, plundering the Temple and murdering tens of thousands of Jews. Altars were erected with statues of the Greek gods and goddesses in every city and town. Soldiers forced Jews to make offerings, to eat forbidden foods, and to engage in other immoral acts.

REVOLT

Many other Jews resisted, and refused to follow Greek practices, and would not bow down to the Greek's pagan idols. The Greeks tried to get Jews to abandon the Torah and commandments, but God was in charge. Many times God had fought the Jewish battles, against all odds, delivering the evil to the righteous and the outnumbered. God helped the Jews to organize the common people, farmers, workers, and servants, and they began to fight the Syrian persecutors.

THE MACCABEES

This small group of Hasmoneans, under the leadership of Judas Maccabee, employed guerrilla warfare and drove the Syrians out. The Maccabees regained control of the Holy Temple, and began the task of purifying it. The altar which had been defiled by the sacrifice of a pig upon it was torn down and rebuilt. All new holy vessels were crafted. A date for the rededication of the Temple was set–the twenty-fifth day of the Hebrew month of Kislev, which occurs approximately in the Roman month of December (A.T.O.M. 1995).

Taking unhewn stones, as the law commands, they built a new altar on the model of the previous one. They rebuilt the Temple and restored its interior, and consecrated the Temple courts. They renewed the sacred vessels and the lampstand, and brought the altar of incense and the table into the Temple.

They burnt incense on the altar and lit the lamps on the lamp-stand to shine within the Temple. They decorated the front of the Temple with golden wreaths and ornamental shields. They renewed the gates and the priest's rooms, and fitted them with doors. When they had put the Bread of the Presence on the table and hung the curtains, all their work was completed (Killian 1996). The Temple was then rededicated to God with festivities that lasted eight days.

THE MIRACLE

When the Jews cleaned out the temple idols, they found only one small cruse of oil with only enough oil for one day to light their holy lamps. They decided to light the Menorah (the Temple candelabra) even with the small amount of oil. To everyone's amazement the menorah miraculously burned for eight days until new oil was available!

CELEBRATION

The congregation of Israel decreed that the rededication of the altar should be observed with joy and gladness at the same season each year, for eight days, beginning on the twenty-fifth of Kislev. The light of the menorah is the symbol of the light of Yahweh. The fact that the light burned even when no supply was left is a perfect symbol of the eternity of God's Word. The heart of the celebration, is not only the Rabbis retelling of the saga of revolt and renewal, but also the retelling of the divine experience of the miracle of the oil.

Jewish Customs of Hanukkah Today

Jewish tradition sought to embellish these days of celebration. It is the practice to have festive meals for the eight days, and in addition to Latkes, jelly doughnuts fried in oil became popular. (Both symbolize the miracle of the oil.) Other popular sources of joy are the Hanukkah gifts and Hanukkah gelt (money.)

The major ritual ceremony of the holiday is the lighting of the Hanukkah menorah. The eight days are marked by prayers of thanksgiving, special songs of praise (for the miracles and redemption), the Shmoneh Esrei (the central silent prayer) three times a day, and grace after meals.

LIGHTING THE CANDLES

Some Jews light one candle the first night and add one additional light every subsequent night. Others Jews start with all eight candles lit and decrease one every night.

Since the object of the lighting is to publicize the miracle, the candles are usually placed near windows: to remind others of the holiday and the redemption. It is customary to light the candles right after sundown.

After the destruction of the temple the menorah became the most important Jewish pictorial motif: what had been a holy implement became the symbol of Judaism. The main prophetic reading of Hanukkah is the prophecy of Zechariah, which ends, "*...Not by might, nor by power, but by my spirit, saith the Lord of hosts*" (Zech. 4:6).

HALLEL

A Hallel is a song of praise celebrating God's mighty acts on behalf of His Chosen People, the nation of Israel. The complete text of the song is contained in Psalms 115 through 118. The complete HALLEL is recited in the morning service throughout the eight days of Chanukah.

AL HANISIM

The prayer of "Al Hanisim," in which we give thanks to God for all the miracles of Chanukah, is recited in the Shmone Esrei (Amidah) as well as in the Birkat Hamazon (grace after meal) each day of Chanukah.

READING THE TORAH

The Torah is read each day of Chanukah, specifically, the story of the dedication of the Tabernacle in the desert and the special gifts donated by the leaders of each of the twelve tribes of Israel in connection with the dedication. This Torah portion is read on Chanukah because the Tabernacle was completed on the twenty-fifth of Kislev, the same day in which the miracle of Chanukah took place close to one thousand years later.

SPINNING THE DREIDEL

Those who would like to quickly part with their gelt play the game of Dreidel (spinning top). On the Dreidel are Hebrew letters Nune, Gimel, Shin, and Hay. On the surface, those letters stand for *"Nes Gadol Hayah Sham - A great miracle happened there"* Each player puts the same amount of something— nuts, raisins, pennies, or chocolate coins in the middle, which is called "the pot". Play proceeds clockwise around the circle of players. Each player takes a turn spinning the Dreidel. Whatever the Dreidel lands on decides what you are to do.

    HAY: .... you get half of the pot.

    GIMEL: .... you get ALL of the pot.

    NUNE: .... you get nothing.

    SHIN: .... you must put 1 (nut, or raising, or penny, etc.) in the pot.

Whoever has the most in the end wins! The Rabbis are opposed to gambling games and it became customary to give any Dreidel money to charity.

Messianic Significance of Hanukkah

The law did not require Jews to be at the Temple in Jerusalem, as this was not one of the pilgrimage festivals. Every one observed it in his own place, not as a holy time. Jesus was there that He might improve those eight days of holiday for good purposes.

Jesus walked in the temple in Solomon's porch when the Sadduciens asked him *"How long dost thou make us to doubt? If thou be the Christ tell us."* They pretended to want to know the truth, as if they were ready to embrace it; but it was not their intention.

Jesus answered them, I told you, and ye believed not: the works that I do in my Father's name, they bear witness of me. But ye believe not, because ye are not of my sheep, as I said unto you. My sheep hear my voice, and I know them, and they follow me (John 10:25-27).

He had told them, and they believed not; why then should they be told again, merely to gratify their curiosity?

MIRACLES

Hanukkah's theme is of a miracle. During Hanukkah Jesus spoke of His miracles: *If I do not the works of my Father, believe me not. But if I do, though ye believe not me, believe the works: that ye may know, and believe, that the Father is in me, and I in him* (John 10:37-38).

Jesus wanted the people of his day to see His miracles and believe in Him as a result. His miracles point to his divine and messianic identity. In this way Yeshua personifies the message of Hanukkah: God actively involved in the affairs of his people. Hanukkah reminds us that God is a God of miracles, not just of concept and religious ideals. He has broken through into human history and continues to do so today. All of us who know Yeshua can speak of God's working in our lives (Gilman 1995).

JESUS IS THE LIGHT OF THE WORLD

Jesus preached three sermons in which he declared Himself the "light of the world," and all three would be during Hanukkah, the Festival of Lights.

Then Jesus said unto them, Yet a little while is the light with you. Walk while ye have the light, lest darkness come upon you: for he that walketh in darkness knoweth not whither he goeth. While ye have light, believe in the light, that ye may be the children of light. These things spake Jesus, and departed, and did hide himself from them (John 12:35-36).

During Hanukkah—The Feast of Lights— Jesus brought literal light to the blind. *As long as I am in the world, I am the light of the world. When he had thus spoken, he spat on the ground, and made clay of the spittle, and he anointed the eyes of the blind man with the clay, And said unto him, Go, wash in the pool of Siloam, He went his way therefore, and washed, and came seeing* (John 9:5-7).

ENDTIMES

The story of Hanukkah can be compared with end-time happenings described in the books of Revelation and Daniel. Antiochus is a type of the antichrist. Just as happened under the rule of Antiochus, Daniel prophesied in Daniel 9:27 *And he shall confirm the covenant with many for one week: and in the midst of the week he shall cause the sacrifice and the oblation to cease, and for the overspreading of abominations he shall make it desolate, even until the consummation, and that determined shall be poured upon the desolate.*

The same powers promoted by Antiochus are in the world today. Worldwide immorality, and idolatry are the norm. We must come out and be separate. *And what agreement hath the temple of God with idols? for ye are the temple of the living God; as God hath said, I will dwell in them, and walk in them; and I will be their God, and they shall be my people. Wherefore come out from among them, and be ye separate, saith the Lord, and touch not the unclean thing; and I will receive you.* The deceiver stands waiting to devour in this present culture (2 Cor. 6:16-17).

WAS JESUS CONCEIVED ON HANUKKAH?

Many believe that our Messiah, the "light of the world," was conceived on the festival of lights—Hanukkah. The Bible does not specifically say the date of

Jesus' birth. It was not during the winter months because the sheep were in the pasture (Luke 2:8). A study of the time of the conception of John the Baptist reveals he was conceived about Sivan 30, the eleventh week (Luke 1:8-13, 24). Adding forty weeks, for a normal pregnancy reveals that John the Baptist was born on or about Passover (Nisan 14). Six months after John's conception, Mary conceived Jesus (Luke 1:26-33); therefore Jesus would have been conceived six months after Sivan 30 in the month of Kislev—Hanukkah. Was the "light of the world," conceived on the festival of lights?

Starting at Hanukah, which begins on Kislev 25 and continues for eight days, and counting through the nine months of Mary's pregnancy, one arrives at the approximate time of the birth of Jesus at the Festival of Tabernacles. (See the Tabernacle chapter.)

Suggestions for Celebrating Hanukkah

If you decide to celebrate Hanukkah in your home you'll need a menorah. Beautiful multi-colored Israeli-made candles are available for those who light menorahs. Any library or bookstore should have a good selection of illustrated books telling the story of Hanukkah for children.

Have festive meals for the eight days, say silent prayer three times a day and each night while lighting the menorah, talk to your children about Jesus being the light.

BLESSINGS FOR LIGHTING THE CANDLES

1. Blessed are you, Lord our God, King of the universe, who has sanctified us by His commandments, and has commanded us to kindle the lights of Chanukah.

2. Blessed are you, Lord our God, King of the universe, who wrought miracles for our fathers in days of old, at this season.

3. The following blessing is said only on the first evening (or the first time one kindles the lights this Chanukah):

   Blessed are you, Lord our God, King of the universe, who has kept us alive, and has preserved us, and enabled us to reach this season.

After Kindling the Lights the Hallalu is Recited. The Hallalu: "We kindle these lights (to commemorate) the saving acts, miracles and wonders which You have performed for our forefathers, in those days at this time, through Your holy kohanim. Throughout the eight days of Chanukah, these lights are sacred, and we are not permitted to make use of them, but only to look at them, in order to offer thanks and praise to Your great Name for Your miracles, for Your wonders and for Your salvations."

WORK

Hanukkah is not considered sacred, so all work is allowed during the eight-day period except for the weekly Sabbath.

GIFTS

Gift giving on each of the eight nights is an American tradition that probably came from the pressures American Jews faced from their children missing Christmas. If you'd like to give a small gift each night, or a large gift the first or last night of Hanukkah, it is up to your family. Create your own family tradition.

Each night read verses about the light, the commentary, and talk of the different symbolism.

HANUKKAH READING NIGHT ONE

The Lord is Our Light

The sun shall be no more thy light by day; neither for brightness shall the moon give light unto thee: but the LORD shall be unto thee an everlasting light, and thy God thy glory (Isa 60:19).

From Matthew Henry's Commentary:

> God shall be all in all in the happiness here promised; so he is always to true believers: The sun and the moon shall be no more thy light. God's people, when they enjoy his favour, and walk in the light of his countenance, make little account of sun and moon, and the other lights of this world, but could walk comfortably in the light of the Lord though they should withdraw their shining. In heaven there shall be no occasion for sun or moon, for it is the inheritance of the saints in light, such light as will swallow up the light of the sun as easily as the sun does that of a candle. "Idolaters worshiped the sun and moon (which some have thought the most ancient and plausible idolatry); but these shall be no more thy light, shall no more be idolized, but the Lord shall be to thee a constant light, both day and night, in the night of adversity as well as in the day of prosperity." Those that make God their only light shall have him their all-sufficient light, their sun and shield. Thy God shall be thy glory.

The LORD is my light and my salvation; whom shall I fear? the LORD is the strength of my life; of whom shall I be afraid? (Ps 27:1).

From Matthew Henry's Commentary:

> The Lord is my light. David's subjects called him the light of Israel,

(2 Sam. 21:17). And he was indeed a burning and a shining light: but he owns that he shone, as the moon does, with a borrowed light; what light God darted upon him reflected upon them: The Lord is my light. God is a light to his people, to show them the way when they are in doubt, to comfort and rejoice their hearts when they are in sorrow. It is in his light that they now walk on in their way, and in his light they hope to see light for ever.

HANUKKAH READING NIGHT TWO

The Word is Our Light

Thy word is a lamp unto my feet, and a light unto my path (Ps. 119:105).

The entrance of thy words giveth light; it giveth understanding unto the simple (Ps 119:130).

For the commandment is a lamp; and the law is light; and reproofs of instruction are the way of life (Prov 6:23).

From Matthew Henry's Commentary:

> The nature of the word of God, and the great intention of giving it to the world; it is a lamp and a light. It discovers to us, concerning God and ourselves, that which otherwise we could not have known; it shows us what is amiss, and will be dangerous; it directs us in our work and way, and a dark place indeed the world would be without it. It is a lamp which we may set up by us, and take into our hands for our own particular use. The commandment is a lamp kept burning with the oil of the Spirit; it is like the lamps in the sanctuary, and the pillar of fire to Israel.

> It must be not only a light to our eyes, to gratify them, and fill our heads with speculations, but a light to our feet and to our path, to direct us in the right ordering of our conversation, both in the choice of our way in general and in the particular steps we take in that way, that we may not take a false way nor a false step in the right way. We are then truly sensible of God's goodness to us in giving us such a lamp and light when we make it a guide to our feet, our path.

HANUKKAH READING NIGHT THREE

We Should Be a Light to Others

Matt. 5:16 *Let your light so shine before men, that they may see your good works, and glorify your Father which is in heaven.*

No man, when he hath lighted a candle, putteth it in a secret place, neither under a bushel, but on a candlestick, that they which come in may see the light (Luke 11:33).

From Matthew Henry's Commentary:

> They had the light with all the advantage they could desire. For God, having lighted the candle of the gospel, did not put it in a secret place, or under a bushel; Christ did not preach in corners. The apostles were ordered to preach the gospel to every creature; and both Christ and his ministers, Wisdom and her maidens, cry in the chief places of concourse, v. 33. It is a great privilege that the light of the gospel is put on a candlestick, so that all that come in may see it, and may see by it where they are and whither they are going, and what is the true, and sure, and only way to happiness.

> All believers in Christ are light in the Lord (Eph. 5:8), and must shine as lights (Phil. 2:15), but ministers in a special manner. Christ calls himself the Light of the world (John. 8:12), and they are workers together with him, and have some of his honour put upon them. Truly the light is sweet, it is welcome; the light of the first day of the world was so, when it shone out of darkness; so is the morning light of every day; so is the gospel, and those that spread it, to all sensible people. The world sat in darkness, Christ raised up his disciples to shine in it; and, that they may do so, from him they borrow and derive their light.

> As the lights of the world, they are illustrious and conspicuous, and have many eyes upon them. A city that is set on a hill cannot be hid. The disciples of Christ, especially those who are forward and zealous in his service, become remarkable, and are taken notice of as beacons. They are for signs (Isa. 7:18), men wondered at (Zech. 3:8); all their neighbors have any eye upon them. Some admire them, commend them, rejoice in them, and study to imitate them; others envy them, hate them, censure them, and study to blast them. They

are concerned therefore to walk circumspectly, because of their observers; they are as spectacles to the world, and must take heed of every thing that looks ill, because they are so much looked at. The disciples of Christ were obscure men before he called them, but the character he put upon them dignified them, and as preachers of the gospel they made a figure; and though they were reproached for it by some, they were respected for it by others, advanced to thrones, and made judges (Luke 22:30); for Christ will honour those that honour him. As the lights of the world, they are intended to illuminate and give light to others.

HANUKKAH READING NIGHT FOUR

The Light of the Body is the Eye

The light of the body is the eye: therefore when thine eye is single, thy whole body also is full of light; but when thine eye is evil, thy body also is full of darkness (Luke 11:34).

To open their eyes, and to turn them from darkness to light, and from the power of Satan unto God, that they may receive forgiveness of sins, and inheritance among them which are sanctified by faith that is in me (Acts 26:18).

From Matthew Henry's Commentary:

> Having the light, their concern was to have the sight, or else to what purpose had they the light? Be the object ever so clear, if the organ be not right, we are never the better: The light of the body is the eye (v. 34), which receives the light of the candle when it is brought into the room. So the light of the soul is the understanding and judgment, and its power of discerning between good and evil, truth and falsehood. Now, according as this is, so the light of divine revelation is to us, and our benefit by it; it is a savour of life unto life, or of death unto death.

> If this eye of the soul be single, if it see clear, see things as they are, and judge impartially concerning them, if it aim at truth only, and seek it for its own sake, and have not any sinister by-looks and intentions, the whole body, that is, the whole soul, is full of light, it receives and entertains the gospel, which will bring along with it into the soul both knowledge and joy. This denotes the same thing with that of the good ground, receiving the word and understanding it. If our understanding admits the gospel in its full light, it fills the

soul, and it has enough to fill it. And if the soul be thus filled with the light of the gospel, having no part dark,— if all its powers and faculties be subjected to the government and influence of the gospel, and none left unsanctified,— then the whole soul shall be full of light, full of holiness and comfort. It was darkness itself, but now light in the Lord, as when the bright shining of a candle doth give thee light, v. 36. Note, The gospel will come into those souls whose doors and windows are thrown open to receive it; and where it comes it will bring light with it. But, if the eye of the soul be evil,— if the judgment be bribed and biased by the corrupt and vicious dispositions of the mind, by pride and envy, by the love of the world and sensual pleasures,— if the understanding be prejudiced against divine truths, and resolved not to admit them, though brought with ever so convincing an evidence,— it is no wonder that the whole body, the whole soul, should be full of darkness, v. 34. How can they have instruction, information, direction, or comfort, from the gospel, that wilfully shut their eyes against it? and what hope is there of such? what remedy for them? The inference hence therefore is, Take heed that the light which is in thee be not darkness, v. 35. Take heed that the eye of the mind be not blinded by partiality, and prejudice, and sinful aims. Be sincere in your inquiries after truth, and ready to receive it in the light, and love, and power of it; and not as the men of this generation to whom Christ preached, who never sincerely desired to know God's will, nor designed to do it, and therefore no wonder that they walked on in darkness, wandered endlessly, and perished eternally.

HANUKKAH READING NIGHT FIVE

The Messiah is the light of the World

In him was life; and the life was the light of men. And the light shineth in darkness; and the darkness comprehended it not (John 1:4-5).

Then spake Jesus again unto them, saying, I am the light of the world: he that followeth me shall not walk in darkness, but shall have the light of life (John 8:12).

Then Jesus said unto them, Yet a little while is the light with you. Walk while ye have the light, lest darkness come upon you: for he that walketh in dark-

ness knoweth not whither he goeth. While ye have light, believe in the light, that ye may be the children of light. These things spake Jesus, and departed, and did hide himself from them (John 12:35-36).

From Matthew Henry's Commentary:

> Jesus Christ is the light of the world. One of the Rabbis saith, Light is the name of the Messiah, as it is written, (Dan. 2:2), And light dwelleth with him. God is light, and Christ is the image of the invisible God; God of gods, Light of lights. He was expected to be a light to enlighten the Gentiles (Luke. 2:32), and so the light of the world, and not of the Jewish church only. The visible light of the world is the sun, and Christ is the Sun of righteousness. One sun enlightens the whole world, so does one Christ, and there needs no more. Christ in calling himself the light expresses, 1.) What he is in himself— most excellent and glorious. 2.) What he is to the world— the fountain of light, enlightening every man. What a dungeon would the world be without the sun! So would it be without Christ by whom light came into the world (John 3:19).

> The light shineth in darkness. Light is self-evidencing, and will make itself known; this light, whence the light of men comes, hath shone, and doth shine.

> The eternal Word, as God, shines in the darkness of natural conscience. Though men by the fall are become darkness, yet that which may be known of God is manifested in them; (see Rom. 1:19-20). The light of nature is this light shining in darkness. Something of the power of the divine Word, both as creating and as commanding, all mankind have an innate sense of; were it not for this, earth would be a hell, a place of utter darkness; blessed be God, it is not so yet.

> The eternal Word, as Mediator, shone in the darkness of the Old-Testament types and figures, and the prophecies and promises which were of the Messiah from the beginning. He that had commanded the light of this world to shine out of darkness was himself long a light shining in darkness; there was a veil upon this light (2 Cor. 3:13).

> The Jews, who had the light of the Old Testament, yet comprehended not Christ in it. As there was a veil upon Moses's face, so

there was upon the people's hearts. In the darkness of the types and shadows the light shone; but such as the darkness of their understandings that they could not see it. It was therefore requisite that Christ should come, both to rectify the errors of the Gentile world and to improve the truths of the Jewish church.

HANUKKAH READING NIGHT SIX

Paul Saw the Light

Whereupon as I went to Damascus with authority and commission from the chief priests, At midday, O king, I saw in the way a light from heaven, above the brightness of the sun, shining round about me and them which journeyed with me. And when we were all fallen to the earth, I heard a voice speaking unto me, and saying in the Hebrew tongue, Saul, Saul, why persecutest thou me? it is hard for thee to kick against the pricks. And I said, Who art thou, Lord? And he said, I am Jesus whom thou persecutest. But rise, and stand upon thy feet: for I have appeared unto thee for this purpose, to make thee a minister and a witness both of these things which thou hast seen, and of those things in the which I will appear unto thee; Delivering thee from the people, and from the Gentiles, unto whom now I send thee, To open their eyes, and to turn them from darkness to light, and from the power of Satan unto God, that they may receive forgiveness of sins, and inheritance among them which are sanctified by faith that is in me (Acts 26:12-18).

From Matthew Henry's Commentary:

> Paul saw a heavenly vision, the circumstances of which were such that it could not be a delusion— deciptio visus, but it was without doubt a divine appearance. He saw a great light, a light from heaven, such as could not be produced by any art, for it was not in the night, but at mid day; it was not in a house where tricks might have been played with him, but it was in the way, in the open air; it was such a light as was above the brightness of the sun, outshone and eclipsed that and this could not be the product of Paul's own fancy, for it shone round about those that journeyed with him: they were all sensible of their being surrounded with this inundation of light, which made the sun itself to be in their eyes a less light. The force and power of this light appeared in the effects of it; they all fell to the earth upon the sight of it, such a mighty consternation did it put them into; this light was lightning for its force, yet did not pass away as lightning, but continued to shine round about them.

Christ himself appeared to him (v. 16): I have appeared to thee for this purpose. Christ was in this light, though those that travelled with Paul saw the light only, and not Christ in the light. It is not every knowledge that will serve to make us Christians, but it must be the knowledge of Christ.

Christ made himself known to him, he said, "I am Jesus; he whom thou hast despised, and hated, and vilified; I bear that name which thou hast made so odious, and the naming of it criminal." This convinced him that the doctrine of Jesus was divine and heavenly, and not only not to be opposed, but to be cordially embraced: That Jesus is the Messiah, for he has not only risen from the dead, but he has received from God the Father honour and glory; and this is enough to make him a Christian immediately, to quit the society of the persecutors, whom the Lord from heaven thus appears against, and to join himself with the society of the persecuted, whom the Lord from heaven thus appears for.

HANUKKAH READING NIGHT SEVEN

If Christ is Your light, You are No Longer in the Darkness of This World

For ye were sometimes darkness, but now are ye light in the Lord: walk as children of light: (For the fruit of the Spirit is in all goodness and righteousness and truth;) Proving what is acceptable unto the Lord. And have no fellowship with the unfruitful works of darkness, but rather reprove them (Eph. 5:8-11).

But ye, brethren, are not in darkness, that that day should overtake you as a thief. Ye are all the children of light, and the children of the day: we are not of the night, nor of darkness. Therefore let us not sleep, as do others; but let us watch and be sober (1Thess. 5:4-6).

But ye are a chosen generation, a royal priesthood, an holy nation, a peculiar people; that ye should shew forth the praises of him who hath called you out of darkness into his marvellous light (1 Peter 2:9).

And have no fellowship with the unfruitful works of darkness, but rather reprove them. For it is a shame even to speak of those things which are done of them in secret. But all things that are reproved are made manifest by the light: for whatsoever doth make manifest is light. Wherefore he saith, Awake thou that sleepest, and arise from the dead, and Christ shall give thee light. See then that ye walk circumspectly, not as fools, but as wise (Eph. 5:11-15).

This then is the message which we have heard of him, and declare unto you, that God is light, and in him is no darkness at all. If we say that we have fellowship with him, and walk in darkness, we lie, and do not the truth: But if we walk in the light, as he is in the light, we have fellowship one with another, and the blood of Jesus Christ his Son cleanseth us from all sin. If we say that we have no sin, we deceive ourselves, and the truth is not in us. If we confess our sins, he is faithful and just to forgive us our sins, and to cleanse us from all unrighteousness (1 John 1:5-9).

From Matthew Henry's Commentary:

In your unregenerate state you were darkness, you have now undergone a great change. You lived wicked and profane lives, being destitute of the light of instruction without and of the illumination and grace of the blessed Spirit within. A state of sin is a state of darkness. Sinners, like men in the dark, are going they know not whither, and doing they know not what. But the grace of God had produced a mighty change in their souls: Now are you light in the Lord, savingly enlightened by the word and the Spirit of God. Now, upon your believing in Christ, and your receiving the gospel. Walk as children of light. Children of light, according to the Hebrew dialect, are those who are in a state of light, endued with knowledge and holiness. "Now, being such, let your conversation be suitable to your condition and privileges, and accordingly live up to the obligation you are under by that knowledge and those advantages you enjoy— Proving what is acceptable unto the Lord (Also see John 3:19-22).

HANUKKAH READING NIGHT EIGHT

We Need to Shine

Do all things without murmurings and disputings: That ye may be blameless and harmless, the sons of God, without rebuke, in the midst of a crooked and perverse nation, among whom ye shine as lights in the world; Holding forth the word of life; that I may rejoice in the day of Christ, that I have not run in vain, neither laboured in vain (Phil. 2:14-16).

From Matthew Henry's Commentary:

We should have a cheerful obedience to the commands of God: "Do all things, do your duty in every branch of it, without murmurings.

A Family Guide to the Biblical Holidays©

Do it, and do not find fault with it. Mind your work, and do not quarrel with it." God's commands were given to be obeyed, not to be disputed. This greatly adorns our profession, and shows we serve a good Master, whose service is freedom and whose work is its own reward.

We should have peaceableness and love one to another. "Do all things without disputing, wrangling, and debating one another; because the light of truth and the life of religion are often lost in the heats and mists of disputation."

Observe, where there is no true religion, little is to be expected but crookedness and perverseness; and the more crooked and perverse others are among whom we live, and the more apt to cavil [quibble], the more careful we should be to keep ourselves blameless and harmless. Among whom you shine as lights in the world. Christ is the light of the world, and good Christians are lights in the world. When God raises up a good man in any place, he sets up a light in that place. Or it may be read imperatively: Among whom shine you as lights (compare Mt. 5:16). Let your light so shine before men. Christians should endeavor not only to approve themselves to God, but to recommend themselves to others, that they may also glorify God. They must shine as well as be sincere—Holding forth the word of life.

One of our favorite family traditions is to watch *Lamb Chop's Special Chanukah Video* by Shari Lewis. Even though it designed for young children, we all look forward to it. Our favorite Hanukkah song is the Maccabee story in rhyme that we learned from this tape. Ask your bookstore to order it for you through Youngheart (price runs about $15.00).

Centerpiece

To assemble your centerpiece for Hanukkah (see "Multi-Holiday Centerpiece" in *Preliminary Activities & Crafts* section), use **Star of David** and **Dove** flags. Cover the base with white drape. Set your Menorah craft (instructions follow) in the center. If you plan to light the candles on occasion, put a neatly-cut piece of plastic wrap on the cloth, below the candle row. Position **Star of David** and **Dove** flags in opposite corners.

SYMBOLISM IN THE CENTERPIECE

White base and menorah—light itself and the festival of lights; purity and the cleansing of the temple on this occasion.

Star of David flag—reminder of God's hand in helping the Jewish nation on this occasion.

Dove flag—represents the work of the Holy Spirit in keeping our hearts aflame with passion for Jesus; see Revelation 4:5 for reference of the seven "lights" of the Holy Spirit. Isaiah 9:2 speaks of the light that Messiah would bring and Isaiah 11:2 relates seven aspects of the Spirit that would be present in Him.

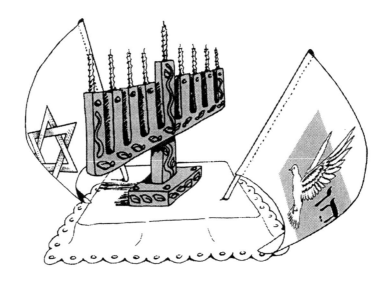

Menorah Craft

Use clay-doh or purchase an air-drying craft clay to create a menorah to a scale that will use birthday candles. Do **NOT** light unless parents approve and check to see that candles are secure. This size candle will only last a brief time, such as during a Bible verse reading, etc. If you do light candles, remember to put down a piece of clear plastic wrap to catch drips.

- Roll the dough evenly to 1/2" thick. Make sure the opening in the base is <u>slightly larger</u> than the stem of the menorah. With pointed table knife cut out base and holder, <u>keeping each in one piece</u> if possible. If not, make sure parts fit together well and plan to glue after baking. Cut both pieces as they rest flat on a cookie sheet.

- Insert a candle 1/4" deep in top of each "branch" to make indention for holding candles later. **Remove candles.**

- Bake at 200 degrees for two hours. Turn over and bake another hour or more, or leave in warm oven (turned off) overnight. Cool.

- Insert stem into base and glue.

- Use spray or craft paint in silver or gold. Use a cotton swab to make sure your candle indentations do not fill with paint. Air dry as directed on paint label. Add craft crystal sequins or use puffy paint in gold to decorate with leaves, branches or other patterns, if desired.

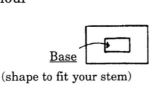

Base
(shape to fit your stem)

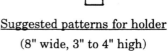

CLAY-DOH

1 cup all-purpose or wheat flour
1/2 cup salt
1/2 cup corn starch
2 tbsps. oil
1 cup water

<u>Suggested patterns for holder</u>
(8" wide, 3" to 4" high)

Mix well. Teen or parent should cook over medium heat for about 2 minutes until rubbery, and it pulls away from sides of pan. Scoop out quickly onto wax paper and knead as soon as tolerable <u>with the paper around it</u> (it's hot!) for one minute. Shape and bake as necessary for project. To smooth edges after baking, use emery board or medium sandpaper if necessary. Store unused portion in airtight bag.

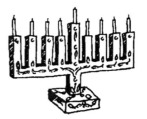

Design-a-Dreidel

Two symbols stand out at this celebration. They are the dreidel, a four-sided spinning top, and the menorah, the oil lamp used in the temple. You can purchase these from suppliers listed in the back of this book, or make a simple replica on your own.

To make your own **Dreidel** from a top you already have, see the following directions.

1. Use an ordinary top (tall ones work best) and cut a long card that will bend at four corners and touch the top when the ends come together. Be sure you can still spin the top–it is most important that the tip extends below the card. Measure around top to get the circumference. Use the formula $C = \pi d$ to compute the diameter. This diameter will equal one side. Multiply by four to get the length of the card needed.

2. Place the Hebrew alphabet letters for N (nun), G (gimmel), H (heh), and SH (shin) which stand for the Hebrew words *Nes Gadol Hayah Sham:* **A Great Miracle Happened Here.** Use white glue (or rubber cement if you plan to reuse the top without the cards. Rub unwanted dried rubber cement off with an eraser or your fingers.)

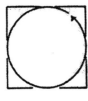
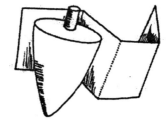

HOW TO PLAY

See "Spinning the Dreidel" in the *Jewish Customs of Hannukah Today* section on page 388 for instructions.

Making the Most of Music

This is a psaltery, a 10-stringed lyre. Might it have been the "guitar" of Bible times? You could carry it easily and pick or pluck its strings. What is your favorite musical instrument? Did it have an "ancestor" in Bible times? Look it up and write about it or make up a story. Include a paragraph about a psalm you like to sing; tell why. (Many praise and worship choruses are actually Psalms. Ask a parent or older brother or sister if you need help.) Tell what you learned in your research at a meal during this feast. Invite your family to sing a Psalm with you.

Star of David Craft

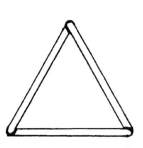

A simple star of David can be made from 6 craft sticks, one yard of gold cord or very narrow ribbon, markers and craft or hot glue.

1. Use a marker to color front, back and sides of 3 craft sticks. Color another set of 3 in a contrasting color. Suggestions are one set in yellow gold to use in front, and a set in teal or blue to use behind.

2. Form two equilateral triangles by gluing an exact match at each corner of three adjoining craft sticks. The best procedure is to make one end under and the opposite end on top as you go around the triangle. Plan the positions before you glue. Allow to dry. Either a small dot of hot glue (parents to supervise) or craft-type glue will work. Do not use "school glue" for wood bonding.

3. Position the triangles to form a Star of David, then glue in place. Let dry.

4. Begin from underneath the horizontal stick on the front triangle. Using the gold cord (or substitute) wrap clockwise around the star, going over the joints from underneath each time. If you leave about 12 inches before you start wrapping, you will have less to adjust when you are finished.

5. Adjust ends to match in length and tie knot behind the stick so it will not show. Bring ends up and tie a bow above the point of the rear triangle. Trim ends to match. Hang from the loop below the bow.

See "Symbolism in the Centerpiece" on the Centerpiece page, in the Pentecost section.

A Family Guide to the Biblical Holidays©

Recipe

MENORAH TORTIZZAS

This is a fun recipe for using the menorah, the focal symbol for this feast. Get the family or friends involved by letting each person create his own.

Tortilla dough:
> 2 c whole wheat flour (or 1 c each white and wheat, omit gluten)
> 4 t wheat gluten
> 1 t salt
> 1/4 c lukewarm water

Stir well, then knead 2 to 3 minutes. Divide into 12 portions and roll into balls. With rolling pin, roll ball into 6 to 7-inch tortilla and place on lightly sprayed cookie sheets.

Toping:
> 1 can, 15 oz. pizza sauce
> 2 to 2 1/2 c shredded mozzarella cheese
> 2 cans (14.25 oz.) cut green beans
> 2 T whole kernel corn

Spread tortillas with 1-1/2 to 2 tablespoons of pizza sauce. Sprinkle with about 3 tablespoons of mozzarella cheese. Bake at 425 degrees for approximately 4 minutes (until cheese bubbles but edges are not brown).

Remove from oven (also remove from hot cookie sheet if younger children are creating the menorahs). Use 14 to 15 green bean pieces to construct menorahs, placing a kernel of corn to make each "light". See illustration.

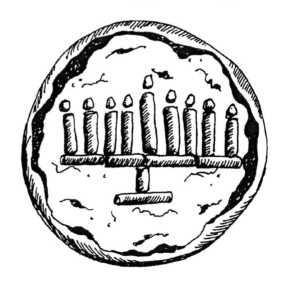

Pop back into oven for 3 to 4 more minutes until crust and cheese edges begin to brown. Sprinkle with parmesan cheese if desired.

Word Search

```
Y K J G S O I L G F R L A M A
C T I U N U L F S X I I E L Z
R A S S D I E T P G S N E E S
E N N A L E K Z H R O D N Y B
D O C D N E A T E R I O R T R
N M L I L Y V P A E I I F Z A
A O A M T E D H R T A O T X N
X L D M P S S D A Y S Q N Q C
E O T O D H I C E S A H V H H
L S R I A D I N G L P I I N E
A C V L A D S U E R C I D N S
H A L N E T B S M L E A R E E
D E I D A R B A G X L E R I M
L E E R O L Y M P U S E K I T
L R N O I T A C I D E D H S M
```

ALEXANDER	HALLEL	OLYMPUS
BRANCHES	HELLENISTIC	PERSIA
CANDLES	JUDEA	PORCH
DANIEL	KING	REDEDICATION
DAVID	LIGHT	SHINE
DEDICATION	MEDIA	SOLOMON
DREIDEL	MENORAH	SPIRIT
DYNASTY	MIRACLE	STAR
GREEKS	OIL	SYRIA

Crossword Puzzle

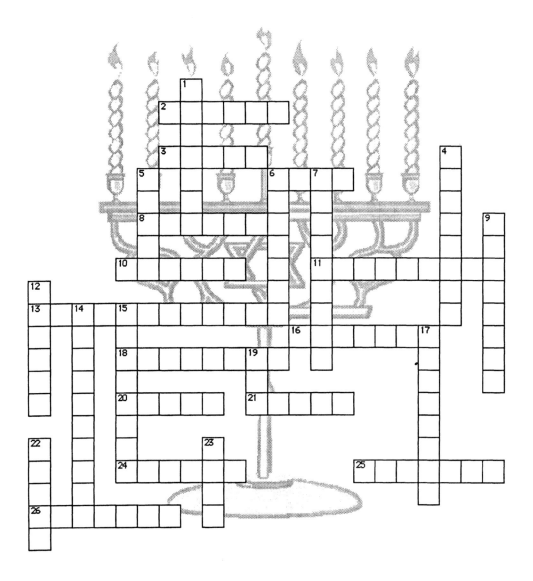

Across

2. Third month
3. God's anointed, who led after King Saul's death
6. Celestial body
8. Spinning top
10. Faithful prophet that God spared from the lions
11. Profaned the Temple of Israel
13. To recommit oneself
16. Candelabrum
18. Christ, our ___
20. To emit light
21. Not dark
24. God's Holy ___
25. A succession of rulers
26. Lighted one at a time

Down

1. An event that appears inexplicable by the laws of nature
4. The Menorah has several
5. Jewish countryside, region
6. King ___ , son of David
7. Young world conqueror
9. Early historian
12. Men from Greece
14. To set apart and consecrate to God
15. A city in the story of Hanukkah
17. Feast of Lights
19. Lamp fuel
22. Portico, covered walk
23. Sovereign

Coloring Page

PURIM

And Mordecai wrote these things, and sent letters unto all the Jews that were in all the provinces of the king Ahasuerus, both nigh and far, To establish this among them, that they should keep the fourteenth day of the month Adar, and the fifteenth day of the same, yearly, As the days wherein the Jews rested from their enemies, and the month which was turned unto them from sorrow to joy, and from mourning into a good day: that they should make them days of feasting and joy, and of sending portions one to another, and gifts to the poor. And the Jews undertook to do as they had begun, and as Mordecai had written unto them; Because Haman the son of Hammedatha, the Agagite, the enemy of all the Jews, had devised against the Jews to destroy them, and had cast Pur, that is, the lot, to consume them, and to destroy them; But when Esther came before the king, he commanded by letters that his wicked device, which he devised against the Jews, should return upon his own head, and that he and his sons should be hanged on the gallows. Wherefore they called these days Purim after the name of Pur.

Therefore for all the words of this letter, and of that which they had seen concerning this matter, and which had come unto them, The Jews ordained, and took upon them, and upon their seed, and upon all such as joined themselves unto them, so as it should not fail, that they would keep these two days according to their writing, and according to their appointed time every year; And that these days should be remembered and kept throughout every generation, every family, every province, and every city; and that these days of Purim should not fail from among the Jews, nor the memorial of them perish from their seed.

Then Esther the queen, the daughter of Abihail, and Mordecai the Jew, wrote with all authority, to confirm this second letter of Purim. And he sent the letters unto all the Jews, to the hundred twenty and seven provinces of the kingdom of Ahasuerus, with words of peace and truth, To confirm these days of Purim in their times appointed, according as Mordecai the Jew and Esther the queen had enjoined them, and as they had decreed for themselves and for their seed, the matters of the fastings and their cry. And the decree of Esther confirmed these matters of Purim; and it was written in the book.

(Esther 9:20-32)

PURPOSE OF PURIM

Purim, the Feast of Lots, is observed on the fourteenth day of the Hebrew month of Adar (February-March). This is a celebration of the deliverance of the Persian Jews over one of the most dastardly plots in history to exterminate the Jewish people. The book of Esther in the Old Testament tells the story of how the beautiful Jewish woman Esther (Hadassah) and her cousin Mordecai thwart the evil Haman, who plots to massacre the Jews.

The book of Esther has been referred to as "a monument in the history of anti-Semitism." The anti-Semitism shown in the book of Esther is religiously based. The anti-Semitism shown in later Hellenistic-Roman literature through today is purely ethnic hatred. The Jewish people have faced elimination as a group many times through ancient, medieval, and modern societies. *They have said, Come, and let us cut them off from being a nation; that the name of Israel may be no more in remembrance* (Ps 83:4).

At this time, the Hebrew people lived in Persia. Many of the Jews socialized with the Persians and became more and more worldly. They were accepted, integrated citizens who blended in to Persian life. In fact, a Jewish woman became the Queen. Imagine their shock, in a moment their lives were drastically changed. Out of the blue, the Prime Minister convinces the King to destroy the entire Jewish nation.

The Jews had a rude awakening! In a brief instant, they went from their normal daily routines to persecution to the point of death. They were hated, on the verge of destruction because of their race. During these years, the Jews were divided into two kingdoms, Israel and Judah. Both kingdoms had fought with each other. The prophets had tried to get the two groups together. Now that the Hebrews faced extinction, they joined kingdoms and turned to God for mercy.

IMAGINE A PARALLEL

Think about how you would feel if a similar situation would happen to Christians in America today. What if the nation decided all Christians should be destroyed just because there are a certain people scattered around the country who keep laws other than the state laws, and they are separate from *normal* people because of their radical religious beliefs (Esther 3:8). What if they were persecuted because they remain a different, distinct group, with morals and values that do not line up with the world's standards? Not just persecuted—the entire group receives the death sentence! Maybe it would wake up some worldly-leaning Christians!

COVENANT AND PROMISE

Purim is a story of when the Jews lived outside the land of Israel. The Jews are the people chosen to live in the promised land. It was God's land, and he chose one people to live in it to the exclusion of all others. Displacement from the land was punishment for sins, a jail sentence. The Bible explains, when the Jews failed to keep God's commands and betrayed the covenant, He sent them out of the land. *I will deliver them to be removed into all the kingdoms of the earth ...And I will send the sword, the famine, and the pestilence, among them, till they be consumed from off the land that I gave unto them and to their fathers* (Jer. 24:9-10). The Jews restoration to the land is a sign that God kept His promise. The covenant of the Promised Land is still valid.

BACKGROUND AND STUDY

The name *Feast of Lots* comes from the fact that the day was chosen for the Jews to die by way of lottery. It is interesting to note that the word *pur* is not Hebrew, but Persian. Thus the Torah, when mentioning it, translates into Hebrew: "Pur: That is, the goral (lot)." All other festivals, including Chanukah (another post-Mosaic holiday) have Hebrew names.

While God's name never appears *directly* in Esther, it does appear in acrostic form in Esther 5:4. It is the first letter of each of four successive words - yod hay vav hay, YHWH. This is the only book of the Bible that does not *directly* contain God's name. There is no doubt, though, that God was clearly in charge behind the scenes!

Purim in Bible Times

The story starts with a beauty contest in which Esther is chosen to be the new queen. *And the king loved Esther above all the women, and she obtained grace and favor in his sight more than all the virgins; so that he set the royal crown upon her head, and made her queen* (Esther 2:17). During that time, the Jews lived peacefully in the Persian (modern-day Iran) land. Mordecai was a descendent of King Saul, and advisor to the King and Esther's cousin. Esther was raised by Mordecai. He advised Esther not to tell the king she was of Hebrew descent.

The villain of the story is Haman, an arrogant, treacherous, egotistical advisor to the king. Haman demanded all the king's servants bow down to him. But Mordecai would not. Haman was full of jealousy and bitterness. A descendant of the Jew-hating tribe of Amalek, Haman devised his scheme to solve the Jewish "problem" once and for all by annihilating every Jew. Haman told the king, *"...There is a certain people scattered abroad and dispersed among the people in all the provinces of thy kingdom; and their laws are diverse from all people; neither keep they the king's laws: therefore it is not for the king's profit to suffer them"* (Esther 3:8) Haman convinced powerful Ahasuerus (Xerxes) that the Jews did not keep his laws and they should all be wiped out.

By lottery, the day was chosen for the Jews to die. Haman suggested that anyone who killed a Jew would be rewarded by keeping the victim's property. People responded well to this anti-Semitism. It was decreed that all Jews, both young and old, little children and women, in one day, were to be annihilated on the thirteenth day of the twelfth Hebrew month, Adar.

Mordecai "clothed himself in sackcloth and ashes and went out into the midst of the City." He turned to repentance, and urged the rest of the Jews to do likewise. Then he sent Esther to come to the King to beseech him and plead with him for her people. The first thing she did was to tell Mordecai to "Go and gather all the Jews . . . and they should fast for me, and neither eat nor drink for three days and nights." In addition, Esther included herself: "I also . . . will fast likewise." On the third day Esther went uninvited to the king's royal throne (taking her life in her hands). Queen Esther "found grace and favor in his sight." The king asked Esther, "What wilt thou, queen Esther? and what is thy request? it shall be even given thee to the half of the kingdom." Esther answered, "If it seem good unto the king, let the king and Haman come this day unto the banquet that I have prepared for him." The king agreed.

That day, Haman saw Mordecai in the king's gate. Again, Mordecai did not bow down to Haman. Haman was enraged! He and his wife devised a plot to have the king order Mordecai hanged. He gave the instructions for special gallows to be constructed for Mordecai's death.

That evening the king could not sleep. He sent for his court records and through them found out that Mordecai had never been repaid for saving his life. The king decided to honor Mordecai.

At the evening of the banquet the king again asked Esther, "What is thy petition? and it shall be granted thee: and what is thy request? even to the half of the kingdom it shall be performed." Esther answered, "My petition and my request is; If I have found favor in the sight of the king, and if it please the king to grant my petition, and to perform my request, let the king and Haman come to the banquet that I shall prepare for them, and I will do to morrow as the king hath said."

The king was aware that Esther was willing to die in order to bring a request to him and he was willing to grant her request. He would know that it was a most serious request. This also accounts for him repeating his question at the two banquets. He knew that she would not have risked death just to invite him to dinner.

The king and Haman came to the second banquet with Esther the queen. And the king said again "What is thy petition, queen Esther? and it shall be granted thee: and what is thy request? and it shall be performed, even to the half of the kingdom." Esther then exposed Haman as the king's adversary and enemy and besought the king to spare the Jewish people. The King was full of rage. He commanded Haman to be hanged on the gallows made for Mordecai.

Neither Esther nor the Jewish people sat around waiting for God to send His angels, but, rather, trusting in God to answer the prayer, they *acted boldly*. In both cases we do see an expression of the humility of men not being willing to trust their own strength, but imploring God for help. The community was also involved in the prayer:

The law decreeing the Jews to be killed could not be canceled, so the king gave a new decree that the Jews were now allowed to defend themselves when attacked. Therefore, the day that was to be destruction became a day of deliverance. Because of Mordecai's and Esther's loyalty and devotion, the entire Jewish nation was saved. The Jews also showed their devotion, for, throughout the duration of the year, not one single Jew chose to convert, even to save his life! The Jewish people had shown their character. They had earned the right to leave Exile, to return to the Holy Land, and to rebuild the Temple.

The king gave his ring, which he had taken from Haman, to Mordecai. Mordecai became the king's chief minister. Mordecai declared this rescue would be called Purim, to be celebrated each year (Esther 9:20-32).

TIME LINE OF PURIM EVENTS

Nisan 13
- Haman ordered the destruction of the Jews (Esther 3:12).
- Sometime towards the end of the day, the Jews repented and began to fast (Esther 4:16).

Nisan 14
- Day 1 of a 3-day fast.

Nisan 15
- Day 2 of a 3-day fast.

Nisan 16
- Day 3 of a 3-day fast.
- Esther went to the King uninvited (Esther 5:1).
- Esther had a banquet with Haman and the King (Esther 5:4).

Nisan 17
- Esther had the second banquet with Haman and the King (Esther 5:8).
- Adar 13, is decided to be the day for the destruction of the Jews (Esther 3:13).
- Haman's plans are spoiled.

Jewish Customs of Purim Today

To commemorate the miraculous turn of events recorded in Esther, Purim is celebrated with feasts, sending gifts of food to friends and the needy, and with the reading of Esther, the story of Purim. The earliest descriptions of Purim celebrations, from the Second Temple and Mishnaic eras, offer no indication of the partying that is associated with the festival today. The emphasis was on the formal reading of the Scroll of Esther, which was to be conducted with great care and seriousness. Later customs originated in late fifteenth century Italy, such as donning masks, drinking, parody, and costumes.

Purim is a joyous day celebrated by the entire family. The following are main traditions of Purim:

1) Listening to the Megillah reading in the evening and again in the morning.
2) Sending at least two ready to eat foods to at least one friend.
3) Giving charity to at least two poor people.
4) Eating a festive meal during the day of Purim in honor of the holiday.
5) Reciting "Al Hanisim" in prayer and in grace after meal.

FASTING

To commemorate the day of prayer and fasting that the Jews held before their victory, Jews fast on the day before Purim from approximately three hours before sunrise until forty minutes after sunset.

GIVE TO CHARITY

It is a tradition to give to charity to commemorate the half-shekel given by each Jew in the time of the Holy Temple.

PRAYERS

Special prayers are said for evening, morning and afternoon, as well as in the grace after meals. The morning of Purim, there is a special reading from the Torah Scroll in the synagogue.

PLAY

One of the most entertaining customs of the Purim holiday is the children dressing up as the characters found in the story of Esther. The *Megillah* (the Scroll of Esther) is read aloud as it is acted out in a play or acted out with puppets.

The custom of donning masks and costumes on Purim probably originated in late fifteenth century Italy as an imitation of Christian carnivals. It was tied to the idea of God's "hiding his face" as found in the Talmud!

NOISEMAKERS

Groggers are the noisemakers used during the reading of the Megillah. Every time the name of Haman is mentioned, everyone boos, hisses, stamps their feet, and twirls their groggers. Any type of noisemaker can be used. In medieval Europe, children would write Haman's name on stones or wood blocks, and bang them until the name was erased. When the name Mordecai is mentioned, the people cheer.

FOOD

Family and friends gather together to rejoice in the Purim spirit by having a special festive meal. As with other holidays, there is a traditional food. During Purim, *Hamantaschens* are served. *Hamantaschen* means "Haman's pockets." These are triangle-shaped cookies that supposedly look like the hat Haman wore. The cookies are sweet, filled with a fruit (usually prune) or poppy seed mixture.

WORK

Work is permitted as usual on Purim unless, of course, it falls on a Saturday.

Messianic Significance of Purim

This was one of many episodes in God's dealings with His people. The Jews were saved physically at this point in their history. The time of their full salvation and the complete fulfillment of God's prophecies given to Abraham was drawing nigh. It happened five hundred years later with the coming of adon Yeshua HaMashiach (the Lord Jesus, the Messiah). He was the greater Mordecai. Condemned to die for His people, Jesus the Messiah became the supreme sacrifice of atonement for the sins of Jew and Gentile alike. In Him were truly fulfilled the prophecies of old, *"...All the nations of the earth shall be blessed in him"* (Genesis 18:18). Today we see millions of people in all parts of the earth who have received these blessings through Abraham's seed, the Messiah, flesh of our flesh and bone of our bone (Frydland 1996).

Mordecai and Esther knew for certain that Haman's decree was not an accident of history, but a consequence of failings within the Jewish people. That is why Mordecai's response was "[He] *clothed himself in sackcloth and ashes and went out into the midst of the City.*" He turned to repentance, and urged the rest of the Jews to do likewise. Only then did he send Esther *"to come to the King and entreat him and plead with him for her people."*

Esther was also repentant. She asked Mordecai to *"Go and gather all the Jews . . . and they should fast for me, and neither eat nor drink for three days and nights."* In addition, Esther included herself: *"I also . . . will fast likewise."*

Just as the Jews were rescued, we are redeemed by our Righteous Messiah. True and complete redemption lies in our own hands, as we must turn to God in complete repentance.

SYMBOLISM

1.) The picture of the three-day resurrection is shown. Esther fasted for three days, and on the third day she arose to go before the king.

2.) The story of Esther is a depiction of a Christian's walk in a new life. Exposing Haman is symbolic of exposing sin. The new decree triumphs. The old decree symbolizes Jesus triumphing over the law of sin and death. Once Haman (sin, flesh) was put to death, Mordecai (Holy Spirit) is given unlimited command.

3.) The Jews were again delivered on the seventeenth of Nisan—Firstfruits—the same day that deliverance for the Israelites in Egypt began, and the same day Jesus arose!

Suggestions for Celebrating Purim

Get together with friends and family for a Purim party. Let the children dress up as the characters found in the Scroll of Esther (King Ahasuerus, Vashti, Queen Esther, Mordecai, and the evil Haman.)

Use groggers (instructions later in this section), and serve Hamantaschen cookies.

A HAMANTASHEN HAPPENING

One year, our family (Robin speaking) was making Hamantashen for a Purim party. I was making a quadrupled batch of batter. Our three smallest children were standing on chairs helping. I usually put out all the ingredients for the children to hand to me when they help. I needed the vanilla, so I got down a plastic container filled with several bottles of spices and seasonings, from the cabinet, and placed it on the counter. Of course, the phone rang, and as I was talking on the phone, my eighteen-month-old dumped an entire, large bottle of imitation bacon bits into the batter. Bacon bits—in a Jewish cookie batter! I was speechless. I had used the last of my eggs and butter and we were attending a Purim party that night. I started digging out the bacon bits before they got mixed into the batter. It looked like I got most of the red bits out—until I baked them. Each of the cookies had a few red bits showing. The cookies still tasted good, and the bacon wasn't real, so I took them to the party. Ever since we laughingly refer to those cookies as the "Pagan Bacon Haman Cookies." (See recipe this section—without the bacon bits!)

GIFTS TO OTHERS

Gifts of food and clothing to the ill or needy are also a custom established by the Jewish people in Esther's time. Let your family think of someone special that you could bless. A small package of goodies, or a larger food basket will depend on your income or the number of families you want to remember on this holiday.

Centerpiece

To assemble your centerpiece for Purim (see "Multi-Holiday Centerpiece" in the *Preliminary Activities and Crafts* section), use the **Star of David** and **Cup & Bread** flags. Cover base with bright colorful calico. Place **Crown and\or Scepter** craft (instructions follow) in the center. Insert flags in diagonally opposite corners.

SYMBOLISM IN THE CENTERPIECE

Bright Calico—Represents the happiness and joy of escaping destruction.

Crown and/or Scepter—the royal position through which God chose to rescue His people; God's sovereign hand in history (Rom. 13:1-7).

Star of David flag—God's rescue of the nation of Israel through miraculous grace, even though they were in captivity.

Cup & Bread flag—the nature of this festival to share food with the poor and with neighbors, and the puzzling fact that this opportunity for sharing came about because of a 3-day fast.

Scepter Craft

To use your centerpiece, you may want to select only the STAR OF DAVID and CROWN to signify the Lord's rule and protection over His chosen people, as well as to indicate this holiday was established by God's people to remember a special act of mercy.

Follow the Clay-Doh directions in the Hanukkah section or paper Maché in Tabernacles section and make a scepter or crown for your centerpiece. After baking, paint and sprinkle on glitter. NOTE: shape your scepter or crown out of a single clump if using doh, or you may need to glue parts together after baking. You can also glue small craft beads or sequins on later.

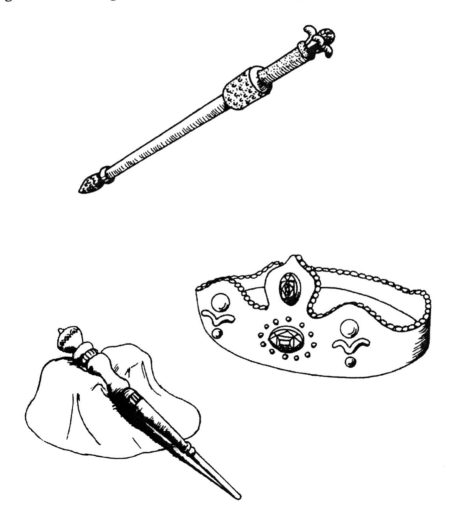

GROGGERS

Groggers are the noisemakers used during the reading of the Megillah. You can make a simple grogger by just putting a few dried beans in a pill bottle. Or spend some time making special personalized groggers. You will need: juice cans; jingle bells; scissors; adhesive backed paper such as contact paper; stickers or colored tape; glitter; and white glue.

1. Wash and dry the juice can and lid you removed. Trace the circular end on the adhesive paper. Draw another circle 1" larger than the outline circle. Cut out the outer circles. With scissors make cuts spaced 1" apart around the circle, from the outer edge in. Make two for the end caps for the can.

2. Cover attached end of the juice can with adhesive paper. Place a few jingle bells inside. Attach the lid on the open end and put other paper circle over it, sealing the jingle bells inside.

3. Cut a strip of adhesive paper which is the width of the can and is long enough to wrap around the can with 1" of overlap. Wrap around the can, covering the entire outside of the juice can.

4. To decorate the grogger, use colored tape, stickers, draw decorative lines with white glue and sprinkle them with glitter.

 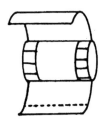 

Recipes

HAMANTASHEN COOKIE RECIPE

2 sticks margarine - softened
2 cups sugar
2 large eggs
2 tsp. vanilla
4 tsp. baking powder
4 cups of wheat flour or 2 cups white flour and 2 cups wheat flour

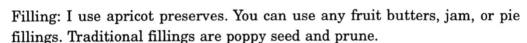

Filling: I use apricot preserves. You can use any fruit butters, jam, or pie fillings. Traditional fillings are poppy seed and prune.

Cut butter into sugar. Blend thoroughly. Add eggs and blend thoroughly. Add flour, 1/2 cup at a time, blending thoroughly between each. Put the batter in the refrigerator overnight or at least a few hours. Roll it out to about 1/4 inch thickness and then cut circles with a cookie cutter or use a drinking glass. Put a tablespoon of filling in the middle of each circle. Fold up the sides to make a triangle, overlapping the sides as much as possible so only a little filling shows through the middle. Bake at 375° for about 10-15 minutes, until golden brown.

ESTHER'S BANQUET BARS

Cookie Crust Base:
   2/3 cup oats
   2/3 cup whole wheat flour
   1/3 cup oat bran or ground
   almonds
   1/3 cup fructose or sugar
   1/3 cup brown sugar
   1/3 cup butter

Cut together as for pie crust and press into well-sprayed or oiled broiler pan or jelly-roll pan (approx. 11in. by 15 in). Bake in preheated 325° oven for 10 to 12 minutes.

Fruit Topping:
   29 oz can (lg.) sliced peaches,
   drained
   3/4 cup sour cream
   1/2 cup fructose or sugar
   1 egg
   cinnamon

On warm crust, arrange all peach slices into three vertical rows. Mix remaining ingredients, except cinnamon. Drizzle over and between slices. Dust with cinnamon to taste. Return to oven for twenty minutes. While still warm, cut in bars. Refrigerate leftovers.

Paper Dolls

Make copies onto card stock if possible. If not, use rubber cement and bond doll to card stock (discarded manila folder). Do not mount clothes on card. Carefully color and cut out these figures and their clothes. For added durability, cover with clear contact plastic. Use doll furniture or shoe boxes to create a throne, bed, banquet table and other props you may want.

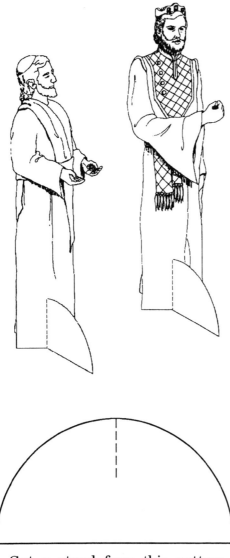

Cut a stand from this pattern using the same card stock you are using for the doll backing. Trace and cut out one for each doll. Cut slit on base and figures to slide in.

Card-weight paper stock (as in a file folder) is easiest to cut for a backing. To increase sturdiness, glue two craft sticks vertically to the center back when you have finished. Overlap as shown to help keep the figure upright.

A Family Guide to the Biblical Holidays©

ESTHER

Put sash over sackcloth dress below to make outfit at beginning of story

Cut on dotted line

This page left blank for cut-out

Mordecai

This page left blank for cut-out

King Ahasuerus

Cut between
fingers across base
of black area.

This page left blank for cut-out

Haman

1. Put brass brad in lowest necklace ornament, then in arm.

2. Use arm to gesture when Mordecai wears King's clothes.

3. At banquet, insert goblet in hand.

4. After Esther speaks truth, remove goblet, raise hand to cover eyes.

This page left blank for cut-out

Crossword Puzzle

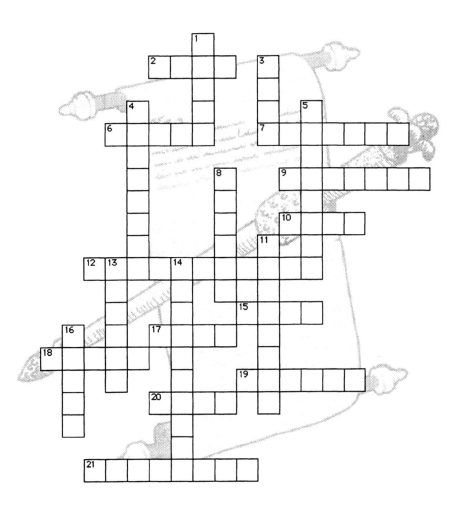

Across

2. Sixth month
6. King's headdress
7. The King's staff
9. Allegiance
10. Small, circular, jeweled band
12. Great damage
15. Ruler
17. Mordecai saved them
18. King's wife
19. King X___
20. Prince Jonathan's father
21. Helped Queen Esther

Down

1. Received a ring from the King, planned to destroy the Jews
3. Objects used to make a random determination
4. Noise makers
5. Ardent affection
8. The King's home
11. A person who serves as an agent for another
13. Queen
14. Remorse or contrition for past conduct
16. Feast of ___

Word Search

```
O X L I M C B R S G W D P P
S I R O R D N P N S Y A D T
D E N A V P J I W C L Y E E
R E X A D E R E R A D T V C
E F D R M A J E C E J L O N
T N K I E A M E S I U A T A
P T I O C X H T S W M Y I T
E P Q L Q A R P E A R O O N
C Y O U N U T E U E U L N E
S T E W C A Y I S R G L L P
S E O T J P Y P O T I N S E
N R I H R D Z M H N H M I R
C O G R O G G E R S T E C K
N S A C R I F I C E D H R O
```

ADAR	LOYALTY
CROWN	MERCY
DEDICATION	PALACE
DESTRUCTION	PURIM
DEVOTION	QUEEN
ESTHER	REPENTANCE
GROGGERS	RING
HAMAN	SACRIFICE
JEWS	SAUL
KING	SCEPTER
LOTS	XERXES
LOVE	

A Family Guide to the Biblical Holidays©

Coloring Page

פורים

Section 6: The Seventh Day Holiday

- SABBATH

I was glad when they said unto me,
Let us go into the house of the LORD.
Psalm 122:1

446

Sabbath

Shabbat

Purpose of The Sabbath

God sanctifies places and things to communicate to His people. He set apart the ark of the covenant and tabernacle. He set apart His holy book—the Bible. He set apart His Holy Son—Jesus, and He set apart a holy day—the Sabbath. *God blessed the seventh day, and sanctified it...* (Gen. 2:3). The Sabbath is the celebration of God's complete and perfect creation. As Judah Halevi explains, "The observance of the Sabbath is in itself an acknowledgment of His omnipotence, and at the same time an acknowledgment of the creation in His divine word."

The Sabbath was held in high esteem in both in Jewish circles and in early Christianity. The Sabbath was made at creation, two thousand years before there were any Jews. After Abraham's time the Sabbath applied to all people, aliens, and animals within the gates of the Israelites. (An alien is someone who is not a native of the land. This is the Hebrew "ger," a righteous non-Hebrew who has been grafted into Israel. See Romans 11:13-21.)

> **The Sabbath is not a yoke of bondage.**
>
> **It's a day of joy, rest, eating, enjoying Scriptures, and fellowship.**

God intends that the Sabbath be regarded as something honorable, something significant, not for its own sake, but because of what it represents. Keeping the Sabbath is the only one of the holy days to be ordained in the Ten Commandments. It is tied to two specific and highly significant acts in history: 1.) God's "resting" after six days of creation (Gen. 2:2) and 2.) Israel's deliverance from Egypt (Deut. 5:15).

God's model of work and rest demonstrates how much of our lives is to be spent in labor and how much is to be spent in worship. In both the Old and New Testaments, the Sabbath calls to mind God's sovereign rule and His merciful redemption.

The Sabbath is not a yoke of bondage. It's a day of joy, rest, eating, and enjoying Scriptures, fellowship, etc. The Sabbath was never intended to be a restraining time of punishment. What would your reaction be if your boss came to you and said, "I want you to take tomorrow off to rest. Enjoy yourself, eat, rest, read, just don't even think about work." Would you feel burdened?

The Sabbath is a holy time of resting from our weekly work in order to come into a joyous worship of God. It is a time of release from the stress and pressure of making a living. It is a time to rest from our normal pursuit of physical gain and to remember our Creator.

Keeping the Sabbath honors God, our Creator, who also rested on the seventh day (Genesis 2:3). It also unifies our families and sets priorities for them. This day of rest refreshes us spiritually and physically—providing time when we can gather together and when we can reflect on God without the stress of our everyday activities.

HISTORY

The study of when the Sabbath was changed to Sunday is very interesting. The New Testament is totally silent with regard to any change of the Sabbath day or any sacredness for Sunday. The adoption of Sunday observance in place of the Sabbath did not occur in the early Church of Jerusalem by virtue of the authority of Christ or of the Apostles, but rather took place several decades later.

In 132 A.D. Bar-Kokhba led a revolt against the Romans. When he was done, 50 percent of the population of Judea was dead and tens of thousands of men and women who remained alive were sold into slavery. Jews were forbidden to set foot in Jerusalem, and the province was renamed *Palestine*. It was a dangerous time to be identified with the Jews. During this period, the predominate day of worship among Christians gradually began to change from the Sabbath to Sunday. The day changed, in part, because of the need to disassociate the Christian movement from the Jewish nation.

Years later, the Church of Rome: Canon 29, Council of Laodicea, 364 C.E., worried about Judaizing and gave the following statement: "Christians shall not Judaize and be idle on Saturday, the Sabbath, but shall work on that day; but the Lord's day (Sunday) they shall honor, and as being Christians, shall, if possible, do no work on that day. If, however, they are found Judaizing, they shall be shut out from Christ."

The Catholic Encyclopedia states that it was the Catholics who changed the day of worship from Sabbath to Sunday and claims this as a mark of its authority. Converts Catechism of Catholic Doctrine said, "Sunday observance is from when the Catholic Church transferred the solemnity from Saturday to Sunday."

The Jew looks at the Sunday worship as abandoning the law. The Jewish rejection of Christ was triggered by the Christian rejection of the law as said by historian Jules Isaac, "To ask a Jew to reject the law is like asking them to tear out their heart."

To ask a non-Jew to keep the strict Jewish rituals, they were not accustomed to, could be an obstacle to salvation.

Acts 15:28-29 explains Council of Jerusalem decided not to put obstacles in the way of non-Jewish believers to turn to God (v. 19). The landmark decision released converts from circumcision and being bound to the Old Testament Sabbath rituals. However, the new converts could choose to benefit from the special weekly Sabbath worship and rest.

Jesus Himself said the Sabbath was made for the man. Every day is to be holy unto God. Our Father does not want His children divided by focusing on a day. He wants them united, focusing on Christ. Whatever day you observe as a day of family worship and rest is between you and God. Enjoy it as a day of rest, family worship and strengthening relationships. Let it bring unity and focus to your home.

A Family Guide to the Biblical Holidays©

The Sabbath in Bible Times

The *Encyclopedia of Judaism* explains;

> Bible does not mention that the Patriarchs observed the Sabbath (although rabbinical sources do). During their wanderings in the Wilderness of Zin and with the introduction of manna, the Israelites were first commanded to observe the Sabbath; they were told that five days of the week they were to collect a single portion of manna, but on the sixth they should collect a double portion, for *"...Tomorrow is the rest of the holy sabbath unto the LORD..."* (Ex. 16:23). When some searched on the seventh day for manna and found none, *"And the LORD said unto Moses, How long refuse ye to keep my commandments and my laws? See, for that the LORD hath given you the sabbath, therefore he giveth you on the sixth day the bread of two days; abide ye every man in his place, let no man go out of his place on the seventh day"* (Ex. 16:28-29). Three weeks later, the Israelites received the Ten Commandments, the fourth of which is devoted to the Sabbath.
>
> Little information is available about Sabbath observance during the First Temple period, although something may be gleaned from statements in Amos and Hosea. There is no prohibition against trading on that day in the Pentateuch, but Amos (8:5) implies that it existed in his time. Hosea (2:13) includes the Sabbath in the happy times which will cease. Isaiah (1:13) bears witness to the Sabbath being a national institution. Jeremiah (17:21-22) exhorts the people to observe the Sabbath as it was commanded, for the future of Jerusalem depended on it. Nehemiah (chap. 10) tells of the covenant he made with the returned exiles, one point of which was not to buy items on the Sabbath. However, upon his return from Persia he saw that the covenant had not been adhered to and introduced changes to insure Sabbath observance (Neh. 13:15-22). Ezra and his disciples began to systemize rules and interpretation of the Bible and tradition to preserve and encourage Sabbath observance.
>
> The residents of Jerusalem would not defend themselves on the Sabbath when besieged by Ptolemy I. Some 150 years later,

however, during the Maccabean wars, Mattathias the Hasmonean ruled that the laws of the Sabbath may be transgressed to save lives, therefore the Jews could defend themselves on the Sabbath (1 Macc. 2:40-41). After the Sanhedrin began to function, Sabbath laws became more formalized in the Halakhah, and the rabbinical laws became the touchstone for all further development of these rules until modern times. Work is prohibited on the Sabbath. The basic feature of the Sabbath is to refrain from "work," following the injunction in Exodus 20:10, *"But the seventh day is the sabbath of the LORD thy God: in it thou shalt not do any work."*

Jewish Customs of the Sabbath Today

The Hebrews call the Sabbath *Shabbat*. It is one of the best known but least understood of all Jewish observances. Many think of the Sabbath negatively to be associated with "killjoys" who want a day filled with suppressing restrictions. To appreciate the Sabbath day with God we need to get rid of this negative image. To those who observe Shabbat, it is a precious gift from God, a day of great joy eagerly awaited throughout the week, a time when one can set aside all of their weekday concerns and spend time for spiritual enrichment.

Observant Jews translate this command into practical observance by refraining from any act of creation or destruction on the Sabbath. Shabbat is a day devoted to rest, reflection, prayer and Torah study. The order of the activities vary, especially among non-Orthodox communities—just as Thanksgiving varies in American homes.

FRIDAY AFTERNOON

In traditional Jewish homes, Sabbath preparations begin well before sunset on Friday evening. Cooking and cleaning are typical Friday afternoon affairs. It is much like preparing for the arrival of a special guest: the house is cleaned, the family bathes and dresses up, the best dishes and tableware are set, a festive meal is prepared.

Strict Jews remove the light bulb from the refrigerator (so it does not turn on when you open it), set timers for appliances to come on, etc. There are even elevators in Israel that will automatically open on Sabbath so a Jew does not have to push a button.

FRIDAY NIGHT SHABBAT DINNER

Sabbath begins at sunset. Shabbat candles are lit and a blessing is recited no later than eighteen minutes before sunset[1]. This ritual, performed by the woman of the house, officially marks the beginning of the sabbath.

The most picturesque tradition associated with the Sabbath is the candle lighting. The candle lighting marks the beginning and end of all Sabbaths, weekly or annual celebrations.

The tradition of lighting candles to begin and end the Sabbath started in a very practical way. Scripture says, *"You shall not kindle a fire in any of your dwellings on the Sabbath day"* (Exodus 35:3). In ancient times, the only form of light available at night was an oil lamp or candle. In order to have the supply of oil burn longer into the Sabbath, the lamps were lit at the very last moment before the Sabbath began - at or before the beginning of sundown. Once they burned out, they could not be relit until after the Sabbath was over. That time is marked by the lighting of the Havdalah candle (described below) (Taylor 1996).

Some families attend a brief evening service. In many synagogues, the Friday evening prayers are recited at dusk. After services, the family comes home for a festive, leisurely dinner. Before dinner, the man of the house recites a prayer over wine (Kiddush) sanctifying the sabbath. There are no specific requirements or customs regarding what to eat except for the challah bread, a sweet, eggy bread shaped in a braid. Covers made of linen or other fine fabric are used for covering the Sabbath loaves (challah covers). They are often embroidered with words such as "In honor of the Sabbath" or another relevant phrase, decorative floral patterns, or Sabbath themes.

BLESSINGS

A beautiful Shabbat tradition is the parental blessing. The father places both hands on each child as he says a blessing over them. Examples:

A traditional Jewish blessing for a son is: May God make you like Ephraim and Manasseh.

A traditional Jewish blessing for a daughter is: May God make you like Sarah, Rebekah, Rachel and Leah.

Or a personal blessing is said for each child using a format similar to this:

"May God bless you with _____ and _____. May you be (like) _____ and _____. May this Sabbath fill you with _____ and _____."

Some families say a husband and wife blessing. Husbands read Proverbs 31:10-31 to their wives and wives read Psalm 112 to their husbands.

Then everyone joins hands and sings or recites a phrase similar to the following: May Adonai bless you and guard you. May Adonai shine Divine light upon you and be good to you. May Adonai face you and give you peace."

SATURDAY

Many Jews spend Saturday morning in the synagogue. Upon returning home, traditional Jews repeat several of the Friday evening customs as they enjoy their Sabbath lunch. Cooking is prohibited on Shabbat so lunch is usually prepared the day before (in crock pot or slow cooker).

Saturday afternoon is unstructured, designed for relaxation and visiting. Activities include: telling uplifting stories at meals, studying the weekly Torah portion (individually, as a family or with friends, or in a special class or study) reading other suitable study materials, taking a nap, playing games with the children, a walk in the park, worship services, telling stories, singing songs, visiting relatives and friends, and if possible, visiting the sick, the shut-in, and the elderly.

In the evening, when three stars are seen, the Havdalah service is performed.

SATURDAY EVENING HAVDALAH SERVICE

The Havdalah ceremony is held on the Sabbath evening just after dark. This is a man-made short ceremony to formally mark the end of Shabbat. The Hebrew word havdalah means separation or distinction. The following items are used to perform the ceremony: a cup of wine, a braided candle, and a box of sweet-smelling spices.

Participants stand close together in a circle. Blessings are said over each item as they are passed around the circle. The wine is poured until it overflows and then the cup is lifted up again. Psalm 116:13 is recited: *I will take the cup of Salvation and call upon the name of the Lord*. Then the braided candle is lit. It is customary for the child to hold the candle. A blessing is said over the wine. The spices are shaken and passed around for all to enjoy the aroma. A blessing is said over the spices. The wine is passed around for everyone to sip. The candle is extinguished in the remaining wine as the final blessing is said. The ceremony is concluded with a song.

Messianic Significance of the Sabbath

- The Sabbath reminds us that God created the world.
- The Sabbath reminds us that God delivered Israel from bondage in Egypt.
- The Sabbath reminds us that Christ delivered us from the penalty of sin at Calvary.
- The Sabbath reminds us that God will make us holy, just as He made the Sabbath holy.
- The Sabbath reminds us that God will finish His work in our lives, just as He finished His work of creation and redemption.
- The Sabbath reminds us that God is our Lord and God.
- The Sabbath reminds us that we have rest in Christ.

The rest that God intended for us to receive on Sabbath is not just a physical rest from our work or a mental and emotional rest from the stress of life. When Jesus said, *Come unto me . . .I will give you rest* (Matt. 11:28), He also said, *ye will find rest unto your souls* (Matt. 11:29). Entering that rest requires that we stop trying to save ourselves and rest in the finished work of Jesus.

The image of the joyless, somber restricting Sunday stems from the 16th century. Jesus defines the Sabbath in Matthew 12:8, *For the Son of Man is Lord of the sabbath day* [(!)] The Sabbath, as with the rest of the Bible finds fulfillment in Christ. *For Christ is the end of the law for righteousness to every one that believeth* (Rom. 10:4).

Everything about the Sabbath teaches us something about the Messiah (Lancaster 1996).

THE CANDLES

The Sabbath is full of customs and traditions far predating the time of Jesus. The two candles that are lit to mark the beginning of the Sabbath are called the witness candles and they are symbolic of the two witnesses that stand before the Lord in Revelation 11 and Zechariah 4. They are Moses and Elijah, the personifications of the Torah and the Prophets. These same two witnesses appear with Messiah in the transfiguration. Each Friday evening the lighting of the two witness candles reminds us that Messiah is witnessed throughout the Torah (first five books of the Bible) and the Prophets.

THE WINE

When the family is seated around the table, a declaration of the holiness of the Sabbath and the blessing of the wine is recited (Kiddush). The father lifts a cup of wine and says "Blessed are you, Lord our God, King of the Universe, who brings forth fruit from the vine." Jesus says in John 15:5, *I am the vine, ye are the branches,* and in Mark 14:24, Jesus said unto them, *This is my blood of the new testament, which is shed for many.*

THE BREAD

The special bread called Challah is covered with a cloth while Kiddush is recited. Then the cloth is removed from the bread and the loaves are lifted up while a blessing is said: "Blessed are you Lord our God, King of the Universe, who brings forth bread from the earth." In the same way, the Messiah was laid in the earth and covered with a cloth, *And he took it down, and wrapped it in linen, and laid it in a sepulcher that was hewn in stone, wherein never man before was laid* (Luke 23:53). Then He was lifted up from the dead, brought forth from the earth, and exalted. The bread is broken and dispersed around the table.

The Sabbath blessings have not changed since before the time of Jesus. So when we read in the gospels that Jesus took a piece of bread, made the blessing, broke it, gave it to them and said, "Take it! This is my body," we know what that blessing was: Blessed are you Lord our God, King of the Universe, who brings forth bread from the earth. It was a prophecy regarding his resurrection!

HAVDALAH CEREMONY

Jesus is revealed even in the Havdalah ceremony. The wine is poured until it overflows and then the cup is lifted up again. Psalm 116:13 is recited, *I will take the cup of Salvation and call upon the name of the Lord.* The Hebrew word for Salvation is Jesus, so the above verse can be recited: *"I will take the cup of Jesus and call upon the name of the Lord."* At the end of Havdalah, the lit candle is extinguished into the wine which has run over the cup. We see how in the same way the life of our Messiah was extinguished with the spilling of His blood. It is an awe-inspiring picture of our Lord's sacrifice.

PROPHECY

Just as at the completion of six days of work there comes a seventh day of rest, Messiah will reign over the earth for a thousand years at the completion of the age.

But, beloved, be not ignorant of this one thing, that one day is with the Lord as a thousand years, and a thousand years as one day (2 Pet. 3:8).

We are approximately six thousand years from creation and the thousand-year Sabbath reign of Jesus is at hand.

The Sabbath is a mirror of the World to Come.

Suggestions for Celebrating the Sabbath

God intended the Sabbath to be more than a "day off" after six days of work. The Sabbath is a day when we rest and rebuild our emotional, physical, mental, and spiritual resources. The Sabbath was a day to enjoy God, our Creator and His creation. Christ declared "it is finished" at Creation and at the Cross, telling us that we cannot add anything to what God has done for us. So we are able to rest in God's finished work.

God adds another element to this instruction on Sabbath keeping: "And call the sabbath a delight, the holy day of the Lord honorable..." The word translated delight is the Hebrew term *oneg*, meaning "daintiness." This term comes from a root meaning "soft, delicate." This is an interesting way to describe the Sabbath. God speaks of attributing a quality to the Sabbath. The quality represented by this word *oneg* is preciousness or fragility; it denotes something that is highly valued. Therefore, God says that keeping the Sabbath is not a matter of mere perfunctory behavior (that is, behavior done in a mechanical fashion without care) it involves a worshipper in an intellectual process whereby he renders a judgment concerning a thing's worth (in this case, the "worth" of the Sabbath) (Bordwine n.d.).

You can start a wonderful family worship in your home each week by sanctifying the Shabbat as a special day - making it distinct, or separate, from the rest of the week. Use this day to deepen your relationship with God, your spouse, children, and friends. Have a special candlelight dinner on Friday evening and bless your children. You can use the Traditional Jewish Observance for a model but don't get burdened down by man's laws—just use it as a guide.

The degree to which a child will delight in the Sabbath depends on the example set by the parents. This is true especially for younger children. By deliberate design and by default, parents communicate values, opinions, ethics and attitudes to their children. If a parent wants to see a child delight in the Sabbath, let that parent delight in it himself. Teaching reinforced by example is forceful; teaching contradicted by example is mere rhetoric (ibid).

THURSDAY

If you did not grow up in a family keeping Sabbath, it takes a little getting used to. Many of us usually use Saturday as a house cleaning or shopping day. I find it helpful to shop on Thursday for ingredients for a special Sabbath dinner and ingredients for effortless meals on Saturday (muffins, sandwiches, etc.). Prepare the challah bread (see recipe in this section) or pick up two loaves at a bakery Thursday evening or Friday morning.

FRIDAY

Get the house all clean just as if you were having guests. If you set the goal to have the house clean by noon, the Sabbath will go much smoother. Rushing around hurriedly at the last minute is not a good way to start off Sabbath. Remember this is preparation for a joyful rest day—don't make it a burden. Saturday's lunch can be prepared Friday in crock pot or slow cooker. Try rewarding the children with a special lunch or outing on Friday afternoon for having the house clean by lunch time. Choose a simple, but nice dinner (a roast or roasted chicken or vegetables or casserole) that can be cooking in the oven with little attention. As dinner cooks, set a special table including two candles and have everyone dress in nice clothes.

FRIDAY NIGHT SABBATH DINNER

Mother lights the candles as she says a verse or prayer or one of the following:

Let your light so shine before men, that they may see your good works, and glorify your Father which is in heaven (Matthew 5:16).

Then spake Jesus again unto them, saying, I am the light of the world: he that followeth me shall not walk in darkness, but shall have the light of life (John 8:12).

Blessed are you, oh Lord our God, King of the universe, Who has sanctified us by Your commandments.

Before dinner the father can say a blessing over each child (see blessings in previous section). Think of individual gifts and abilities, present needs and future goals. Husband and wife can exchange blessings. This would be an excellent time for children to recite memory verses they have worked on during the week.

During dinner share what God has done for each of you during the week and personal thoughts with the rest of the family. Ask each of the children to share something special, something they really liked, and something they did not like about their week. Encourage them to reflect.

Conclude dinner by reading a Bible passage or devotional. Make after dinner special with your own family traditions. Read aloud, watch a special video, play board games, etc.

SATURDAY

Rest

Alter your pace whatever you do. Take longer to eat, walk slower, etc. Refrain from all weekday and weekend work-type activities. If you must work, keep the Sabbath in mind. Do as little work as is necessary. Try to spend lunch time reading God's word, break time in prayer, etc.

Your Sabbath morning and afternoon can be spent studying God's Word, reading aloud, telling stories, sleeping in, taking a nap, playing games, walking in the park, at worship services, singing songs, and visiting relatives and friends, etc.

Take a Trip Down Memory Lane

Since Sabbath is a day for family, why not study yours? Let every one help as you arrange family photo albums. The youngest members will enjoy just looking through completed pages. If your collection is complete, use a relaxing browsing time to spur discussions about the special memories they represent.

Consider making a family tree and sharing your information about past generations. Even if unpleasant memories or facts arise, remind your children that when they become members of the family of God, they can choose their spiritual inheritance. Example: you may want to identify with your grandfather's generosity, but reject your great aunt's fear. Keep your great grandma's hospitality, but reject a great grandpa's dishonesty, etc. Because we are heirs with Jesus (Rom. 8:14-17, Gal.3:29, 4:6, Tit. 3:7, Jas. 2:5), we don't have to walk in the sins and errors of past generations. *"Therefore, if any man be in Christ...behold, all things are become new"*(2 Cor. 5:17).

Teach your children how to enjoy the happy memories and give the painful ones to Jesus. This is not the same as denying them. Allow your children, and yourself time to grieve losses, wrongdoing and other unhappiness, then prayerfully ask Jesus to take the sad memories and cover them with a healing touch that only He can give.

Visit a Shut-In

Reach out to someone who is of lower socio-economic background and embrace them as members of the family of God. Our "adopted grandmother" [Linda speaking] is an elderly, blind, black lady who is full of the love of God. Helping to clean her house, run errands for her, paint, prepare food, sing or read scripture (or let her recite scripture to us!) is a special opportunity to serve in God's kingdom. The work we do for her does not violate the Sabbath, according to Isaiah 58. Shut-ins need to be set free from the "bondage" of loneliness, helplessness and fear. Your rejection of pride and prejudice will bring great blessing to you as well as them. Just to visit and offer friendship and encouragement will glorify God and begin to fulfill this scripture.

Give a Cup of Water

Use your Sabbath to extend a "cup of cold water" to someone in Jesus' name. (Mark 9:41; Matt. 25:34-40) Consider a ministering to the poor, nursing home invalids, those of another culture, etc. who don't know Jesus, and use your friendship or servanthood as a door to some day introduce them to Him. You can pray and ask the Lord to show you how to reach out—even for just an hour—on your Sabbath. It is good for children to see parents model an unbiased, humble heart. *"For God so loved the world...but not willing that any should perish, but that all should come to repentance."* (John 3:16, 2 Pet. 3:9) Make your Sabbath a day of rest... and sharing God's love.

HAVDALAH

If you decide to try the Havdalah service you can follow the order described in the Jewish Customs section and add New Testament verses to the blessings. Special spice boxes and the traditional braided Havdalah candle can be purchased at most synagogues or Judaic shops, or you can make the Havdalah candle easily by taping three candles together, or warm in oven and twist together, and use a potpourri box for the spices.

464

Look up Bible verses together as a family and determine your own traditional Sabbath blessings. Here are a few examples:

Blessing for the candle: *Ye are the light of the world. A city that is set on an hill cannot be hid. Neither do men light a candle, and put it under a bushel, but on a candlestick; and it giveth light unto all that are in the house. Let your light so shine before men, that they may see your good works, and glorify your Father which is in heaven* (Matt. 5:14-16).

Blessing for the wine: *And he took the cup, and when he had given thanks, he gave it to them: and they all drank of it. And he said unto them, This is my blood of the new testament, which is shed for many* (Mark 14:23-24).

Blessing for the spices: *For we are unto God a sweet savour of Christ, in them that are saved, and in them that perish* (2 Cor 2:15).

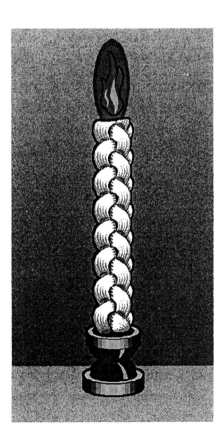

Star of David Potato Stamp

Here are two basic designs of the Star of David (see facing page). The solid design is easiest. The open design will have to be done by older children or teens and requires a <u>large</u> baking potato.

Mom or dad or teen will need to supervise. This activity requires an EXACTO® knife, although a paring knife with a good point can be used for the smaller, solid design.

- Trace design on next page onto other paper and cut it out. Cut the potato in half. Pin the design to your potato in the center and cut down into the potato about 1/4" as you follow the outline.

- After you have cut the entire outline of your star, cut carefully across your potato, parallel to the sliced surface, to remove at least 1/8 inch depth **only on areas that are NOT the star.** When you are finished, the star should be left standing <u>at least</u> 1/8 inch higher than the rest of the surface.

- Pour tempera or acrylic paint (thin with water to the consistency of gravy) on a saucer or in a jar lid that is larger around than the potato. Dip the design into the paint, then press onto a sample paper. If you discover any flaws, wash the potato gently, pat dry, and correct the flaws. Now complete your project.

- Once your stamp is cut, if you want to **reuse it another day,** wrap it in plastic and store in the refrigerator. The potato will usually stay firm for a week or more. Before storing you may want to rinse off excess paint. When using different colors, rinse the potato gently under cool running water and blot dry carefully.

Below are options for using your potato stamp.

1. On the next page is an example of a design you could use on Sabbath dinner place cards. Make several and store them to replace soiled cards as necessary.

2. Print the design on 2- to 3-inch circles or rectangles. Punch hole and thread yarn or gold cord through and use as doorknob ornaments to

A Family Guide to the Biblical

remind you to pray for the light of the gospel to come to the Jews.

3. Place the design in the corner of sheets of writing paper. To make your own, cut regular typing paper in half crosswise to make 5 1/2" x 8 1/2" sheets or fold in half a second time and have notecards. Standard size envelopes to fit can be purchased from a printing office.

4. Make a border on 11" x 17" paper placemats, or come up with your own ideas!

Simple Star   Difficult Star

Sabbath Recipe

Challah "IN A BAG"

2 1/2 cups whole wheat flour
3 cups unbleached or all-purpose flour
2 pkg. of Rapid Rise yeast or 1 1/2 tbsp. instant-active bulk yeast
1 1/2 tsp. salt

Put half of the flour, all the yeast and salt in a gallon size zipper-lock bag or a large sturdy plastic bag (younger child may need another person to hold it tightly). Force all the air out of the bag, close and work the bag with your fingers to mix the ingredients together.

ADD:

1 2/3 cups very warm water (120°F. Use candy thermometer to make sure it isn't too hot. If it is too hot the bread won't rise; if too cool, it will take longer to rise.)

1/4 cup oil or softened margarine

1/4 cup honey

Carefully squeeze out air, seal bag and work bag with fingers until well mixed.

ADD:

Add the other half of your flour. You will mix well, then watch to see if you need any extra flour. If you do, only add 1/4 cup at a time. The dough should feel soft like new "play-dough," and will pull away from the sides of the bag and stick to itself. If you add too much flour the dough will be too hard, like clay, and will not rise as well. Work the bag, mixing well.

Rest the dough (and you) for ten minutes. Spray or lightly oil cookie sheet.

TURN OUT:

Turn out dough onto light floured surface (about one cup of either flour). Sprinkle some flour on top and knead several minutes until smooth and elastic. 'Knead' means pushing the dough forward with the 'heel' of the palm of your hand, then using your fingers to pull it back over itself. Repeat, turning dough as needed.

BREAK OFF:

Break off about one third dough. This will be for your top braid. Separate it into 3 equal parts and roll between your hands to shape into 8" or 9". long ropes. Braid the ropes. Now take the big portion of dough and divide it into 3 parts. Shape these into 14" to 15" ropes and braid. Place the larger braid on cookie sheet first and put the smaller one lengthwise on top.

LET RISE:

Let rise until double in size. This will take 45 minutes to 1 hour away from a draft.

PREHEAT:

Preheat your oven to 325°. This takes 7 to 8 minutes. If you don't, the bread will get too brown on the bottom before it's done on top.

FOR ADDED SHINE:

For added shine and color, you can beat one egg white and use a basting brush to gently 'paint' your challah braids on the top and sides.

BAKE:

Bake on the middle rack for 45 to 55 minutes until nicely brown (ovens vary). This loaf is equal to two medium loaves. It weighs about 2 1/4 pounds. If your family is small, you may want to halve the recipe.

Games

Not all families enjoy the same activities. Choose those which enable you to appreciate one another, encourage one another, or focus on things in God's kingdom. Sabbath is not to appear as another day of school — it is a time set apart and special: freeing and restful.

These games are a few suggestions for stimulating times when nearly the whole family can participate. For other ideas in addition to games, there are a number of Christian and secular idea books. We recommend *Together at Home* by Dean & Grace Merrill, *Let's Make a Memory* by Shirley Dobson and Gloria Gaither, *Family Walk* Magazine by Bruce Wilkinson.

WHO AM I? MYSTERY GAME

This game is played by having some of the family members taking turns in guessing what Bible characters the other members are pretending to be. Those who are guessing ask clue questions that can only be answered by a "yes" or a " no."

To avoid going down lists of kings, prophets or disciples, a limit to two or three names may be guessed before being disqualified. Example: "Are you in the Old Testament?" No. "Are you a disciple?" Yes. (At this point the limit of two or three names is allowed. Other questions should provide clues, such as "Did you write a book in the Bible?" or "Do you have a brother who is also a disciple?" or "Were you a tax collector?," etc.)

This game is excellent for subtly reinforcing biblical information, and developing thinking skills and problem solving.

THE MINISTER'S CAT

This is an alphabet game that has been around for more than a century, but there are different variations and it is not familiar to all. It is sure, however, to bring fun. Based on the alphabet, each player must take the letter that falls on his turn and think of a word for the "minister's cat." Example: The minister's cat is an Adorable cat... NEXT... The minister's cat is a Bothersome cat..., etc.

Have a limit of 30 seconds to come up with your word. For older children or teens, a more difficult variation is to clap in time, as you speak, with four claps to the phrase. (Clap on "min-," "cat," your adjective, and final "cat.") Continue to clap in time, while players are thinking up answers, with a limit of fifteen to twenty claps. When a player cannot come up with a word, he becomes "one third of a cat." After failing to come up with a word a total of three times, he "meows" when it falls his turn. Repeat the alphabet as long as you wish.

NOTE: Omit K, X and Z as there are so few adjectives to choose from. Younger children may need to be helped to make describing words from their suggestions such as *often-gone* or *yarn-chasing* or adding -y to the word they have chosen. Have as your motto "Just chuckle and go on."

SONGFEST

School-age family members can pick their own tune (one familiar to the whole family) and make up a new set of words. Younger children may want to use simpler nursery rhyme tunes such as "Mary had a Little Lamb," and older folks can go for tunes like "This Old Man" or "She'll be Comin' Round the Mountain."

To bring unity to the activity, choose a single subject like joy, prayer, God's love, etc., or center around a Bible character you have recently read about. You may want to make up different verses if a story is being told. When you are finished, sing and share as you go. Younger family members will likely spend less time and want to do theirs first. Listen, then sing it again with them. Older children or teens who find this a challenging creative outlet may use the entire afternoon or evening. Perhaps the family can hear it before the next mealtime, think on the words, and sing together before leaving the table. Praise everyone's efforts and the Lord for His gift of music.

DINNER MUSIC

This is nice to sing at the end of your Sabbath dinner. Sing to the tune of "Jesus Loves Me"

Bless this home and bless this food.
Lord you will to do us good.
Keep us faithful, kind, and true.
So that we may be like you.

Chorus: Lord bless this Sabbath;
Lord bless our family.
Lord bring your presence.
That we may rest in you.

Coloring Page

To Parents: We suggest the purchase of a special Bible story coloring book which younger children will only use on Sabbath. Reserving it for once a week will make it seem more important. If wish, you could pull out pages that relate to your devotional or study time that day and keep the book in a "safe spot."

Crossword Puzzle

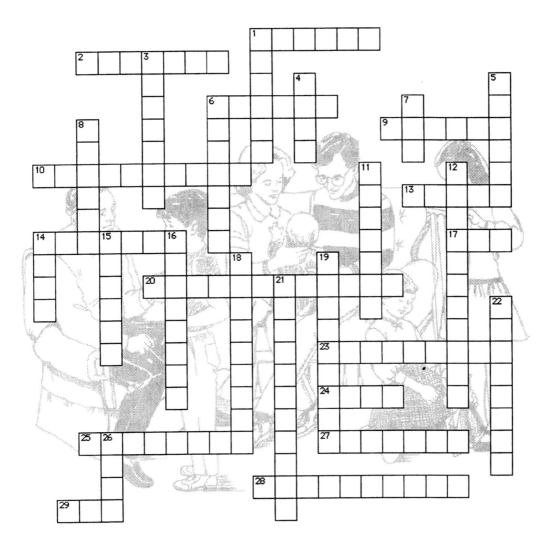

Across

1. Day before the Sabbath
2. Uttering sounds in a series of tones
6. Aromatic plant substances
9. Vegetable plot
10. Cleansed by God
13. Favor rendered by God
14. Reverent love and devotion
17. Twenty-four hour period
20. One of ten edicts
23. Jewish meeting place for worship
24. A king
25. Small sons and daughters
27. Anticipated deliverer
28. Word of God
29. Ecstatic happiness

Down

1. Household
3. Contains the story of creation
4. We will enter into God's ___
5. Burned to provide light
6. Sabbath
7. Created in His Image
8. Evening meal
11. The seventh day
12. Illumination from a candle
14. Seven days
15. Disappearance below the western horizon
16. Solomon's precepts, inspired by God
18. Holy deliverance
19. The Holy city
21. Free from entanglement
22. The world and all the things in it
26. God's sacred character

Challah Cloth

To continue a tradition, you may want to make a special cloth that is only used to cover your Sabbath challah. There are numerous symbols you can use to create a design to cross stitch, applique, or embroidery paint.

Begin with a 14"x18" piece of white or pastel cloth and launder to pre-shrink. You may choose to turn under 1/4" twice to make a finished hem or stitch 1/2" to 1" away from edge and ravel the cloth out to make a fringed edge. Adding any washable trim to the finished hem is also an option.

Trace off design on next page and use needlework, fabric paint or crayons to create the design.

- For needlework we suggest:

Basic Backstitch	2 strands overlap $\frac{1}{16}$" at beginning of each stitch. Use this for outline of the shield.
Basic Chain Stitch	3-4 strands (return needle to nearly same hole, don't pull loop through. Come up from bottom $\frac{1}{8}$" away, into the loop). Use this on large outer border.
Basic Button Hole	4 or more strands close horizontal stitches. Use for Psalm 84:11 and wheat in corner.

- Refer to a needlework book for specific stitch work. To use iron-on approach, or fabric paint, see flag instructions in the "Preliminary Activities and Crafts" section.

- Younger children may render in crayon. Parent may iron between several layers of paper towel to absorb wax and fix dye. Put butcher paper at bottom to protect ironing board. To launder later, hand wash with minimal agitation.

Suggested colors:

Purple . . . . .straight border lines, or fill-in shield.
Blue . . . . .dove's curved banner, Ps. 84:11, ties on wheat (for added detail, use two shades of blue on dove's banner).
Green . . . . .shield's narrow banner
Yellow and/or **Gold** . . . . . .sunbeams, outline of dove.
Brown and/or **Orange** . . .wheat symbols in corners, cross.

PSALM 84:11

Word Search

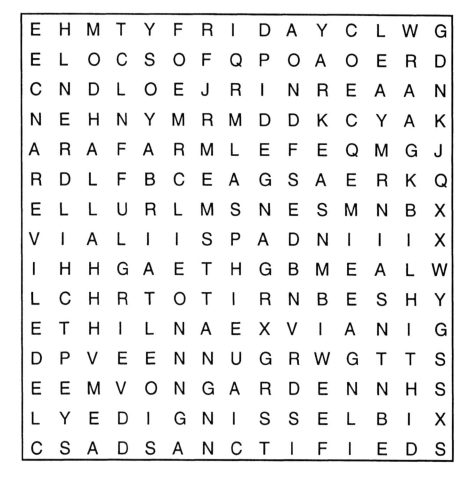

```
E H M T Y F R I D A Y C L W G
E L O C S O F Q P O A O E R D
C N D L O E J R I N R E A A N
N E H N Y M R M D D K C Y A K
A R A F A R M L E F E Q M G J
R D L F B C E A G S A E R K Q
E L L U R L M S N E S M N B X
V I A L I I S P A D N I I X
I H H G A E T H G B M E A L W
L C H R T O T I R N B E S H Y
E T H I L N A E X V I A N I G
D P V E E N N U G R W G T T S
E E M V O N G A R D E N N H S
L Y E D I G N I S S E L B I X
C S A D S A N C T I F I E D S
```

ADONAI	GENESIS	PROVERBS
BLESSING	GRACE	PTOLEMY
CANDLE	HALLAH	REST
CANDLELIGHT	HAVDALAH	SABBATH
CHILDREN	HOLY	SALVATION
COMMANDMENTS	JERUSALEM	SANCTIFIED
CREATION	JOY	SCRIPTURES
DAY	LEVITES	SEVENTH
DELIVERANCE	LORD	SINGING
DINNER	MAN	SPICES
EPHRAIM	MANASSEH	SUNSET
FAMILY	MESSIAH	SYNAGOGUE
FRIDAY	ORTHODOX	WEEK
GARDEN	PRAYER	WINE
	PROPHECY	WORSHIP

CROSSOUT

Cross out every other letter and discover the hidden verse. Use a Bible concordance to help you look up the reference. Who said this? What do you think this verse means?

TXHUERSBAMBKBEACTRHYW
ZATSNMQAKDJELFPOTRNMC
AHNFNUOYTRMGADNVFEOPR
LTGHXEBSZAWBQBTANTZHD

Write the verse here:

_____

_____

MATTERS OF THE HEART

Read God's description of fasting and Sabbath activities in Isaiah 58. Instead of focusing on work or school or keeping house, these appear to be times to think about, build upon and improve relationships:

Relationships with the poor or needy, relationships within our family, relationship with the family of God, and especially relationship with God Himself.

Pray and ask God to give YOU some ideas toward each of these relationships.

GOD'S IDEAS FOR ME:

Sabbath is a time for matters of the heart.

_____

_____

_____

_____

Section 7:
Holidays Across The Curriculum

- ◆ INTRODUCTION TO UNIT STUDIES
- ◆ SPRING HOLIDAYS ACROSS THE CURRICULUM
- ◆ FALL HOLIDAYS ACROSS THE CURRICULUM
- ◆ POST MOSAIC-HOLIDAYS ACROSS THE CURRICULUM
- ◆ RESOURCES FOR UNIT STUDIES

Heart of Wisdom Publishing

The Biblical Holidays Across the Curriculum

This special Home School Section includes a variety of thematic units for home schoolers to use to expand the study of the Biblical holidays into other subjects. The units can be used in a variety of ways and for different amounts of time. A thematic unit can be a study for one or two days, a few weeks or for an entire year.

THEMATIC UNIT STUDY

More and more school systems are using unit studies due to the tremendous reaction from the students. Students enjoy studying subjects that relate to each other across the curriculum. Studies show that students who examine subjects thematically retain up to 40 percent more of the material.

STUDYING THE WHOLE, NOT THE PARTS

America's Greek educational system is failing. The Greeks took a topic and divided it into isolated parts, taking away the relationship to the Creator. The Greeks are responsible for the subject divisions with which we are familiar today. For example, under what subject should the sun be studied? Yes, the sun falls under Science—astronomy. However it is also much more.

- Bible—Creation, scientific discoveries in Bible times, etc. Symbolism: Jesus is the light of the world, Christians are lights to the world, rainbows, discernment, etc.

- Biology—Humans, animals, and plants need light and heat.

- Meteorology—Weather, climate, zones, evaporation, etc.

- Chemistry—Chemical reactions of light and heat, etc.

- History—Theological beliefs of the sun in different time periods (ancient times, Middle Ages, and modern times). Scientific studies and effects during each period.

- Physics—light waves, microscopes, mirrors, bending light, etc., photon theory of light, quark, Big Bang and other false theories, etc.

- Geology—Sun's effect on earth's environment.

- Geography—Different locations of the globe, time zones, effects of no sunlight, etc. Effects of natural resources, industries, etc.

- Language Arts—Simile, metaphors, idioms, etc. Dictate passages learned about the sun for handwriting practice, capitalization, punctuation, etc. Reading assignments.

- Composition—Emotions, day and night, dark and light, poetry, classics

- Literature—Fiction, myths, fables, etc.

- Political Science—Government regulations, day and night laws, effects, etc.

- Math—Distance, radius, calendars, speed of light calculations, etc.

- Geometry—Spheres, orbit, rotation.

- Health—Light, vitamins, minerals, burns, sunscreens, sleep, diet, etc.

- Ecology—Greenhouse effect, sun's energy.

- Art—Colors of the spectrum, reflection and refraction, beautiful photos or paintings of a sunset or sunrises, sunlight.

- Studying and Thinking Skills—Research, reference, reason, record, problem–solving, etc.

TEACHING SEVERAL AGES TOGETHER

If God meant for children to learn with only children their own age, He would have given us children in litters. Unit studies are popular with home schoolers because mother can teach history, science, Bible, etc., together to all ages—simply on different levels. Here are two families, each with three children, grades 1, 3, and 6. Look at the two schedules. Which mother spends more time planning and teaching?

MOTHER A - TEXT BOOK SUBJECTS

	Bible	**Science**	**History**
Child 1	Obedience	Plants	Colonial Days
Child 2	Abraham	Human Body	Civil War
Child 3	Paul	Solar System	Ancient Egypt

MOTHER B - UNIT STUDY: HUMAN BODY

All children: Unit Study of the human body looking at creation, man, anatomy, and medical discoveries through History, etc.

Children interact and teach each other, reading and writing at their own levels in more detail. Each child learns as he or she is able, but is not limited. For example: all children learn that God created man, that we have a sinful nature, that we are hindered by the lust of the flesh, etc. Child 1 learns the five senses and about illness and doctors in pioneer days. Child 2 learns the body systems, major medical discoveries in the last two hundred years. Child 3 learns how each body system functions and details about medical discoveries and how they affect life in different time periods.

The thematic unit studies in this section look at the topics as a whole and the relationship to God, then looks at individual aspects of that topic. Instead of studying isolated parts of topics that do not relate to each other, students learn all parts of a topic and how the topic relates to the whole. In this way, subjects make sense to the student. Students are motivated to learn.

Studying school topics around God's Word and God's Holy Days is an excellent way for first-time unit study users to get their feet wet in this strange thematic land. It's also a terrific, fresh approach for veteran unit study users.

REPRODUCIBLE PLANNING PAGES

For your convenience, pages are included in this section to plan the dates you will use the unit studies—**Planning for the School Year** or **Seasonal.** There are also pages to plan individual lessons with spaces for materials, books, Bible verses, field trips, etc. There are also **Lesson Planning Pages** included in this section, which you can use for each individual holiday.

CREATING A PORTFOLIO

Use this Biblical Holidays Study to create a portfolio of your child's work. A portfolio is an accumulation of your child's work, made with the child's input, in an organized manner. A portfolio highlights and records aspects and progression of a child's quality work. A portfolio is a collection of samples of a child's interest, and evidence of his or her God-given abilities. A portfolio can show others more about your child's learning than any grade. Most children absolutely love building portfolios. The portfolios can center on the Biblical Holidays as a whole study, or your child can make an individual portfolio for each holiday. This method encourages children to be active learners, learning through a variety of means (living books, audio cassettes, videos, field trips, writing, etc.). When a child's experience is rich and diverse, it invites him or her to display initiative, and engages his or her curiosity. This performance assessment will help you learn about your child as you watch him learn about his world. Portfolios include items such as:

Art Work	Bible Studies	Book Reviews
Brochures	Computer Disks	Computer Printouts
Displays	Essays	Field Trip Reports
Formal Letters	Journal Entries	Maps
Photographs	Play Dialog	Poetry
Projects	Recipes	Research Papers
Songs	Writing Samples	

CO-OPING

Many home schoolers decide to do the same unit study at the same time as one or more families in their support group or church group. The Biblical Holidays Unit Study works well in this fashion. Not only can you get together one day a week to share activities or field trips, but you'll also be preparing for a special celebration time together!

USE THE THEMATIC UNITS WITH YOUR CURRICULUM

Incorporate the holiday into your regular curriculum. Skim the "Across the Curriculum" section. Choose and mark activities you will be studying this year. For example: while studying plants in your normal curriculum, you can incorporate plant activities from one or more of the holidays and include a study of the holiday that relates to your curriculum.

PREPARATION

First you'll need to decide the amount of time you want to spend in each unit.

1. **During Holidays:** You can simply spend a few days in each unit as you study the holidays.

2. **Seasonal:** Spend approximately two weeks studying each unit.

3. **School Year:** Use the units for entire year for your entire family.

Schedule the unit around your family. Feel free to spend more or less time in each unit. You are never required to do every activity. If you're concerned about the National Standards, see the Home School Resources in the back of this book for *What Your Child Needs to Know When*. (You'll need to supplement math and language arts for each grade level.)

PLANNING

We've included several suggestions on the next few pages. Each schedule is approximate because the holidays dates change year to year. Once you choose a schedule (the amount of time to spend in a unit), you'll need to adapt your schedule to the appropriate calendar year. This will organize you to gather materials, plan library trips, order books, etc.

Use a pocket or wall school calendar (beginning in the fall). Assign a color to each holiday and color code the calendar. Mark the appropriate date with the appropriate color. See one-month sample below.

WALL CALENDAR

Sun	Mon	Tue	Wed	Thu	Fri	Sat
	1	2	3	4	5	6
7	8	9	10	11	12	13
14	15	16	17	18	19	20
21	22	23	24	25	26	27
28	29	30				

Lamb **Bread** **Plants**

SCHOOL YEAR SCHEDULE

ACTUAL DATES	MONTH	HOLIDAYS	THEMATIC UNIT
	August	Fall Holidays Overview	Overview
	September	**Trumpets**	Praise & Worship
	October	**Day of Atonement**	Grace
	November	**Tabernacles**	Trees
	December	**Hanukkah**	Oil
	January	**Purim**	Fruit
	February	Spring Holidays Overview	Overview
	March	**Passover/Unleavened**	Sheep/Bread
	April	**Firstfruits/Omer**	Plants
	May	**Weeks**	Law

SUGGESTED FALL SCHEDULE

ACTUAL DATES	WEEK	HOLIDAYS	THEMATIC UNIT
	1 and 2	Trumpets	Praise and Worship Unit
	3 and 4	Day of Atonement	Grace Unit
	5 and 6	Tabernacles	Trees Unit
	7 and 8	Prepare for Fall	Overview
	Actual Holiday Date		**Celebrate Trumpets**
	Actual Holiday Date		**Celebrate Atonement**
	Actual Holiday Date		**Celebrate Tabernacles**

A Family Guide to the Biblical

SUGGESTED WINTER SCHEDULE

ACTUAL DATES	WEEK	HOLIDAYS	THEMATIC UNIT
	1 and 2	Hanukkah	Oil Unit
	Actual Holiday Date		**Celebrate Hanukkah**
	3 and 4	Purim	Fruit Unit
	Actual Holiday Date		**Celebrate Purim**

SUGGESTED SPRING SCHEDULE

ACTUAL DATES	WEEK	HOLIDAYS	THEMATIC UNIT
	1 and 2	Study Passover	Sheep Unit
	3 and 4	Study Unleavened B.	Bread Unit
	5 and 6	Study Firstfruits	Plants Unit
	7 and 8	Study Spring Holidays	Preliminary Activities
	Actual Holiday Date		**Celebrate Passover**
	Next Seven Days		**Celebrate Unleavened B.**
	Day After Sabbath	Celebrate Firstfruits	
	9-16 (Seven Weeks)	Count The Omer	Plants and Law Unit
	Actual Holiday Date		**Celebrate Shavuot**

RESOURCES

One trip to the library before each unit will provide you with plenty of material to study each theme at each child's level. (Realize most library books include evolution and the big bang theory). Books are suggested in each unit. Those marked with an * are available through Family Christian Academy. Textbooks make good reference books, but the students usually enjoy the library books and pictures more. Those who have a good home library and encyclopedia can probably use what is on hand. For computer users, CD ROMs and on-line material are available for all topics. Literature is recommended in each unit in order of reading level; however, we suggest you all enjoy reading aloud together.

Home School Lesson Planer

Holiday:		
Date of Celebration:	Date to Start:	No. of Weeks:
		Material Needed List
Lesson #	**Date:**	**Lesson #**
Read Aloud Pages:		
Activity Sheet Pages:		
No. of Copies to Make:		
Bible Verse to Memorize:		
Lesson #	**Date:**	**Lesson #**
Read Aloud Pages:		
Activity Sheet Pages:		
No. of Copies to Make:		
Bible Verse to Memorize:		
Lesson #	**Date:**	**Lesson #**
Read Aloud Pages:		
Activity Sheet Pages:		
No. of Copies to Make:		
Bible Verse to Memorize:		
Lesson #	**Date:**	**Lesson #**
Read Aloud Pages:		
Activity Sheet Pages:		
No. of Copies to Make:		
Bible Verse to Memorize:		
Lesson #	**Date:**	**Lesson #**
Read Aloud Pages:		
Activity Sheet Pages:		
No. of Copies to Make:		
Bible Verse to Memorize:		

Family Christian Press 1-800-788-0840   *A Family Guide to the Biblical Holidays©*

Spring Holidays Across the Curriculum

PASSOVER: LAMB UNIT STUDY
BIBLE

Discuss: Talk about the Figurative Uses of the Words Sheep and Shepherd. Jesus is our Passover Lamb. *Sheep* is also figurative of believers who follow the shepherd. One without a leader is like a sheep without a shepherd. Jesus is our Shepherd. Discuss the responsibilities of a shepherd: protect, feed, shelter, etc.

Compare: Talk about the lambs in each of these Bible verses: John 1:29-36: Isaiah 53:7; Revelation 5:6.

Read: Read aloud *A Shepherd Looks at the Psalms** by Phillip Keller. This book is a beautiful portrayal of how our Shepherd cares for us.

Take a Field Trip: Visit a sheep farm. Make a list of all the things the shepherd does for his sheep.

LIFE SCIENCE OR BIOLOGY

Classify: Learn the classification system. Make a chart showing the classification of sheep. INCLUDE: Animal Kingdom: Mammals: Order Artiodactyla; Suborder Ruminantia; Family Bovidae; Genus Ovis.

Research: Some of a sheep's characteristics includes hoofs, cud-chewing, four-compartmented stomach. They are also placentals. Find out about these and other characteristics and write a definition of each.

Classify: Make a list of several types of sheep and classify by breed. Include wool breed, hair breed, and merino strains.

Study: Complete "The Animal Kingdom" reading and activities lessons 21 through 26 in *Considering God's Creation.*

Write a Report: Choose one of the following sheep behaviors to research and write about: life cycle; lambing; breeding; gestation; and life span.

ANIMAL HUSBANDRY/AGRICULTURE

Study: Agriculture is the science and industry of managing the growth of plants and animals for human use. Agriculture includes the breeding and raising of livestock and dairying, under the science of Animal Husbandry.

Brainstorm and List: What would it be like to have a commercial sheep farm? Think about what is involved with purchasing, raising, and caring for sheep (feeding, lambing, shearing, sheltering, etc.).

Calculate Expenses: Calculate the cost per lamb: original cost, grain cost, hay cost, veterinary cost, show fees, etc.

Discuss: What are the advantages and disadvantages of animal supplements such as hormones, antibiotics, vitamins, and other substances used to increase growth or productivity? What are the health risks to humans who consume meat grown with such additives? Find out how much of the meat in a grocery store has been raised with additives.

Discover: Research the sheep dog and its relationship with the sheep and with the master (a fascinating study!), necessary training, innate ability, and dog shows. Read Phillip Keller's *Lessons From a Sheep Dog**. Check your local video store; Disney has a few excellent black and white documentaries about sheep farming.

Chart Statistics: Research the number of breeds; how many in the world, and the number in the United States. Make a chart recording your findings.

Investigate the Sheep Industry and Products: Research wool manufacturing. Include different types of wool; textiles, production; clothing, manufacturing, labeling, pelts, carpeting, and sheep skins. Research sheep in the food industry. Include lamb and mutton; food processing; preservation; or the world food supply. Sheep also provide milk for drinking and making cheese. Sheep are also used to make parchment.

HISTORY

Each of these time periods and countries were involved with sheep or sheep farming. Use the *Kingfisher's Illustrated Book of History* to find out what other events in the same period.

World History

6000 B.C.	Assyria
3000 B.C.	Macedonia
2000 B.C.	The Hittites
1250 B.C.	Moses outside of Egypt
1000 - 961 B.C.	David in Israel
1200-1400 A.D.	Mongol Empire
1100 A.D.	England (Enclosure began)
1212 A.D.	Children's Crusade
1722	Easter Island

American History

1700+	Modern Pueblo Period
1840-1850	Native Americans - Navajo
1860-1900	American Reconstruction
1990s	Sheep Farming Today

GEOGRAPHY

Explore a Country, State: The leading sheep producers in the world are: 1. Australia 2. USSR 3. China. In the United States, the leading sheep-producing states are Texas, California, Wyoming, South Dakota, and New Mexico. Choose one each of these countries and states to study.

Compare and Chart Ecosystems: Make a chart showing the variance in the ecosystems sheep live in: grasslands, prairies and plains of North America, the pampas and paramos of South America, the veld of South Africa, and the steppes of Eurasia. Mountain Areas: Various species of wild goat and sheep abound in the Himalayan Mountains of India. Bighorn Sheep, also called Rocky Mountain sheep, are found in the North American continent.

LANGUAGE ARTS

Learn to Research: Research involves the generation, collection, organization, retrieval, and reporting of recorded knowledge. Look up in the encyclopedia: sheep, sheep farming, animal husbandry, zoology, shepherds, and wool. Include these periodicals in your research: *Ranger Rick* and *National Geographic* Magazines.

Books and Stories: Bible stories of Jesus, Moses, or David, are sources of references to sheep. You can also find references to sheep in many nursery Rhymes, like "Baa, Baa, Black Sheep," and "Mary had a Little Lamb."

Creative Writing: Write about a shepherd and his relationship with his sheep, or sheep and sheep farming. Or write an allegory, a folktale, or a story for children. Then write a poem about a lamb. Find out about different types of poetry, figurative, narrative, epics, ballads, dramatic, or lyrics). Younger children can dictate their stories or draw illustrations and explain it.

Add to your Vocabulary: Record all the new words you have heard during this unit. Discuss the meanings or look them up and write the definitions.

Resources for the Lamb Unit Study

	TITLE	AUTHOR	DESCRIPTION	PUB
*	A Shepherds Look at the Psalm 23	Phillip Keller	A compelling look at the sheep and shepherds relationship comparing our relationship to Jesus, our Shepherd. Excellent. 6 grade and up or read aloud.	Word Publishing
*	Lessons From a Sheep Dog	Phillip Keller	Heartwarming, spiritual, educational story about sheep, sheep dogs and the Shepherd. 6 grade and up or read aloud.	Word Publishing
A	Alone on the Mountain	Patti Sherlock	The subtitle reads: *Shepherding in the American West.* A fascinating look at sheep and shepherds in the mountains in Idaho. 144 p. Ill.	Doubleday, c1979
A	Sheep Husbandry	J. B. Killebrew	Sub title: A Work Prepared for The Farmers of Tennessee. 301 p. For teens or adults.	Eastman & Howell, 1880.
A	This Was Sheep Ranching: Yesterday And Today	Virginia Paul	A look at sheep ranches in the history of the United States. For teens or adults. 176 p. Ill.	Superior Pub. Co., c1976
E	Charlie Needs a Cloak	Tomie de Paola	A shepherd shears his sheep, cards and spins the wool, weaves and dyes the cloth, and sews a beautiful new red cloak. 32 p. Ill.	Prentice-Hall c1973
E	The Snow Lambs	Debi Gliori	Because she is on a rescue mission, Bess, the sheep dog, fails to respond when Sam's dad calls her to return home as winter storm approaches. 32 p. Ill.	Scholastic, 1996.
J	Away to Me, Moss!	Betty Levin.	Ten-year-old Zanna becomes involved in working with a spirited sheep dog that belongs to the stroke patient her mother is helping to rehabilitate. 161p.	Greenwillow Books, c1994
J	Dogs Working for People	James L. Stanfield.	Photographs and brief text describe the skills of retrievers, sheep and cattle dogs, Seeing Eye dogs, greyhounds, bloodhounds, police dogs, and other canines that work for man. 40p. Ill.	National Geographic Society, c1972
J	From Sheep to Scarf	Ali Mitgutsch.	Highlights the step-by step process of shearing sheep, spinning wool, and knitting a scarf. 24 p. Ill.	Carolrhoda Books, 1981
J	Goats, Sheep, and How They Live	Marie M. Jenkins	Describes the physical characteristics, habits, natural environment, and relationship to humans of goats, sheep, and their relatives. 157 p. Ill.	Holiday House, c1978
J	Here's To Ewe: Riddles About Sheep	Diane L. Burns	From the You must be joking! Series. A collection of humorous riddles about sheep. 32 p. Ill.	Lerner Co., c1990.
J	Sheep	Tessa Potter	Illustrated book about raising of sheep for wool. 32 p. Ill.	SteckVaughn, c1990
J	Smudge, The Little Lost Lamb	James Herriot	After leaving Farmer Cobb's flock and exploring the outside world, Smudge the lamb has trouble returning home. Unpaged, Ill.	St. Martin's Press, c1991.
J	The Parables Of Jesus	Tomie dePaola	An illustrated retelling of seventeen parables used by Jesus Christ in his teachings. Includes "The Lost Sheep."	Holiday House, c1987
J	The Tale Of Tawny And Dingo	William H. Armstrong	Tawny, the runt sheep of the flock, discovers a friend in Dingo, the dog, and gains an unusual kind of courage and leadership. 44 p. Ill.	Harper & Row, c1979
J	Wonders of Sheep	Sigmund A. Lavine	Traces the history and habits of the various kinds of sheep, notes their appearances in folklore, literature, and art, and the raising of sheep for wool, food, and other uses. 80 p. Ill.	Dodd, Mead, c1983.
J	Your Sheep: A Kids' Guide To Raising And Showing	Paula Simmons	A guide to the choosing, handling, care, breeding, and showing of sheep. A Garden Way Publishing book. Includes index. 120 p. Ill.	Storey Communi, c1992.

* Possibly in the library, available through Family Christian Academy. Library Codes: A - Adult Section; J – Juvenile Section; E – Easy Reading Section; P- Periodical.

UNLEAVENED BREAD: BREAD UNIT STUDY

BIBLE

Study the Bible: Discuss symbolism of bread and leaven. *Daily bread* in the Lord's Prayer sums up all that we really need for our earthly existence (Matt. 6). Stop now and say a prayer to thank God for providing our daily bread. Unleavened bread is a symbol of Our Savior (John 6:33-35). When unleavened bread is broken, it is symbolic of the death of Christ (Matt 26:26). Bread can be symbolic of poverty (when in want of) or abundance (when full of). The bread of adversity shows heavy affliction. Sometimes bread is even symbolic of idleness or wickedness in Proverbs. Leavening is symbolic of growth—good and bad. The rapid spread of the gospel is wonderful (good growth). Bad growth is the spread of false doctrines.

SCIENCE

Investigate Grains: Bread is made from flour. Grinding grain such as wheat or rye into a powder makes flour. Make a list of the number of grains used to make breads.

Classify: Learn how plants are classified. Grains are in *Plantae* Kingdom and family *Gramineae* (the Grass Family).

Explore Agriculture: Research crop farming: Crop rotation, environment, erosion, pest control, pollution, depletion of minerals in soil, etc.

Make a List: Study Biblical rules of farming: the soil to be selected and prepared. Only pure seed and good plants are to be used, and the land should rest every seventh year. Scientists now know that, if the land does not rest, the minerals in the land will deplete and produce lower quality foods. Find out the effects on humans deficient in minerals. Make a list of mineral deficiencies and symptoms in animals and in humans.

Study Chemical Reactions: Yeast is called the "pet" of modern molecular biology. It is single-celled, fast growing, cheap to keep, insensitive, and easy to manipulate. Find out how fermentation causes chemical changes in organic substances produced by the action of enzymes.

Use the Scientific Method: Make two loaves of bread, one loaf with yeast and one loaf without. Write down your observations and predictions about each loaf before baking. What conclusions did you come to because of this experiment? Look up: bread, fermentation, bacteria, enzyme, gluten, and yeast.

Do an Experiment: Use the book *Cooking and Science** to learn about carbon dioxide production by yeast.

Study: Bread sustains life. Use this unit as a spring board to learn about the human body. Read and complete all activities in "Man Made in God's Image" lessons 27 through 36 in *Considering God's Creation**.

HEALTH

Research Nutritional Values: Bread is a food source for three-fourths of the world. Where is grain on the Food Pyramid? Compare white bread's and wheat bread's nutritional values. The most nutritional bread is that made from fresh whole wheat ground within 48 hours of baking.

Compare: The average life span for an American today is 75.5 years. The average life span for a doctor is 58 years. Do research to compare life spans in the U.S. and other countries. Compare diets of people in different income brackets and people in different countries. Record your findings.

Make a Display: Find pictures or examples of each of these grains: wheat, barley, quinoa, spelt, bulur, kamut, rye, teff, triticale, rice (brown, white, Basmati, Wehani, long and short grains), Make a display with samples and nutritional values of each.

A Family Guide to the Biblical Holidays©

HISTORY AND TECHNOLOGY

Investigate: There is an excellent CD-ROM available for younger children called *How Things Work in Busytown*. In it, the Busy Town characters plant a crop of wheat. They prepare the field, plant the seed, water the field, make sure it has sun, wait for it to grow, harvest the wheat, take it to the mill, grind the wheat, take the flour to the baker, bake the bread, and take the bread to the grocery store!

Look Back: In Bible times, Israelites depended on the hand-mill for daily bread. Eventually millstones were used. In Early America, farmers took grain to mills. Today, electric grinders are available. Find any method of milling today to observe.

Bake: In Bible times, people baked in open fire, then stone ovens. Today, commercial bakeries use mixing machines; chain conveyors; automatic baking ovens; and cooling, slicing, and wrapping machines. Today small mills are available for home use.

Look Back: Interview your parents and grandparents or older friends about the changes in bread in the last 100 years.

Go on a Field Trip: Visit one or more: a commercial bread bakery, a mill, a university's Department of Food And Nutrition.

HISTORY

Choose one of these time periods and countries that were involved with specific events dealing with wheat or bread. Use the *Kingfisher's Illustrated Book of History* to find out what other events in the same period.

5000 B.C.	Evidence of farming communities
Bible Times	Crop failures and food shortages due to disobedience
100 B.C. - 200 A.D.	Ancient Rome used public ovens
100 A.D.	Roman engineers introduce the water mill
7th century A.D.	Windmills invented in Persia (now called Iran)
1436 -63	The Corn Laws of England
1700-1950	Industrial Revolution
1795	French Revolution—bread riots
1917	The Russian Revolution of 1917
1912	Bread and Roses strike in Massachusetts
1930s	Dust Bowl
1990s	Grain farming and industry today

GEOGRAPHY

Explore: Choose a country and a U.S. state to study in-depth. **Countries:** The world's leading producers of wheat are: the USSR, China, and the United States. **States:** The leading wheat-producing states are North Dakota, Kansas, Montana, and Oklahoma.

LANGUAGE ARTS

Read a Bible Story: Manna given in the desert (Ex. 16); Jesus fed the five thousand with two loaves and five fishes (Mark 6:38); Jesus answered Satan's temptation (Matt. 4:3-4).

Read a Book: Chose one or more of the exciting books to read from the included resource page. Read aloud with the family or assign independent reading.

Write a short story: Write about living on a crop farm or owning a bakery. Rewrite *The Little Red Hen* in your own words. Younger children can dictate their stories or draw illustrations and explain it. Write a poem about Passover, bread, or wheat.

Add to Your Vocabulary: List all the new words you have heard during this unit. Discuss the meanings or look them up and write the definitions.

Resources for the Bread Unit Study

	TITLE	AUTHOR	DESCRIPTION	PUB
*	Cooking and Science	J. Julicher	Learn to write a lab report, answer application questions, and enjoy these recipes.	Castle Heights
*	Louis Pasture	John H. Taylor	A biography, from the Sower Series, about an unknown scientist. Grades 5 and up or read aloud. 176 p.	Mott Media
*	Science in Creation Week	David Unfred	Use this unit as a springboard to study the human body and digestive system. Read and complete lessons 27 through 36. 137 p.	Noble Publisher, 1994
A	Wheat, Millet and Other Grains	Beatrice Trum Hunter	Brief history and use of each grain, brief discussion of milling process, table of nutrients. For more information see books by same author *Whole Grain Baking Sampler*, or *The Great Nutrition Robbery*. 26 p.	Keats Publishing, Inc.
E	Everybody Bakes Bread	Norah Dooley	A young boy helps his aging grandfather complete a basket to be used by their Garifuna village to carry on the tradition of making cassava bread. 40 p. Ill.	Carolrhoda Books, c1996.
J	A Grain Of Wheat: A Writer Begins	Clyde Bulla	The author describes his early years up until the age of ten, growing up on a Missouri farm and how he decided to be a writer. 49 p.	D.R. Godine, 1985.
J	All About Bread	Geoffrey Patterson	Traces the history of bread. Describes the growing of the wheat and how it is ground into flour and eventually made into different kinds of bread. 71p. Ill.	A. Deutsch, 1984.
J	Bread	Dorothy Turner	Describes how bread is produced, prepared, and eaten and presents some background history, as well as two recipes. 32 p. Ill.	Wayland Publishers
J	From Grain to Bread	Ali Mitgutsch.	Highlights the step-by-step process of planting wheat seeds, harvesting the crop, grinding wheat into flour, and baking bread. 24 p. Ill.	Carolrhoda Books, 1981.
J	Grasses and Grains	Theresa Greenaway.	Discusses the characteristics of different kinds of grasslands in the world and describes the structure of grasses, how they grow and develop, the grains they produce, and their importance to animals and humans. 47 p. Ill.	Steck-Vaughn Library, 1990.
J	I Know a Baker	Chika A. Iritani	A boy visits his uncle's bakery and learns how bread, cakes, and cookies are made in large quantities. 45 p. Ill.	NY, Putnam 1969.
J	Messing Around with Baking Chemistry	Bernie Zubrowski	Presents experiments and projects to explore what happens when batter and dough turn into bread. Emphasizes the properties of baking powder, soda, and yeast. 63p. Ill.	Little, Brown, c1981.
J	The Bread Book: All About Bread And How To Make It.	Trina Hyman	Describes the history and important ingredients of bread making. Includes customs and legends about bread and discusses breads popular in different countries.	Harcourt Brace Jovanovich, 1971.
J	The Bread Dough Craft Book	Giulio Maestro	Instructions for making jewelry, decorations, mobiles, sculpture, and other items from a mixture of bread dough and glue. 128 p. Ill.	Lee and Shepard 1972.
J	Wheat	Sylvia A. Johnson	Explains the life cycle of wheat, its varieties, its cultivation, its harvesting, and its importance in feeding millions of people all over the world. 48 p. Ill.	Children's Press, c1977.
J	Where Food Comes From	Dorothy Patent	Shows how all food—grains, vegetables, fruits, and dairy and meat products—begins on the farm as sun, earth, air, and water combine to grow plants. 40 p. Ill	Holiday House, c1991.
M	How Things Work in Busytown.	Richard Scarry CDROM	Interact with the Busy Town characters to prepare the field, plant seed, water the field, wait for it to grow, harvest the wheat, grind it, take the flour to the baker, bake the bread, and take the bread to the grocery store! Includes many other activities. Ages 3 to 7.	Novatrade, 1994.

* Possibly in the library, available through Family Christian Academy. Library Codes: A - Adult Section; J – Juvenile Section; E – Easy Reading Section; P- Periodical.

494

FIRSTFRUITS: PLANTS UNIT STUDY

BIBLE

Read and Discuss Parables: There are many parables about plants in the Bible—about sowing and reaping, abiding in the vine, grafting, and others that help us understand our relationship to Christ. The sower (Matt. 13-38; Mark 4: 3-20; Luke 8: 5-15); the vineyard (Matt. 20); the wicked vine-growers (Matt. 21:33-41); and the parable of the mustard seed (Luke 13:19) .

Read and Discuss: God gives us plants for food, shelter, and pleasure. Read Genesis 1:29-30; 2:9; 9:3; Psalm 104:14-17; Jonah 4:6. We see the effects of sin in the condition of plant life. Read Genesis 3:17-19; Proverbs 24:30-34.

Do an Experiment: Find a branch, with leaves, from a bush or tree (one with fruit or a flower would be ideal). Place the branch in a visible area for at least a week as you study this unit. At the end of the week, talk about what has happened to the branch, the leaves, and the flowers (by this time students should know where a branch's life and nourishment comes from). Explain why. Discuss how our lives are like the branch. Read John 15:1-8. What does the gardener do to the branches that bear fruit as opposed to the branches that do not? What did Jesus say the branches must do to bear fruit? Who are the branches?

SCIENCE

Draw and Label: Draw a plant and label the parts: roots, seeds, leaves, and stems.

Study Photosynthesis: Discuss and explain this process needed for plants to grow. Explain the roles that water, air, and sunlight play in the process.

Contrast and Compare: Compare several types of seeds: bean, sunflower, brown rice, corn, celery, almond, pecan, etc. Discuss the parts of a seed: embryo, seed coat, endosperm.

Read a book: Chose one or more of the exciting books to read from the included resource page. Read aloud with the family or assign independent reading.

Study: Do all the reading and activities in "The Plant Kingdom," lessons ten through twelve in *Considering God's Creation*.

Color: Learn more about botany by coloring the pages of the ecological coloring book *Forests* made by a botanist.

Sprout Seeds: You will need: 1.) Dried beans such as: navy beans, field peas, garbanzo beans, lentils, kidney beans, etc., 2.) A glass jar, 3.) a rubber band, and 4.) a piece of hosiery, netting, or cheese cloth. Soak the beans on a wet paper towel overnight. The next day, put the beans in a clear jar. Place a piece of hosiery or cheese cloth over the top of the jar. Rinse and drain the beans every day.

Brainstorm and List: Plant growth and development follow God-given laws. Read and discuss: Genesis 1:11-12; 8:22; Deuteronomy 22:9; Isaiah 28: 24-25; Luke 6:44; 2 Corinthians 9:6; Galatians 6:7-8; James 3:1; Leviticus 25:2-22. Make a list of the laws in each of the listed verses. Try to find or think of an example for each verse physically and spiritually.

Observe Roots: Grow a sweet potato, carrot tops, or violet leaves in water and observe the roots. Place in the sunlight.

Research Life Cycles: Look up and define each: *seed, germination, growth,* and *death.*

Investigate: Find out about *monocots* and *dicots* (types of seeds).

Brainstorm and list: Make a list of specific plant uses in these categories: food, clothing, shelter, medicine, and any other category you can think of.

Watch a video: *The Journey of Life*, From Moody, is a fascinating video which shows how a seed travels through floods, fire, and storms to exotic places, where it lives and grows. It is a picture of the living seed taking root in the human heart.

Investigate: Many of the crop failures and food shortages in Israel's history were due to disobedience to God. Read and discuss the following verses: Deuteronomy 28:1-6; 11:18; 38-42; 2 Kings 8:1; Isaiah 17:10-11; Jeremiah 8:13; Haggai 1:9-11; 2:17; Malachi 3:8-11.

HISTORY/ SCIENCE TECHNOLOGY

Investigate crop farming: Find out how farm tools have changed through history. Early civilizations used sickles and primitive plow sticks. Today's farmers use plows, tractors, harrows, drills, planters, broadcasters, manure spreaders, cultivators, mechanical dusters, etc., to plant fields. To harvest, they use combines. To keep records, they use personal computers.

Take a field trip: Visit a grain farm or get a video or book on farming. Try to imagine how chores would be done without technology.

Take a look back: Take a look at farming through history using the timeline below. Find out what other events were going on in these places, during these times. Use the *Kingfisher's Illustrated Book of History* to find out what other events in the same period.

6000 B.C.	Jericho
3100-2150 B.C.	Egyptian Peasant Farmers
300 B.C. - 300 A.D.	Roman Slave Farmers
300-900 A.D.	Mayan Farmers
960-1280	Chinese Rice Farmers
1100-1400	English Serfs
1400-1700	Benin Farmers
1730-1830	British Farmers
1900-1900s	Modern Western Farmers

GEOGRAPHY

Find and Discuss: The total land area of the United States is about 917 million hectares (about 2.27 billion acres), of which about 47 percent is used to produce crops and livestock. There are several major farming areas that vary by soil, slope of land, climate, and distance to market, and in storage and marketing facilities. Biomes are large-scale divisions of the biosphere into regions of different growth patterns. Find a map of the U.S. with the principal agricultural areas marked (or make your own). Find and discuss each biome. Make a list of plants found in each of these biomes: Grassland, Desert, Swap, Rain Forest, Tundra.

LANGUAGE ARTS

Read a Story: Read the fascinating story about George Washington Carver and his scientific contributions to agriculture.

Write a Story: Write a short story about one of these subjects: sowing, reaping, farming, or gardening. Or write an allegory, a folktale, or a story for children about plants. Younger children can dictate their stories or draw illustrations and explain it. Write a poem about a plant's life cycle. Find out about different types of poetry.

Add to Your Vocabulary: Record all the new words you have heard during this unit. Discuss the meanings or look them up and write the definitions.

Resources for the Plant Unit Study

	Title	AUTHOR	DESCRIPTION	PUB/DISTR
*	Botany Coloring Book	Paul Young	Learn the structure and function of plants, survey the plant kingdom, and botanical vocabulary through coloring. High school level.	
*	Botany for All Ages	Globe Pequot	Great introduction to botany introducing principles of observation, experimentation, and self-expression. Everything you ever need to know about plants in every subject.	Globe Pequot, 1994.
*	Drawing from Nature	Jim Arnosky	Instructions for drawing water, land, plants, and animals. Home school favorite. 64 p. Ill.	Lee & Shepard Books, c1982.
*	Fall And Winter in the North Carolina Forrest	Rosa Mullet	Companion to the book below. Full of Christian short stories of the Wilson boys as they camp out. Includes instructions for ant farm, casting animal tracts, etc. 244 p.	Rod and Staff
*	George Washington Carver	David R. Collins	Sub title: Man's Slave Becomes God's Scientist. A biography of Carver's fascinating life. This biography, from a Christian view includes details about his spiritual life that other biographies leave out. Grades 5 and up.	Mott Media
*	God's Power Plants: Energy That Grows On You (Video)	Walter Schnaegel	See how the sun in the sky fuels the power plant deep in the heart of all green life and how we are dependent on plants to sustain life, just as they are dependent on us. 30 min.	Moody Video
*	Kids Gardening	Klutz	A guide to messing around in the dirt indoors or outdoors. Each book comes with a variety of seeds, and trowel. Good for any climate or any season.	Klutz, 1995
*	Mysteries And Marvels Of Plant Life	Barbara Cork	Take an exciting detailed look at many amazing, mysterious plants, the behavior, species, habitat, etc. Elementary ages. 34 p. Illustrated in Usborne's distinguished artistic style.	Usborne, c1983
*	Science In Creation Week	David Unfred	For this unit read the sections about the third day of creation, lessons ten through twelve, explaining the fundamentals of plant biology.	
*	Spring And Summer In The North Carolina Forrest	Rosa Mullet	The Wilson children live in the mountains of N.C. This book is a collection of short stories of how they view God observing His creation. Stories of their experiences with plants, animals, the stars and more. Includes crafts and illustrations. 240 p.	Rod and Staff
*	The Country Diary of an Edwardian Lady	Edith Holden	A beautiful work of art. A record of the countryside through the change of seasons. Beautiful paintings on every page, perfect to inspire a child to start their own nature journal.	
*	The Power in Plants (Video)	Video	A bean sprouts and spirals upward. A flower splits the sidewalk with Herculean strength. Delight in the mysterious mechanisms God has planted all around us. Also includes It's a Small World and enjoy an award-winning look at an active insect in Busy as a Bee.	Moody Video
J	Linea's Windowsill Garden	C. Bjork & Anderson	Easily-understood book on how to grow (incl. water and fertilize) many kinds of seeds cuttings, flower bulbs, garlic, carrots, fruit trees and a host of other ideas you can incorporate into this unit. Adaptable grades 1-6. 59 p. 2-color Ill.	R & S Books
J	Agriculture Careers	Gene & Clare Gurney	Review of general types of jobs available in this field. Suitable springboard for upper elementary and junior high research. Use in across curriculum science or independent study. 66 p. incl. college & further information list, b/w photos.	Franklin Watts, 10978

* Possibly in the library, available through Family Christian Academy. Library Codes: A - Adult Section; J – Juvenile Section; E – Easy Reading Section; P- Periodical.

497

Plants Continued

	Title	Author	Description	Publisher
J	All About Seeds	Susan Kuchalla	Brief text and pictures present several kinds of seeds and show how they grow into plants. 32 p. Ill	Troll Associates, c1982.
J	All Around Me	Sally Hewitt	Covers a wide variety of scientific facts about the world around us, including plants, with suggested mini-projects. From the "Now I Know" series. 47 p. Ill	Thomson Learning, 1995.
J	Atlas of Plants	Gallimard Jeunesse	Laminated pages with transparent overlays introduce over fifty plants from around the world and give details about their growth, life cycles, and value. 36 p. Ill	Cartwheel Books, 1996.
J	Being a Plant	Laurence Pringle	This examination of plants includes a discussion of their internal structure, their ability to make their own food, and their complex relationship with other organisms. 88 p. Ill.	Crowell, c1983.
J	Biology Project Puzzlers	A. Harris Stone	Projects which enable the beginning scientist to observe the effects of food, sunlight, water, oxygen, and temperature on living plants and animals. 64 p. Ill	Prentice-Hall 1973.
J	Consider The Lilies: Plants Of The Bible	J &K Paterson	Presents botanical illustrations of familiar and exotic flowers, trees, and plants mentioned in the accompanying Bible verses and selections. 96 p. Ill.	Crowell, c1986.
J	Dining on a Sunbeam; Food Chains & Food Webs	Phyllis S. Busch.	Explains the interrelationship and interdependency existing between all animals and plants and the sun. Learn about food chains. 60 p. Ill.	Four Winds Press 1973.
J	Does Candy Grow on Trees?	Karen Rice	Describes some of the plants used in making candy.	Walker, 1984.
J	Fly Traps!	Martin Jenkins	Subtitle: Plants That Bite Back. Describes the habitat and physical characteristics of various insect-eating plants. 28p. Ill.	Candlewick Press, 1996.
J	How Seeds Travel	Cynthia Overbeck	Describes how seeds are moved from place to place by wind, water, and animals, and how they function in plant reproduction. 48 p. Ill photos.	Lerner PubCo., 1982.
J	Hummingbirds in the Garden	Roma Gans	Describes the general migratory and feeding habits of the hummingbird emphasizing the amount of fuel necessary to sustain the small high-powered body weighing less than a penny. 33 p. Ill.	Crowell, c1969
J	The Secret Garden	Frances Hodgson	This classic is available in several different reading levels, with or with out illustrations. There are also two videos with this title. Ten-year-old Mary comes to live in a lonely house on the Yorkshire moors and discovers an invalid cousin and the mysteries of a locked garden.	various
P	Ranger Rick	Magazine	Plants, allergy-causing: A/S 76, 36-39; alpine meadow: Jul 82, 10: attract hummingbirds: Apr 93, 8; carnivorous: Nov 70, 42-47; Nov 77, 26-32; Aug 82, 24; Oct 82, 36; Aug 87, 36-38; chemical defenses of: May 84, 35 ; cuttings: Oct 82, 12; definition of: Dec 70, 4-9; edible: Apr 93, 37-39; Feb 94, 43; endangered: Jan 83, 32-33; fastest growing: May 93, 41; fuel-producing: Mar 82, 14-15; heat-producing: May 82, 20-22; house plants, care of: Dec 88, 18-19; making food: Jun 94, 41; medicine: Feb 90, 4-9; poisonous: May 87, 39, 41; Dec 94, 20-21, 27; pollination. Aug 94, 3-11, 33 rainforest: Apr 93, 22-23; record-breaking: May 93, 40-41; stinky: Jun 83, 16-21; survival trick: Oct 94, 36; water: Aug 81, 30-33; Feb 82, 43-47 (see also separate species)	Ranger Rick

* Possibly in the library, available through Family Christian Academy. Library Codes: A - Adult Section; J – Juvenile Section; E – Easy Reading Section; P- Periodical.

WEEKS: LAW UNIT STUDY

BIBLE

Read and Discuss: The law is a system of commands designed to allow a society to function. The Hebrew word *Torah*, literally "teaching, doctrine," is rendered in the Bible by the Greek word *nomos*, which means "law." Consequently, most Christians look upon the *law* as a negative thing. It has mistakenly come to be thought of by Christians as legalistic, or as a curse to the Jews. Judaism divides the Bible into the Law, the Prophets, and the Writings, "Law" reflecting the Greek understanding of the Hebrew word *torah*. But *torah* is more properly translated "instruction." The Bible explains the law is a gift and a blessing—The Psalmist said, "Oh, how I love the law." Read Psalm 119 aloud. The entire chapter is a collection of various prayers, praises, and professions of obedience of God's law.

Define: In the Bible, the term *Torah* is used for law in general—the book of the law. In many cases, law is used for commandments in the vetitive ("you shall not do this"), the imperative ("do this"), and the jussive ("you shall do this"). It is a commandment from a person of higher authority to a person of lower authority. In the religious sphere, it is the Lord; in the legal sphere it might be the king, judge or elders; in the family sphere it might be the father or mother. Look up *law* in a Bible dictionary. Look up the different types of law: commandments; dietary laws; international law; slavery laws; civil and criminal law; Mosaic law; the Noahide laws, law of sin and death; etc.

Study: Read Bible verses about the law. The law is blessed (Ps. 1:1-3; 32:1, 2; 112:1; 128:1; Matt. 5:3-12; Luke 11:28; John 13:17; James 1:25; Rev. 22:14.). The law is undefiled, or, perfect, or sincere (2 Kings 20:3; 2 Chron. 31:20, 21; Job 1:1, 8; John 1:47; Acts 24:16; 2 Cor. 1:12; Titus 2:11, 12.). God's law inscribed in a heart is reflected in actions, consciences, and thoughts.

Study: *The Heart of the King* explores the intense hunger which dwells in all of us, and our search for God. It is a commentary on each of the 176 verses in Psalm 119 that reveals the incredible longing King David had for God and God's law (instruction). This is an excellent book to use as a short daily devotional for the entire family.

Study: Did Jesus or Paul teach against the law of God? *Harper's Bible Dictionary* shows that there is no hint of contradiction between law and grace in the teachings of Jesus. Paul was not in opposition to *law* (e.g., Rom. 7:12); rather, he was in opposition to *observance* of the law as the means to divine redemption (e.g., Gal. 5:4). Paul's audience, unlike that of Jesus, was mainly Gentile, and his mission to convert them was likely to be encumbered by insistence upon observance of the Mosaic Law.

Research: Jesus said that not so much as a jot or tittle would pass from the law. Look at the Hebrew alphabet to find out the meanings of *jot* and *tittle*.

Brainstorm and Discuss: Is it breaking the law of gravity if a man jumps off a twenty-story building? No, it is an illustration of the law of gravity. Jesus said *"Do not think that I have come to abolish the Law or the Prophets; I have not come to abolish them but to fulfill them."* Jesus fulfilled the law in such a way as to perfect a foundation. Jesus is the law—the perfect life—our instruction, our example. God's instruction to His children was that, each year, the Jewish people were to rejoice in God's instructions (law) during Simchat Torah. The only negative thing about the law is the consequences of breaking it —receiving our deserved punishment—death!

Christ came and died as our replacement, receiving *Himself* our punishment. If we accept His free gift, then we are set free from the law of sin and death! Jesus did not come to kill, steal, or destroy. He came that we might have life more abundantly—an *extraordinary* life surrounded by His love.

Read and Discuss: Read Mark 2:25-26. Jesus shows the Pharisees that their narrow interpretation of the Law blurred God's intention in creating the law. The spirit of the Law in respect to human need took priority over its ceremonial regulations in the case of David. Read Luke 13:10-16 and James 2:5-25 also.

Read and Discuss: Jesus summed up all the laws in these two: Love the Lord your God with all your heart, soul, and mind, and love your neighbor as yourself. Make a list of ways we can show God that we love Him. Make a list of your neighbors; then read the story of the Good Samaritan. Read about the relationship between the Jews and Samaritans in John 4:9.

Read and Discuss: Paul taught against Judaizing (insisting that Jews and Gentiles alike obey the letter of the law). He taught that the *spirit* of the law is what is important, and he condemned those who put their trust in rituals instead of in God. Read Acts 21:14-26 and Romans 2:1-29.

Discuss: Talk about the following verse: *"Jesus said unto him, Thou shalt love the LORD thy God with all thy heart, and with all thy soul, and with all thy mind. This is the first and great commandment. And the second is like unto it, Thou shalt love thy neighbour as thyself. On these two commandments hang all the law and the prophets."*

Look Up and List: In the Bible times, the family was regarded as very important. The father was the head of the family. Find the verses related to the family, and list the laws of the family. Some examples include the rules of marriage and inheritance, laws against beating and cursing parents, and laws regarding the authority of the father, the submission of the wife, and the obedience of the children. Make another list of ways to follow the Bible's rules of instruction for the family.

SCIENCE

Research and Record: Find out about Newton's three laws of motion. Study them until you can give an example of each.

Watch a Video: Watch the *Facts of Faith* video (Moody) for fascinating demonstrations of the harmony of science and faith.

Study: Newton's theories of force and gravity.

Study: Learn about atoms, molecules and the Periodic Table using Usborne's *Atoms and Molecules*. Make a model of an atom using materials in your home.

Read a Biography: Read *Isaac Newton* and/or *Johannes Kepler* from the Sower Series.

Investigate: Kepler's laws explain planet orbits, planet speeds and distances from the sun. Do research to find out more about Kepler, his findings, and his spiritual beliefs. Make a chart showing his discoveries.

Enjoy a Story: Read *Voyage to the Planets* by Richard B. Bliss. This book present creation science-content material in an interesting story of young people in a fictional voyage into planetary space.

Write a Song: Johannes Kepler would become so excited about his scientific discoveries that he would write songs to praise God while recording his findings in his scientific journals. Write a song praising God for what you have learned about His creation during this unit.

Make a Display: Make a mobile of the nine planets orbiting around the sun.

Study: Study the solar system reading the text and doing the activities in *Considering God's Creation:*. Complete lessons one through five.

Watch a Video: Discover how God wonderfully ordered the solar system often referred to as the Law of the Universe, by watching one or both of the videos in the Journey of God's Creation series: *Our Solar System* and *The Milky Way and Beyond* (Moody).

Investigate: Learn about astronomy using the book *Astronomy and the Bible* by DeYoung. Chapters include: The Earth and Moon; The Solar System; The Stars; Galaxies and the Universe; General Science; Technical Terms and Ideas.

AMERICAN HISTORY

Read and Discuss: Examine the rights guaranteed by the first ten Amendments to the Constitution. Create a list with three headings: (1) Rights of Children in Our Home, (2) Rights of Adults, and (3) Rights of Children at a Public School. Name ten rights for each column. The rights should include things such as music, Bible reading, coming and going, traveling distances, friends, prayer, etc. (Your home may have a different list compared with other homes. For example: we feel the right to own a pet, or to talk on the phone at home is *not* a right. It is a privilege). Discuss each of the items in the three lists and write the number of the amendment which corresponds to the right next to it. If there are any amendments not used, think of some rights for them also. Discuss which *one right* is most important.

Memorize: Commit to memory the titles or summary statements of the Bill of Rights.

Study: Use the Commandments as a springboard to study the Constitution of the United States. Read aloud the Constitution, stopping to explain it as you read. Have your child(ren) write down any questions or comments they might have. Using the Constitution as a guide, write up a home constitution or bill of responsibilities (emphasizing rights can produce rebellion). You may also want to attach a Bill of Rights. When a dispute begins over a rule, discuss it together using your constitution as a guide.

Dramatize: Act as if your family is the Congress. Make up laws (house rules) to be signed by the President (Dad). Make up some mock lawsuits that challenge these laws, for the Supreme Court (your family, again) to try. For instance, one of the laws passed (house rule) says no one can call anyone else names. If one of your children calls another child a name, have a mock trial, where Father is now the judge. The child at fault will claim that he was exercising freedom of speech. Try different cases with different rules and different children as the perpetrators. Appoint a prosecutor and a defense attorney for each court case. The defense attorney must show that the law violated his client's rights.

Watch a Video: Watch the *Story of America's Liberty**. This video is an inspirational documentary of America's Christian Heritage featuring accounts of God's miracles in the founding of America. Or watch *Faith and Freedom* a video that traces the pilgrim's voyage across the ocean to Plymouth Rock with little more than their Bibles.

Take A Field Trip. Attend an actual trial that is open to the public. Later, discuss the outcome of the trial and if everyone in your household agreed with the verdict.

Write a Summary: Explain the purpose of the law. In other words, why did God lay upon man any commands at all? Read Romans 3:20 and 21.

Research: In the thirteenth century, Saint Thomas Aquinas formulated a fourfold classification of types of law: 1. eternal law—God's plan for the universe; 2. natural law—that part of the eternal law in which humans participate by their reason; 3. divine law—God's direct revelation to humankind through the scriptures; and 4. human law—particular determinations of certain matters arrived at through the use of reason from the general precepts of the natural law. Brainstorm and list ten laws in each category.

Debate: In 1962 and again, in 1963, the U.S. Supreme Court ruled that permitting prayer in public schools was a violation of the First Amendment "establishment of religion" clause. Read the First Amendment. Discuss this with your parents. Does it make sense?

Investigate: The police are government agents charged with maintaining order and protecting persons from unlawful acts. Find out the requirements to become a police officer in your state.

Research: Most developed societies have had some kind of law enforcement agency. Do research and write a report about at least one of the following agencies: Royal Canadian Mounted Police, The French Police Nationale, Texas Rangers, International Criminal Police Organization.

Discuss: Would your parents home school if it were against the law? Discuss why or why not with your parents. Brainstorm and discuss other scenarios concerning the law. The Chinese government reinforced its restriction of one child per family with laws that make birth control compulsory for newlyweds. If you lived in China, would you obey that law? Discuss this with your parents.

Brainstorm and Discuss: Read Matthew 5:25, Luke 12:58, and 1 Corinthians 6:1-8. How should a Christian handle litigation? By the time of the establishment of the Roman Republic (509 b.c.), a considerable amount of customary law existed. It was not written but oral law. Brainstorm and make a list of problems we would have today if laws were not written. Read these instances of arbitration: the two harlots before Solomon (1 Kings 3:16-28), and the manner urged by Paul, as a mode of action for Christians (1 Cor. 6:1-8). Think of a circumstance when you would use arbitration today.

Research: Call your local pro-life organization. Find out how many babies are killed daily in America since the *Roe vs. Wade* decision. Ask how many O.B./GYN. doctors are in your area that *do not* perform abortions.

Language Arts

Write a Paragraph: Write a persuasive essay about the necessity of passing laws eliminating adult book stores and nude dancing in your town. Include all the benefits your town would receive.

Write A Summary: Read about obeying God's law using the following passages: Psalm 19:7-9; Psalm 119:1-8; and Proverbs 28:4 and 5. Older children should write a summary of their findings.

Resources for the Law Unit Study

Resources about God's natural law or universal law, Torah (God's instruction), America's legal system, the Constitution, rules in the home, etc.

	Title	AUTHOR	DESCRIPTION	PUB
*	**21 Rules of this House**	Greg Harris	21 good rules that define exactly what good behavior is. An excellent training tool. Wall chart, coloring book and study guide. Highly recommended. Ill.	Noble Publishing, c1994.
*	**Astronomy and the Bible**	Donald B. DeYoung	One hundred questions on astronomy and the universe are answered from the Christian perspective. Divided into six sections ranging from earth and moon, the solar system and the stars, to general science and technical terms. 136 p.	Baker Book House, c1989.
*	**City of Bees** (Video)	Video	Marvel at the amazing sophistication and order of bees and why God's design for humans is vastly superior.	Moody
*	**Democracy for Young Americans**	Victoria Shrerow	This workbook explores the historical background, values, and implications of the American system. Local, state, and national governments presented. 112 p. Grades 4-8+.	Good Apple
*	**Facts of Faith** (Video)	Video	Floating rings of steel. An egg frying in a cold pan. Fascinating demonstrations reveal the harmony between science and faith.	Moody Videos
*	**From Bondage To Freedom**	D. Fuchs & H. Sevener	Subtitle: *A Survey of Jewish History from the Babylonian Captivity to the Coming of the Messiah.* The blank page between the Old Testament and the New represents 400 years of history. This book is a fascinating look at this period in Israel's history. Teen/Adult.173 p.	Chosen People Ministries
*	**God of Creation** (Video)	Video	Revel in the order, power and majesty of God's creation from microscopic organisms to the brilliant stars of the universe.	Moody Video
*	**God's Rockin' World** (Video)	Video	Subtitle: *Foundations You Can Build Upon.* From microscopic crystals to the magnificent Grand Canyon, see how the Creator watched over every little detail, just as He watches over the tiniest details of our life today.	Moody Video
*	**Issac Newton**	John H. Taylor	A devout Christian and great mathematician, Newton is remembered as the discoverer of the law of gravity. Includes details about his spiritual life. Grades 5 and up.	Mott Media
*	**It Couldn't Just Happen**	L. Richards	Solid Biblical answers to evolution and our world. Examine God's orderly world in this fascinating book and refute evolution in easy to understand language. Excellent! 191 p.	Word Publishing, c1989.
*	**Johannes Kepler**	John H. Taylor	This giant of astronomy considered his studies to be a way of looking at God's creation. Includes details about his spiritual life that other biographies leave out. Grades 5 and up.	Mott Media
*	**Moses and the Law**	K Merrill & K Christian	An excellent nondenominational Bible study for all ages studying the historical period during the life of Moses. Includes: Origin of the Torah, Bible timeline, Commandments, Tabernacle, maps, charts, flash cards, activity sheets, teacher's notes, and more. 192 p.	Infinite Discovery, c1991.
*	**Our Constitution: Then and Now**	Jerry Allen	A workbook. The original constitution in one column with interpretation in another. Includes review sheets, writing assignments, and games. Grades 5-8+. 168 p.	Good Apple
*	**Our Solar System** (Video)	Video	As long as man has gazed into the night skies, we've wondered at the world of space. Now you can see for yourself in this remarkable exploration of the universe. 40min.	Moody Videos
*	**Shhhh, We're Writing the Constitution**	Jean Fritz	Delightful illustrated book for children, by this renowned author and illustrator, telling the story of the writing of the Constitution. 64 p.	Putnum, 1974

	Title	Author	Description	Publisher
*	The Bill of Rights And Landmark Cases	Edmund Lindop	Discusses landmark cases regarding the Bill of Rights. 144 p. ill	Watts, c1989.
*	The Heart of the King	Ron Auch	A wonderful a commentary on each of the 176 verses in Psalm 119 that reveals the incredible longing King David had for God and God's law (instruction). This is an excellent book to use as a short daily devotional for the entire family. HB. 178 P.	New Leaf Press, 1995
*	The Magic School Bus Explores the Solar System		A special field trip on the magic school bus allows Ms. Frizzle's class to get a first-hand look at major parts of the solar system. Colorful comic book style. Workbook available.	Scholastic
*	The Magic School Bus Explores the Solar System	CDROM	Based on the book above this interactive CDROM is full of games, and activities to teach children ages 6 to 10 about the solar system. Includes video clips from NASA, the Jet Propulsion Laboratory, and details about the planets.	Microsoft Home.
*	The Milky Way & Beyond (Video)	Video	The birth of a star. The creation of a black hole. Quasars, nebulae and exploding stars. See them all. Thrill to the vastness of God's creation as this incredible video brings the deepest regions of space into sharper focus than ever before in history. 40 min.	Moody Videos, 1997
*	God Created the World and the Universe	E. and B. Snellenberg	Ideal nutshell presentation from creation through Apollo mission, moon phases, seasons, solar system, atmosphere, etc. 32 p. coloring and sticker book with in-depth text	Master Books
*	The Spirit of the Law	Ron Mosley	Many Christians have a distorted view of the law. This book explains the law is God's instruction in a straightforward and insightful approach. Quotations from the book appear in the Feasts of Weeks section (Nine-fold Purpose of the Law). Excellent!	
*	The Story of Liberty	Charles Coffin	Beginning with the Magna Carta in 1215 through the story of John Wycliffe translating the Bible into English, through Columbus, the Pilgrims. Timeless classic by a godly historian. Adult or read aloud. 415 p.	Reprinted Mantle Ministries, 1890
*	Voyage to the Planets	Richard B. Bliss.	This book present creation science-content material in an interesting story of young people in a fictional voyage into planetary space. Grades 5 + up.	
A	Careers in Law Enforcement and Security	Paul Cohen	Discusses career possibilities as private investigators, police, and in the field of law enforcement. 128 p.	Rosen Pub. Group, 1990.
J	Free Speech, Free Press, and the Law	Jethro K. Lieberman.	Fifty controversial cases decided by the Supreme Court show how the First Amendment protects freedom of speech and freedom of the press. 160 p.	Lee & Shepard, c1980
J	It is Illegal to Quack Like a Duck & Other Freaky Laws	Barbara Seuling	An overview of some unusual laws from all over the world. 70 p. Ill	Lodestar Books, c1988.
J	It's the Law	Annette Carrel.	Subtitle: A Young Person's Guide to Our Legal System. 187 p.	Volcano Press, c1994.
J	The FBI and Law Enforcement Agencies of the United States	Michael Kronenwetter	Explores the diverse responsibilities and powers of various law enforcement agencies in the United States, including the FBI, the DEA, and the United States Marshals.	Enslow Publishers, 1997.
P	National Geographic	various	Space exploration: Apr 68, 12-15; March, 1981 - Space Shuttle; Sept., 1983 - Satellites, Spacelab; Jan, 1980 - Jupiter, AUG 1990 - Solar System Supplement, NW Passage, Voyager, NASA: Feb 92, 34-37; Mission to Planet Earth, NASA: Feb 92, 34-37;	National Geographic
P	Ranger Rick	various	Constellations, star: Jan 77, 10-12 ; Canis Major: Feb 87, 10; Big Dipper: Jun 89, 16-17; Number of stars in universe (relate to Abraham's children): Aug 92, 17	Ranger Rick

504

Fall Holidays Across the Curriculum

TRUMPETS: PRAISE & WORSHIP UNIT STUDY

Bible

Research Singing: Search in your Bible concordance for verses that contain *sing, singing,* or *singers*. Copy five of your favorite.

Brainstorm and List: God's gifts of music, drama, dance, and art, are all forms of worship to Him. The secular world has corrupted each of these art forms to glorify sin. Title a paper "Be ye Separate" and make a list of secular art forms Christians can avoid.

Research Musical Training: Listen to the excellent audio cassette *How to Provide Excellent Musical Training for Children*. The practical suggestions and easily obtained materials can make it possible for anyone with little musical background to learn along with the children.

Research Singers: Songs in scripture are attributed to Moses, Deborah, Hannah, David, Mary, angels, Simeon, and "the redeemed." Read the songs they sang or wrote. Who wrote praise about God? Who wrote worship songs to God? Do some songs contain both?

Research Dancing: Biblical dancing was not done by paired couples with romance in mind. It was done by individuals or entire groups with only the praise of God in mind. It included everything from clapping and skipping to ballet-type movements. Read the account of Miriam's praise song and dance in Exodus 15:20-21. Then read about the rejoicing over David's victory in 1 Samuel 18:6 and about David's dancing "with all his might" in 2 Samuel 6:14. Also read Psalms 149:3 and 150:4, and the Lord's special touch in Psalm 30:11. If God has given you a heart to worship Him in this way, find a time and place to give Him your offering.

Classify Psalms: Read several Psalms. Choose one of the following categories for each. 1.) Psalms of lamentation or complaint cry out for help in a situation of distress or frustration; 2.) Psalms of thanksgiving; 3.) Hymns praising God; 4.) Wisdom; 5.) Kingship Psalms (God's rule over His people and also pointing ahead to the Messiah—God's kingdom); 6.) Songs of Zion praise; and 7.) Prophetic Psalms.

Investigate Hebrew Words: The ancient Hebrews used seven words that mean praise, each with its own flavor: 1. *Halal* means to celebrate loudly (Ps. 150); 2. *Yadah* is that of giving thankful praise (Ps. 108:3); 3. *Towdah* is also the praise of thanksgiving but it is the joyful sacrifice of praise (Ps. 100:4); 4. *Barak* means to bless kneeling down (Ps. 103); 5. *Shabach* means loud adoration, shouting praise (Ps 47); 6. *Zamar* is sung praise or using a musical instrument (Ps. 33); 7. *Tehillah* is translated as extemporaneous praise. (Ps. 40).

Investigate the Psalms: Service of song is encouraged in James 5:13. How many melodies do you already know (some choruses are only 2-4 verses of a psalm)? Singing scripture is an excellent alternative way to "hide God's Word in your heart". Sing a psalm together as a family to conclude your devotion time or at bedtime nightly as you work this unit.

Science

Learn About Sound: Use an encyclopedia to see how it is created, measured, and recorded. Look at patterns of sound waves made by different instruments. Learn about decibels.

Learn About Harmony: Learn the difference between harmony and discord. What is cacophony and why has it been referred to as "the devil's music" (it is often incorporated into some hard rock)? What are its ill effects? Babies can differentiate between harmony and discord. Test three babies (using low volume) to see their responses.

Learn about the Ear: Learn and illustrate its parts. Learn also the part of the brain that interprets the stimuli.

Learn about Voice: Research the vocal cords. How do they work in speaking and singing? What part of the brain regulates speech? What part controls singing? Learn why persons who have suffered a stroke and cannot speak may still be able to sing.

Watch a Video: Learn about the five senses watching the Christian video *Windows of the Soul* (Moody).

Look at Math in Music: Learn how beats are counted in music and how tempo works.

Study Music Technology: Learn how electronic music is created. Learn how stringed, brass, woodwind, and keyboard instruments work.

Investigate Music Made by Planets: Research the "harmony of the spheres"—sound patterns made by the planets—and other sounds mysteriously emitted by non-living as well as living things in creation. Truly all creation praises Him!

HISTORY

Read a Biography: Study the lives of great Christian composers such as Vivaldi, Haydn, Johann Sebastian Bach or George Frederick Handel. Study the lives of great hymn writers such as Charles Wesley, Isaac Watts, John Newton, or Fanny Crosby. Read about Use *Color the Classics—Godly Composers* materials or Sower Series biographies.

Listen to Music: Listen to Handel's "Messiah," following the entire life of Christ or to any of the composers listed above.

Research Spirituals: During the days of slavery in the United States, slaves who became Christians found strength and hope in singing spirituals. They frequently had echo-type patterns similar to West African music.

Make a Timeline: Create a timeline which shows dates for the advent of different musical instruments, the first written music, the first musical staff, great works of music, and lives of outstanding composers. Modern-day musicians will be much a matter of your family's taste, as the world abounds with exceptional praise and/or worship music writers and composers. Keep in mind that all good music (harmonious sound and uplifting, constructive lyrics) is from the Lord's inspiration—whether the composer knows it or not.

GEOGRAPHY

Label a Map: Study musical instruments that are native to certain parts of the world. Include guitar, violin, banjo, sheng, concertina, waisted drum, highland bagpipes, sitar, tablas, vina, didgeridoo and balalaika. Use a map to locate their "homes."

Learn a Song in a Foreign Language: Obtain a praise tape for children which features languages around the world. Memorize one or more. One source: Far East Broadcasting Company, Box 1, La Mirada, CA 90637. Request *A World of Praise* or a similar production. Suggested gift $5. Locate furloughing missionaries and ask them to demonstrate and teach you native songs they know.

Learn a Dance: Learn a Jewish dance to a praise song.

Learn Praise Songs: Call 1-800-533-6853 to order any of the following cassettes: *Up to Zion, Shalom Jerusalem, Messianic Praise, Songs of Zion* or *Best of Hosanna.*

Visit a Church: Visit a black, white, Hispanic, or Korean church that worships Jesus. Enjoy praise and worship in a different approach than that to which you are accustomed. Remember, God likes it all! His "appreciation factor" is not limited by culture. He's looking at hearts, and has an unbiased ear. One day we will stand together before the throne (Rev. 5:9) singing in worship—why not prepare your heart ahead of time?

LANGUAGE ARTS

Creative Writing: Write a praise song about God. It can be about an account in scripture, His hand in creation, or something He has done for you personally. Younger children can dictate and illustrate.

Write a Song: Write lyrics for a worship song. Remember, worship is when you are singing to God. When you refer to Him, use His name or the words *you* and *your(s)*, and when you refer to yourself use *I, me, my,* and *mine*.

Write a Paper: Write a summary about a concert you have attended or an outstanding music video you have watched. What types of music were included? How did they make you feel? Did they draw attention to Jesus, or His Word, or only the performer?

Research Poetry: Read "I Hear America Singing" by Walt Whitman. Search English literature texts for original verses to read by Charles Wesley, Augustus Toplady, and William Cowper. Sing them in modern hymn versions.

Learn a Song in Sign Language: Learn the sign language for a praise or worship song you already know.

Research and Write: Compare and contrast *praise* and *worship* and draw the relationship between them. Summarize the concepts of praise and worship in writing.

Vocabulary: list all the new words you have heard during this unit. Discuss the meanings or look them up and write the definitions. *Selah* appears in the Psalms. *Selah* (seh-lh') is a verb that means "to pause and reflect" or a noun meaning "a burst of musical praise."

Learn to Spell Homophones: Play the game "Teakettle." Make up a sentence that includes a homophone. Say the sentence aloud replacing the word Teakettle for the homophone. For example, "The boat had a large blue Teakettle." The answer is sail! S-a-i-l, not s-a-l-e. To get the answer correct, the person guessing must: 1. Guess the homophone, 2. Spell the homophone, and 3. Use the sound-alike homophone in a sentence. The one with the correct answers supplies the next sentence. Or Mother can make up all the sentences as children guess the answers. Teakettle is a good car game.

Resources for the Praise and Worship Unit Study

	TITLE	AUTHOR	DESCRIPTION	PUB
*	Provide Excellent Musical Training For Children	Inge Cannon	Audio cassette. Order by sending $5 to Education Plus, P.O. Box 1029, Mauldin, SC, 29662.	Education Plus
*	Francis Scot Key	C. Ludwig	A biography about this courageous Christian who penned the Star Spangled Banner. 113 p.	Mott Media
*	George Fredrick Handle	Charles Ludwig	A biography about a child prodigy and musical genius inspired but God to write "The Messiah." Be sure to listen to this beautiful famous recording also.	Mott Media
*	Samuel Francis Smith	Marguerite Fitch	A biography about this New England pastor who wrote the lyrics to "America: My Country 'Tis of Thee" 154 p. 5th grade and up or read aloud.	Mott Media
*	Windows Of The Soul	Video	Enjoy an amazing look at the five senses in this 50th Anniversary Special Release from Moody.	Moody Video
A	David's Harp: The Story of Music in Biblical Times	Alfred Sendrey	Presents a panorama of the history of music, especially as related to the Old Testament. Sponsored by Jewish Heritage Foundation. Teens and adult. 276 p.	New American Library
J	Alexander Graham Bell	Kathy Pelta	Presents a biography of the speech teacher whose study of sound and human voice led to the invention of the telephone. 137 p.	Silver Burdett Press, c1989.
J	Amazing Grace: The Story Behind The Song	Jim Haskins	Relates the story of the British slave trader who rejected his calling, became a minister, and wrote the words to the popular hymn "Amazing Grace." 48 p. Ill.	Millbrook Press, c1992.
J	Ears And Hearing	Doug Kincaid	Explains how sound can be modified by the shape of the ear, with the use of technical aids, and insulation. 24 p. Ill photos.	Rourke Pub., 1983.
J	Elijah, Brave Prophet	Angeline J. Entz	Relates the persistent efforts of the prophet Elijah to convert the people of Israel from idol worship to the worship of one true God. 47 p. Ill.	Broadman Press, c1978
J	Exploring Sound	Ed Catherall.	Explores the many aspects of sound, including how it travels, is received by the human ear, and can be recorded, and provides simple projects and experiments. 48 p. Ill.	Steck-Vaughn Library, c1989.
J	Homographs	Hanson, Joan.	Introduces words that look but do not sound the same like bow and bow and sew.	
J	Music From Strings	Josephine Paker	Traces the development of stringed instruments through various cultures. Includes projects for making instruments and exploring how sound is made on strings. 48 p. Ill.	Millbrook Press, 1992.
J	Silent Sound: The World Of Ultrasonics.	David C. Knight	Examines extremely high frequency sound known as ultrasound and discusses its use in navigation, industry, and medicine. 93 p. Ill.	Morrow, 1980.
J	Slave Songs	Jerry Silverman	A collection of more than two dozen songs sung by African American slaves. Nobody Knows The Trouble I See, Slow Your Trumpet, Gabriel, Go Down, Moses and more.	Chelsea House Publishers, c1994.
J	The Story Of Your Ear	Alvin Silverstein	Describes the structure of the ear, what sound is and how the ear receives it, the ear's role in maintaining balance, and how the ear can be damaged. 64 p. Ill.	McCann & Geoghegan, 1981.
J	What Instrument is This?	Rosemarie Hausherr.	Identifies an array of popular musical instruments and discusses how they are made, how they sound, and the styles of music for which they are best suited. 38 p. Ill.	Scholastic Inc., 1992.
J	What Makes A Telephone Work?	Len Darwin	Explains how: sound is made and transmitted, the human voice makes sound, human ear perceives it, each part of a telephone instrument works and a network functions. 58 p. Ill.	Little, Brown, c1970.

* Possibly in the library, available through Family Christian Academy. Library Codes: A - Adult Section; J – Juvenile Section; E – Easy Reading Section; P- Periodical.

ATONEMENT: GRACE UNIT STUDY

BIBLE

Think About: The fullness of God's grace is beyond our appreciation or comprehension. The riches of His mercy are overwhelming. We cannot really explore its depths. Read what Paul said in Romans 11:33-36.

Discuss: The word *grace* comes from the Greek *charis*, equivalent to the Hebrew word *chen* ("grace, favor") or *chesed* ("loyal love and kindness"). **Grace** and **truth** are personal attributes of God that Jesus revealed during his earthly lifetime.

Create a Booklet: Read and discuss Genesis 3:15. This is the first time a promise of a Saviour is mentioned. To keep man from forgetting this promise, God established the sacrificial service. Fold four or more sheets of paper in half to make a booklet. Illustrate the story of Cain and Abel on each page using crayons or markers. As you know, Abel's offering was acceptable to God, and was sweet to Him. On the other hand, Cain's offering was not accepted because there was no blood shed, and "without the shedding of blood there is no remission for sins." Choose Bible verses to write on each page of your booklet.

Think: What is more important, God's grace, or our conduct? Nothing man can do apart from God can force God to consider man righteous. God's grace and man's conduct *are not* alternatives or opposites. We should live an obedient life in gratitude to God for his grace (see Ephesians 2:8–10). If man could work his way to heaven, the death of Christ would have been in vain. The battle against sin (without going to God through Jesus) is doomed to failure because it is actually a struggle against God. When a person acknowledges God's remedy, the desire to do His will is more than enough motivation to lead to both eagerness and productiveness in the struggle against sin.

Illustrate: Cut large drops of blood out of red construction paper. Put captions on each droplet demonstrating the reason Jesus shed His blood for us. For example: "my sin," "for me," "because He loves me," "my disobedience," or list specific areas of sin. After hanging the droplets up, pray over each, thanking God for His shed blood and asking forgiveness for specific sins.

Find Out: Read Exodus 24:4-8 and Leviticus 16:1-22. Discuss the ritual of sprinkling the blood of animals on the altar. *Atonement* means "to cover." The blood of the sacrificed animal was a temporary covering for our sins. Why don't we sacrifice animals today?

Brainstorm: We can see Jesus in the picture of the sacrificed animal and a picture of the High Priest. Discuss how Jesus is like the High Priest, for example, in His willingness to lay aside beautiful robes for plain white linen robes, or his being the link between God and man. Can you think of any more? Think of the arms of the high Priest over the goats (one for God, one for Azazel). Is it a picture of Jesus on the cross and the two thieves?

Play a Game: Write these words on index cards: *mediator, advocate, intercession, ascension, tabernacle, Temple, Mercy Seat, Ark of the Covenant,* and *Holy of Holies.* Ask each member of the family to define the word on the card. If someone does not know an answer, continue to the next member. Decide on your own rules (younger child can be given hints. Older children may need to find a Bible verse to illustrate the meaning, etc).

Imagine and Discuss: Imagine a man being sentenced to death because he committed murder. Just as they strap him in the electric chair to give him his just punishment, the Governor calls and grants the man a pardon. The man is released. Does this gift of freedom allow the man to go out and murder again? Did the pardon release him from the law or the punishment? Paul wrote: "Therefore, there is now no condemnation for those who are in Christ Jesus, because through Christ Jesus the law of the Spirit of life set me free from *the law of sin and death.*" (Rom. 8:1-2). We are free of the law of sin and death when we place

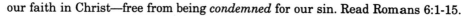

our faith in Christ—free from being *condemned* for our sin. Read Romans 6:1-15.

Read, Contrast and Compare: There once was a man who owned several slaves. He was mean and wicked to his slaves They were beaten and starved so badly that they could scarcely work. He decided to sell his slaves to buy new ones. He took them to the slave market. A rich, generous man came into the crowd as the auction began. His heart leaped for joy as he recognized one of the boys as his *own* son, who was kidnapped many years earlier. He bid the highest, and was able to buy his son. The son had a new owner—his true father. How different his life would be. He was no longer a slave to evil but now a slave to love. Read Romans 6:15-23. Grace is no excuse to sin. We are no longer slaves to sin but are slaves to righteousness. Make a list of what the boy's life was like under each master. Now make two lists, one of a life as a slave to sin and one as a slave to righteousness. Discuss Matthew 6:24, "No one can be slave to two masters." Exodus 6:6-7 explains God's promises: "Wherefore say unto the children of Israel, I am the Lord, and (1) I will bring you out from under the burdens of the Egyptians [the world], (2) I will rid you out of their bondage [sin], (3) I will redeem you with a stretched out arm and with great judgments [bought with a price]; and (4) I will take you to me for a people, and I will be to you a God [our new loving Master]"

Write: Lessons in Titus show us that God's Grace is a Holy Teacher. Write about a character that displayed qualities taught in Titus, like saying "No" to ungodliness; saying "No" to worldly passions; and learning to live self-controlled, upright, and Godly lives in this present age. Think of several difficult situations the character may have had to face and how these lessons would shine through in his or her life.

Read: David recognized grace. Read Romans 4:6-8. Grace was brought to the Gentiles. Romans 11:11,12.

Read and Discuss: Matthew 10:29-31; 1 Peter 1:18-19 and 1 Corinthians 7:23. Jesus paid for (ransomed) us. God loved us enough to pay the ultimate price for us. *Redemption* is a word taken from the slave market. The basic idea is that of obtaining release by payment of a ransom. On the cross, Jesus took the wine and said, "It is finished!" (John 19:30). Then he bowed his head and died. According to the *Bible Knowledge Commentary: Tetelestai* is the word in Greek translated here "it is finished." Papyri receipts for taxes have been recovered with the Greek word *Tetelestai* written across them, meaning "paid in full." God proved His love and concern for us by giving us His Greatest Gift. He did not spare His son, but gave Him up for us—you and me. Since He did that, He'll **graciously** give us all things. The word *graciously* means that God does what He does for us out of a heart of grace. Illustrate this by designing a T-shirt or sweatshirt with a giant SOLD sign on the shirt. Be prepared to answer when someone asks you what it means by memorizing one of these verses: 1 Corinthians 7:23; 1 Corinthians 6:19-20; Romans 6:20-22. Romans 3:24-25; Colossians 1:14; Acts 20:28; Ephesians 1:7.

SCIENCE AND HEALTH

Study Blood: Use the studies of grace, blood, bondage, and freedom to springboard to studies on blood banks, blood poisoning, blood transfusions, blood clots, the cleansing effects of blood, etc.

Watch a Video: Learn about the circulatory system watching this remarkable video *Red River of Life* from Moody.

Discuss: If you are ever worried about God's grace being sufficient to cover *all* your sins. think about the creation of time, space, and matter. Einstein's General Theory of Relativity reveals that time itself is a created physical property as one of four dimensions of our universe. Quantum physics and astrophysics provide remarkable evidence of God's ongoing involvement in our lives. God's grace eternally existed for us literally "before time existed." *According as He hath chosen us in Him* (Christ) *before the foundation of the world...."* (Eph. 1:4). Grace was given to us outside of our time domain of cause-and-effect relationships and before there were cause-and-effect connections. Use this dis-

A Family Guide to the Biblical Holidays©

covery of grace to further investigate the theory of relativity or cause and effect.

HISTORY

Study Slavery: Use the studies of grace, blood, bondage and freedom (liberty) to springboard to history by events such as slavery (ancient history, middle ages, modern times) and America's freedom.

Investigate: The first theological conflict over the nature of sin and grace occurred in the late fourth century between St. Augustine and the British theologian Pelagius. Find out what each man believed and why. Have two children, or a parent and child, take one of the two position and have a debate.

Read a Biography: The sixteenth-century Protestant reformers dissociated grace from the sacraments. John Calvin emphasized the personal quality of grace. Read a biography about one of these men.

Investigate: The Statue of Liberty is the form of a woman, wearing flowing robes and a spiked crown, who holds a torch aloft in her right hand and carries in her left a book inscribed "July 4, 1776." Find out what each item represents.

Take a Look Back: There is a period of four hundred years between the Old and New Testaments, frequently referred to as the four hundred Silent Years. Daniel, Isaiah, and Jeremiah all prophesied about this period. Use the book *From Bondage to Freedom* to study this time period. Include the study of prophetic scriptures; the Jewish nation under Babylon, Persia, Greece, the Hasmonean dynasty, and Rome. Also look at God's promises in Exodus 6:6, 7, and you will see that this fascinating look at this silent period reminds us of the spiritual bondage to freedom journey.

Research: Immunity is an exemption or freedom from liability or penalty under criminal or civil law. Through Christ we have immunity from the penalties of sin (although we may suffer consequences of sin). Study the privileges and immunities of U.S. citizens in the U.S. Constitution in Article IV, in the 14th Amendment, and in the 5th Amendment.

Language Arts

Read Bible Stories: Noah's Ark (Gen. 6:8); God sparing Lot from Sodom and Gomorrah (Gen. 19:1-29); God keeping covenant with Israel (Ezek. 16:8 and Isa. 49:14-18). The divine grace rests on the infant Jesus who subsequently grows in grace, speaks gracious words, and is the ultimate "mercy and truth." (Luke 2:40, 52; 4:22; John 1:14; Ex. 34:6).

Practice Handwriting: Choose one or more of the following verses to practice handwriting: Prov. 14:31; Eccles. 7:33; Psalms 6:2; 41:4, 9:13, 119:29.

Write a Card: To be pardoned is an act by which an individual is freed from the consequences of having committed a breach of the law. Pardons can be conditional or unconditional. Christ's blood bought us an unconditional pardon. Read Ephesians 4:1-3 and write a thank you card to show gratitude to God for the sacrifice of His Son. What can we do in our lives to show gratitude?

Write a Parable: Show your understanding of grace by writing or narrating a parable about a mother and/or father showing grace to their child who broke a rule. Include repentance and the giving of a gift (because God gave us a gift), and why parents make rules (laws). Discuss: should you obey your parents' rules if you can be forgiven easily and get gifts anyway (greasy grace)?

Add to Your Vocabulary: List all the new words you have heard during this unit. Discuss the meanings or look them up and write the definitions.

Resources for the Grace Unit Study

	TITLE	AUTHOR	DESCRIPTION	PUB
*	Blood And Guts: A Working Guide To Your Own Insides	Linda Allison	Discusses the elements of the human body. Includes suggestions for related experiments and projects. 127 p. Ill.	Little, Brown, c1976.
*	A Drop Of Blood	Paul Showers	Let's-read-and-find-out science book. A simple, fun introduction to the composition and functions of blood. 32 p. Ill	Crowell, c1989.
*	Fearfully And Wonderfully Made	Dr. Paul Brand	Referred to as "The finest medical presentation of the functions of the body." Careful sensitive interweaving of spiritual applications in the body of Christ. Grade 9 and up.	Zondervan
*	Red River of Life (Video)	Video	Compelling macrophotography takes you on a remarkable journey inside the human circulatory system.	Moody Videos
*	The Wonder Of You (Video)	Video	Discover the inner workings of the world's most complex machine-the human body from a Christian view. Also on this video Mystery Story and A Matter of Taste.	Moody Videos
J	Adam: The Inside Story	CDROM	Explore the human body aboard the interactive story. A.D.A.M. stand for Animated Dissection of Anatomy for Medicine. Includes narrated animations, medical illustrations, video clips, sound, commentaries, puzzles, and more. Modest setting available.	A.D.A.M. Software, 1995
J	Amazing Grace: The Story Behind The Song	Jim Haskins	Relates the story of the British slave trader who rejected his calling, became a minister, and wrote the words to the popular hymn "Amazing Grace." 48 p. Ill.	Millbrook Press, c1992.
J	Blood	Herbert S. Zim	Discusses such aspects of the composition and functions of blood as the manufacture of red blood cells, blood type and Rh factor, lymph, clotting, disease and antibodies, and the transportation of oxygen, hormones, and food. 63 p. Ill.	W. Morrow, 1968.
J	Blood	Anna Sandeman	Explains what blood is, what it does, and how it circulates in the human body. 31p. Ill.	Copper Beech Books, 1996.
J	The Body: And How It Works	Steve Parker	Examines the systems and parts of the human body and how they work, including the skin, blood, bones, lungs, and heart. 64 p. Ill.	Houghton Mifflin Co., c1992.
J	Circulatory Systems: The Rivers Within	A. & V. B. Silverstein	Describes the organs of the circulatory system and their functions and discusses the composition of the blood. 74 p. Ill.	Prentice-Hall 1970.
J	The Human Body For Every Kid	Janice VanCleave	Subtitle: Easy Activities That Make Learning Science Fun, A fun-filled activity book that will encourage learning.	Wiley, c1995.
J	Secrets of the Heart and Blood	Anne Terry	Comprehensive information on circulatory system and blood. Brief introduction to Jenner, Pasteur and Fleming. Mention of evolution. 80 p. Spot-color illus.	Garrard Publishing Co.
J	Your Heart And Blood	Leslie Jean LeMaster	Discusses the composition of the blood and its importance to body function and describes the structure of the heart and its role in pumping the blood through the body. 45 p. Ill.	Child-rens Press, c1984.

* Possibly in the library, available through Family Christian Academy. Library Codes: A - Adult Section; J – Juvenile Section; E – Easy Reading Section; P- Periodical; Au—Audio.

TABERNACLES: TREE UNIT STUDY

BIBLE

Read and Discuss: Read Genesis 1:29 and chapters 2 and 3 for the original plan for trees and their involvement in man's fall. The Tree of Life theme is repeated in Ezekiel 47:12 and Revelation 22:2, 7, and 14. Read Jotham's parable of the trees. Discuss the symbolism of trees in Proverbs 3:18 and 11:30.

Read a Bible Story: 2 Samuel 12-18 relates a long account of how the sin in David's life opened the door for other wickedness within his family. One chief offender was his son Absalom who was killed after he was caught by his hair in an oak tree (18:9). Parents may condense the story as necessary and discuss how rebellion and pride played parts in his death.

Study Symbolism: Read Nebuchadnezzar's vision of a tree in Daniel 4. Illustrate the before and/or after appearances of the tree.

Research: In Peter Michas' book, *The Rod of an Almond God's Master Plan (see page 549)*, he explains a very interesting view that the Tree of Life in the Garden of Eden was an almond tree. (He believes the tree of good and evil was a fig tree) The author shows documentation from Jewish resources and the Bible that trace a rod from the Tree in the Garden of Eden to Adam to Moses to David and ends up being the actual tree upon which Christ was crucified.

Memorize: Psalm 1 and Isaiah. 55:12, which younger children can learn and/or illustrate. Take a nature walk through a well-treed area and listen for different sounds of "applause" from various species.

Investigate a Parable: Jesus said to learn a parable of the fig tree (Matt. 24:32; Mark 13:28). Fig trees are mentioned thirty-three times in the Bible.

SCIENCE

Study and Learn: Study the four main parts of the tree and learn their purposes.

Research Grafting: Romans 11:27 explains how believers are grafted into Israel. The root of the tree is the source of life and nourishment to all the branches, and Abraham is "the father of all who believe." (Rom. 4:11-12, 16-17).

Watch a Video: Watch the video *God's Earth Team (Moody)*. A delightful video to teach about stewardship, environmental protection.

Study: Complete all reading and activities in lesson 11 "Trees" in *Considering God's Creation*.

Watch a Video: This fascinating video Hidden Treasures (Moody) reveals how seeds of different trees travel through floods, fire, and storms to exotic places, where they live and grow. It is a picture of the living seed taking root in the human heart.

Plant a Tree. Research which trees in your area grow best by contacting your state or city forester. Be sure there is adequate irrigation.

Color Trees: An excellent botany source for older students is the coloring book *Forests** (a Running Press book by Elizabeth Dudley Ph.D.).

Investigate Grafting: Trees can grow without starting as a seed. This process is called asexual propagation. Grafting is one process of asexual plant propagation. When a portion of a plant is physically attached to a seedling or plant (of the same species) it is called grafting. For example: a branch of a yellow apple tree is attached (using a string, rubber band or wax) to an actively growing red apple tree. After several weeks, if the graft is successful, the branches will have grown together, making a new type of apple. Do research to find out about grafting and other asexual propagation: budding, root cuttings, tissue culture, marcottage (air layering). Visit a nursery or interview a gardener to find out more about grafting. Romans 11:27 explains how believers are grafted into Israel. The root of the tree is the source of life and nourishment to all the branches, and Abraham is "the father of all them that believe." (Rom. 4:11-12, 16-17).

Collect Specimens: Make a personal leaf collection. Preserve the color of specimens by pressing them between newspapers or blotting paper and changing the paper every other day. Dried blotting paper can be reapplied. A heavy book on top will assure flatness. Use a field guide to identify.

Go on a Field Trip: Locate the nearest relatives or examples of biblical trees in your locale. Include cedar, fir, pine, willow, oak, almond, palm, pomegranate, apple, fig, myrtle, and olive. Use a Bible concordance to find others. Learn their family groupings. Example: most fruit trees are in the rose family. Fringetree, adelia ,and ash are in the olive family.

Go on a Field Trip: Visit a sugar maple farm that makes syrup.

Research: Study the vascular system in trees. How do rings in a slice of trunk relate to growth?

Study the Ecosystem: Learn and illustrate the five layers of a forest.

Watch a Video: Learn about stewardship and environmental protection by watching the video *God's Earth Team* (Moody).

HISTORY

Learn About Arbor Day: The Jews have an "Arbor Day" and so does the United States (and perhaps your country). Research to see who began these practices of planting new trees, when, and why. (Arbor Day may occur on different days in different parts of the country to accommodate climate.)

Study Wood Materials: Trees have been used for basic housing for centuries. Read the account of Pa and Ma building the cabin in *Little House on the Prairie* by Laura Ingalls Wilder or another account of building cabins from earlier historical accounts.

Investigate Craftsmanship in History: Use a book such as *Reader's Digest Back to Basics* (a book about the simple life) or *Foxfire* to learn about converting trees into lumber, building a log cabin, raising a barn, constructing a fence, using wood as fuel, cooking with wood, and woodworking.

Create a Timeline: Make a timeline showing furniture, tools, machines, or other inventions that are crafted primarily from wood. Include the processing of wood pulp into paper and the printing of books. Include interesting items such as Viking ships and the Trojan horse. Draw illustrations to affix to the line.

GEOGRAPHY

Search a Map: On a world map, locate deciduous, evergreen, Olympic rain forest and tropical rain forest areas.

Make a Map: Draw a map of your country and color in national forest areas, basic forested regions, and privately protected forests, if possible.

Investigate Biomes: Learn the differences between virgin and second growth forests. Where do virgin forests remain in the world?

LANGUAGE ARTS

Read a Book: Read *one of the books in the resource section*.

Enjoy Poetry & Music: Read Robert Frost's "Birches" and/or Paul Hamilton Hayne's

"Aspects of the Pines." Memorize any or all of these three poems: "Woodman, Spare That Tree" by George Perkins Morris, "Loveliest of Trees" by Alfred Edward Houseman, and "Trees" by Joyce Kilmer.

Write a Poem: Write a poem about the glories of autumn or a special tree.

Brainstorm and List: Make a list of products made from wood. Write a research paper on these products. Younger children may illustrate.

Write an Essay: Write about the environmental value of trees: homes for animals, wind buffers, moderate the sun's effects, slow down moisture loss from wind. Include wise conservation techniques, and what your family can do personally to contribute to their health or care. (Many U.S. Soil Conservation districts have essays and posters contest.)

Vocabulary: List all the new words you have heard during this unit. Discuss the meanings or look them up and write the definitions.

Listen to Music: Listen to Antonio Vivaldi's "Autumn" concertos from *The Four Seasons*, a group of violin concertos, each based on a poem. Since Vivaldi is known to have often quoted the Psalms as he worked at the Pieta conservatory, consider reading Psalm 1 or others at certain points in the performance.

Resources for the Tree Unit Study

	TITLE	AUTHOR	DESCRIPTION	PUB
*	*Johnny Appleseed*	David R. Collin	Sub title: *God's Faithful Planter*. In his knapsack he carried his Bible and as many apple seeds that would fit as he headed out for the West. Grades 5 and up. 160 p.	Mott Media
*	*Tree in the Trail*	Holling Clancy Holling	Beautifully illustrated as all Holling's books are. A cottonwood tree watches the parade of history on the Santa Fe Trail for 200 years. All ages read aloud.	Houghton Mifflin, c1942.
A	*1001 Questions Answered About Trees.*	Platt, Rutherford Hayes	Illustrated with drawings and with photos.	Dodd, Mead, 1959.
E	*Be a Friend to Trees*	Patricia Lauber	Discusses the importance of trees as sources of food, oxygen, and other essential things. 32 p. col. Ill.	Harper Collins Pub., c1994.
E	*Hello, Tree!*	Joanne Ryder	Describes, some of the unique characteristics of trees. 32 p. Ill.	Lodestar, c1991.
E	*Mighty Tree*	Dick Gackenbach	Three seeds grow into three beautiful trees, each of which serves a different function in nature and for people.	Harcourt Brace J, c1992.
J	*Around the Oak*	Gerda Muller	Fiction story about three children that observe the forest, including a giant oak, throughout the year. 39 p. Ill.	Dutton Children's Books, c1994.
J	*Consider the Lilies: Plants of the Bible*	John & Katherine Paterson	Presents botanical illustrations of familiar and exotic flowers, trees, and plants mentioned in the accompanying Bible verses and selections. 96 p. col. Ill.	Crowell, c1986.
J	*Crinkleroot's Guide to Knowing the Trees*	Jim Arnosky	An illustrated introduction to trees and woodlands with information on how to identify the bark and the leaves, the many ways that animals use trees, and how to read the individual history that shapes every tree.	Bradbury Press; c1991.
J	*Everyday Trees*	Gertrude E. Allen	Simple information on the uses, seeds and species of the apple, maple, willow, birch, oak, pine and firtrees. 47 p. Ill.	Houghton Mifflin, 1968.
J	*Outside And Inside Trees*	Sandra Markle	Discusses various parts of trees and their functions, including the bark, sapwood tubes, roots, and leaves. 39 p.	Maxwell Macmillan Int'l, 1993.
J	*The Blossom on The Bough: A Book of Trees*	Anne Ophelia Dowden	Discusses the importance of forests, the parts and cycles of trees, the functions of flowers and fruits, the distinctive features of conifers, and the forest regions in the United States. 71 p. Ill.	Crowell 1975.
J	*Walden*	adapted by Steven Lowe	In this illustrated adaptation of Thoreau's famous work, a man retreats into the woods and discovers the joys of solitude and nature. Ill.	Philomel Books, 1990.
P	*Ranger Rick Magazine*	various	Tree: Jan 68, 16-19; Jan 73, 38-39; Feb 80, 9-11; May 80, 32-35; Oct 80, 13-16; Sep 82, 9; May 88, 10-11; Feb 91, 30; Sep 94, 17; acacia: Sep 81, 45-47;vv; Adopt-a-Tree program: Feb 80, 10-11; catching tree thieves: Oct 91, 33; leaves: Oct 81, 4-8; collecting: Mar 70, 10-11; pest-fighting: May 84, 35; rainforest: Apr 82, 18-21; rings: Jan 71, 30-32; saving for wildlife: May 90, 36-39; (see also individual species)	Ranger Rick
V	*Tree (video)*	Anne McLeod.	A CAFE production for BBC Worldwide Americas, Dorling Kindersley Vision in association with Oregon Public Broadcasting. 35 minutes.	Eyewitness videos. DK Vision, c1996.

* Possibly in the library, available through Family Christian Academy; Library Codes: A - Adult Section; J — Juvenile Section; E — Easy Reading Section; P- Periodical; Au—Audio.

Post-Mosaic Holidays Across the Curriculum

HANUKKAH: OIL UNIT STUDY

BIBLE

Read Bible Stories: Read and discuss how the widow feeds Elijah (1 Kings 17:12-16) and the parable of the good Samaritan in Luke 10:34.

Watch a Video: Watch the Maccabees: The Story of Hanukkah, an animated Hero Classic available from Nest Entertainment.

Read a Parable: Read and study the parable of wise and foolish virgins (Matt. 25). Five of the virgins had made adequate preparation, for they possessed the necessary lamps and extra oil in jars (Matt. 25:4). Five others had lamps but no extra oil.

1. The Bridegroom . . . . .Jesus
2. The Wise Virgins . . . . .Christians
3. The Foolish Virgins . . . . . .Professing "Christians"
4. Lamp .Outward Christian Profession
5. Oil . . . . .The Holy Spirit
6. Arrival of Bridegroom . . . .Second Coming of Christ

Watch a Video: Get a better understanding of how important it is to keep our lamps full of oil ready for the bridegroom by watching the video *Beloved Thief: A Musical Love Story*. Learn the customs of a young Jewish couple as they fall in love and are betrothed. The same customs apply to Christians who, as the bride of Christ, wait for our beloved.

Investigate: The Bible mentions oil hundreds of times. Read and discuss the symbolic verses about oil. Oil is considered a blessing (Deut. 8:7-8), and symbolic for the Holy Spirit (2 John 2:27). Oil was used for comfort, spiritual nourishment, or prosperity (Deut. 33:24; Job. 29:6; Ps. 45:7). The presence of oil symbolized gladness (Ps. 45:7, Isa. 61:3), while its absence indicated sorrow or humiliation (Joel 1:10). Mourners did not use oil on their bodies during their period of sadness (2 Sam. 14:2; Isa. 61:3; Dan. 10:2-3). Oil was used to bestow honor and refreshment, and for grooming. "Pure oil signified the gifts and graces of the Spirit, which are communicated to all believers from Christ, of whose fullness we receive (Zech. 4:11, 12), and without which our lights cannot shine before men." (Henry, 1991)

Discover: Read the domestic references to oil. The expressed product of the olive fruit except when cosmetic ointments (Ruth 3:3; 2 Sam. 14:2; Ps. 104:15) or oil of myrrh (Esther 2:12) are indicated. The abundance of olive trees (*Olea europaea*) in ancient Palestine enabled a flourishing trade in oil to be carried on with Tyre and Egypt. Oil was used for many domestic purposes. Those who lived in Bible times cooked with and ate oil like we use butter today (Lev. 2:4-5 1 Kings 17:12-16). Oil was also used for cosmetic purposes. Oil could be compounded with perfumes to make aromatic ointments (cf. Esther 2:12; Song 1:3; 4:10). Oil was used as personal care for the head and face (Ps. 23:5, Luke 7:46, Matt. 6:16, Ps. 104:15). It was also used as a wound dressing for healing as shown in Luke 10:34's parable of the Good Samaritan.

Research: Read the anointing uses of oil. Priests and kings (Ex. 28:41; Ps. 133:2; 1 Sam.10:1, 16:1,13; and 1 Kings 1:39) were anointed with oil. *The Spirit of the Lord God is upon me, because the Lord hath anointed me.* (Isa. 61:1) The Spirit is called *the oil of gladness* because of the delight wherewith Christ was filled in carrying on His undertaking. He was anointed with the Spirit *above all his fellows*, above all those that were anointed, whether priests or kings." (Henry, 1991). Oil is used as anointing for healing. (God consecrates the common, making it holy for His purpose [James 5:15.]) Oil of prosperity is thought to be petroleum, as indicated in Job 29:6 (rock-based petroleum).

Research: Read the uses of oil in the Tabernacle. Sacred anointing oil was used for the tabernacle and the furnishings (Ex.30:23-3). Oil was used for light in the tabernacle (Ex. 27:20-21, Lev. 24:2-4) (pure olive oil, beaten) "To supply light in the tabernacle, the lampstand with its seven lamps required a continual provision of olive oil. The Israelites were to provide this oil so that the priests could keep the lamps burning continuously as a lasting ordinance." (Walvoord, John F., and Zuck 1985)

Discuss: Before Jesus was crucified, He went to pray in Gethsemane, which means "an oil press." Oil presses were used to extract oil from the fruit. Find and read about this event in one of the gospels.

Research: The Bible Knowledge Commentary states: "In Deuteronomy. 33:25, when Moses said of Asher, 'Let him dip his foot in oil,' he was speaking prophetically of the wealth from petroleum that would come in 1935 when the Great International Iraq-Petroleum Enterprise would cross the "toe area" of the foot-shaped map of Asher's territory. Oil brought nearly 1,000 miles across sands from Mesopotamia poured through Haifa harbor at a million gallons per day." Study petroleum uses today. Discuss what would happen to your country if it did not have access to oil.

Research: Older children: look up oil throughout the Old and New Testaments, using a concordance.

Make a Game: Develop a concentration-type game using pairs of examples for the different uses of oil.

SCIENCE

Study Olive Trees: The olive tree is cultivated for its edible fruit, its foliage, and its wood. The olive tree produces tiny white flowers with immature, green, edible olives that turn bluish or purplish when ripe. The olives are quite acidic and must be prepared for human consumption. Oil is extracted from the olives to be used for cooking and other purposes.

Brainstorm and List: Oil is any substance that does not dissolve in water, but can be dissolved in ether. God has made many different examples of oils. Make a list of several oils, then use your encyclopedia to add to it.

Classify: The olive tree family contains about nine hundred species, placed in twenty-four genera. Olives make up the family Oleaceae. The representative genus is *Olea*. Make a chart showing the classification of the olive tree.

Classify: Classify your oils into *animal, vegetable,* and *mineral.* Separate your "brainstorm" list into *fixed* and *volatile* oils, according to their behaviors when heated.

Find and List: Find out the different ways of processing oil. Include the differences between virgin olive oil, extra virgin olive oil, and cold pressed olive oil.

Research Friction: Oil lubrication brings freedom from friction. Ask someone familiar with cars to explain the importance of oil in the moving parts of a car engine. Ask how the oil pump works. Watch the next time someone puts oil in your family car.

Investigate: Look up oil lubrication, oil lamp, and oil rig in *The Way Things Work* or any general science books.

Compare: Learn examples of *drying oils, semidrying,* and *nondrying oils.* Separate your list into these categories.

Make Butter: Put whole cream in a baby food jar and shake until it turns into butter. Read Chapter 2 on butter making from *Little House in the Big Woods* by Laura Ingalls Wilder. Find out what makes the cream turn to butter.

Have a Scavenger Hunt: Look in your home and garage to locate as many oil-based products as possible, then group them into the three main classes.

Research and List: Discover twenty uses for oil. Have middle- and upper-level students research one of these uses and report about the source of oil(s) used, how they are incorporated into the product, and the benefits derived from its use.

Make a Candle: Use a craft book for directions on making a floating oil candle.

Make Soap: See *Reader's Digest Back to Basics* for instructions on several soap recipes.

Research: Read about the perfumery's arts in your encyclopedia. Purchase a vial of rose oil or a similar fragrance. and make potpourri.

HEALTH

Study Nutritional Value: Read the chapter "The Fat of the Land" in *What the Bible Says About Healthy Living* by Rex Russell, M.D. or a similar book for insight on the healthful benefits of olive oil and butter.

Have a Taste Test: Taste as many edible oils as possible. Prepare them in recipes, if desired.

HISTORY

Create a Time line: Create a timeline demonstrating the discovery or important events related to each of the twenty uses from the science section. Examples: chart the date of the first manufactured soap, the historical impact of the victory of the Maccabees and the miraculous temple oil remembered at Hanukkah. Research the impact of petroleum-based products in the World Wars. Trace the importance of printer's inks in history. In past times whale oil was commercially important. Read about whale oil's past to present usage.

Learn About a Scientist: George Washington Carver is a famous Christian scientist who found hundreds of uses for the peanut. Which of these uses involve peanut oil, and how did each impact history?

GEOGRAPHY

Make a Map: Make a world map showing where base products can be found. Include olives, spices (such as nutmeg and/or clove), fish (choose salmon, sardine or herring), walnuts or linseed, and petroleum. Use a different dot or line pattern to shade in areas. Mediterranean Study: Read about Mediterranean countries whose economies and diets depend on olive oil.

Investigate Trade: Read about oil trade between Tyre and Egypt in Bible times.

Watch a Video: Watch *Yanni, Live at the Acropolis* (PBS performance) for a taste of Greek and international music.

Make a Dinner: Enjoy a Spanish, Italian, Greek, or middle-eastern dinner made with dishes that contain olive oil.

LANGUAGE ARTS

Write a Story: Girls should write their thoughts as though they were the young woman who anointed Jesus' feet with the ointment from her alabaster box (Luke 7:36-50). Boys should write as though they were George Washington Carver—awake night and day in a passionate discovery of things to make with peanut oil. See a biography for hints.

Create a Poem: Write a poem about the wonder or blessing of any (or all) oils.

Add to Your Vocabulary: List all the new words you have heard during this unit. Discuss the meanings or look them up and write the definitions.

DRAMA, MUSIC

Act Out : Younger children may dramatize the daily entrance into the temple by priests who witnessed the miracle remembered at Hanukkah. Scenes of cleaning the temple and mixing new anointing oil are also possibilities.

Learn a Song: Sing the chorus "Give Me Oil in My Lamp, Keep Me Burning."

Listen to a Ballad: Midnight Oil is performed by Phillips, Craig and Dean. (Words and music by Joy Becker and Shawn Craig.)

Resources for the Oil Unit Study

	Title	AUTHOR	DESCRIPTION	PUB
*	*Energy and Power*	Science and Experiments Book	Explains different kinds of energy and how it's used. Describes basic scientific facts, latest technology, environmental problems, advantages and disadvantages of each. Using Usborne's colorful artistic illustrations. 48 p. Ill.	Usborne
J	*Alaska: Indians, Eskimos, Russians, and the Rest*	Cora Cheney	A history of Alaska from the arrival of its native peoples to the building of the oil pipeline in the 1970's, with special emphasis on its Russian period. 143 p. Ill.	Mead, c1980.
J	*America the Beautiful: Texas*	R. Conrad Stein.	Introduces the vast and diverse state with deep historical roots in the lore of cowboys and oil tycoons. 143 p. Ill.	Childrens Press, 1989.
J	*America the Beautiful: Oklahoma*	Ann Heinrich	Introduces this central state that has been a "Dust Bowl," Indian Territory, oil rich, and a promised land to settlers.	Childrens Press, c1989.
J	*An Introduction to Exploration Economics*	R. E. Megill	Text and illustrations describe the physical layout, operations, and personnel of a drilling platform or oilrig. production.	Petroleum Pub. Co., c1979.
J	*Black Diamonds: A Search for Arctic Treasure*	James Houston	While searching for a gold mother lode, the Morgans and friends come upon a pool covered with iridescent oil. "Black diamonds," oil is known by those who seek it?	Atheneum, 1982.
J	*Cinderella of the New South: A History of the Cottonseed Industry*	Lynette Boney Wrenn	Beginnings of the American cottonseed industry, expansion of cottonseed milling in the South, buying, selling, crushing, oil refining, manufacturing, organization, price fixing, politics, WW I, postwar, hydraulics and more.	University of TN Press, c1995.
J	*Doodlebugging, the Treasure Hunt for Oil*	Elaine Scott	Discusses the different methods used by geophysicists to locate petroleum.	F. Warne, c1982.
J	*From Oil to Gasoline*	Ali Mitgutsch	Follows crude oil from its underground bubbles to the refinery then converted into fertilizer, plastic, records, paint, medicine, gasoline, jet oil, and heating oil. 24 p. Ill	Carolrhoda Books, 1981.
J	*Gib Morgan, Oilman*	A. Dewey	The adventures of the legendary oilman as he travels all over the world drilling for oil.	Greenwillow c1987.
J	*How Did We Find Out About Oil?*	Isaac Asimov	Describes the origin, composition, and historical and modern uses of petroleum. 61 p. Ill.	Walker, 1980.
J	*Iran and Iraq : Nations at War*	Lisa Mannetti.	Surveys the historical background and recent events of the war between Iran and Iraq and considers the resulting political and economic complications for the region and for oil-dependent countries. 87 p. Ill.	F. Watts, 1986.
J	*Oil Rigs*	Neil Ardley	Describes the construction and operation of an oilrig and the search for and discovery of petroleum.	Garrett Ed Corp., 1990.
J	*Oil Rigs*	R. Stephen	Photographs and brief text examine how oil rigs are used to drill for oil on land and at sea.	F. Watts, 1986.
J	*Oil Spills: Damage, Recovery, and Prevention*	Laurence Pringle	Describes petroleum and its uses, examines the harmful effects of oil spills, and discusses how such environmental disasters can be cleaned up or prevented	Morrow Junior Books, c1993.
J	*Plastics*	Terry Cash	Describes how plastics are made into many different products from bottles and bags to tubes and toys. Includes ideas for a variety of simple projects and experiments. 25 p. Ill.	Garrett Ed. Corp., 1990.
J	*The Story of the New England Whalers*	R. Conrad Stein	The history of whaling in New England from the early eighteenth century to its decline when oil was discovered in mid- nineteenth century. 31 p. Ill.	Childrens Press, c1982.
J	*Undersea Technology*	Ralph Rayner	Surveys the technology used in underwater exploration, mining, oil production, describes submarines, bathyscaphes, and other vehicles, and undersea environment. 47 p. Ill.	Bookwright Press, 1990.

* Possibly in the library, available through Family Christian Academy. Library Codes: A - Adult Section; J – Juvenile Section; E – Easy Reading Section; P- Periodical.

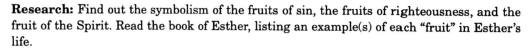

PURIM: FRUIT UNIT STUDY

BIBLE

Research: Find out the symbolism of the fruits of sin, the fruits of righteousness, and the fruit of the Spirit. Read the book of Esther, listing an example(s) of each "fruit" in Esther's life.

Read: *A Gardener Looks at the Fruit** by Philip Keller or *Fruits of the Spirit** by Ron Hembree. Keller explains the physical attributes of growing fruit compared to producing spiritual fruit while Hembree illustrates the impact of the nine spiritual fruits produced by God in the life of a believer.

Investigate Fruit From the Bible: Purchase a Bible fruit you have never (or seldom) eaten. Locate the scripture passage(s) where it is mentioned. Then, after holding, smelling, and tasting, see if you gain new insight into the passages. For example: olive trees live longer than most other fruit trees. Spaniards brought them to the U.S. in 1769. Some of them are still alive, as are some of the ones in the Holy Land, which were living in Bible times.

Make a Display: Paul lists the fruit of the spirit in Galatians 5:22: love, joy, peace, patience, kindness, goodness, faithfulness, gentleness, self-control. Make a giant tree out of brown and green construction paper, to hang on the wall. Use red construction paper to cut out circles of "fruit," then, using a black marker, write one of the names of the fruit of the spirit on each. Now, cut out brown paper circles to represent shriveled-up, dead fruit. Write the names of undesirable fruits such as lying, unkindness, selfishness. Put the dead fruit under the tree on the ground. This is a picture of what should happen when you come into the family of God. The nasty fruit should fall away and be replaced with new fresh fruit.

Give a Gift: When you give gifts of food to friends and to the needy to celebrate Purim, consider recipes with fresh or dried fruit in them, or just fruit itself. Include a piece of paper with one or more of the "fruit" passages written on it—God's Word is food, too!

SCIENCE

Fruit: Commonly the term *fruit* is often restricted to succulent, edible fruits of woody plants, to melons, and to such small fruits as strawberries and blueberries. Ripe fruits are divided into two groups, dry and juicy. Fruit is the part of a plant that contains seeds. All flowering plants begin with a seed.

Study Fruit Properties: Learn the values and purposes of fruit sugars, pectin, tannins, vitamins, enzymes, and fiber found in most fruits.

Classify Fruits: Write the names of these fruits on a card and classify them any way you choose: acorn, apple, avocado, banana, blackberries, cantaloupe, dates, figs, grapefruit, grapes, honeydew melon, kiwifruit, lemon, lime, mango, nectarine, orange, papaya, peach, pear, pineapple, plums, tangerine, tomato (yes, it is a fruit), strawberries, summer squash, watermelon. Which do you think belong in these groups: berries, drupes, and pomes? Find out how the scientists classify them.

Taste Fruits: Try fruits from the above list that you have not tried before. Predict how it will taste by its looks (kiwi may surprise you).

Research Fruit Preservation: Which preservation techniques preserve the most nutrients? Read about freezing, canning, and drying. Study the process of making orange or other fruit juice. Visit a place that makes old-fashioned apple cider.

HEALTH

Investigate Nutrition: Read the chapter on fruits and vegetables *in What the Bible Says About Healthy Living* by Rex Russell, M.D.

Investigate Fruit Types: Fruit is classified by several characteristics, the most significant being the number of ovaries included (simple fruit, aggregate, multiple fruit). Simple fruits are divided into dry or fleshy.

Research Nutrition: Fruits are eaten raw or cooked, dried, canned, or preserved. Fruits provide many essential vitamins and minerals. Use a nutrition book or read labels to compare the nutritional value of fresh fruit to canned or frozen fruit.

INDUSTRY

Investigate Employment and Career Opportunities: Interview someone with a career dealing with the fruit industry: farmer, picking, harvesting, processing, marketing, factory worker, or engineering. Ask about: careers, current and future employment needs, job descriptions, training requirements, working conditions, opportunities for advancement, etc.

Research Cultivation: Find out the benefits and drawbacks of using pesticides and growing fruit organically. How are hybrids such as tangelos, seedless varieties, or oversized fruits developed?

Research Economic Importance: Find out from your agricultural agency or library the economics in the foreign, national, state, and local areas, as well as the fruit crop statistics of each.

Take a Field Trip: Go to a local canning factory, a wholesale produce warehouse, a fresh vegetable market, or a commercial greenhouse that grows fruit for truck gardeners. If possible, visit a farm during either planting or harvesting that grows fruit for food-processing plants or for the fresh market.

HISTORY

Make a Timeline: Brainstorm to list other people or events in history associated with some kind of fruit. Create a timeline to record these events, plus those from the Bible (example: Abigail brings fruit on food-laden donkeys to David and his troops).

Research and Compare: Crop farming through history and today; soils and soil conservation; plant structure and processes; plant propagation; land preparation; planting; cultivation; irrigation; weed identification and control measures; insect and disease control; harvesting; storage; marketing; and shipping.

GEOGRAPHY

Label a World Map: On a world map, locate the areas where these fruits grow: grapes, dates, coconuts, bananas, persimmons, and pineapple.

Label a National Map: Map the United States (or your country) and color in the areas where major fruit production takes place. Label the color code in the legend on the map. Examples: melons, berries, cherries, plums, pears, apples, peaches, or citrus varieties.

Research: Find out which fruits are only grown in the New World, and which were brought here by explorers or fruit marketers.

Research Biomes: Research the climate and soil restrictions for growing a crop of dates. Study soil composition in your area (contact a soil conservation office, or take in a soil sample, etc.) to learn which fruits may best be grown in your community or on your property.

Take a Field Trip: Visit a commercial fruit-growing operation nearby and ask about fertilization, disease control and weather protection.

Investigate Trade: Discover what fruits your country imports and exports.

Investigate: Research the history of dates and grapes.

Draw: Pictures of pomegranates appeared on Solomon's temple pillars. Research to find their descriptions and illustrate one of the pillars.

Read a Legend: Read the account of William Tell, who was remembered for shooting an apple off his son's head. Get the facts about the cherry tree George Washington supposedly cut down.

Research: Research the discovery of using fresh fruits to prevent scurvy and other diseases on long voyages.

LANGUAGE ARTS

Discuss: Talk about the difference between a fiction, nonfiction, biography, autobiography, etc.

Read A Nonfiction Book or Story: Bible Stories: The sower (Matt. 13. 2); the vineyard in Matthew 20; the wicked vine-growers in Matthew 21:33-41; and the parable of the mustard seed in Luke 13:19.

Write a Story: Write a story for young children based on the fruit of the spirit in Esther's life. Younger children can dictate their stories or draw illustrations and explain it.

Write a Decree: Pretend you are King Ahasuerus and write out the decree for celebrating Purim, which will be published far and wide throughout your kingdom. (You have a camel express to deliver it—forerunner of the Pony Express in America.) Using your best penmanship, incorporate adjectives and adverbs abundantly in your royal proclamation. Younger children may dictate.

Read Poetry: Read the poem "When the Frost Is on the Pumpkin" by James Whitcomb Riley, or "In the Garden of the Lord," a poem by Helen Keller.

Draw: Create menus for Esther's banquets. Use middle eastern dishes, fresh or dried fruits, etc. Use a calligraphy pen and your design ability.

Record Vocabulary: Record all the new words you have heard during this unit. Discuss the meanings or look them up and write the definitions.

Resources for the Fruit Unit Study

	TITLE	AUTHOR	DESCRIPTION	PUB
*	*Alabaster Doves*	Linda Holland	Eight quiet heroines who lived godly lives. Self controlled, caring missionaries, martyrs, wives and mothers who gave love, joy, peace and kindness in the name of Jesus. 166 p.	Moody Press, 1995
*	*A Gardner Looks at the Fruits of the Spirit*	Phillip Keller	A practical look at the how and why of fruit production in our lives. God's people are likened to a carefully cultivated garden, tendered, and tilled with loving care. Watered and hedged with undivided devotion. 186 p.	Word Publishing, c1986
*	*Fruit of the Spirit*	Ron Hembree	Illustrations of spiritual fruit from literature, history and the lives of fellow Christians and the impact the fruit has on the world. Read aloud or teens/adult.	Baker Book House, 1995
*	*Gaining Favor with God and Man*	William Theyer	Complete short stories about great men and their character. Each page dripping with wisdom explains the importance of dozens of character traits. Over 100 years old. Read aloud or teens/adult. 455 p. Some photos.	Reprint from Mantle Ministries.
*	*God Made them Great*	John Tallach	Inspiring stories of five great men of faith (missionaries) and the spiritual fruit in their lives. Jr high/adult.	Banner of Truth, 1992
*	*Moral Lessons of Yesteryear*	A. L. Byres	Revisited Christian centered era looks at obedience, helpfulness, respect, honesty, gratefulness, responsibility, and many more through stories and poems. Great read aloud.	Mantle Ministries, 1995
*	*Wisdom from the Millers*	Mildred Martian	Children 4 to 12 love these short stories based the wisdom in Proverbs shown through a loving family and their true-life experiences on the farm. Delightful! 159 p.	Green Pasture, 1993
J	*Alexander: the Grape Fruit and Vegetable Jokes*	Charles Keller	A collection of humorous riddles incorporating fruits and vegetables, such as, "What's a raisin? A worried grape." 44p. Ill.	Prentice-Hall, c1982.
J	*The Apple Pie Tree*	Zoe Hall	Describes an apple tree as it grows leaves, flowers and fruit, while in its branches robins make a nest, lay eggs, and raise a family. Includes a recipe for apple pie. 32 p. Ill.	Scholastic, 1996.
J	*Apple Trees*	Sylvia A. Johnson	Discusses the growth and cultivation of apple trees and the development, harvesting, and storage. Excellent photography including microscopic. Glossary. Elem. to adult. 48 p. Ill.	Lerner Pub Co., 1983.
J	*Apple Orchard*	Irmengarde Eberle	Story of an apple orchard in New York. Follows seasonal activities year-round. Lower elementary.	Walck, Inc.
J	*Eat The Fruit, Plant the Seed*	Millicent E. Selsam	Gives directions for growing plants from the seeds found inside avocados, papayas, citrus fruits, mangos, pomegranates, and kiwis.	New York: Morrow, 1980.
J	*From Flower to Fruit*	A. Dowden	Text and drawings explain how flowers mature into seed-bearing fruit. 56 p. Ill.	Fields, 1994.
J	*The Life and Times of The Apple*	Charles Micucci	Presents a variety of facts about apples, including how they grow, crossbreeding and grafting techniques, harvesting practices, and the uses, varieties, and history of this popular fruit. 32 p.	Orchard Books, c1992.
J	*Plants Give Us Many Kinds of Food*	Jane Belk Moncure	Introduces some of the seeds, leaves, roots, and fruit of plants that can be used as food by man and animals. Ill.	Child's World; c1975.
J	*Science Experiments You Can Eat.*	Vicki Cobb	Experiments with food demonstrate various scientific principles and produce an eatable result. Includes fruit drinks, grape jelly, muffins, chop suey, yogurt, and junket. 127 p. Ill.	Lippincott, 1972
J	*Treasured Tales: Great Stories Of Courage and Faith*	Compiled by Laura E. Cathon	Collection of stories and poems of brave tales, strong decisions, and brave actions. Stories of noble deeds and great accomplishments. Rich with wisdom and human understanding. Apple Dumpling and others fit this unit study. 256 p. Ill.	Abbington Press, NY 1960

* Possibly in the library, available through Family Christian Academy. Library Codes: A - Adult Section; J - Juvenile Section; E - Easy Reading Section; P- Periodical.

Appendixes

- CONTROVERSIES OR WHY ALL THE FUSS?

- FESTIVAL DATES

- NEW MOON

- GOD'S AND JESUS' NAMES

- SYMBOLISM IN NUMBERS

- HEBREW ROOTS RESOURCES

- HOME SCHOOL RESOURCES

Heart of Wisdom Publishing

Appendix A: Controversies or Why All The Fuss?

If you decide to celebrate God's holy days, you may be surprised to discover some of the opposition our family experienced (explained in the Preface). Many people are simply concerned that celebrating the holidays may be an "earning salvation" type of works belief. They are afraid of the negative term *law* and being labeled "legalistic." They do not fully understand that the Biblical Holidays are a beautiful picture of God's grace, His unmerited favor.

The following are some of the questions you may encounter:

Q: *Isn't the keeping of the holidays an attempt to earn one's way with works?*

A: *No, the holidays are a picture of God's grace!* The grace of God shines forth clearly in the holidays and their stories of blessing, preservation, promise, and fulfillment. God delivered an undeserving people before they entered into His covenant. Before God gave Israel the law, He gave them Himself as their redeemer when he liberated them from Egypt. He didn't send the Ten Commandments and tell them to obey them before He saved them. He first saved them, then sent His law in response. His instruction (law) is His guidance for our own good, for a good life here on earth.

The Passover story, and other holidays, show God's grace in action. Obedience is a response to grace. Grace cannot be bought; it is given. Obedience is the fruit of grace. God wants us to tell the story of His grace to our children.

And when thy son asketh thee in time to come, saying, What mean the testimonies, and the statutes, and the judgments, which the LORD our God hath commanded you? Then thou shalt say unto thy son, We were Pharaoh's bondmen in Egypt; and the LORD brought us out of Egypt with a mighty hand: And the LORD shewed signs and wonders, great and sore, upon Egypt, upon Pharaoh, and upon all his household, before our eyes: And he brought us out from thence, that he might bring us in, to give us the land which he sware unto our fathers. (Deut. 6:20-23).

By studying the Old Covenant shadows through the Passover or the other holidays, we can appreciate the New Covenant (John 1:17).

Q: *We have grace. Why keep any law?*

A: Of course we are saved by grace, through faith in Christ. Is grace a license to go the world's way and not follow God's paths? Many of today's churches are adopting the world's standards in the name of grace. An unbalanced view of grace results in emptiness, a hollow relationship with God.

*Being justified freely by his grace through the redemption that is in Christ Jesus: Whom God hath set forth to be a propitiation through faith in his blood, to declare his righteousness for the remission of sins that are past, through the forbearance of God; To declare, I say, at this time his righteousness: that he might be just, and the justifier of him which believeth in Jesus. Where is boasting then? It is excluded. By what law? of works? Nay: but **by the law of faith**. Therefore we conclude that a man **is justified by faith without the deeds of the law**. Is he the God of the Jews only? is he not also of the Gentiles? Yes, of the Gentiles also: Seeing it is one God, which shall justify the circumcision by faith, and uncircumcision through faith. **Do we then make void the law through faith? God forbid: yea, we establish the law.** (Rom.3:24-31).*

A desire to worship and gain more understanding of God should not be thwarted by a fear of being legalistic. Our standard should be holiness, living our lives dedicated to God, not living our lives dedicated to the traditions of men. Praise God, believers are coming to realize that we need to "come out from the world" and be separate. Jesus taught his disciples, *"No one can serve two masters; for either he will hate the one and love the other, or he will hold to one and despise the other. You cannot serve God and mammon."* (Matt. 6:24). True godliness, and purity can only come from a biblical relationship with God. That relationship is shown to us through our father Abraham's love and devotion.

Q: *Aren't the holidays only for the Jews?*

A: The biblical holidays were commanded to the Hebrew people in Leviticus. Notice these are not "Jewish" holidays. God said they were *His* feasts.

"And the Lord spake unto Moses, saying, Speak unto the children of Israel, and say to them, Concerning the feasts of the Lord, which ye shall proclaim to be holy convocations, even these are my feasts. Six days shall work be done: but the seventh day is the sabbath of rest, an holy convocation; ye shall do no work therein: it is the sabbath of the Lord in all your dwellings. These are the feasts of the Lord, even holy convocations, which ye shall proclaim in their seasons. In the fourteenth day of the first month at even is the Lord's passover. And on the fifteenth day of the same month is the feast of unleavened bread unto the Lord: seven days ye must eat unleavened bread. In the first day ye shall have an holy convocation: ye shall do no servile work therein. But ye shall offer an offering made by fire unto the Lord seven days: in the seventh day is an holy convocation: ye shall do no servile work therein."

Paul explains in Galatians that, because of God's grace, Gentiles who came to salvation were *not* required to keep the feasts. The Gentiles were not raised keeping the Jewish commands and were not expected to keep the 613 laws that identify the Jews as God's chosen people. They were expected to give up idolatry and obey the seven Noahide laws (see Appendix F: Law for the Noahide laws.). They were glad to be a part of God's family. The Gentile had the freedom to celebrate the holidays and did sometimes at the risk of persecution. In the year 339, it was considered a criminal offense to convert to Judaism. Several decades later, the Synod of Laodicea ruled against Christians feasting with Jews, classifying those that did as heretics.

God's mercy and grace through Christ's death and resurrection saves the Jews and Gentiles—then and now.

Q: *Are Believing Gentiles Part of Israel?*

A: *(see below.)*

1. It is explained in Romans 2 that a born-again Gentile, one who has come to faith in the God of Israel through trusting Jesus the Messiah, is a Jew inwardly because his heart is circumcised even though his flesh is not; he is a true God-worshiper, whose praise comes from God—in many senses a real Jew. Some Gentiles claim Jews are no longer the chosen people—so they don't need to celebrate.

2. Romans 2 has been used to prove Gentiles *are commanded* to keep the holidays—because believers are Jews and God commanded the holidays to be kept forever.

3. Romans 2 has also been used to say Gentiles *are not commanded* to keep the holidays because Gentiles do not need to be circumcised.

It has also been argued that just as certain Scripture (Exodus 13:2; Deuteronomy 21:15-17) is given only to the "first-born," the holidays are only for the Jews. Others believe because we are grafted into God's family (Romans 11), we are accountable for all of God's commands. Does God have different rules for His children? Yes, He has different commands for priests, for women, and for men. To whom much is given, much is required.

Q: *Isn't it True there is No Longer Jew nor Greek in Christ?*

A: Galatians 3:28 says, *"There is neither Jew nor Greek, there is neither bond nor free, there is neither male nor female: for ye are all one in Christ Jesus."* This secluded verse has been twisted to say a Jew must give up his culture. There are differences between male and female, a slave and a free man. According to this verse, all should be treated as equals, thus fulfilling Jesus' command to love others as yourself. Jewish and Gentile believers (male or female, slave or free) are all equals before God. Continue reading the rest of Galatians 3. *And if ye be Christ's, then are ye Abraham's seed, and heirs according to the promise.*

Again, look at Romans 3:25: *"Is he the God of the Jews only? is he not also of the Gentiles? Yes, of the Gentiles also..."*

The law (guidance) was given for the people's sake, not for God's sake. It was a gift, a treasure, as explained all through Psalm 119. Jesus never condemned the law. He only rejected what the legalistic men had turned it into. For example, the Sabbath was made for all to benefit. The law specifically said the slaves, domestic workers, and even animals were not to work. It was to be a rest for all, for the *benefit* of the entire community. Jesus was criticized for healing on the Sabbath. Jesus said, "Man was not made for the Sabbath but Sabbath for the man." He was recapturing the original point of the law—the spirit of the law—for man's benefit. Jesus summed up all of the laws in two commands, loving God with all we have and loving others as ourselves. On these two commands hang all the law and the prophets. (Matt. 22:34-40).

Q: *Didn't Christians Replace the Jews as the Chosen People?*

A: The Jews are the chosen people of God. They were chosen because they accepted God when other peoples rejected Him. Some religions believe the Jews lost that promise. Other groups claim that *they* are now God's chosen people.

Replacement theology is a *false belief* that another group of people have replaced the Jews because the Jews gave up the opportunity to believe in Christ. We must remember the *entire* first church was completely Jewish. Hundreds of thousands of Jews accepted Christ. Peter and Paul took the gospel to the Gentiles and, praise God, many Gentiles accepted Christ. But remember also, *many Gentiles rejected Christ!* If someone feels the Jews gave up the right to be God's people—that person believes that works—not even personal works, but works of a race—save us! We all fall short; all our righteousnesses are as filthy rags. The Jews are God's chosen people because of God's covenant to

A Family Guide to the Biblical Holidays©

Abraham. God never broke His promises to the Jews. Revelation is full of references to the Israelites during the end time.

Q: *Isn't keeping the holidays Judaizing?*

A: Another huge misunderstanding in the traditional Christian churches is when a Gentile accuses a Jew of Judaizing. The Bible is clear Gentiles are not to Judaize. If a Gentile believes he earns God's approval by conforming to Jewish practice, he violates the message of Galatians and is involved in true legalism. There are cults that cultivate such legalistic Judaizing of Gentiles.

David H. Stern explains Judaizing and other misunderstandings between Jews and Gentiles, in *The Jewish New Testament Commentary*:

The Greek word "*Ioudaizein*" can be rendered, "to Judaize, to Judaize oneself, to become a Jew, to convert to Judaism, to live like a Jew, to live as a Jew;" there is enough variety here to cover all three of these heresies. But all meanings of "*Ioudaizein*" assume that those who get "Judaized" are Gentiles, never Jews. In spite of this fact, one of the most tenacious and pernicious phenomena in Christendom is the application of the term "Judaizers" to Messianic Jews attempting to establish for Jewish believers a Jewish way of following the Jewish Messiah.

Messianic Jews, with very rare exceptions, are guilty of none of these heresies. They do not press Gentile Christians to get circumcised or convert to Judaism but usually discourage it on the basis of 1C 7:18. They do not force Gentile Christians to adopt Jewish practices, although Gentiles who voluntarily choose to are welcomed, provided their motives are sound, because they are "free in Christ" to make that choice. Finally, Messianic Jews do not claim that observance of customs developed in non-Messianic Judaism is either necessary for salvation or a sign of greater spirituality. Instead, Messianic Jews try to develop a Messianic mode of celebrating the Jewish festivals, a Messianic form of Jewish worship, and a Messianic Jewish lifestyle wherein Jewish believers can express both their Jewishness and their Messianic faith.

Yet for obeying the Great Commission (Mt 28:18–20), so often neglected by the Church in relation to the Jewish people, Messianic Jews are stigmatized among Gentile Christians as "Judaizers." Yet how can a Jew, who is already Jewish, be "Judaized"? This is a contradiction in terms, an absurdity. Nowhere in the New Testament are Jewish believers criticized for living like the Jews they are. On the contrary, when Sha'ul [Paul] was accused of teaching Jews not to observe circumcision and the Mosaic Law, he demonstrated that the accusation was false (Acts 21:20–27). Was Sha'ul [Paul] therefore a "Judaizer" for encouraging Jewish believers to continue circumcising their children and observing the *Torah*?

One of the most frequent and bothersome accusations made by uninformed Christians against Messianic Judaism is that Messianic Jews "are trying to build up again between Jews and Gentiles 'the middle wall of partition' which the Messiah has broken down." Without exception the charge is made by those who do not understand what Sha'ul is saying or what Messianic Judaism is really trying to accomplish.

Sha'ul's point is that Gentiles are no longer separated but can now join the Jewish people and be one with them as God's people through faith in the Jewish Messiah, Yeshua. The partition is down, the Gentiles can join us! The critics understand it the other way round: the partition is down, so that once Jews believe in their own Messiah they no longer have the right to maintain their Jewish identity but must conform to Gentile patterns. Amazing! And certainly not what Sha'ul himself did (Acts 13:9).

The object of Messianic Judaism is not to destroy fellowship between Jews and Gentiles in the Messiah's Body but to preserve it; a review of the notes at 1C 7:18b; Ga 1:13, 2:14b, 3:28 will suffice to show that. At the same time Messianic Judaism seeks to provide a framework in which Jewish believers can express their faith in Yeshua through and along with their Jewishness. The Scriptural warrant for this is not only Sha'ul's own practice but also his principle of presenting the Gospel in a way that minimizes the obstacles to its acceptance by its hearers (Ga 1:17, 1C 9:19–22). Messianic Judaism ought to have been preserved continuously since the time of Yeshua, for there have always been believing Jews; there should have been no need to create it afresh. The movement is assertive today only because anti-Jewish pressure within the Church did away with and continued to oppose Jewish expressions of New Testament truth. That the New Covenant itself was made with Israel (v. 12, Jeremiah 31:30–33) adds irony to insult.

On the other hand, frequently those Gentiles who raise the bugaboo of the "middle wall of partition" are themselves the ones who are building it! For they would have Jews enter the Body of the Jewish Messiah only if they will conform to Gentile customs and ways and give up their Jewishness. Members of no other culture are put upon in this way, only Jews. Their idea of Sha'ul's remark that the Messiah **has made us both one** is that the "one" is Gentile!

HOW TO HANDLE QUESTIONS OR CRITICISM

Meet any opposition as a chance to lovingly share God's Word. Don't debate opinions— look to Scripture. As with any other problem in our lives, the answer is found in Scripture. Be it Jew or Gentile, our job as believers is to:

1. **Explain you are not celebrating the feast to earn favor. Share this book with anyone who accuses you of being legalistic.**

2. **Pray, ask for wisdom, knowledge, and understanding. Ask God to direct your paths.**

   In all thy ways acknowledge him, and he shall direct thy paths. (Prov. 3:6).

   All the paths of the Lord are mercy and truth unto such as keep his covenant and his testimonies. (Ps. 25:10).

   Because my people hath forgotten me, they have burned incense to vanity, and they have caused them to stumble in their ways from the ancient paths, to walk in paths, in a way not cast up; (Jer. 18:15).

   Concerning the words of men, by the word of thy lips I have kept me from the paths of the destroyer. Hold up my goings in thy paths, that my footsteps slip not (Ps.17:4-5).

3. **Remember, we are not struggling against human beings but against the unseen agents**.

   For we wrestle not against flesh and blood, but against principalities, against powers, against the rulers of the darkness of this world, against spiritual wickedness in high places. (Eph. 6:12).

4. **Strive for unity**.

   Behold, how good and how pleasant it is for brethren to dwell together in unity! It is like the precious ointment upon the head, that ran down upon the beard, even Aaron's beard: that went down to the skirts of his garments; As the dew of Hermon, and as the dew that descended upon the mountains of Zion: for there the Lord commanded the blessing, even life for evermore. (Ps. 133:1-3).

5. **Give glory to God** (I Cor. 10:31, I Peter 4:11).

   And be not drunk with wine, wherein is excess; but be filled with the Spirit; Speaking to yourselves in psalms and hymns and spiritual songs, singing and making melody in your heart to the LORD; Giving thanks always for all things unto God and the Father in the name of our LORD Jesus Christ; Submitting yourselves one to another in the fear of God (Eph. 5:18-21).

6. **Encourage and uplift one another in the Lord**.

   And let us consider one another to provoke unto love and to good works: Not forsaking the assembling of ourselves together, as the manner of some is; but exhorting one another: and so much the more, as ye see the day approaching. (Hebr. 10:24-25).

Summary

No matter what we do or who we are, if we are obedient, if we give sacrificially, if we give our all, it means *absolutely nothing*—if we lack love for the Father or for one another.

Though I speak with the tongues of men and of angels, and have not charity [love], I am become as sounding brass, or a tinkling cymbal (1 Cor. 13).

Appendix B: The Festival Dates

2009-2010
Trumpets (Rosh Hashanah) 9/19/2009
Day Of Atonement (Yom Kippur).............. 9/28/2009
Tabernacles (Sukkoth) 10/3/2009
Hanukkah 12/12/2009
Purim.. 2/28/2010
Passover (Pesach) 3/30/2010
Pentecost (Shavuot)............................... 5/19/2010

2010-2011
Trumpets (Rosh Hashanah) 9/9/2010
Day Of Atonement (Yom Kippur).............. 9/18/2010
Tabernacles (Sukkoth 9/23/2010
Hanukkah 12/21/2011
Purim.. 3/20/2011
Passover (Pesach) 4/19/2011
Pentecost (Shavuot)............................... 6/8/2011

2011-2012
Trumpets (Rosh Hashanah) 9/29/2011
Day Of Atonement (Yom Kippur).............. 10/8/2011
Tabernacles (Sukkoth) 10/13/2011
Hanukkah 12/21/2011
Purim.. 3/8/2012
Passover (Pesach) 4/7/2012
Pentecost (Shavuot)............................... 5/27/2012

2012-2013
Trumpets (Rosh Hashanah) 9/17/2012
Day Of Atonement (Yom Kippur).............. 9/26/2012
Tabernacles (Sukkoth) 10/1/2012
Hanukkah 12/9/2012
Purim.. 2/24/2013
Passover (Pesach) 3/26/2013
Pentecost (Shavuot)............................... 5/15/2013

For more on dates go to BiblicalHolidays.com

Special Notes

WORK ON FEAST DAYS

Not all feast days prohibit work (the same activities that are forbidden on the Sabbath) but some do, including cooking, baking, transferring or carrying firewood. Work is not permitted on the Feast of Trumpets, the Day of Atonement, the first and second days of the Feast of Tabernacles, Pentecost, and the first, second, seventh and eighth days of Passover. When a holiday occurs on a Sabbath, the full Sabbath restrictions are observed.

EXTRA DAY OF FEASTING

The Jews celebrate some feast days one more day than the Bible requires. There is a reason for this additional day. The Jewish calendar is lunar, with each month beginning on the new moon, determined by observation. The Sanhedrin declared the beginning of a new month, and notice was sent out by messengers to tell people when the month began. People in distant communities could not always be notified of the new moon, so they did not know the correct day to celebrate. They knew that the old month would be either twenty-nine or thirty days, so if they didn't get notice of the new moon, they celebrated holidays on both possible days.

The Feast of Trumpets is celebrated as two days because it occurs on the first day of a month. Messengers were not dispatched on the holiday, so even people in Israel did not know whether a new moon had been observed, and everybody celebrated two days. The Day of Atonement is celebrated only one day because of the holiday's fasting restrictions. In Israel, and among Reform Jews, festivals last one day only, except for the Feast of Trumpets.

POSTPONING FEAST DAYS

To prevent the Day of Atonement falling on Fridays or Sundays (which would create problems of Sabbath observance), the rabbis ordained that the first day of the New Year could not fall on a Sunday, Wednesday, or Friday. Sometimes, the Sanhedrin would deliberately postpone the announcement of the New Year on Tishri 1 for a day, and sometimes for two days (Easton's Bible Dictionary).

In the fourth century, the Rabbis used a correctly computed equinox to fix the first month of spring, Aviv (Nisan on their calendar); however, they did not know that the equinox moved through the heavens making one cycle between 25,000 and 30,000 years. As a result the equinox date upon which the Rabbinical calendar is based is now out of phase with the actual equinox. This causes the month of Aviv to fall a month late, in many cases throwing the high holy days off for the entire year. Rabbis who study the calendar are well aware of these problems and freely admit that the calendar does not follow the methods laid down in the Talmud, but they are reluctant to change back to the old system (Holeman Bible Dictionary).

Appendix C: The New Moon

The first day of each new month was considered holy. Hence the association in the Old Testament of the monthly new moon with the weekly Sabbath (e.g. Isa. 1:13). This fresh beginning was marked by special sacrifices (Num. 28:11-15) over which the trumpets were blown (Num. 10:10; Ps. 81:3). Amos depicts the merchants of his day anxiously awaiting the end of the new moon and of the Sabbath so that they could resume their fraudulent trading. It seems therefore to have been regarded, like the Sabbath, as a day on which normal work was not done. The reference may be, however, to the new moon of the seventh month, regarding which the law stated specifically that no servile work was to be done on it (Lev. 23:24-25; Num. 29:1-6). 2 Kings 4:23 suggests that both new moon and Sabbath were regarded as providing opportunity for consulting the prophets, and Ezekiel (46:1, 3) marks out the new moon as a special day for worship (*The New Bible Dictionary*, 1962).

The moon is mentioned as marking by its behavior the coming of the Messiah (Mark 13:24; Luke 21:25). Psalm 121:6 suggests that it was recognized as capable of affecting the mind, and in the New Testament Greek words meaning, literally, moonstruck are used in Matthew 4:24 and 17:15 (ibid).

In the fourth century, Hillel II established a fixed calendar based on mathematical and astronomical calculations. This calendar, still in use, standardized the length of months and the addition of months over the course of a nineteen-year cycle, so that the lunar calendar realigns with the solar years. Adar II is added in the third, sixth, eighth, eleventh, fourteenth, seventeenth and nineteenth years of the cycle. The new year that began Monday, September 25, 1995 (Jewish calendar year 5756) was the eighteenth year of the cycle. Jewish year 5758 (beginning October 2, 1997) will be the first year of the next cycle.

IMPORTANCE

Before the introduction of a fixed permanent calendar, the identification and designation of Rosh Hodesh — the day of the New Moon — was of crucial importance for the timely observance of festivals during that month. In Temple times, to avoid the possibility of festivals being observed in different communities on different days, the Sanhedrin in Jerusalem insisted on retaining its centralized and single authority for fixing the date of the new moon as well as for the intercalation of the thirteenth month of the leap year when they thought it was necessary. Originally, the beginning of the new month was decided after eyewitness evidence to the appearance of the new moon had been accepted by the Sanhedrin. Distant communities were informed of the date by means of a chain of fire signal from one hilltop to another (*Encyclopedia Judaica 1997*).

In non-technical language the new moon is the first night in which the first thin crescent of light can be seen of the moon. The Hebrew scholars call this the *Hodesh*, which means literally means "fresh," or "renewed," — because the moon is really the old moon with a renewed crescent. The *Hodesh* can be seen just after sunset for a few minutes at the beginning of the new lunar cycle (Gregg 1994).

TODAY'S NEW MOON

In modern astronomy the new moon is when the moon earth and sun line up, and the moon cannot be seen. More precisely the astronomer's new moon is when the arc of distance between the sun and moon viewed from the center of the earth reaches a minimum on each orbit of the moon around the earth; it is also called the "conjunction." The astronomer's new moon is called *molad* (birth) by the Hebrew scholars. The *molad* or astronomer's new moon can never be seen (Achtemier 1985).

According to early rabbinic sources, the new moon was originally fixed by proclamation of witnesses regarding the reappearance of the moon's crescent. If the crescent had not been sighted on the thirtieth day of the month, the new moon was proclaimed for the thirty-first day. Beacons were kindled on the Mount of Olives to mark the arrival of the new moon crescent. This system was extended throughout the Diaspora until the Samaritans began to light misleading beacons to confuse the calendar and the observance of the new moon. The high court countered this attack on rabbinic authority by sending messengers to remote communities with the announcement of the new moon (Achtemier 1985).

Note: There are two versions of computer software available to calculate the new moon. The evaluation version which operates only for the years 5750 (1990) to 5755 (1995) and the full version which operates for the years 5344 (1583) to 7000 (3239). If you have the evaluation version and want the full version or if you have obtained a free copy of the full version you should send the registration fee of $18 to the address below.

Pennant Enterprises, 25 Shadow Lane, Great Neck, NY 11021, (516) 466-5509. Send only U.S. currency or checks drawn on U.S. banks. You may send questions to Lester Penner at the same address or to CompuServe 75236,1572 or Prodigy TMDB08A.

Appendix D: God's and Jesus' Names

YHWH is often referred to as the Ineffable Name, the Unutterable Name or the Distinctive Name. Linguistically, it is associated with the Hebrew root *Heh-Yod-Heh*, "to be," which shows that God is eternal. In the Bible, this Name is used when discussing God's relation with human beings, and when emphasizing His qualities of lovingkindness and grace.

Judaism does not prohibit writing the name of God; it prohibits only erasing or defacing a name of God. So, observant Jews avoid writing any name of God casually because of the risk that the written name might later be defaced, obliterated or destroyed accidentally by one who does not know better.

WHERE DID JEHOVAH COME FROM?

In Exodus 3:14-15, it says, "And God said unto Moses, I AM THAT I AM: and he said, Thus shalt thou say unto the children of Israel, I AM hath sent me to you. And God said moreover unto Moses, Thus shalt thou say unto the children of Israel, The LORD God of your fathers, the God of Abraham, the God of Isaac, and the God of Jacob, hath sent me unto you: this is my name for ever, and this is my memorial unto all generations." The same Hebrew word translated "I AM WHO I AM", "I AM" and "LORD" is YHWH.

The Ancient Hebrew used no vowels. The actual pronunciation of YHWH was quickly lost. When the Masoretes in late medieval times decided to make the Hebrew more readable by adding vowels, they changed YHWH to JHVH (there was no J in the Hebrew). They used the vowels they assigned to Adonai. Thus they created "Jehovah" to be used in place of YHWH.

PRONUNCIATION OF YHWH

Since Hebrew was written without vowels in ancient times, the four consonants YHWH contain no clue to their original pronunciation. In traditional Judaism, the name is not pronounced, but Hebrew-*Adonai* ("Lord") or something similar is substituted. YHWH was probably pronounced *ahiyhwah* during the Temple period. We do not know what vowels were used, or even whether the *Vav* in the Name was a vowel or a consonant. Some Bible scholars use the names *Yahweh* and *Yahveh* but other scholars do not find these pronunciations correct.

TODAY'S BIBLES TRANSLATE YHWH AS LORD

Each time you see the name LORD or GOD in all caps in the King James Version of the Bible, it is a translation of YHWH. (If you see "Lord GOD" it is a translation of "Adonai YHWH"). In A few English versions of the Bible the tetragrammaton is represented by Jehovah.

OTHER NAMES

Without doubt, the tetragrammaton, YHWH, is the most significant name in the Old Testament. As one writer observed, "no single word in Hebrew has ever evoked such a torrent of discussion as . . . YHWH, the personal name of the Hebrew God" (Gianotti, 1996). Let's look at other names used to designate God in the Old Testament:

English	Hebrew	Example in Scripture
God	Elohim	Genesis 1:1
God	El	Genesis 14:18
God	Eloah	Nehemiah 9:17
God	Elah (Aramaic form)	Daniel 2:18
GOD	YHWH (Yahweh)	Genesis 15:2
LORD	YHWH or YH	Genesis 2:4
JEHOVAH	YHWH	Exodus 6:3
JAH	YH (Yah)	Psalm 68:4
Lord	Adon	Joshua 3:11
Lord	Adonai	Genesis 15:2

English	Hebrew	Example in Scripture
I AM THAT I AM	Eheyeh asher Eheyeh	Exodus 3:14
I AM	Eheyeh	Exodus 3:14
Most High God	El-Elyon	Genesis 14:18
The Lord Sanctifies	Yahweh-Mekaddesh	Ex. 31:13
The Lord is my Banner	Yahweh-Nissi	Ex. 17:15
The Lord is Peace	Yahweh-Shalom	Judg. 6:24
The Lord of Hosts	Yahweh-Sabaoth	1 Sam. 1:3; Jer. 11:20
The Lord is my Shepherd	Yahweh-Rohi	Ps. 23:1
The Lord is Our Righteousness	Yahweh-Tsidkenu	Jer. 23:5-6; 33:16
The Lord is There	Yahweh-Shammah	Ezek. 48:3
Almighty God	El-Shaddai	Genesis 17:1
Everlasting God	El-Olam	Genesis 21:33
The Most High God	El-Elyon	Num. 24:16; 2 Sam. 22:14
God of Eternity	El-Olam	Gen. 21:33; Isa. 26:4; Ps. 90:2
God of the Covenant	El-Berith	Judg. 9:46
God of Vision	El-Rohi	Gen. 16:13

Jesus employed a form of El when he cried from the cross, "Eloi, Eloi" ("my God, my God,") quoting Psalm 22.

Many of the names for God are symbolic, illustrative, or figurative.

Shield	Gen. 15:1; Ps. 84:11
Ancient of Days	Dan. 7:9,13,22
Rock	Deut. 32:18; Ps. 19:14; Isa. 26:4
Refuge	Ps. 9:9; Jer. 17:17
Fortress	Ps. 18:2; Nah. 1:7
Refiner	Mal. 3:3

Descriptions of God come from everyday life.

King	Zech. 14:9
Judge	Gen. 15:14
Shepherd	Ezek. 34; Psalms 23

Descriptions refering to God as Father:

God the Father	Ps. 103:13
Father of Israel	Jer. 31:9
Our Father (how we are to pray)	Matt. 6:9
Father of Mercies	2 Cor. 1:3
Father of Lights	James 1:17
Father of Glory	Eph. 1:17

GOD'S NAME WAS ON THE SIGN ON THE CRUCIFIXION TREE!

Studies have shown the Tetragrammaton probably appeared over Jesus when He hung on the cross. During Bible times, messages were commonly written with the first letter of each word. An example in English: UPS, stands for United Parcel Service. The phrase "Jesus of Nazareth and King of the Jews" was written in three languages on a sign above Jesus as He hung on the cross (John 19:19) . "Jesus of Nazareth and King of the Jews" initials in Hebrew was YHWH. That is why the priest asked Pilate to change the writing. *Then said the chief priests of the Jews to Pilate, Write not, The King of the Jews; but that he said, I am King of the Jews. Pilate answered, What I have written I have written* (John 19: 22). For details see *God's Master Plan* or *7 Feasts of Israel Video* in the resources section.

GOD'S NAME IS HIDDEN IN THE TORAH!

The Jews were to preserve the Hebrew text. Scribes went through strenuous training to insure the characters were written perfectly and without error in even one jot or tittle (two small Hebrew characters). While God's name never appears directly in Esther, it does appear in acrostic form in Esther 5:4. It is the first letter of each of four successive words - yod hay vav hay, YHWH. This is the only book of the Bible that does not directly contain God's name; however by using the code method the name YHWH is found five times.

There are hidden codes in the Torah. These codes were found by a process called "Reading with Equal Intervals." First, you eliminate the spaces between words of Torah. Then the computer can locate various words hidden in the text at regular number intervals. For example: The first time you see the letter *T* ("*T*" or "*Tav*") in the book of Genesis and every fiftieth letter spells: H R 1 T (Torah). The same thing happens when you use the book of Exodus. With Leviticus, go to the first *Y* ("*Y*" or "*Yod*"). Count to the subsequent eighth letter, and so on. The Hebrew (and correct) name of God emerges: H W H Y ("YHWH"), which most Jewish scholars believe should be pronounced as "Yahweh"). In Numbers and Deuteronomy, "Torah" is spelled out again, but backwards. It is like having the first two books and last two books pointing to YHWH in the middle book! Daniel Michelson, Professor of Mathematics at Hebrew University, computed the odds of such a coincidence in just Genesis and Exodus at about one in three million (Chaimberlin 1996).

Genesis	Exodus	Leviticus	Numbers	Deuteronomy
TORH	TORH	YHWH	HROT	HROT
—->	—->	YHWH	<——	<——

JESUS' NAME

Jesus' Hebrew name is transliterated *Yeshuwa*. The Hebrew word for *salvation* is *Yeshuwah*, or *Y'shua*. It was given to Him as His personal name, in obedience to the command of an angel to Joseph, the husband of His mother, Mary, shortly before He was born (Matt. 1:21). Y'shua is the name his mother, disciples, and everyone called Him while He walked on earth. The *Ya* portion of His name is from His Father, Yahweh. Jesus' name would have been said as Yaishwu'a, Yahshwu, or in Aramaic, Ehshu.

Jesus is the culmination of all the Old Testament names of God. It is the highest, most exalted name ever revealed to mankind. (Jesus fulfills all the eleven compound names of Jehovah.) The name of Jesus is the name of God that He promised to reveal when He said, "Therefore my people shall know my name" (Isaiah 52:6). It is the one name of Zechariah 14:9 that encompasses and includes all the other names of God within its meaning (Bernard 1996).

There is not now nor was there ever an equivalent letter *j* in the twenty-two letters of the Hebrew alphabet. Nor is there any Hebrew letter that carries even an approximate sound of the consonant letter *j*. Neither is there a letter *j* in the Greek alphabet. Even our English *j* is of recent origin, appearing in English only five hundred years ago, when it often replaced the letter *i*, usually at the beginning of a word.

We must know and have faith in the One represented by that name (Acts 19:13-17). The name of Jesus is unique because unlike any other name it represents the presence of the owner. It represents God's presence, power, and work. When we speak the name of Jesus in faith, Jesus Himself is actually present and begins to work. The power does not come from the way the name sounds, but it comes because *the utterance of the name in faith demonstrates obedience* to the Word of God and faith in the work of Jesus. When we call His name in faith, Jesus manifests His presence, performs the work, and meets the need (Collin 1996).

The name *Jesus* is the English translation of the Greek *Iesous* from the Hebrew *Y'shua*. It also happens to be the first name of many other Jews including Barabbas (Barabbas means "son of a father or master"), the captive robber whom the Jews begged Pilate to release instead of Christ (more of this in the Atonement chapter), but our Father in Heaven knows our hearts and He knows those who love His Son, though we may use a translation of His Hebrew name, rather than the Hebrew name itself.

YESHUA'S NAME IS HIDDEN IN THE TORAH!

A Torah code program shows Yeshua encoded in Torah at seven different locations. The Hebrew data uses the Michigan-Claremont transliteration scheme. At these locations once the name starts with the *Yod*, the next letter is found forty-two characters later, each of the seven locations: (1.) Genesis 28:6,7,8; (2.) Genesis 38:8,9,10,11; (3.) Exodus 20:3,4,5; (4.) Numbers 14:17,18,19; (5.) Numbers 27:16,17,18; (6.) Numbers 33:8,9,10; (7.) Deuteronomy 34:9,10,11. This is fairly new information now that we have computers that can locate various words hidden in the text at regular number intervals. It will be very interesting to see how Jewish non-believers react to this information.

The name YHWH points to God's relationship to Israel in both His saving acts and His retributive acts, manifesting His phenomenological effectiveness in Israel's history. What God says, He will do. His Name promises that. And He will act on behalf of His people. But YHWH does not ultimately limit the significance of His name to the children of Israel. As Eichrodt succinctly states, "it is in the person of Jesus that the function of the Name of Yahweh as a form of the divine self-manifestation finds its fulfillment." Truly Jesus is the par excellence manifestation of God's active effectiveness in the history of the world! (Gianotti, 1996).

For details about Y'shua's name in the Torah and other names found such as Hitler, Rabin, Sadat see *Yeshua: The Name of Jesus Revealed in the Old Testament* by Yacov Rambsel or *The Signature of God* by Grant R. Jeffrey

"YAHWEH AND Y'SHUA-ONLY" GROUPS

Very rarely there are small groups who will not even use the name Jesus, saying it is another name for Zeus[1], the principal god of the ancient Greeks. This theory comes from a lack of study and lack of understanding translations. This attitude usually starts out as a zeal for God, wanting to please Him, but usually turns into an attitude of arrogance to the point of dissociation of all believers who do not use "the sacred name." No one is absolutely sure of the pronunciation of YHWH. These groups say "Yahweh" but they may be pronouncing it wrong. The groups who insist on only using the names YHWH and Y'shua would never have known how to find out the name of God if they hadn't studied English reference books that use the names God and Jesus.

Beware of any group thinking they are the only ones that will be saved because they use "God's real name." *All* of our righteousness is as filthy rags. No one is better than another. We are ALL sinners that need salvation. One is saved by an active belief in the Father's Son, that His blood was shed, and that He died and arose. Our responsibility is to make Him Lord of our lives and follow His Word. Yes, God's name is YHWH and Jesus' name is Y'shua, but will YHWH condemn those who serve Him to hell, just because they pray to "Dear Lord," "God" or as Y'shua directed, "Our Father"? Our Father in Heaven knows our hearts and He knows those who love His Son.

The preface of this book explains how to tell if something is legalistic or pleasing to God. The fruit of legalism is easily recognized—arguments, jealousy, selfish ambition, and envy. The resulting strife and confusion of the "Yahweh only" groups are far from what Y'shua taught. Y'shua taught us to love one another. Love is the fruit of a believer. When a person thinks higher of himself than others, especially to the point of disassociating himself with other believers because of a translation of a name, it is cruel judgment and an attitude of superiority—not love.

USING ONLY HEBREW NAMES

The word *Jew* is the English translation of *Yehuwdiy*. A Jew is a `Ibri` or Hebrew, a descendant of *Yehudah* (*Judah* in English). If you only speak English and have only grown up hearing English names, it difficult to understand writings or teachings using the Hebrew names. It is difficult enough to get people to read the Bible. Can you imagine what it would be like if they had to read all the names in Hebrew? It doesn't mean we shouldn't study Hebrew–far from it. It is a precious thing to understand Scripture in its original language; however, if it is easier to use terms that people understand to lead them to the Savior or teach a truth, why not?

In the first chapter of this book, I explain the significance of Jewish roots. If I had used the term *Yehuwdiy's Sheoesh*, 99.9 percent would not understand what I was referring to. In the same way, using Yahweh and Y'shua could be a real stumbling block for some. We must be able to communicate to share God's Word. At the time of this writing two denominations have shown an interest in using this book in their Sunday School classes nationwide. If this book only used the Hebrew names, I seriously doubt they would have any interest.

CONCLUSION

YHWH is God's Hebrew name. Y'shua is Jesus' Hebrew name. God and Jesus are just two of the many, many titles English-speaking people use.

My name is Robin Scarlata Sampson. I also answer to Mommy, Mom, Ma, Aunt Robin, Honey, Sweetheart (my Grandmother's name for me), Sis, Mrs. Sampson, Mrs. Robin, and Sister Sampson. My son-in-law never has been too sure of what to call me, so I still answer to his hesitant, "Hey, look at this." I also answer, with all the love I have to offer, to the uplifted hands of my granddaughter, who is too young to say "Grandmother." She just started saying something that sounds close to "gamaa." I enthusiastically answer, because I am full of love for her no matter what she calls me. I loved her before she could ever say my name or even recognize me. I know that I know YHWH is full of love for me, unworthy sinner that I am. Usually I call Him Father, sometimes I call Him God, Lord, or Yahweh. He is happy that I read His Word and I call on Him.

YHWH is our Healer, Provider, Protector, Sustainer, Guide, Shepherd, Keeper, etc., as well as our Savior through His Son Jesus. I have no problem calling Y'shua— "Y'shua," "Lord," or "Jesus." He is the Son of God our Redeemer, therefore, it is really irrelevant what His name is translated into, since we know very well Who is being spoken of. If one grows in his or her Christian walk and has always been taught God's Son's name is Jesus, I have a very hard time believing that our wonderful, just, merciful YHWH would be so petty as to fault us for our vocal characteristics, even when our intent is pure. ....*If we love one another, God dwelleth in us, and His love is perfected in us* (1 John 4:12).

Hereby know we that we dwell in him, and he in us, because he hath given us of his Spirit. And we have seen and do testify that the Father sent the Son to be the Saviour of the world. Whosoever shall confess that Jesus is the Son of God, God dwelleth in him, and he in God. And we have known and believed the love that God hath to us. God is love; and he that dwelleth in love dwelleth in God, and God in him (1 John 4:13-16).

NOTES: WHAT REFERENCE BOOKS SAY ABOUT GOD'S NAME:

This subject of God's name may be new to you. To help you study this subject on your own, we've included some reference book definitions of God's and Jesus' names.

Nelson's Illustrated Bible Dictionary explains:

Yahweh. One of the most important names for God in the Old Testament is Yahweh, or Jehovah, from the verb "to be," meaning simply but profoundly, "I am who I am," and "I will be who I will be." The four-letter Hebrew word YHWH was the name by which God revealed Himself to Moses in the burning bush (Ex. 3:14). This bush was a vivid symbol of the inexhaustible dynamism of God who burns like a fire with love and righteousness, yet remains the same and never diminishes. Some English translations of the Bible translate the word as Jehovah, while others use Yahweh.

A popular custom of Bible times was to compose names by using the shortened forms of the divine name El or Ya (Je) as the beginning or ending syllable. Examples of this practice are Elisha, which means "God is salvation"; Daniel, "God is my judge"; Jehoiakim, "the Lord has established"; and Isaiah, "the Lord is salvation."

Vine's Expository Dictionary of Biblical Words explains:

Yahweh— "Lord." The Tetragrammaton YHWH appears without its own vowels, and its exact pronunciation is debated (Jehovah, Yehovah, Jahweh, Yahweh). The Hebrew text does insert the vowels for "adonay," and Jewish students and scholars read "adonay" whenever they see the Tetragrammaton. This use of the word occurs 6,828 times. The word appears in every period of biblical Hebrew.

The divine name YHWH appears only in the Bible. Its precise meaning is much debated. God chose it as His personal name by which He related specifically to His chosen or covenant people. Its first appearance in the biblical record is (Gen. 2:4): "These are the generations of the heavens and of the earth when they were created, in the day that the Lord God made the earth and the heavens." Apparently Adam knew Him by this personal or covenantal name from the beginning, since Seth both called his son Enosh (i. e., man as a weak and dependent creature) and began (along with all other pious persons) to call upon (formally worship) the name of YHWH, "the Lord" (Gen. 4:26). The covenant found a fuller expression and application when God revealed Himself to Abraham (Gen. 12:8), promising redemption in the form of national existence. This promise became reality through Moses, to whom God explained that He was not only the "God who exists" but the "God who effects His will": "...Thus shalt thou say unto the children of Israel, The Lord [YHWH] God of your fathers, the God of Abraham, the God of Isaac, and the God of Jacob, hath sent me unto you: this is my name for ever, and this is my memorial unto all generations. Go, and gather the elders of Israel together, and say unto them, The Lord [YHWH] God of your fathers, the God of Abraham, of Isaac, and of Jacob, appeared unto me, saying, I have surely visited you, and seen that which is done to you in Egypt: And I have said, I will bring you up out of the affliction of Egypt unto the land of the Canaanites..." (Exod. 3:15-17). So God explained the meaning of "I am who I am" (Exod. 3:14). He spoke to the fathers as YHWH, but the promised deliverance and, therefore, the fuller significance or experienced meaning of His name were unknown to them (Exod. 6:2-8).

Original Greek or Hebrew Translation:

The definition for the original Greek or Hebrew version of the current word or phrase, based on its corresponding Strong's number. A Greek-Hebrew definition includes the following elements: 1.) the Strong's number. 2.) the original Greek or Hebrew word, with pronunciation guides. 3.) a definition of the word or phrase. 4.) an indication of the word(s) from which this word or phrase was derived, or to which it is related. 5.) examples of the different ways this word or phrase has been translated in the King James Version:

About 100 years ago, Dr. Strong keyed the English text of the Authorized (King James) Version of the Bible to the Hebrew and Greek language using numbers. The resulting numerical index from the King James English to the Greek and Hebrew is called the Strong's Concordance, and the numbers which are used are called the Strong's Numbers.

Strong's Definitions of God's Name

3050 Yahh (yaw); contraction for 3068, and meaning the same; Jah, the sacred name: KJV— Jah, the Lord, most vehement. Compare names in "-iah," "-jah."

3068 Yehovah (yeh-ho-vaw'); from 1961; (the) self-Existent or Eternal; Jehovah, Jewish national name of God: KJV— Jehovah, the Lord.

3069 Yehovih (yeh-ho-vee'); a variation of 3068 [used after 136, and pronounced by Jews as 430, in order to prevent the repetition of the same sound, since they elsewhere pronounce 3068 as 136]: KJV— God.

Brown Drivers Briggs Thayers' Definitions of God's Name:

3050 Yah-Jah (Jehovah (Yahweh) in the shortened form) a) the proper name of the one true God b) used in many compounds: 1) names beginning with the English letters `Je-' 2) names ending with `-iah' or `-jah'

3068 Yehovah (yeh-ho-vaw'); from 1961; (the) self-Existent or Eternal; Jehovah, Jewish national name of God: KJV— Jehovah, the Lord. Compare 3050, 3069.

3069 Yehovih-Jehovah (Yahweh), used primarily in the combination `Lord Jehovah (Yahweh)' equal to 3068 but pointed with the vowels of 0430.

Encarta Encyclopedia definition of Jesus' Name:

Jesus Christ —The name Jesus is derived from a Greek rendering of the Hebrew name Joshua, or in full Yehoshuah ("Jehovah is deliverance"). The title Christ is derived from the Greek christos, a translation of the Hebrew mashiakh ("anointed one"), or Messiah. "Christ" was used by Jesus' early followers, who regarded him as the promised deliverer of Israel and later was made part of Jesus' proper name by the church, which regards him as the redeemer of all humanity.

Vine's Expository Dictionary of Biblical Words definition of Jesus' Name:

Iesous — is a transliteration of the Heb. "Joshua," meaning "Jehovah is salvation," i. e., "is the Savior," "a common name among the Jews, e. g., (Ex. 17:9; Luke 3:29) (RV); (Col. 4:11). It was given to the Son of God in Incarnation as His personal name, in obedience to the command of an angel to Joseph, the husband of His Mother, Mary, shortly before He was born, (Matt. 1:21). By it He is spoken of throughout the Gospel narratives generally, but not without exception, as in (Mark 16:19,20; Luke 7:13), and a dozen other places in that Gospel, and a few in John.

Strong's Definition of Jesus' Name:

Hebrew—# 3091 Yehowshuwa` (yeh-ho-shoo'-ah); or Yehowshu`a (yeh-ho-shoo'-ah); from 3068 and 3467; Jehovah-saved; Jehoshua (i.e. Joshua), the Jewish leader: -Jehoshua, Jehoshuah, Joshua. Strong's #3442 Yeshuwa` (yay-shoo'-ah); for 3091; he will save. This name in Greek is interpreted as 2424 Iesous (ee-ay-sooce') then translated into English as Jesus.

Greek— #2424 Iesous (ee-ay-sooce'); of Hebrew origin [3091]; Jesus (i.e. Jehoshua), the name of our Lord and two (three) other Israelites: KJV— Jesus.

Brown Drivers Briggs Thayers' Definition of Jesus' Name:

2424 Iesous-Jesus = "Jehovah (Yahweh) is salvation" 1) Joshua was the famous captain of the Israelites, Moses' successor 2) Jesus, son of Eliezer, one of the ancestors of Christ 3) Jesus, the Son of God, the Savior of mankind, God incarnate 4) Jesus Barabbas was the captive robber whom the Jews begged Pilate to release instead of Jesus Christ 5) Jesus, surnamed Justus, a Jewish Christian, an associate with Paul in the preaching of the gospel.

Appendix E: Symbolism and Numbers

The following list is a brief description of the symbolic meaning of primary numbers.

One: The symbol of unity, and commencement (beginnings) and primacy in all languages.

Two: The number of difference. First number that can be divided from itself, it symbolizes division as on the second creation day; witness; testimony.

Three: Is the number of divine perfection, completeness. It is the number of the Trinity. The number for resurrection. It has the necessary dimensions for substance, length, breadth, and height.

Four: Represents creative works in reference to the material creation—all things under the sun. 3 + 1, the number of beginning, thus 4 is the symbol of creation.

Five: 1 Divine grace (4+1) God adding the blessings to the works of His hands. Creation plus, a new beginning.

Six: Is the human number. Man works six days, was created on the sixth day. The number of imperfection. Creation plus division 4+2, or Grace with man's addition to it 5+1.

Seven: Is the number of completion. It is the number of spiritual perfection. Creation lasted six days, God rested on the seventh. (See below for more on the number seven.)

Eight: Is the number of resurrection, 7+1, completion plus newness.

Nine: Symbolizes judgment; completeness; fullness; finality. Akin to the number 6, six being the sum of its two factors (3x3=9 and 3+3=6), it is significant of the end of man.

Ten: Symbolizes completeness of order; law; restoration. After ten the numbers repeat.

Eleven: If ten is the completeness of order, then eleven is the subversion and undoing addition to that perfect order; disorganization; lawlessness.

Twelve: Is the symbol of governmental perfection or rule (3x4) God's rule over his creation. There are 12 apostles, 12 tribes of Israel, 12 months in a year, 12 members of a jury, 12 hours on a clock face, etc.

SYMBOLISM OF THE NUMBER SEVEN

Many of the holidays are timed according to cycles of seven. The cycle of the week with its climax on the seventh day provided the cyclical basis for much of Israel's worship: as the seventh day was observed, so was the seventh month, and the seventh year, and the fiftieth year (the year of Jubilee), which God declared would follow seven cycles, each of seven years. Not only were the festivals as a whole arranged with reference to the cycle of the week (Sabbath), two of them (the Feast ofUnleavened Bread and the Feast of Tabernacles) lasted for seven days each. Each began on the fifteenth of the month—at the end of two cycles of weeks and when the moon was full. Pentecost also was celebrated on the fifteenth of the month and began fifty days after the presentation of the firstfruits—the day following seven times seven weeks.

Seven symbolizes completeness and perfection. God's work of creation was both complete and perfect—and it was completed in seven days. Another multiple of seven used in the Bible is seventy. Seventy elders are mentioned (Ex. 24:1,9). Jesus sent out the seventy (Luke 10:1-17). Seventy years is specified as the length of the Exile (Jer. 25:12). The messianic kingdom was to be inaugurated after a period of seventy weeks of years had passed (Dan. 9:24).

In the creation narrative God rested from his work on the seventh day, and sanctified it. This gave a pattern to the Jewish sabbath on which man was to refrain from work (Ex. 20:10), to the sabbatic year (Lev. 25:2-6), and also to the year of jubilee, which followed seven times seven years (Lev. 25:8). The Feast of Unleavened Bread and the Feast of Tabernacles lasted seven days (Ex. 12:15, 19; Nu. 29:12). The Day of Atonement was in the seventh month (Lev. 16:29), and seven occurs frequently in connection with OT ritual, e.g. the sprinkling of bullock's blood seven times (Lev. 4:6) and the burnt-offering of seven lambs (Nu. 28:11); the cleansed leper was sprinkled seven times (Lev. 14:seven), and Naaman had to dip seven times in Jordan (2 Kings 5:10). In the tabernacle the candlestick had seven branches (The New Bible Dictionary). Look at a few examples of the number seven in the Bible:

- There are seven days in the creation week.

- God blessed the seventh day and made it holy (Gen 2:3).

- Major festivals such as Passover and Tabernacles lasted seven days.

- During Unleavened Bread the people were commanded to eat bread made without yeast for seven days (Ex. 12:15).
- During the Feast of Tabernacles the people are commanded to live in booths for seven days (Lev. 23:42).
- Wedding festivals lasted seven days (Judges 14:12,17).
- Noah took seven of every kind of clean animal on the ark (Gen 7:2).
- Noah waited seven days (twice) to send out the dove from the ark (Gen 8:10).
- Abraham set apart seven ewe lambs from the flock (Gen 21:28).
- So Jacob served seven years (twice) to get Rachel (Gen 29:20).
- Pharaoh's dreams had seven fat cows, seven thin cows, seven full heads of wheat, and seven thin heads of wheat (Gen. 41).
- Moses was called on the seventh day (Exodus 24:16).
- Psalm 119:164 says, *Seven times a day do I praise thee because of thy righteous judgments*.
- The counting of the Omer is seven full weeks (Lev 23:15).
- In the Tabernacle there were seven gold lamp stands, with seven branches each for seven candles.
- Seven priests carry the rams' horns in front of the ark.
- On the seventh day Joshua had the people march around the walls seven times.
- The fiery furnace was made seven times hotter.
- In the Ten Commandments three refers to God and seven to man.
- The First and Second Temples were completed in seven years.
- The Lord's Prayer contains seven petitions.
- Jesus asked how many times we should forgive. He answered, seven times seventy (490).
- Revelation is full of the number seven.
- The seven churches (Rev. 2-3).
- And many others too numerous to print here.

Appendix F: Law

There are many different laws. The law of sin and death was nailed to the cross. The laws dealing with sacrifices were only for the Temple period. The intention of ceremonial laws is to bring holiness to God's people. *"And the Lord spoke unto Moses and said, 'Speak to all the congregation of the children of Israel and say to them; You shall be holy, for I the Lord you God am holy.'"* Jesus became the ultimate sacrifice–no more sacrifices are needed (Hebrews 8).

We are not without the law but under "the law of Christ" (Gal. 6:2). There are laws that apply to believers today that deal with our relationships with other people. The law is good and just and perfect–there is a problem with the law–there is a problem with man. Man, with his sin nature, is unable to keep the law.

The New Testament verses concerning God's law explain that those who love God will follow God's instructions—His ways, His paths (Romans 2:23; Ephesians 6:2-3; Exodus 20:12; Deuteronomy 5:16; Hebrews 10:16; James 1:25; 2:11; 8-26; 1 John 2:3-4, 24; 3:22; 5:2,3; 2 John 6; Revelation 22:14). The law was *never* meant to save—only to guide. Without God's instruction, it would be impossible for people to live together. Without God's law, there could be no grace. As David said in Psalm 119, God laid down precepts that are to be obeyed. He said he meditated on God's precepts and ways, and if we walk in God's paths our hearts are set free.

The Jews never believed that anyone could earn their way to salvation. They know salvation is only by grace through Messiah (and we are praying they will have their eyes opened to see the Y'shua is the Messiah). Neither Jesus nor Paul ever taught God's law was "done away with." Paul's letters to the Gentiles speak against upset with those who twisted the law––those who abused it such as making it a prerequisite for salvation. Paul made it clear the Gentiles did not have to live by the law to attain salvation. He did encourage the Jewish believers to keep the law–but never made it a condition of salvation. Paul never implied that believers in Christ were to start a "new religion" that did away with the Old Testament. In fact, Paul explains we should thank God for His mercy that by faith we are grafted into Israel and we are not to boast for their eyes are blinded, in part, until the fullness of the Gentiles– see Romans 11:16-36. We are under a new covenant but we still have the same King and His Word says obedience is better than sacrifice. The law exposes sin, measures man, and actually shows us how full of mercy God is. Luther, Wesley, Spurgeon, Finney, Moody and other Christian leaders all taught the importance of God's law.

The idea that grace replaced the law began in the second century. The first section of this book explains how the Early Church left their Hebraic roots. During the second century, Marcion, a heretic who twisted Paul's writings, caused a radical opposition between the Law and the Gospels. He suggested the entire Old Testament be omitted from the cannon. He broke away from the Roman church in 144 and set up his own very successful group. Polycarp referred to Marcion as the Son of Satan. Marcion believed the God described in the Old Testament was cruel, so he refused to acknowledge the God of the Old Testament but embraced the portions of the New Testament that expressed God's love. Marcion created a reduced version of the New Testament consisting of Luke and parts of Paul's letters–purposely leaving out all Jewish interpolations. Marcion's legacy lives on. A study of Marcion and his immense influence on Christian leaders in church history is highly advisable to anyone serious about studying God's law.

Roy Blizzard summed up the law, as it is used in the Bible, in these two sentences:

> "The idea of law in Hebrew is not something that,
> if transgressed, is going to get you zapped.
>
> Torah [Law] is instruction,
> that if followed, will enrich one's life,
> if ignored will diminish it."

Ron Mosley's book *The Spirit of the Law* sums up the purpose of the Law:

The Nine-Fold Purpose of the Law of God

1. To teach the believer how to serve, worship and please God [Psalm 19:7-9; Acts 18:13, 14].

2. To instruct the believer how to treat his fellow man and have healthy relationships with him [Leviticus 19:18; Galatians 5:14; Galatians 6:2].

3. To teach believers how to be happy and prosper here on earth by manifesting the power and authority of God's reign in their lives [Joshua 1:8; Psalm 1:1-3; Luke 12:32].

4. The Law was given, not to save, but to measure man's deeds both toward God and his fellow man, straightening out all matters contrary to sound doctrine [I Timothy 1:8-10; II Timothy 2:5; I Corinthians 6: 1- 12; I Corinthians 3:13; Romans 2:12; Revelation 20:12, 13].

5. The Law is a schoolmaster showing that we are guilty and then leading us to Christ our Messianic justification [Galatians 3:21-24; Romans 3:19].

6. The Law gives us both the knowledge and depth of our sin [Romans 3:20; Romans 4:15; Romans 7:7, 8; Luke 20:47 - greater damnation].

7. The Law reveals the good, holy, just, and perfect nature of God and serves as the visible standard for God's will [Romans 2:17, 18; Romans 7:12; II Peter 1:4].

8. The Law is to be established or accomplished by our faith, therefore, it is called the Law of faith [Romans 3:27; Romans 3:31].

9. The same Law today is written on our hearts, and through God's Spirit we can delight and serve the Law of God [Romans 7:6-25] (Mosley 1996).

THE WHOLE LAW CAN BE WRAPPED UP IN TWO COMMANDMENTS

Master, which is the great commandment in the law? Jesus said unto him, Thou shalt love the Lord thy God with all thy heart, and with all thy soul, and with all thy mind. This is the first and great commandment. And the second is like unto it, Thou shalt love thy neighbor as thyself. On these two commandments hang all the law and the prophets (Matt. 22:36-37).

The moral law is more clearly revealed in the New Covenant. The believer's standard of conduct should be holiness (Col. 3:1). We are not without law but we are under "the law of Christ" (Gal. 6:2), the law of love (James 2:8), and "the law of liberty" (James 2:12).

613 LAWS

According to orthodox Jewish tradition, there are 613 commandments in the law of Moses. These are divided into 248 affirmative laws and 365 negative laws. Moses Margoliouth, who was one of the translators of the English Revised Version, published a catalog of the 613 commandments in English in 1743. It is common to divide the Mosaic law into three parts: the Ten Commandments (often called the moral law), the ordinances, and the judgments. The ordinances are the laws governing Israel's religious life while the judgments are the civil laws. These divisions are sometimes helpful for analysis and study but actually have no Scriptural authority. Many of Israel's laws would belong in two of the suggested divisions. For example, the law of the tithe is both religious and civil. The Ten Commandments have a prominent place in the law but Christ taught that the greatest commandment was not one of the ten (Aldrich 1959). Each of the 613 laws can be classified into the two commandments above.

If you are interested in the 613 instructions of the Torah you can order a copy from The Arkansas Institute of Holy Land Studies, 9700 Highway 107, Sherwood, AR 72120, 501-834-9426.

NOAHIDE LAWS

Since the time of Noah there are seven laws non-Jews were required to "keep" after becoming a worshiper of the God of Abraham. Keeping the Noahide laws did not save you—even the Jews know that keeping the law does not save. Only the Messiah can save. These laws are simply instructions for our own good. The word law means instruction. The Noahide Laws based on Genesis nine are:

1. To behave justly in all relationships, and to establish courts of justice.

2. To refrain from blaspheming God's name.

3. To refrain from practicing idolatry.

4. To avoid immoral practices, specifically incest and adultery.

5. To avoid shedding the blood of one's fellow man.

6. To refrain from robbing one's fellow man.

7. To refrain from eating a limb torn from a live animal.

(For more information see The *Spirit of the Law* in the resources section.)

Appendix G: Resources to Study Hebrew Roots

Many resources available from Homeschool-Books.com

Our Father Abraham

By Marvin R. Wilson

This is a stunning achievement as well as a life-changing book! Although the roots of Christianity run deep into Hebrew soil, many Christians are regrettably uninformed about the rich Hebrew heritage of the church. This volume delineates the link between Judaism and Christianity, between the Old and New Testaments, and calls Christians to examine their Hebrew roots.

Upon completion of this course you will be able to:

◆ Understand the importance of reading and interpreting Scripture from the context in which it was written.

◆ See the 66 books of the Bible telling the same story, not 39 books (Old Testament) telling one story and 27 books (New Testament) telling another.

◆ Have a general understanding of the first century believers and how Christianity became separate from Judaism.

Chapters include: "Abraham's Children," "Jewish Heritage," "The Earliest Church and Judaism," "Theological Conflict and Persecution," "Heretics and the Synagogue," "The Jewish Revolts," "Anti-Semitism and the Church," "Understanding Hebrew Thought," "Hebraic Foundation of the Church," "Christianity is Jewish," and much more.

Yeshua

A Guide To The Real Jesus And The Original Church

By Dr. Ron Moseley

This is a well researched and fascinating study of the Jewishness of the historical Jesus. The author explores the structure and mission of the original church in the Jewish culture of the first century. The book combines scholarship with an understandable writing style resulting in a book that can be easily read but challenging to the reader. This book is a must for every serious student of the Bible in enlightening us as to our Jewish heritage. With forwards by Brad Young, Ph.D., Dr. Marvin Wilson, and Dwight Prior.

Chapters include:

◆ Jewish Background of the Early Church
◆ Jewish Customs of the Early Church
◆ Jewish Idioms and the Teachings of Jesus
◆ Misconceptions that have Hindered Our Understandings
◆ Torah and Grace
◆ Purpose of the Law
◆ Noachide Laws
◆ Delivered from the Bondage of the Law
◆ Pharisees
◆ The Puritans
◆ And much, much more.

I can promise that this remarkably impacting book will help you understand difficult Hebraic phrases and theological dilemmas by investigating the original Jewish roots of the early church.

The Spirit of the Law

By Dr. Ron Mosley

Many Christians appear to choke when they hear the word "law"; to them it essentially represents some type of dead legalistic bondage of another age. That is a distorted view of the precious teachings of Jesus in the early church. This book explains the underlying idea of the law in the Bible–*teaching and instructing*. Law is instruction, that if followed, will enrich ones life, if ignored will diminish it. Mosley explains that Luther, Wesley, Spurgeon, Finney, Moody and other Christian leaders never taught against the law.

Author, Ron Mosley, founder of Arkansas Holy Land Studies (see page 555), and excellent teacher, presents a straightforward and insightful approach to a sometimes perplexing subject. Includes: The nine fold purpose of the law, explanation of different types of law, and who should be keeping the law. A must for *every* Christian. See the excerpt *The Nine-Fold Purpose of the Law of God* from *The Spirit of the Law* on page 547.

UnPromised Land

By Gary and Shirley Beresford

A story of the incredible struggle of Messianic Jews Gary and Shirley. Because of their faith in Yeshua they were betrayed by their family, rejected by Irrael immigration, tormented by court trials, and more. Their battle to claim their righful inherheritance in the promised land was waged not only for themselves but for all Messianic Jews who wish to return to their homeland. A true and facinating saga.

Our Hands are Stained With

Blood *By Michael Brown*

From the first "Christian" persecutions of the Jews in the fourth century to the unspeakable horrors of the Holocaust, from Israel-bashing in today's press to anti-Semitism in today's pulpits, this shocking painful book tells the tragic story of the "Church" and the Jewish people. It is a story every Christian must hear! It will leave you pained, provoked, and tear-stained, but with a new love for all God's people. "No one can be the same towards the Jewish people after reading this book"—Don Wilkerson. 241 pp.

Our Father Abraham Study Guide

A Study Guide Outline developed to accompany the book OUR FATHER ABRAHAM. Developed by Bob Edwards, and revised by Eric and Lori Swim, James Coots, MG, and Margaret Todd. You may print out an older copy of this study guide from HaY'Did (The Friend) Ministries, Inc. website at http://www.haydid.orgsite. Order the new revised version in spiral book form from HaY'Did.

HaY'Did Ministries, Inc., PO Box 804, Independence, KS 67301
shalom@haydid.org • http://www.haydid.org • 1-316-331-7712

549

ANCIENT HISTORY
ADAM TO MESSIAH

Seven unit studies available individually or in one combined volume.

Multi-Level: Grades 4-12

SEVEN UNIT STUDIES

❖ **Adam to Abraham**

❖ **Mesopotamia**

❖ **Ancient Egypt**

❖ **Ancient Israel**

❖ **Ancient Greece**

❖ **Ancient Rome**

❖ **The Messiah**

This valuable world history teaching resource covers a time frame from Creation through the time of Christ in two unique ways:

WORLD HISTORY WITH A BIBLE FOCUS

This book is your introduction to the history of the world beginning with God's Creation. It follows the *ultimate* living book as you learn of the Mesopotamian world of the patriarchs, the Egyptian world of the Exodus, the Babylonian world of Daniel, the Persian world of Esther, and other Bible stories that show us not only the faithfulness of our God and the greatness of our privileges, but also the marvelous wisdom of the plan of salvation. Seventy-eight percent of the entire Bible concentrates on Israel. God's focus was on Abraham and his family; shouldn't our study of world history have the same focus?

THEMATIC UNIT STUDY

Lead your student(s) chronologically on a fascinating journey through the Bible and other living books as they learn to study, write, research, and reason through many subjects including: Bible, world history, geography, literature, government, composition, agriculture, religion, science, economics, art history, economics, and more. The giant combined volume is 787 pages. Avaialable as a three-ring course binder or download and print the hyperlinked Ebook.

I was drawn to these studies because of the focus on the Bible. But quite honestly, what is keeping me is the quality of content and the ease in lesson preparation!! I would highly recommend Heart of Wisdom to anyone who has been intimidated by the preparation involved...

See more customer comments at HeartofWisdom.com

SUBJECTS

❖ BIBLE

❖ HISTORY

❖ GEOGRAPHY

❖ LITERATURE

❖ GOVERNMENT

❖ COMPOSITION

❖ AGRICULTURE

❖ RELIGION

❖ SCIENCE

❖ ECONOMICS

❖ AND MORE

IT STUDIES

Seven Ancient History Unit Studies available individually or in one combined volume.

Adam to Abraham Unit Study Begin your history study with the foundation God gave us—the fascinating stories in Genesis! The first eleven chapters describe Creation, the Fall, the Flood, and the origin of nations. Genesis 12-50 is the ancestral story beginning with Abram. The focus of this unit study is on the memorable stories from Creation to Abraham entering Canaan and how each of the events foreshadows Jesus, the Messiah! This book is a great way to try out Heart of Wisdom Unit Studies to see if they fit your family. You'll never regret time in God's Word. Each HOW Unit Study includes hundreds of links to worksheets, puzzles, Bible studies, book excerpts and more on the Internet. **120 Pages.**

Mesopotamia Unit Study In order to properly understand the biblical periods, we must examine the beginnings of culture in the ancient Near East. The Mesopotamia unit is central to understanding the beliefs, social norms, and material traits of the Old Testament world. (Early civilizations are also spoken of in the NT. Read Rev. 17:9-11). Several early civilizations developed in Mesopotamia at different places and times simultaneously with Egypt. This unit's focus in on Bible geography and the Hebrews' interaction with the Sumerian, Babylonian, Assyrian, and Medo-Persian civilizations of Mesopotamia. Full of maps and activities that will give your student a good grasp of Biblical geography! **102 Pages.**

Ancient Egypt Unit Study It is impossible to properly understand the history of God's people without knowing something about ancient Egypt. The children of Israel were brought into Egypt and settled, living there for centuries before becoming an independent nation. Their removal from contact with the people of Canaan and their time of affliction prepared them for inheriting the land promised to their fathers—Israel. **136 Pages.**

Ancient Israel Unit Study As we study how God dealt redemptively with the Hebrews, our spiritual ancestors by faith, we gain insight into the plans and purposes of God for mankind. Three things must be held in common by a society in order for it to be a people: religion, education, and law. In all history, there is only one civilization that bases its religion, education, and law on Scripture—Israel. Secular history studies focus on reading stories and legends about ancient mythical gods and exclude Israel—**the stories from the ultimate Living Book— God's Word**. As you learn about the roots of the Christian faith, you deepen your personal walk and relationship with Christ. **190 Pages.**

Ancient Greece Unit Study Learn about Greece's political history, social systems, cultural achievements, and economic conditions. Also learn how the Greeks affected the secular view of Scripture and the church in ancient times and today. These lessons will address the key events, ideas, aspects, and issues of culture in ancient Greece to enhance your overall understanding. **136 Pages.**

Ancient Rome Unit Study The history of Rome covers a massive empire, a rich culture, a profound philosophical legacy, and a lengthy era. The New Testament era was influenced by Hellenistic ideas, customs, religion and language, but dominated by Roman law, governmental forms, ideas of class and the military. A study of ancient Rome will give you a better understanding of Jesus and the early church, because Christ lived His entire human life under the Roman empire. Paul was also a Jew living under the Roman authorities in Jerusalem. **151 Pages.**

Messiah Unit Study All the treasures of wisdom and knowledge are hidden in the person of the Messiah! You have the opportunity to investigate ancient prophecies, hidden wisdom, things that people longed to know for centuries before the Messiah came to dwell on earth. You are in the privileged position of looking backward through history to see the Messiah as He was described in prophecy, as He dwelt on earth, as He is now, and as He speaks to you through His Word. **88 Pages.**

Tree Book or Ebook??

The combined seven-unit volume is a paper book (tree book) in a three-ring binder.
The individual Unit Studies are available in Ebook format.

How the Cross Became a Sword
By Richard Booker

The events that separated Christianity from its Jewish roots in the first three centuries; A clear survey of the tragic history of Christian anti-Semitism showing where the church went wrong; What Christians and Jews should do in light of current events

Islam, Christianity and Israel
By Richard Booker

Shocking information about the life of Mohammed. Startling facts about the background, teachings, and practices of Islam. How Islam differs from Christianity. How the Arab-Israeli conflict will end.

The Miracle of the Scarlet Thread *By Richard Booker*

The scarlet thread is woven through every book in the Bible. The fabric it forms is God's blood covenant provided for man. This book explains how the Old and New Testament tell the same story—the entire Old Testament is a picture of Jesus! This is one of the most profound books on the

blood of Christ ever written! Considered standard reading for believers. A classic.

The Life and Times of Jesus the Messiah
By Alfred Edersheim

Alfred Edersheim's heritage as a Messianic Jew gives the description of Jewishculture in "The Life and Times of Jesus the Messiah" an authenticity that a non-Jewwould be hard-pressed to duplicate. The culture of Israel during the Roman occupation comes alive in Edersheim's writing in a way that goes beyond scholastic study by blending his own Jewish heritage, archeological fact, and keen spiritual insight. Any serious student of the Gospels or the Epistles would benefit from the insight of Mr.Edersheim because so much of the imagery in the account of Jesus is steeped in the culture of Israel as it progressed from Abraham to Herod. Used as a reference, "The Life and Times" is indexed according to verses and events and gives Bible studies the context for the illustrations of Jesus. Read as a book, Edersheim is ponderous, however, a contiguous reading would give a person a consistent Hebrew framework which the New Testament fit into 2000 years ago.

Jesus Rabbi and Lord: The Hebrew Story of Jesus Behind Our Gospels *By Robert L. Lindsey*

Lindsey tells here the warm, personal account of how he and David Flusser struggled over many years to discover the earliest form of Jesus' words and narratives of His life. They believe that the records, when properly analyzed and studied, show us an authentic picture of Jesus interacting with the people of Jerusalem and Galilee. Jesus clearly heads a movement, the "Kingdom of Heaven," and is a Divine Figure whose actions and words are fully Messianic. (Oak Creek, WI: Cornerstone, 1990) 227 pages. Read about HaKesher Inc - Founded by Ken and Lenore Mullican (daughter of the late Dr. Robert L. Lindsey) on page 555 in this book or at **http://www.hakesher.org/hakesher2/**

Here Comes the Bride
By Richard Booker

One of the most beautiful pictures of God's love is the ancient Jewish wedding. God has called both Jews and Gentiles to a marriage relationship with Him through our Heavenly Bridegroom, the Messiah. God has only one bride, and He has sent the matchmaker from Heaven to make us one with Him. Here the author will warm your heart and give you hope for the future.

Blow the Trumpet in Zion
By Richard Booker

One of the most complete books on the Jewish people available. This book tells the dramatic story of God's covenant plan for Israel as it is recorded in the Bible and revealed in history. A fascinating survey of the history of the Jewish people, their past glory and suffering, present crisis and future hope.

Seven Feasts of Israel (Video)

Did you know that: The miracles during Christ's three and a half year ministry, fall in line with the 7 Feasts and the Torah readings on the Sabbath? The name of God (the Tetragrammaton) is hidden in the Hebrew inscription of the cross? Perry Stone teaches about the seven Feasts in detail and how Christ fulfilled three; the church has fulfilled one, and the church of Israel will fulfill the final three. Very educational, excellent video! Highly recommended.

Jesus the Jewish Theologian
By Dr. Brad Young

Establishing Jesus firmly withing the context of first-century Judaism, Jesus the Jewish Theologian shows how understanding Jesus' Jewishness is crucial for interpreting the New Testament and for understanding the nature of Christian faith. Insights from Jewish literature, archeology, and tradition help modern readers place Jesus withing his original context. Particular attention is given to the Jewish roots of Jesus' teaching concerning the kingdom of God. (Hendrickson, Peabody, Massachusetts, 1995. 308 p, pb).

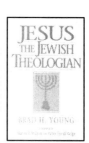

Paul the Jewish Theologian
By Dr. Brad Young

Paul the Jewish Theologian reveals Saul of Tarsus as a man who, though rejected in the synagogue, never truly left Judaism. Author Young contends with long held notions that Hellenism was the context which most influenced Paul's communication of the Gospel. This skewed notion has led to widely divergent interpretations of Paul's writings. Only in rightly aligning Paul as rooted in his Jewishness and training as a Pharisee can he be correctly interpreted. Young asserts that Paul's view of the Torah was always positive and he separates Jesus' mission among the Jews from Paul's call to the Gentiles.

Books by Dr. John Garr

The Hem of His Garment: Touching the Power in God's Word *By Dr. John Garr*

"If I can but touch the Hem of his Garment . . ." These words of desperation formed an axis of faith which brought a miracle into the life of a dying woman when she reached out and accessed the power resident in Jesus the Messiah. But, it was also a key to healing and deliverance for many others who came in faith because "all who touched the hem of his garment" were healed. What was this material object which caused faith to rise in the hearts of citizens of first-century Israel?

This book gives a comprehensive study of the long and interesting Jewish tallit tradition, which required that the four-cornered garment commonly worn in Bible days have tzitzit (fringes) appended to each corner as a means of calling both the wearer and the observer to remember all the Word of God (commandments). You will simply be amazed at the extent of this tradition and its continuing impact upon the Jewish people to this day in the form of the "prayer shawl" that they wear at specific times of devotion and interaction with the Divine Presence. Don't miss *The Hem of His Garment!*

Bless You! Restoring the Biblically Hebraic Blessing *By Dr. John Garr*

Bless You! is a systematic, comprehensive study of the biblically Hebraic concept of blessing. God has forever focused on confirming his covenantal blessings and bringing this good news to all humankind. The blessing that was first given to Adam and Eve is God's intention for everyone!

Original blessing, not original sin, was always God's intention for humanity. In order to fulfill his eternal commitment to bless humankind that God planned before all creation to offer himself in the person of his Son, Jesus Christ, as an atonement for the sins of all the human race. Jesus paid the price for God's blessing to humanity.

God himself composed and prescribed "The Blessing" for his children, a benediction that also places God's personal name on the one who is blessed. This powerful dynamic can now be experienced in every Christian home and in every corporate worship experience. You, too, can restore this vital part from the Hebraic faith of Jesus and the apostles and bring God's blessing upon yourself and your family. Don't miss the amazing blessing of *Bless You!*

God's Lamp, Man's Light: Mysteries of the Menorah *By Dr. John Garr*

God's Lamp, Man's Light is a masterful analysis of the menorah, the only biblical symbol that has the distinction of being designed by God himself.

The only comprehensive study of the menorah in existence, this book is filled with valuable information about the history, design, and function of the menorah in both the Israelite sanctuary and in the earliest church.

Dr. Garr also analyzes biblical themes connected with the menorah, including light, fire, the tree of life. He discusses thoroughly the menorah's messianic imagery. He also evaluates individual men and women, Israel, and the church as God's living menorah, fulfilling the commission of being the light of the world.

You will simply be amazed at the wealth of insight that has been hidden from the historical church because of its separation from Judaism and things Jewish. You will be challenged to embark on a more complete study of the Jewish roots of your Christian faith when you consider this enriching and inspirational teaching on the menorah, God's lamp, man's light. If you're restoring the Jewish roots of your faith, God's Lamp, Man's Light is essential to your quest.

Our Lost Legacy: Christianity's Hebrew Heritage *By Dr. John Garr*

"We've been robbed!" These words of a Methodist bishop in Brazil, an Anglican church leader in India, and a Pentecostal overseer in Africa express the sentiments of thousands of Christians when they discover through the challenging teaching of Dr. John D. Garr the extent to which they have been deprived of the Hebrew heritage of their Christian faith.

For the past nineteen centuries, millions of believers have been denied their biblical legacy, the riches of the Hebrew foundations of their faith. Christian Judaeophobia, anti-Judaism, and anti-Semitism have conspired to rob them of the treasures of their inheritance.Scriptural archaeologists have been digging in the Word of God and have begun to uncover bits and pieces of this lost legacy. Scholars of various denominations have awakened to the realization that our over-Hellenized, over-Latinized Christian faith needs to be restored to its original context. This call to reclaim Christianity's Judaic heritage seems radical and even revolutionary to some; however, it is both scriptural and prophetic, for everything biblical is to be restored at the time of the Messianic age (Acts 3:20, 21).

This volume presents selected essays in which Dr. Garr urges the church to recover its Hebrew heritage, its connection with the Jewish matrix which produced it. These pages call Christians back to the Bible, to the roots of faith that enrich lives and equip believers to achieve greater spiritual maturity through a more comprehensive understanding of Jesus, our Jewish Lord. Restoring Our Lost Legacy is one of the seminal books of our time!

Living Emblems: Ancient Symbols of Faith *By Dr. John Garr*

Living Emblems helps believers everywhere understand the biblical emblems that were designed by God and by his people Israel to emphasize divine truths and to call believers to remembrance of their opportunity and responsibility to worship and honor their Creator. Failure to understand the implications of these important symbols has robbed millions of Christians of vital, spiritually-enriching information.

Restoring the Hebrew foundations of Christianity is essential for individual Christians to understand the roots of their faith. Recognizing the historical and spiritual truths represented by the symbols of the Hebrew Scriptures is a profound means of underscoring the historical and theological truth of Christianity's Jewish connection. with the Jewish matrix which produced it. These pages call equip believers to achieve greater maturity through a more comprehensive understanding of Jesus, our Jewish Lord.

Family Sanctuary: Restoring the Biblically Hebraic Home *By Dr. John Garr*

Family Sanctuary is a provocative look at the modern home that offers clear answers for families in crisis and for those who want to restore their families to biblical foundations. This book is a systematic, comprehensive study of the biblically Hebraic concepts of family. Reviews are calling this by far his best book ever! By helping you understand–as the ancient Hebrews did–that your home is a mikdash me'at (a temple in miniature), Family Sanctuary will equip you to restore your home as a center for spiritual growth. You, too, can restore these powerful dynamics and make your home a family sanctuary.

Don't miss this extraordinary opportunity to recover one of the foundational parts of your biblically Hebraic heritage in the faith of Jesus and the apostles and make your home a true sanctuary of fellowship, study, and worship to God.If you're seeking restoration, *Family Sanctuary* is a must read!

FellowHeirs: Jews & Gentiles Together in the Family of God *By Tim Hegg*

"Jews should do Jewish things and Christians should do Christian things." So says conventional, ecumenical wisdom. But as Jews have begun to discover the Messiah, and non-Jewish believers have begun to discover the Torah, that divisive idea is being challenged.

Tim Hegg's *FellowHeirs* takes on the difficult question of the Gentile believer's relationship to the Torah and to the people of God. A masterful piece of scholarship, Tim Hegg's latest work seeks the biblical perspective on identity within the family of God. Is the Torah for all of God's children, or is it only for Jews? Who are the people the Torah refers to as "strangers"? Do Gentile believers have a legitimate place in Messianic Communities? FellowHeirs answers these questions and more.

The powerful results of Tim's research demonstrate from the biblical text that Jews and Gentiles are both beholden to the same covenant norms and responsibilities. There is only one set of teachings for all of God's people. *FellowHeirs* is a must-read for every serious student of the Bible.

The Letter Writer: Paul's Background and Torah Perspective *By Tim Hegg*

The vast majority of the modern day studies, teachings, and theologies developed concerning the Apostle Paul all disseminate a similar perspective: That Paul underwent a typical conversion from one religion to another, from the Law-based religion of Judaism to the Grace-based religion of Christianity. That Paul preached against the Torah and Judaism and that he

sought to rescue people, both Jew and Gentile, from the clutches of this works-based system. And some even teach that Paul taught that there were two ways of salvation, two ways to gain right-standing before God: the old way (works) and the new (grace).

Has the Body of Messiah missed significant blessing found in the Torah resulting from a skewed perception and misunderstanding of Paul and his writings? It is time for us to take a new and honest look at Paul as an apostle who was Torah observant, faithful to the call of Israel, and a great man that encouraged the followers of the Messiah to embrace the teachings of Moses and with great passion declared Yeshua to be the Messiah of Israel!

The Letter Writer challenges traditional Christian viewpoints of the Apostle Paul, his message and the foundation of his theological approach and understanding. Through this remarkable book Tim Hegg attempts to re-establish a biblical, historical, and cultural understanding of Paul-the Torah observant Apostle.

The Victor Journey Through the Bible

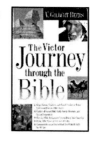

This is a unique resource that approaches the Bible story by story. In these pages you will discover around 250 of your favorite Bible stories presented with background information in word and picture. This storehouse of authentic material includes these features:

- over 400 colorful pages of photographs, drawings, & maps
- more than 100 drawings from objects or monuments
- over 200 photographs of Bible lands today
- photographs of more than 50 archaeological discoveries
- scores of reconstructions and diagrams
- and dozens of colorful maps.

This easy-to-read, visual exploration of the Bible allows you to follow the action from Genesis to Revelation. The stories of Scripture will come alive as you travel story-by-story through Bible lands and times. You will discover how ancient people really lived-the foods they ate, the homes they lived in, the clothes they wore, the work they performed. ISBN: 156476480X . Hard cover, 416 pages.

Nelson's Illustrated Encyclopedia of the Bible

Having this book is like owning an entire library of Bible background works and historical reference tools-in one convenient volume! The "Atlas of Biblical History" provides an overview of significant turning points in biblical history, with maps, timelines, and special features on key people and places. A "Peoples and Empires" section offers intriguing insights on the nations that influenced the culture of the Jews and early Christians.

This information-packed volume also contains a detailed study of the life, ministry, and message of Jesus-plus a comprehensive survey of life in Bible times, including family life, social customs, and religious beliefs and practices from Abraham to the early church. Contemporary graphics visually enhance the biblical and historical images, making this the most complete, accurate, and eye-appealing Bible encyclopedia you'll find anywhere!

Jot & Tittle: Introducing the Hebrew Alefbet through the Weekly Torah
Portions By Pat Feinberg

Want to learn Hebrew straight from the Bible? Then use Jot & Tittle week-by-week-you'll be amazed at what you can learn! Each Torah portion has a quick two-page lesson. By the end of a year, you can know all 54 names of the weekly portions, what they mean, and what goes on in that chunk of scripture. Spell out each name, one letter at a time, then sound out the syllables as the vowel points are added. Practice tracing block and cursive writing, right in the workbook. You can even learn alphabetical order and extra vocabulary. Each time you finish a book (Genesis, Exodus, etc.), word puzzles give you a fun chance to review everything you've learned. It's quick, it's easy, and it's fun, so dig in!

To find out more about Hebrew Roots: Organizations

Arkansas Institute of Holy Land Studies - Homeschool parents, learn about our Hebrew roots as your child attends college via video tapes! Professors include some of the best specialists in Hebrew language, culture, history, and archaeology such as Ron Mosley, Brad Young, Marvin WIlson, Dwight Prior, and Douglas Wheeler. 9700 Hwy 107 Sherwood, AR Phone 1-800-617-6205. Website http://www.HayDid.org/Ark.htm.

Ascend Magazine - is published in conjunction with messiah magazine. This magazine is designed to share the basic concepts of salvation, Messiah and Torah with our Christian brothers and sisters in language that is familiar and friendly to them. The magazine contains great material for those new to the message of Torah. It offers a gentle introduction to the Hebrew Roots message.   Ascend calls us to "Be Faithful; Be Blameless; Be Like Him; Be Holy; ASCEND...and Be Transformed by the Renewing of Your Mind." Published by First Fruits of Zion.

Awareness Ministry - A broad-based Bible teaching ministry encompassing the basic concepts of historic Judeo-Christian teaching. They declare the necessity of returning to the Old Testament for the purposes of establishing New Testament truth concerning moral and ethical standards, as well as Biblical church orders. Robert Somerville is director of Awareness Ministries and also shares pastoral responsibilities at Covenant of Peace Church. P.O. Box 364 - Huntsville, AL 35804 - (256) 776-2732 - Web Site: http://www.awareness.org

Bridges for Peace - A Jerusalem-based, multi-faceted, Christian, non-profit organization dedicated to the building of sincere relationships between the Christian and Jewish communities while encouraging greater concern for the land and people of Israel. It is our desire to see Christians and Jews working side by side for better understanding and a more secure Israel. " Dispatch from Jerusalem" Box 33145, Tulsa, OK 74153 - (800)-566-1998 - Web Site: http://www.bridgesforpeace. com/.

Center for Judaic-Christian Studies - The Center for Judaic-Christian Studies is a research and development organization headquartered in Dayton, Ohio, with extensive work in Israel. Focusing on studies of the Jewish backgrounds of Christian faith, the Center promotes various books and other educational materials which document Christianity's Jewish roots including excellent teaching tapes by Dwight Pryor and Marvin Wilson Write or call for a free catalog. PO Box 293040 - Dayton, OHIO 45429. (800)-308-6506 or (937)-434-4550.

Christian Friends of Israel stands with Israel at a time when their friends are few in the international arena of nations. God has forever promised that blessings will follow obedience to His commands and curses will follow disobedience (Deut. 6,7). Individuals and groups can rise above their government's responses and actions in showing compassion and courage by taking a stand by not bowing to anti-Semitism. PO Box 1813 - Jerusalem 91015, ISRAEL - 972.2.894172, 894187.

Firstf Fruit of Zion - This magazine is dedicated to discovering and living a Biblically- observant Torah lifestyle as believers in Messiah Yeshua. P.O. Box 280827 - Lakewood, CO 80228-0827 - (303) 697- (800) 775-4807.

Friends of Israel was born out of the fires of the Holocaust. Over half a century later, their love and concern for the people so near to the heart of God continues. FOI has home Bible studies, camps, medical clinics, special events, and other activities to share Messiah's love with Jewish people worldwide. PO Box 908 Bellmawr - NJ 08099.

Gospel Research Foundation - dedicated to the scholarly exploration and spiritual restoration of the Jewish roots of Christian faith. GRF seeks to interpret properly the teachings of Jesus in their authentic context giving fresh vitality to Christian experience. The Judaism of Jesus is the root which nourishes the branch. Dr. Brad H. Young is the founder and President of the Gospel Research Foundation. PO Box 703101 - Tulsa, OK 74170 U.S.A. E-mail - bryoung@oru.edu Web Site http://www.gospelresearch.org/

HaKesher - Founded by Ken and Lenore Mullican (daughter of former Jerusalem pastor, the late Dr. Robert L. Lindsey) in 1986 in Tulsa, Oklahoma. HaKesher's main objectives is to promote an awareness of the Judaic heritage of the Christian faith and combat anti-Judaism through mutual understanding and respect. They offer books, audio- and video-cassettes, other study materials, and gifts by mail order, including self-study Hebrew language courses. 9939 South 71st East Ave. - Tulsa, OK 74133-5338 - (918) 298-8816. E-mail hakesher@aol.com Web http://www.hakesher.org/hakesher2/

HaY'Did (The Friend) Ministries, Inc. is a neutral clearing educational house dedicated to train, educate and equip for study both the Jew and the non-Jew in the rich Biblical/Hebraic Heritage. In addition to providing their subscribers with educational materials, HaY'Did gives support to the associate member ministries through an ever growing network of volun-

Find out more about Hebrew Roots-Continued

teers. HaY'Did also helps the associate ministries with conference information and release of information around the world at various levels of learning. The Statement of Faith and Statement of Tolerance are available on th e website. PO Box 804 - Independence, KS 67301 - 1-316-331-7712. E-mail shalom@haydid.org Web Site: http://www.haydid.org,

Heart of Wisdom - publishers of this book and a variety of homeschool materials to help Christian families bring up children with a hearts desire for true wisdom and knowledge from the Lord. Heart of Wisdom materials include an emphasis on studying the Bible in light of understanding our Hebrew roots. Dozens of book excerpts and articles are on HOW's website. 146 Chriswod Lane Stafford, VA 225556. Phone 540-752-2593. http://www.HeartofWisdom.com.

Institute for Hebraic-Christian Studies- Sounds of the Trumpet, Inc. was established in 1979 as a non-profit Christian organization by Richard Booker as the means for providing Bible study materials that would meet the above criteria of depth, with simplicity and practicality. The ministry has functioned with integrity and excellence out of a servant's heart. 8230 Birchglenn Lane - Houston Texas 77070 - (281) 469-1045 E-Mail: shofarprb@aol.com Home Page: www.rbooker.com http://www.rbooker.com/

Jewish Jewels - Neil and Jamie are Bible teachers who host Jewish Jewels, an award winning, nationally syndicated, weekly television program devoted to revealing hidden treasures from the Bible in their original Jewish context. Neil is Jewish by birth, Jamie is Jewish by rebirth, and God has made them "One" in the Messiah. Web sitehttp://www.jewishjewels.org/index.html.

Messiah Magazine - is published 5 times annually. This magazine is dedicated to the study, exploration and celebration of our righteous and Torah-observant king—Yeshua of Nazareth. Each issue provides fresh articles and perspectives on Messiah, the grace we have in Him, the truth He taught us and the 'Torah.' It's not just about having Jewish Roots, its about discipleship to our Jewish King—Yeshua. Each issue brings you cutting-edge teaching. Published by First Fruit of Zion.

Menorah Ministries - A Messianic resource and referral ministry about the Messiah, helping others to know Him, the Bible, Biblical Jewish roots of Christ ianity, Israel, Jesus (Yeshua), and God's plan of eternal redemption. P.O. Box 100931 - Denver, CO 80250-0931 U.S.A. (303)-722-0944, Web Site: http://www.rmii.com/~menorah

Messengers of Messiah -Messengers of Messiah is a Hebraic Roots ministry focused on the interpretation of Scripture within the context of Hebraic culture and language at the time of Jesus. Headquarters is located in Troy, Illinois, with affiliate ministries and individuals in the U.S., England, and Israel. Peter A. Michas is the founder and senior pastor of Messengers of Messiah International Ministries. His unique ministry stimulates greater understanding and appreciation of the richness and beauty of God's Word, as can only be fully revealed by in-depth study of its Hebraic roots. Hundreds of audio and video teaching tapes available. Request a free catalog or visit the Web Site. P.O. Box 125 - Troy, IL 62294, 618-667-1022, fax 618-667-8952, e-mail: Web Site: http://www.ezl.com/~

Messianic Times, The - a quarterly published newspaper. The primary mandate is to exalt Yeshua as Lord and the true Messiah of all, both Jew and Gentile. Subscriptions: 1 Year - free upon request. Suggested donation $20.00. U.S.A.: P.O. Box 42700 - Washington, DC 20015 - (703)-503-5303.

Restoration Foundation - Publisher of the excellent *Restore Magazine*. In order to promote and sustain the growing phenomenon of interest in Christianity's Jewish roots. Robin Sampson contributes to Restore Magazine. The Restoration Foundation is dedicated to research, development, and implementation of the church's Judaic heritage. They are committed to studying and promoting the Hebrew foundations of Christian faith and the profound implications that these historical and theological truths have for the church's life and renewal. Back issues of *Restore Magazine* are available on Restoration Foundation's website. John D. Garr, Ph.D. President, P.O. Box 421218, Atlanta, GA 30342, Phone: 1-423-472-7321, Fax: 1-423-472-1727, E-mail : RestorationFoundation@csi.com, Website: http://www.restorationfoundation.org.

Return to God - Christianity has wandered far from what first century believers understood and practiced. *Return to God* seeks to restore those lost roots. In an era of tremendous moral, social, and spiritual crisis, believers need to be strengthened and prepared to give rational answers for why and what they believe. Return to God seeks to provide that information. P.O. Box 159, Carnation, Washington 98014-0159. E-mail glenna@halcyon.com.

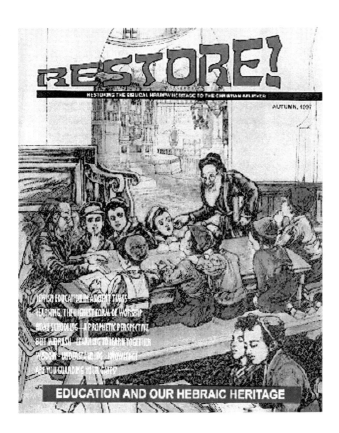

Restore! is published by Restoration Foundation as a service to those in the Christian and Jewish communities who envision the restoration of Christianity's Judaic heritage and the eradication of Christian Judaeophobia and anti-Semitism. In order to promote and sustain the growing phenomenon of interest in Christianity's Jewish roots, Restoration Foundation has been formed as an educational resource to the body of Messiah to bring together an interdenominational network of leaders who are committed to the task of restoring the church's Hebrew foundations.

The Restoration Foundation is dedicated to research, development, and implementation of the church's Judaic heritage. They are committed to studying and promoting the Hebrew foundations of Christian faith and the profound implications that these historical and theological truths have for the church's life and renewal.

Restore! includes articles by Dr. John Garr, Dr. Marvin Wilson, Dr. Brad young, and author of this book, Robin Scarlata Sampson. Back issues of *Restore Magazine* are available on Restoration Foundation's website. E-mail: RestorationFoundation@csi.com, Website: http://www.restorationfoundation.org.

Subscription Information

Price $25 per year (4 issues) in the U.S.; $35 per year for other nations. Please address all communications relating to Restore! and make all checks, drafts, or money orders payable to Restore! P. O. Box 421218 - Atlanta, GA 30342. (423)-472-7321. Send your name and address to receive a free sample issue.

To find out more about Homeschool

HOME SCHOOL RESOURCES

HomeschoolInformation.com - publishers of this book and a variety of homeschool materials to help Christian families bring up children with a hearts desire for true wisdom and knowledge from the Lord. Publications include Heart of Wisdom Unti Studies, What Your Child Needs to Know When. Heart of Wisdom materials include an emphasis on studying the Bible in light of understanding our Hebrew roots.

Home Educators Family Times - P.O. Box 1056, Gray, Maine 04039, (207) 657-2800.

Home School Digest - Excellent, huge magazine full of deeply insightful, full, meaty articles *beyond* the fluff. The focus: fathers who willingly lay down their lives to lead their families into the ways of righteousness; mothers whose hearts desire no higher calling than to know their children are walking in God's truth. Contributors: Johnathan Lindvall, Phil Lancaster, Ruth Beechick, Doreen Claggett, Sam Blumefield, and more. Quarterly issues over 100 pages. $18.00 P.O. Box 154, LaVale, MD 85066-8190.

Home Schooling Today is a magazine published six times per year and is filled with practical help for Christian families. Back Issues for $4.00 each... buy 3 / Get 1 Free! P.O. Box 1425, Melrose, FL 32666.

Homeschool Legal Defense Association, P.O. Box 159, Paeonian Springs, VA 22129, (703) 478-8585.

National Homeschool Association exists to advocate individual choice and freedom in education, to serve those families who choose to homeschool, and to inform the general public about home education. Post Office Box 157290, Cincinnati, OH 45215, (513)772-9580.

Parents' Review - A quarterly magazine offering a touch of culture, old-fashioned wisdom, and introductions to enduring works and lives of great people, all based upon the high ideals and principles of Christian educator Charlotte Mason. Advertisement-free. (P.O. Box 936, Elkton, MD 21922-0936).

Practical Homeschooling is a colorful 96-page quarterly magazine for homeschoolers of all ages and levels of expertise Every issue contains at least 50 to 100 reviews and puts the "practical" in Practical Homeschooling with a wide range of tips and resources. The columnists represent many different philosophies of homeschooling. Subscriptions are $19.95/six issues P.O. Box 1250, Fenton, MO 63026, (800) 346-6322, Fax (314) 343-7203 e-mail address is PRACTIC.@AOL.com.

Patriarch Magazine is a bi-monthly magazine committed to giving men a regular diet of Biblical teaching and application, so that men can once again lead their families, churches and nation for Jesus Christ. Patriarch Ministry is supported by gifts. Suggested donation for one year subscription in print is $25.00 a year. Suggested donation for one year subscription for audio magazine is $30.00. Send to Patriarch, PO Box 725 Rolla, MO, 65402.

Teaching Home is a four color magazine including home education news and articles, curriculum reviews and ads, letters from readers, calendars of state and national events, newsletter inserts from a home education organization in your state and much more. Identify with the joys, trials, and successes of home schoolers, and be inspired and encouraged. Published bimonthly for $15/year. Write for a free copy of answers to some commonly asked questions regarding home schooling. (800) 395-7760 Box 20219, Portland, OR 97220, (503) 253-9633, fax (503) 253-7345.

The Old Schoolhouse Magazine is like a homeschool convention packed into 200 pages! Hear from popular authors, experts, and other homeschool families like you who inform, encourage and inspire. Also win hundreds of dollars worth of free homeschool resources in the process. www.TheHomeschoolMagazine.com

WISDOM

An Internet-Linked Unit
Study

Get on the *right path, now*!

Is your homeschooling on the right path? Are you reaching for the right goal? It does not matter how hard you try or how diligent you are if you don't have the right directions. Are you headed in the right direction?

Suppose you wanted to go to a city in Texas but you were given a Florida map mislabeled Texas? Following the directions would not work—even if you tried harder or increased your speed. You would still be lost! The problem is not your attitude or effort—the problem is you have the wrong map. Many homeschoolers are following the wrong map on their homeschool journey. They follow the state's standards, curriculum scope and sequence, or SAT benchmarks. This unique Unit Study is a map to ***true wisdom***.

There are two ways to live life wisely or unwise. When we follow the path of wisdom the results are joy, peace, contentment, confidence and in the presence of God. The results of living unwisely are conflict, discouragement, disappointment, dissolution, and discontentment. Available as an Ebook (dowload to your computer today!) or bound book.

This study is one of the most important things you will ever do with your children!

LESSONS TEACH:

* How to follow the wise path
* How to stay on it.
* How to stay off the worldly path
* How to set wise goals
* The importance of obedience
* How to pray for wisdom
* How to study God's Word
* How to make wise decisions
* How to choose friends wisely
* How to choose counsel wisely
* How to manage conflict wisely
* How to have the ultimate relationship with Christ
* AND MORE!

What Your Child Needs To Know When

An Evaluation Check List for Grades K-8
By Robin Sampson

Home schoolers often ask the frantic question, "What if there is a concept I haven't taught that is on the test?" No more guess work! This book includes the objectives contained on the five most widely used national achievement tests and a wealth of educational information including:

* A Christian Worldview
* Hebrew VS Greek Education
* Wisdom According to God
* Avoiding Test Anxiety
* What the Achievement Tests Evaluate
* The Accuracy of Achievement Testing
* The terms used in Achievement Testing
* Methods of Evaluation
* Studying God's Word to receive His instruction of wisdom, justice, and righteousness.

This book is for parents who want to teach their children from a Biblical world view and help them become self-motivated, lifelong learners. Compare your curriculum to this book to be sure you are covering all the objectives on the test. Includes everything you need to:

3 Plan Your School Year
3 Overcome Testing Fears
3 Check for Learning Gaps
3 Evaluate Your Child's Progress
3 Cover Each Subject Thoroughly

Includes check boxes to check off each objective as it is studied and again when it is mastered. Also includes: evaluation sheets for Bible reading, character traits, spiritual fruits, social evaluation, work and study habits, glossary of common teaching terms, Dolch sight word list, and the Biblical definition of true wisdom. Also includes instructions on how to use this book with several children so you'll only need one book per family. Grades K to 8.

Don't Miss This Best Seller!

Read Excerpts at Homeschool-Books.com

Answer Keys

Glossary

Works Cited

Bibliography

End Notes

Seder Supper Search

Crossword Puzzles

PASSOVER

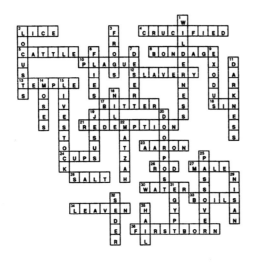

UNLEAVENED BREAD

A Family Guide to the Biblical Holidays ©

Crossword Puzzles

FIRSTFRUITS

WEEKS

TRUMPETS

ATONEMENT

Crossword Puzzles

TABERNACLES

HANUKKAH

PURIM

SABBATH

Word Search

PASSOVER

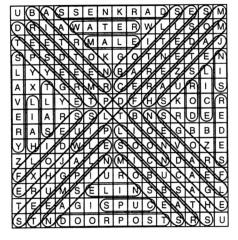

UNLEAVENED BREAD

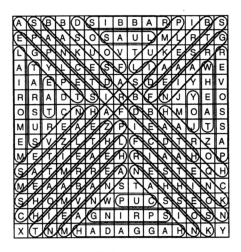

FIRSTFRUITS

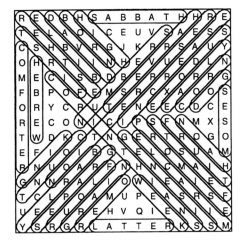

WEEKS

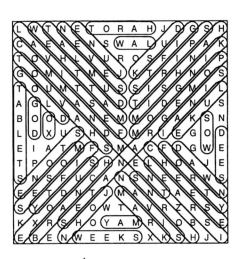

TRUMPETS

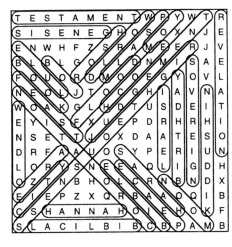

ATONEMENT

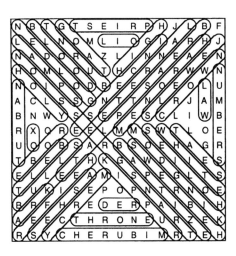

TABERNACLES

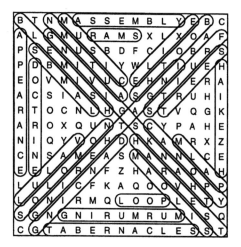

HANUKKAH

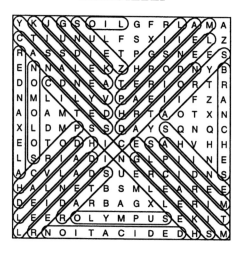

PURIM

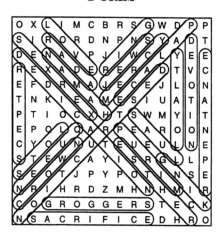

SABBATH

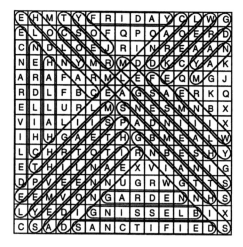

Glossary of Jewish Terminology

Afikoman.........The broken piece of matzah put aside at the beginning of the Passover meal (seder) and eaten at the end of the meal.

Alef-Bet...........The Hebrew alphabet. The name is derived from the first two letters of the alef-bet.

Arbah Minim......Literally *four species*. Fruit and branches used to fulfill the commandment to "rejoice before the Lord" during Sukkot.

Ark...............An acronym of aron kodesh, literally, holy chest. The cabinet where the Torah scrolls are kept. The word has no connection with Noah's Ark, which is "teyvat" in Hebrew.

Atonement ....In Judaism, atonement (Hebrew: kaparah) or reconciliation between God and humanity, is achieved by the process of repentance (Hebrew: teshuvah), seeking forgiveness and making amends with fellow human beings.

Ba'al Tokea........Blower of the shofar (trumpet or ram's horn)

B.C.E...............Before the Common (or Christian) Era. Another way of saying B.C.

Bar Mitzvah.......Literally *son of the commandment*. In Conservative and Reform Judaism, a Jewish boy who has achieved the age of thirteen and is consequently obligated to observe the commandments. Also, a ceremony marking the fact that a boy has achieved this age.

Bat Mitzvah.......Literally *daughter of the commandment*. In Conservative and Reform Judaism, a Jewish girl of 12 to 14 years of age, considered an adult and responsible for her moral and religious duties. Also ceremony that initiates and recognizes a girl as having achieved this status.

Brit Milah........Literally *covenant of circumcision*. The ritual circumcision of a male child before the age of eight days.

C.E................Common (or Christian) Era. Used by Jews instead of A.D., because A.D. means "the Year of our Lord."

Challah ....A sweet, egg, bread, usually braided, which is served on Sabbaths and holidays.

Chol Ha-Mo'ed .....The intermediate days of Passover and Sukkot, when work is permitted.

Chumash.........Literally *five*. A compilation of the first five books of the Bible and readings from the prophets, organized in the order of the weekly Torah portions.

Days of Awe ....Ten days from Rosh Hashanah to Yom Kippur, a time for introspection and considering the sins of the previous year.

Dreidel............a spinning top used in Hanukkah games.

Esther ....One of the heroes of the story of Purim.

Etrog ....A citrus fruit native to Israel, used to fulfill the commandment to "rejoice before the Lord" during Sukkot.

Four Species.......Fruit and branches used to fulfill the commandment to "rejoice before the Lord" during Sukkot.

Gelt...............Money given during Hanukkah. Traditionally chocolate covered in gold foil.

Grogger ....A noisemaker used to blot out the name of Haman during the reading of the Megillah on Purim.

Ha-Shem ....Literally *The Name*. The Name of God, which is not pronounced. The phrase "ha-Shem" is often used as a substitute for God's Name.

Haggadah ....A book containing the story of the Exodus and the ritual of the Seder, read at the Passover Seder.

Halakah...........The legal part of Talmudic literature, an interpretation of the laws of the Scriptures

Haman............The villain of the story of Purim.

Hamentaschen.....Literally Haman's pockets. Triangular, fruit-filled cookies traditionally served or given as gifts during Purim.

Hanukkah.........Literally *dedication*. An eight-day festival beginning on the twenty-fifth day of Kislev, commemorating the victory in 165 B.C. of the Maccabees over Antiochus Epiphanes (c. 215-164 B.C.) and the rededication of the Temple at Jerusalem. Also called *Feast of Dedication, Feast of Lights*. Also spelled Chanukkah.

Haroset . . . . A sweet mixture of apples, nuts, wine and cinnamon served at the Passover Seder.

Hellenism . . . . A name applied to the culture of the ancient Greeks, especially that of Athens at its height in Fifth century B.C. It is also applied to the works of those who later adopted Hellenic values and principles. The Hellenistic Age, a time when Greek culture spread throughout the eastern Mediterranean, is generally dated from the death of Alexander the Great to the rise of Augustus in Rome (323-330 B.C.).

Hoshanah Rabbah . Literally *great hosanna*. The seventh day of Sukkot, on which seven circuits are made around the synagogue reciting a prayer with the refrain, "Hosha na!" (please save us!).

Kiddush . . . . Literally *sanctification*. The traditional blessing and prayer recited over wine on the eve of the Sabbath or a festival.

Kippah . . . . The skullcap worn by Jews during services, and by some Jews at all times. See yarmulke.

Kittel . . . . The white robes in which the dead are buried, worn by some during Yom Kippur services.

Kol Nidre . . . . Literally *all vows*. The evening service of Yom Kippur, or the prayer that begins that service.

Kosher . . . . Literally *fit, proper or correct*. Describes food that is permissible to eat under Jewish dietary laws.

L'Chayim . . . . Literally *to life*. A common Jewish toast.

L'Shanah Tovah . . . . Literally *for a good year*. A common greeting during Rosh Hashanah and Days of Awe.

Latkes . . . . Potato pancakes traditionally eaten during Chanukah.

Maccabee . . . . Judah and his family who led the Jews against Antiochus IV. Also means hammer.

Magen David . . . . . . Literally *shield of David*. The six-pointed star emblem commonly associated with Judaism. See Star of David.

Manna . . . . Special food God gave the Hebrew people when they were in the desert.

Maror . . . . Bitter herbs. Traditionally horseradish served at the Passover Seder.

Matzah . . . . Unleavened bread.

Megillah . . . . Literally *scroll*. One of five books of the Bible (Esther, Ruth, Song of Songs, Lamentations, and Ecclesiastes). Usually refers to the book of Esther.

Menorah . . . . A candelabrum. Usually refers to the nine-branched candelabrum used to hold the Chanukah candles. Can also refer to the seven-branched candelabrum used in the Temple. Instructions for construction of the menorah are found in Exodus 25:31-40.

Messiah . . . . Messiah or Messias, in Hebrew means anointed. *Christ* is Greek for "Messiah."

Messianic . . . . adjective of the noun Messiah.

Messianic Jews . . . . Jews who have accepted Yeshua (Jesus) of Nazareth as the promised Messiah of Israel and Saviour of the world, and maintain Jewish identity and worship style.

Messianic Movement A ministry promoting Jesus (Yeshua) as the Messiah to Jew and Gentile, helping others to know Him, the Bible, Biblical Jewish roots of Christianity, Israel, and God's plan of eternal redemption/salvation. Most Messianics believe it is clear from the Scriptures that salvation is an undeserved and unearned gift from God through His grace. Works of the flesh do not earn one's salvation. They believe the Scriptures also teach that God is a righteous and just God who never changes; therefore the laws given to the Jewish people which have never been abolished stand as a true test of our love for Him.

Mezuzah . . . . Literally doorpost. A case attached to the doorposts of houses, containing a scroll with passages of scripture written on it. The mezuzah is not a good-luck charm nor does it have any connection with the lamb's blood placed on the doorposts in Egypt. It is a constant reminder of God's presence and God's commandments from Deuteronomy 6:4-9.

Midrash . . . . From a root meaning "to study," "to seek out" or "to investigate." Stories elaborating on incidents in the Bible, to derive a principle of Jewish law or provide a moral lesson.

Mishnah . . . . The first section of the Talmud, being a collection of early oral interpretations of the scriptures as compiled about A.D. 200.

Mitzvah . . . . Literally *commandment*. It refers to any of the 613 commandments that Jews are obligated to observe. It can also refer to any Jewish religious obligation, or more generally to any good

Mordecai . . . . One of the heroes of the story of Purim.

Movement . . . . Roughly equivalent to "denomination," although the distinctions between Jewish movements are not as great as those between Christian denominations.

Ne'ilah . . . . Literally *closing*. The closing service of Yom Kippur.

Nisan . . . . The first month of the Jewish calendar.

Omer . . . . A measure of barley. See The Counting of the Omer.

Oral Torah . . . . Jewish teachings explaining and elaborating on the Written Torah, handed down orally until the Second century C.E.

Orthodox . . . . One of the major movements of Judaism, believing that Jewish law comes from God and cannot be changed.

Purim . . . . Literally *lots* (as in "lottery"). A holiday celebrating the rescue of the Jews from extermination at the hands of the chief minister to the King of Persia.

Rabbi . . . . Literally means teacher. A recognized person knowledgeable of Jewish law. Usually ordained at a seminary and empowered to conduct services, weddings, and burials.

Reform . . . . One of the major movements of Judaism, believing that Jewish law was inspired by God and one can choose which laws to follow.

Rosh Hashanah . . . . Literally *first of the year*. The new year for the purpose of counting years.

Rosh Hodesh . . . . . . Literally *first of the month*. The first day of a month, on which the new moon appears.

Sabbath . . . . The most important day of the week is the Sabbath, called *Shabbat* in Hebrew. This begins at sundown on Friday, since the Jewish calendar is based on the lunar calendar and a new day therefore begins at this time. Shabbat is a day for rest and prayer.

Seder . . . . Literally *order*. The family home ritual conducted as part of the Passover observance.

Sekhakh . . . . Literally *covering*. Material used for the roof of a sukkah during the holiday of Sukkot.

Shabbat . . . . Literally *stop,cease, rest*. The Jewish Sabbath, a day of rest and spiritual enrichment.

Shalach Manos . . . . . Literally *sending out portions*. The custom of sending gifts of food or candy to friends during Purim.

Shammus . . . . Literally *servant*. The candle that is used to light other Chanukah candles.

Shavuot . . . . Literally *weeks*. A festival commemorating the giving of the Torah and the harvest of the first fruits.

Shema . . . . Hebrew for "Hear [O Israel]," the first word of Deuteronomy 6:4.

Shemini Atzeret . . . . Literally *the eighth (day) of assembly*. The day (or two days) after Sukkot.

Shevarim . . . . One of four characteristic blasts of the shofar (ram's horn). See Rosh Hashanah.

Shofar . . . . A ram's horn, blown like a trumpet as a call to repentance. See Rosh Hashanah.

Siddur . . . . Literally *order*. Prayerbook. See Jewish Liturgy.

Simkhat Torah . . . . . Literally *rejoicing in the law*. A holiday celebrating the end and beginning of the cycle of weekly Torah readings. Usually considered part of the Feast of Tabernacles.

Star of David . . . . . . The six-pointed star emblem commonly associated with Judaism. It is actually a relatively new Jewish symbol. It is supposed to represent the shape of King David's shield (or perhaps the emblem on it), but there is really no support for that claim in the Bible or in any early rabbinical literature. Today, the Magen David is a universally recognized symbol of Jewry. It appears on the flag of the state of Israel.

Sukkah . . . . Literally *booth*. The temporary dwellings observant Jews in Israel, live in during the holiday of Sukkot.

Sukkot . . . . Literally *booths*. A festival commemorating the wandering in the desert and the final harvest.

Synagogue . . . . From a Greek root meaning "assembly." The most widely accepted term for a Jewish house of worship.

Tallit . . . . A shawl-like garment worn during morning services, with tzitzit (long fringes) attached to the corners as a reminder of the commandments.

Talmud . . . . The most significant collection of the Jewish oral tradition interpreting the Torah.

Tanakh . . . . The Old Testament. Acronym of Torah (Law), Nevi'im (Phophets), and Ketuvim (Writings).

Tashlikh. . . . . Literally casting off. A custom of going to a river and symbolically casting off one's sins. See Rosh Hashanah.

Torah . . . . Literally *the Law*. Torah is Genesis, Exodus, Leviticus, Numbers and Deuteronomy. Bereshit (In the beginning...) (Genesis); Shemot (The names...) (Exodus); Vayikra (And He called...) (Leviticus); Bemidbar (In the wilderness...) (Numbers); Devarim (The words...) (Deuteronomy).

Teshuvah. . . . . A Hebrew word for repentance, about face, or to turn around. It is a time for one to annually examine his life and restore relationships between God and man.

Tzitzit. . . . . Fringes attached to the corners of garments as a reminder of the commandments. Numbers 15:37-41 commands to wear tzitzit (fringes) at the corners of garments as a reminder of the commandments. This is the part of the garment (the hem) the woman who sought a healing from Jesus touched in Matthew 9:20.

Yarmulke. . . . . The skullcap worn by Jews during services, and by some Jews at all times. May derive from Aramaic "Yirei Malka" (Fear of the King). The most commonly known and recognized piece of Jewish garb is actually the one with the least religious significance. It is an ancient practice for Jews to cover their heads during prayer. This probably derives from the fact that in Eastern cultures, it is a sign of respect to cover the head (the custom in Western cultures is the opposite: it is a sign of respect to remove one's hat). Thus, by covering the head during prayer, one showed respect for God. In addition, in ancient Rome, servants were required to cover their heads while free men did not; thus, Jews covered their heads to show that they were servants of God. In medieval times, Jews covered their heads as a reminder that God is always above them. Covering the head is a custom rather than a commandment.

Yom Kippur . . . . Literally *Day of Atonement*. A day set aside for fasting, depriving oneself of pleasures, and repenting from the sins of the previous year.

Zion. . . . . Part of Jerusalem. Defined in the Bible as the City of David. The name is symbolic of Jerusalem, of the Promised Land, of Israel's hope of returning to Palestine (hence the term Zionism).

A Family Guide to the Biblical Holidays©

Works Cited

BOOKS OR CD ROMS

Achtemier, P. J. Th.D. 1985. Harper's Bible Dictionary. San Francisco: Harper and Row, Publishers, Inc.

Avudraham (pp.71-72)

Bean, E. W. 1995. New Treasures: A Perspective of New Testament Teachings Through Hebraic Eyes. Oak Creek, WI: Cornerstone Publishing.

Bernard, D. K. The Oneness Of God. Hazelwood, MO: Word Aflame Press (8855 Dunn Rd. 63042).

———. The Significance Of A Name in The Oneness Of God. ———, ———.

Booker, R. 1996. Here Comes the Bride. Sounds of the Trumpet Inc.

———. 1987. Jesus in the Feasts of Israel. Sounds of the Trumpet Inc.

Bushell, M. S. 1995. Easton's Bible Dictionary.

Chumney, E. 1994. The Seven Festivals of the Messiah, © Edward Chumney.

Edersheim, A. 1993. The Life and Times of Jesus the Messiah. Peabody, MA: Hendrickson Publishers, Inc. II:479-480.

———. 1994. The Temple: Its Ministry and Services. Peabody, MA: Hendrickson Publishing.

Encyclopedia of Judaism. 1989. The Jerusalem Publishing House

Faid, R. W. 1993. A Scientific Approach to Biblical Mysteries. New Leaf Press, 93.

Felton, R. Anti-Semitism and the Church in The Jewish Roots of Christianity. Oklahoma City, OK: Potter's Clay Ministries, Inc. (417 NW 42nd Street, 73118).

Fryland, Rachmiel, 1996, The Lesson of Purim, The Messianic Literature Outreach, PO Box 37062, Cincinnati, OH, 45222

Fuchas, Daniel, Sevener, Harold, 1995, From Bondage to Freedom, Chosen People Ministries, Loizeaux, Neptune, NJ

Glaser, M. and Z. 1987. The Fall Feasts of Israel. Moody Press, 7.

Guinness, A. 1988. Reader's Digest Mysteries of the Bible. Reader's Digest.

Henry, M. 1960. Commentary of the Whole Bible. Grand Rapids, MI: Zondervan Publishing House.

Hook, Cecil, Free in Christ, Chapter 2. Law and Principle. Tigard,OR.

Jewish New Testament Commentary. 1996. Clarksville, MD: Jewish New Testament Publications.

Kollek, T. and Dowley, T. 1995. Next Year in Jerusalem. Eugene, OR: Harvest House.

Levitt, Z. 1979, 12. The Seven Feasts of Israel.

Lesson Maker, NavPress Software, Computer Bible Study Tools, WebMaster@WORDsearchBible.com

Mahzor Vitri, No. 323:54-55.

Mays, J. L., Ph.D., Editor.1988. Harper's Bible Commentary. New York: Harper and Row, Publishers, Inc.

Michaels, J. Ramsey, 1987-96, Holeman Bible Dictionary, Wordsearch 4.06, NavPress Software.

Microsoft (R) Encarta. Copyright (c) 1994 Microsoft Corporation. Funk & Wagnall's Corporation.

Mosley R. 1997. Yeshua: A Guide to the Real Jesus and the Original Church, © R. W. Mosley, Hagerstown, MD: Edbed Publishing (P.O. Box 3595, 21742-3595).

———. 1995. Spirit of the Law.

Nelson's Illustrated Bible Dictionary. 1986. Thomas Nelson Publishers.

Seder ha-Yom, 53-54.

The New Bible Dictionary. 1962. Wheaton, Illinois: Tyndale House Publishers, Inc.

Sevener, H. A, and Fuchs, D. 1995, Passover: Our Price of Freedom, From Bondage to Freedom, Chosen People.

Publishing Company and Dayton, OH: Center For Judaic-Christian Studies.

———. Our Father Abraham. 1989, 26. Dayton, OH: Center for Judaic Christian Studies (P.O. Box 293040, 45429).

Walvoord, J. F., and Zuck, R. B., 1985., The Bible Knowledge Commentary. (Wheaton, Illinois: Scripture Press Publications, Inc.

Wright, C., J.H. 1992. Knowing Jesus Through the Old Testament. Intervarsity Press.

Zimmerman, M. 1981, 118. Celebrate the Feast. Bethany House Publishers.

ARTICLES

A.T.O.M. (Association of Torah-Observant Messianics). 1995. Hanukkah A Minor Festival? Teshuvah. Bowie, MD.

Aldrich, R. L. 1959. Has the Mosaic Law Been Abolished? Vol. 116 # 464

Ari Sorko-Ram, 1996. 04:13, Shmini in First Fruits of Zion Magazine. Lakewood, CO. (P.O. Box 28027, 80228-0827).

Berkowitz, A. and D. January 1996. Cycle of Sanctification in First Fruits of Zion Magazine. ———.

Birnbaum, S. 1996. When You Take Up in First Fruits of Zion. ———.

Booker, R. Celebrating the Lord's Feasts in the Church (an adaptation of a portion of an article from Return to God Magazine, 1: Number 3, page 4. Carnation, WA: Return to God   (P.O. Box 159, 98014).

Bordwine, J. E., Th.D. Winter/Spring 1995. The Doctrine of the Sabbath, (Part II) Keeping the Sabbath, May 96 Contra Mundum No. 14.

Chaimberlin, R. "Aharon." October 1996. Computer Secrets of the Torah, Petah Tikvah, The Messianic Jewish World.

Collin, K. W. 1996. Minor Mysteries. Web Site http://www.kencollins.com/Why-03.htm

Duthie, J., 1996. The Feast of the Leaven. A web page by JD Computer Consulting.

Gerrish, Jim. Dispatch from Jerusalem. Tulsa, OK: Bridges for Peace. (Box 33145, 74153, 1-800-566-1998).

Gilman, A. 1995. Hanukkah—Festival of Lights and Miracles.

Gregg, D. 1994, A Short History of the Hebrew Calendar.

Hillel Foundation, 1995. Introduction to the Jewish Calendar and Holy Days, Stanford University (rabbi@forsythe.stanford.edu)

Hollaway, K. 1995. The Final Countdown? i-open@virtual.co.il (Virtual Jerusalem) hollaway@ghgcorp.com

Jerusalem Sentinel, The. 1995. Vol.4 NO.2.

Johnson, C. 1978, Medical and Cardiological Aspects of the Passion and Crucifixion of Jesus, the Christ, Bol Asoc Med P Rico 70 (3) : 97-102.

Killian, G. 1996. Hag Shavuot in The Watchman. Kent, WA: (P.O. Box 565, 98035).

Lancaster, Daniel, Pictures of the Messiah: The Spring Festivals, First Fruits of Zion Magazine (Lancaster is Pastor at Kehilat Sar Shalom Congregation, 1901 Ford Parkway, St. Paul, MN 55116.)

Langley, T. 1995. The Feast of Dedication - A Message for Today in Return to God Magazine. Carnation, WA: Return to God (P.O. Box 159, 98014-0159). email: glenna@halcyon.com.

Lever, A. B. 1996. Godliness: Forms or Formulas. Parables. Colorado Springs, CO.

Maltz, S. A Tragedy of Errors - a look at Christian Anti-Semitism (e-mail   100126.2467 @compuserve.com)

Michael, B. January 27, 1996. First Fruits of Zion Magazine. Lakewood, CO.

Missler, C. "Isaiah 53" Firefighters for Christ, Westminster, Ca.

Patterson, Dr. R. L., Senior Pastor, Jesus Fellowship. The Study of the Names of God. 1995. (Web Site http://jf.org/sermons/names.htm) Miami, FL (9775 SW 87 Ave, 33176-2900).

Raisdanai, Darab. The End Times - Examining Scripture from a Hebraic Perspective Reveals God's Plan. Return to God Magazine. 1: Number 3, page 9.

Sarna, J., "Passover Raisin Wine," The American Temperance Movement, and Mordecai Noah: The Origins, Meaning, and Wider Significance of a Nineteenth-Century American Jewish Religious Practice, HUCA 59 (1988), 269-88.

Silverman, H. n.d.

Somerville, Robert S. Feast of Pentecost: A Time To Reap, Huntsville, AL: Awareness Ministry, Covenant of Peace Church.

———. The Final Renewal, ———.

———. Why Christians Celebrate the Biblical Memorial Days, ———.

———. At a Galnce Brochure, http://www.Awareness.org/atglance.htm ———.

Terasaka, D., M.D, 1996, Prophecy and Current Events. Syracuse, NY (P.O. Box 31, 13215): "To His Glory Ministries." (Complete article available from)

Thompson, 1984, Unleavened.

Truman, D. M.D., M.S., March 1965, The Crucifixion Of Jesus, The Passion of Christ from a Medical Point of View, Arizona Medicine, Vol. 22, no. 3.

Wiggins, Dr. E., The Final Countdown. Prophecy in Review. television broadcast.

Wagner, C. H., Jr., 1996. The Trumpet Is Sounding In Zion!! Jerusalem Prayer Letter, Tulsa, OK: Bridges of Peace.

Books marked with a 📖 are available through Heart of Wisdom Website

www.heartofwisdom.com

Bibliography

Baer, Ruth Walter, Creation to Canaan. Crockett, KY: Rod and Staff Publishers, Inc., 1979.

Bean, E. William. New Treasures. Oak Creek, WI: Cornerstone Publishing, 1995.

Bible Works for Windows. Big Fork, MT: Hermeneutika Software, 1996.

Bivin, David and Roy Blizzard, Jr. Understanding the Difficult Words of Jesus. Dayton, OH: Destiny Image Publishers, 1994.

Bloch, Abraham P. The Biblical and Historical Background of Jewish Customs and Ceremonies. New York: KTAV Publishing House, Inc., 1980.

Booker, Richard. Blow the Trumpet in Zion. Shippensburg, PA: Destiny Image Publishers, 1985.

——.Here Comes the Bride. Houston, TX: Sounds of the Trumpet, Inc., 1995

——.How the Cross Became a Sword. ——, 1994.

——.How to Prepare for the Coming Revival, Shippensburg, PA: Destiny Publishers, 1990.

——.Islam, Christianity and Israel, Houston, TX: Sounds of the Trumpet, Inc., 1994.

——.Jesus in the Feasts of Israel, South Plainfield, NJ: ——, 1987.

——.The Miracle of the Scarlet Thread, Shippensburg, PA: ——, 1981.

——. The Time to Favor Zion Has Come. Houston, TX: ——., 1996.

Brown, Michael L. Our Hands Are Stained With Blood. Shippensburg, PA: Destiny Image Publishers, 1992.

Bullinger, E. W. Number in Scripture. Grand Rapids, MI: Kregel Publications, 1967.

Chumney, Edward. The Seven Festivals of The Messiah. Shippensburg, PA: Destiny Image Publishers, 1994.

Discovering Exodus. Carmel, NY: Guideposts Associates, Inc., 1988.

Dorsey, John F. A Farmer Looks at the Parables. Shoals, IN: Old Paths Tract Society, Inc.

Drucker, Malka. The Family Treasury of Jewish Holidays. New York: Little, Brown and Company, 1994.

Eldersheim, Alfred. Bible History Old Testament. Peabody, MA: Hendrickson Publishers, Inc., 1995.

——. Sketches of Jewish Social Life. ——: ——, 1994.

——. The Temple: Its Ministry and Services. ——: ——, 1994.

Elwell, Walter and Douglas Buckwalter. Topical Analysis of the Bible With the New International Version. Grand Rapids, MI: Baker Book House, 1991.

Faid, Robert W. A Scientific Approach to Biblical Mysteries. Green Forest, AR: New Leaf Press, Inc., 1993.

——. A Scientific Approach to More Biblical Mysteries. ——: ——, 1994.

Fellner, Judith B. In The Jewish Tradition. New York, NY: Michael Friedman Publishing Group, Inc., 1995.

Freeman, James M. Manners and Customs of the Bible. Plainfield, NJ: Logos International, 1972.

Fuchs, Daniel. Israel's Holy Days in Type and Prophecy. Neptune, NJ: Loizeaux Brothers, 1985.

Good, Joseph. Rosh HaShanah and the Messianic Kingdom to Come. Port Arthur, TX: Hatikva Ministries, 1989.

Goldberg, Louis. Our Jewish Friends. Neptune, NJ: Loizeaux Brothers, 1983.

Greenberg, Rabbi Irving. The Jewish Way. New York, NY: Simon & Schuster, 1988.

Horton, T.C. and Charles E. Hurlburt. Names of Christ. Chicago: The Moody Bible Institute, 1994.

Houghton, S.M. Sketches From Church History. Carlisle, PA: The Banner of Truth Trust, 1980.

Hubbard, Rev. David E. Bible Outlines Teaching Spiritual Truth Through Bible Types and Scriptural Symbols and Shadows. Monroe, NC: Rev. David E. Hubbard, 1973.

Juster, Dan. Jewish Roots. Shippensburg, PA: Destiny Image Publishers, 1995.

Kasdan, Barney. God's Appointed Times. Baltimore, MD: Lederer Messianic Publications, 1993.

Keller, W. Phillip. A Gardener Looks at the Fruits of the Spirit. Waco, TX: Word Incorporated, 1986.

Kolatch, Alfred J. The Jewish Book of Why. Middle Village, NY: Jonathan David Publishers, Inc., 1981.

Kreloff, Steven A. God's Plan for Israel. Neptune, NJ: Loizeaux Brothers, Inc., 1995.

Kreners, Marion F. God Intervenes in the Middle East. Burke, VA: God Intervenes, Inc., 1992.

Kushner, Harold S. To Life! New York, NY: Warner Books, 1993.

Larson, Gary N. The New Unger's Bible Handbook. Chicago, IL: Moody Press, 1984.

Limburg, James. Judaism: An Introduction for Christians. Minneapolis, MN: Augsburg Publishing House, 1987.

Lindsey, Robert L. Jesus Rabbi & Lord. Oak Creek, WI: Cornerstone Publishing, 1990.

Merrill, Eugene H. An Historical Survey of the Old Testament. 2nd ed. Grand Rapids, MI: Baker Book House, 1991.

Merrill, Kathryn L. and Kristy L. Christian. Moses and the Law. Oklahoma City, OK: Infinite Discovery, 1991.

———. In Jesus' Time. Highland City, FL: Rainbow Books, Inc., 1993.

Moseley, Dr. Ron. Yeshua, A Guide to the Real Jesus and the Original Church. Hagerstown, MD: Ebed Publications, 1996.

Mulligan, David. Wisdom in the Christian Community: Far Above Rubies, Marshfield, Vermont: Messenger Publishing, 1994.

Mysteries of the Bible. Pleasantville, NY: The Reader's Digest Association, Inc., 1990.

Paris, Alan. Jerusalem 3000 Kids Discover the City of Gold. New York, NY: Pitspopany Press, 1995.

Richards, Lawrence O. The Teacher's Commentary. Wheaton, IL: Scripture Press Publications, Inc., 1987.

Schaeffer, Francis A. The Church at the End of the 20th Century. Westchester, IL: Crossway Books, 1990.

Settel, Jonathan. Delight in the Shabbat. Jerusalem, Israel: Jonathan & Sharon Settel,

Shepherd, Coulson. Jewish Holy Days Their Prophetic and Christian Significance. Neptune, NJ: Loizeaux Brothers, Inc., 1961.

Steingroot, Ira. Keeping Passover. New York, NY: HarperCollins Publishers, 1995.

Stern, David. Jewish New Testament Commentary. Clarksville, MD: Jewish New Testament Publications, Inc., 1992.

———. Messianic Jewish Manifesto. ———: ———, Inc., 1988.

Strassfeld, Michael. The Jewish Holidays. New York, NY: Harper and Row, Publishers, Inc., 1985.

Strong, James. The Tabernacle of Israel. Grand Rapids, MI: Kregel Publications, 1987.

Wilson, Marvin R. Our Father Abraham Jewish Roots of the Christian Faith. Grand Rapids, MI: William B. Eerdmans Publishing Company, 1989.

Zimmerman, Martha. Celebrate the Feasts of the Old Testament in Your Own Home or Church. Minneapolis, MN: Bethany House Publishers, 1981.

End Notes

HEBREW ROOTS

1. The three ingredients that make a nation are 1.) a system of law, 2.) a religion, and 3.) education. The Biblical Hebrew's law, religion, and education not only focus on God, but are directly from God! The Puritans strived for the same ingredients but the time between the puritans and today has been a steady downhill climb. Now, America has a law that was one time based on God's Word but is de-moralized. America claims to have the freedom of religion, but education system teaches a religion–humanism (based on the pagan Greeks and Romans).

PASSOVER

1. Three Days and Three Nights. Not Friday to Sunday

To understand the chronology of events during the last week of Christ's human life, you need to understand the Bible speaks of two types of Sabbaths. The regular weekly Sabbath and annual high holy days are referred to as Sabbaths.

The Pharisee's asked Jesus for a sign— they wanted evidence that He was the promised Messiah. "But He answered and said unto them, 'an evil and adulterous generation seeks after a sign, and there shall no sign be given to it, but the sign of the Prophet Jonas. For as Jonas was three days and three nights in the whale's belly, so shall the son of man be three days and three nights in the heart of the earth", (Matt. 12:39).

Many think Jesus died on Friday because of this verse: The Jews therefore, because it was the preparation, that the bodies should not remain upon the cross on the Sabbath day, (for that Sabbath day was an high day,) besought Pilate that their legs might be broken, and that they might be taken away (John 19:31).

Friday death to Sunday resurrection is not three days and three nights. If He was risen on Sunday, as is commonly taught, then it leaves us with one hour maximum for Friday (in the grave), plus 24 hours for Saturday, and a maximum of 12 hours for Sunday (reckoning from sunset to sunset). However you count, it leaves us with a maximum total of 37 hours, or one day and two nights in the grave. Let's even count Friday as one whole day: Friday-day= 1 day, Friday Night=1 night, Saturday-day=2 days, Saturday Night=2 nights, Sunday-day=3 days. What about the 3rd night?

We need to understand the chronology of the first Passover to see God's plan. The first Passover lamb was slain on Nisan 14th. Israel emerged from the sea on the 17th. Jonah was in the belly of the great fish from Nisan 14, to Nisan 17 (Mat 12:40). God's plan is so perfect that everything would match down to the day of the week. Three days and three nights. Remember the Jewish time counts 6:00pm to 6:00pm as one day.

Nisan 17, when Israel emerged from the Red Sea, was a shadow of the fulfillment of the day of Firstfruits (Lev. 23:9-14). This was the first of God's people to emerge from sin (Egypt). It was fulfilled almost 1,500 years later on Nisan 17, 30 AD when Jesus was resurrected and ascended to heaven as our High Priest, the Firstfruit of the resurrected (John 20:17).

Note: Other verses can be misunderstood if one does not understand there are seven weeks in the 50 Days of Omer. The first week may be referred to as the first week. The term "the first day of the week" is used many times in the NT. The word "day" is an inserted word; according to Strong's was "added by the translators for better readability in the English. There is no actual word in the Greek text. The word may be displayed in italics, or in parentheses or other brackets, to indicate that it is not in the original text."

UNLEAVENED BREAD

1. The word pascha appears 29 times in the Bible. The KJV translates this word 28 times as Passover and one time as Easter. Easter was a pagan holiday to worship the goddess Ishtar. We chose to use the NIV version of the Bible in this one passage in this book.

FIRSTFRUITS

1. View 1 —The Sadducees felt the "morrow after the Sabbath" meant the day following the weekly Sabbath. The day after the seventh Sabbath can only be the first day of the week or Sunday so First-century Judaism, the Christian Church and many Messianic place Early and Later Firstfruits on Sundays.

View 2—The majority opinion, held by the Pharisees, believed that the "Sabbath" in question was referring to Nisan 15, as the 2nd day of Passover (i.e., the day after the sabbath of Passover instead of during). Josephus and many Bible scholars, including Edersheim, believe that the Sabbath in Lev 23:9 is referring to the 15th of Nisan (no matter what day of the week). This would cause Latter Firstfruits to always fall on Sivan 6. The reformation of the calendar under Rabbi Hillel II in c. 358 AD saw Later Firstfruits set at the sixth of Sivan.

FALL HOLIDAYS

1. Wiggins, Dr., "Prophecy in Review", TBN, Zechariah 6:12-13, Then speak to him, saying, 'Thus says the LORD of hosts, saying: "Behold, the Man whose name is the BRANCH! From His place He shall branch out, And He shall build the temple of the LORD; Yes, He shall build the temple of the LORD. He shall bear the glory, And shall sit and rule on His throne; So He shall be a priest on His throne, And the counsel of peace shall be between them both. He who builds the temple is called the Branch. The Jews will accept the anti-Christ as the Messiah after He re-builds their temple. This temple will be destroyed and the true Messiah will build the Temple of God that will never be destroyed again."

FEASTS OF TRUMPETS

1. Matthew 24:30 And then shall appear the sign of the Son of man in heaven: and then shall all the tribes of the earth mourn, and they shall see the Son of man coming in the clouds of heaven with power and great glory.

DAY OF ATONEMENT

1. It is said that the name Azazel (Lev 16:8-26) either means "Satan" or "complete removal." Moses law did not sanction pushing the goat over the cliff, it was only to be 'let go.'

TABERNACLES

1. You may be as surprised as I was when I looked up Christmas origins in a few different encyclopedias. Microsoft (R) Encarta Encyclopedia explains, "In ancient times, December 25th was the date of the Pagan Roman Bromalia, the final day of the popular week long Saturnalia celebration. Celebrated in honor of the God Saturn. It was the day of the invincible sun, a winter solstice festival. In later legends he was identified with the Greek god Cronus, who, after having been dethroned by his son Zeus (in Roman mythology, Jupiter). Beginning on December 17 of each year, during the festival known as the Saturnalia, the Golden Age was restored for seven days. All business stopped and executions and military operations were postponed. It was a period of goodwill, devoted to banquets and the exchange of visits and gifts. A special feature of the festival was the freedom given to slaves, who during this time had first place at the family table and were served by their masters. Christmas festivals, generally observed by Christians since the 4th century, incorporate pagan customs, such as the use of holly, mistletoe, Yule logs, and wassail bowls."

The New Schaff-Herzog Encyclopedia of Religious Knowledge explains, "In 3000 B.C., after the untimely death of King Osiris (King of Egypt) his wife, Isis propagated (taught) the doctrine -the survival of Osiris as a spirit-being." She claimed a full-grown evergreen tree sprang up over night from a dead tree stump, which symbolized the springing forth unto life of the dead Osiris, then reborn in his son Horus. On each anniversary of his new birth, she claimed Osiris would visit the evergreen tree and leave gifts. The date of his birth was December 25."

Christmas was outlawed in England in 1644 by an act of Parliament and the influence of the Puritans. The Puritans brought this influence to America and by 1659 Massachusetts had passed a law fining anybody who celebrated Christmas. Under the influence of puritanical thought, America suppressed the celebration of Christmas well into the nineteenth century. Puritans did not celebrate Christmas, for these were lingering elements of the papal calendar.

For more information about December 25, order the booklets: Christmas: The Origins; or The Christianizing of Heathen Festivals. Send $4.00 each to PO Box 9887, Colorado Spring, CO 80932. You can also write for a reprint of the article Christmas Remembered, Was Jesus born in December? by Clarence H. Wagner, Jr, Dispatch from Jerusalem a publication of Bridges for Peace, Box 33145, Tulsa, OK 74153.

SABBATH

1. According to the Encyclopedia Americana - 1953 edition, volume 24, page 78: "The Sabbath was the seventh day of the Hebrew week and lasted from sunset on Friday to sunset on Saturday." The Software Toolworks Multimedia Encyclopedia say the Sabbath is: "The seventh day of the Jewish week—from sundown Friday to sundown Saturday—the Sabbath commemorates the seventh day of creation, on which God rested. It is a divinely appointed day of rest (Exodus. 20:8), to be devoted to prayer and study, and its observance is a mark of Jewish faith."

2. That is, to love and protect it, as the husband is the lord of the wife, to love and cherish her.

3. Jesus accused some of the leaders of His day of replacing the law with their own traditions and making the law of no effect. Jesus carefully taught how Sabbath should be observed. He taught that the spirit and attitude were important. The Pharisees had built a "fence" around the law of the Sabbath—adding unnecessary rules. Jesus speaks again against the traditions of men, Matthew 15:3-9 *But he answered and said unto them, Why do ye also transgress the commandment of God by your tradition? For God commanded, saying, Honour thy father and mother, and, He that curseth father or mother, let him die the death. But ye say, Whosoever shall say to his father or his mother, It is a gift, by whatsoever thou mightest be profited by me; And honour not his father or his mother, he shall be free. Thus have ye made the commandments of God of none effect by your tradition. Ye hypocrites, well did Esaias prophesy of you, saying, This people draweth nigh unto me with their mouth, and honoureth me with their lips, but their heart is far from me. But in vain they do worship me, teaching for doctrines the commandments of men.*

4. The Sabbath was made for man (rest for man's benefit). Rejecting the Sabbath is rejecting the benefit.

5. The time of candle lighting is announced for Jews. For example the following would be found in Jewish newspaper: Candle Lighting: Jerusalem 7:09 Miami 7:57 New York 8:08 Kobe 6:52 Singapore 6:28 Hong Kong 6:50 Guatemala 6:14 Honolulu 6:59 Adelaide 5:04 Los Angeles 7:48.

HEBREW NAMES

1. The Romans equated Zeus with their own supreme god, Jupiter. Barnabas was called Zeus by the people after the apostle Paul performed a miraculous healing at Lystra (Acts 14:12-13; 19:35); (Jupiter, KJV). "Zeus" appears in the book of Acts and is translated from the Greek dzyooce.

2. For more information on the hidden Codes in the Torah, see The Heptadic Structure of Scripture, Marshall Brothers Ltd., London, 1923. Chuck Missler's article "The Feasts of Israel," Koinonia House, 1993. *Yeshua: The Name of Jesus Revealed in the Old Testament* by Yacov Rambsel or The *Signature of God* by Grant R. Jeffrey.

Start

S

HANUKKAH P U

U N L E A V E

F I R S T F R U

T R U M P E T

T A B E

FESTIVE FAMILY GAME

© 1997
The Biblical Holidays

THE BIBLICAL HOLIDAYS

© 1997

582

583